Sitting Bull

AN EPIC OF THE PLAINS

BY ALEXANDER B. ADAMS

Thoreau's Guide to Cape Cod
(EDITOR)

First World Conference on National Parks
(EDITOR)

John James Audubon: A BIOGRAPHY

A Handbook of Practical Public Relations

Eternal Quest: THE STORY OF THE GREAT NATURALISTS

Eleventh Hour: A HARD LOOK AT CONSERVATION

Geronimo: A BIOGRAPHY

Still resentful against the Americans' intrusion into his people's lands, Sitting Bull allowed his photograph to be taken against the incongruous background used in nineteenth-century studios.

Sitting Bull

AN EPIC OF THE PLAINS

by

ALEXANDER B. ADAMS

G. P. Putnam's Sons
New York

All the illustrations in this book are from the
collection of the National Archives and Records
Service. Grateful thanks are hereby expressed by
both the publisher and author.

To

George W. Adams and Elizabeth Dore
The Sioux were free spirits, and you are too.
So this book is for you

Contents

Illustrations will be found following page 364.

The Indians have not been without excuse for their evil deeds. Our own people have given them intoxicating drinks, taught them to swear, violated the rights of womanhood among them, robbed them of their dues, and then insulted them! What more would be necessary to cause one nation to rise against another? What more, *I ask. Yet there are many who curse this people, and cry "Exterminate the fiends." Dare we, as a nation,* thus *bring a curse upon ourselves and on future generations?*

—A WHITE WOMAN WHO HAD BEEN DRIVEN FROM HER HOME DURING THE SIOUX UPRISING OF 1862

SOME WORDS OF CLARIFICATION

Those readers who are unfamiliar with the Sioux tribes discussed in this book may find the various divisions confusing, and so I offer them these words of clarification.

The Sioux were also known as the Dakotas. The Teton—or Western—Sioux were divided into seven divisions with the following ranges:

OGLALAS (Those Who Scatter Their Own): eastern Wyoming, southeastern Montana, and across the boundaries into Nebraska and South Dakota.

BRULÉS (Burnt Thighs): Nebraska and southern South Dakota.

MINICONJOUS (Those Who Plant by the Stream): north of the western portion of the Brulés' range in South Dakota.

TWO KETTLES (Two Boilings): to the east of the Miniconjous in South Dakota.

HUNKPAPAS (Those Who Camp by the Entrance): southwestern North Dakota and southeastern Montana. This was the division to which Sitting Bull belonged.

SANS ARCS (Without Bows): approximately the same range as the Hunkpapas.

BLACKFEET SIOUX: also approximately the same range as the Hunkpapas. These should not be confused with the Blackfeet, who lived farther to the north and west in Montana and to whom the Blackfeet Sioux are not related.

13

These ranges, of course, were fluid, and the Sioux often wandered from one to another.

Traditionally, the seven divisions of the Teton Sioux met once a year at a grand council and chose several officers. But they did not have a central government, and each division was free to act as it wished. Thus the white men had to make a treaty with each of the divisions, and even then the division might separate into several bands, each again free to do what it wished.

To the east of the other Sioux in South Dakota were the Yankton Sioux, who do not figure largely in this book.

Further east in Minnesota were the Santee Sioux. They appear in the third chapter, because their uprising stimulated several military expeditions that marched against the Teton Sioux as well.

As for the white men, they also may confuse the reader by their custom of giving out brevet ranks. During the Civil War, these were widely used as awards for bravery and required only routine confirmation by the Senate. After the war, the officers were addressed by their highest brevet rank, although their actual ranks might be considerably lower. Custer, for example, was a brevet major general long before he became a lieutenant colonel, the highest permanent rank he attained. Generally I have referred to the officers by their brevet rank, as was the custom of the day.

An Episode in Wyoming

NIGHT and darkness spread around us, unbroken except for the low flames of our gradually dying campfire. It was too late to put on fresh wood, but nobody was ready yet to spread out his bed roll. For the old man was talking.

He usually did not talk much except in the way of business and then generally because something had gone wrong. Perhaps he had lived so long among the mountains and plains that he had become silent like them. They, not men, had been his lifetime companions.

Unlike most people his age, he did not reminisce freely about the old days, although he had a lot to say. He had known this country for years, was a friend of Jackson, the horse thief who had laid out the Jackson Trail so he could move his stolen livestock swiftly and unseen, and had served as a scout during the wars against the Indians.

There was only one way to start him talking. That was for someone to begin telling a story in which the old man was involved and made mistakes in telling it. If this was done skillfully, the old man would begin correcting the errors. Finally in disgust he would tell the whole story himself.

That was what someone had done that night. The old man had taken the bait, and he was telling how he had carried a message to General Nelson Miles. I was weary, because I had not slept much the previous night. I had placed my bed roll across the trail, so if the pack horses decided to return to their home ranch, they would waken me. The trail, however, ran along the side of a steep slope, so I kept slipping down the hillside, unfolding my bed roll as I went. But, like the others, I was not ready for sleep now.

The story the old man was telling was a simple one. He had ridden for a continuous seventy-six hours through Indian territory with a message for General Miles. The general needed a courier to carry back the reply, and the old man had volunteered.

"But you need some sleep," the general said.

"I need four hours," the old man replied.

So he climbed into a bunk in the general's cabin and closed his eyes. In exactly four hours, he was awake again and swung his feet to the floor.

The general was surprised and said, "I was just about to rouse you."

"You don't need to," the old man replied curtly.

He went outside, saddled his horse, and rode another continuous forty-eight hours with the general's answer.

Like most of the old man's stories, it was a simple one, but it is the simplicity itself that strikes me. He had no heroics, no sense of drama. He was merely proud that he could ride that long without sleep and scornful that a general would think he had to be wakened for the return journey.

At the time, I was just a boy with only two ambitions: to become a good cowhand and some day to write books. I finally realized the second, but events thwarted me in the first. Yet I still remember the old man and others I knew like him. Of course, I listened avidly to their stories. What young boy would not have? But I did not realize that they were telling me history, important history. Like most people, I thought the settlement of the West exciting and romantic, but not basically significant, and none of the schools I subsequently attended ever corrected that impression.

Now, however, I have come to take a different view. The opening of the West played a fundamental role in the development of the American character and in making Americans what they are today. The two greatest forces working on us as a people are probably our inheritance of Anglo-Saxon jurisprudence and political views, and our experience in settling the West. Recognition is given the first but not the second, and our failure to evaluate what happened west of the Mississippi in the nineteenth century is today the cause of unnecessary difficulties. This is why I get somewhat annoyed when the word "Americana"—a slightly derogatory word—is applied to any event that took place west of the Mississippi, while the more dignified word "history" is applied to similar events east of that river.

Unfortunately much of the story of the West is obscured by a fog of myths and sentimentality. Not long ago, an American president publicly lamented that the days of Western justice as depicted by a popular movie actor no longer existed; he meant it, and many people took him seriously. It was as though a British prime minister had gravely expressed a wish to return to the days of the Roundtable as described by Tennyson. Everyone would have laughed, but the parallel is there. The popular conception of much Western history is no more based on fact than Tennyson's fine poems, but in the latter case we recognize the play of imagination.

The story of the West was not a conflict between "good guys" and "bad guys." There were some of each on all sides, and the "good guys" did not always win. More often than not, in fact, they lost. And to this we can attribute much of the harshness and brutality that forms a mean streak in our national character. Dirty tactics and behavior often paid off during those days, and unfortunately they have been paying off ever since.

If we understood Western history, I believe we would understand much about our current position in the world. Perhaps it is not an exaggeration to say that if this part of our past had been better taught in Whittier, California, some years ago, we would have saved many thousands of lives. For one of the students there might have learned the folly of fighting guerrilla warfare by conventional means. It is difficult to do battle with a people when it is almost impossible to distinguish between friends and enemies—a condition that existed when we fought the Indians—and a primitive people can be crushed by large troop concentrations only at the expense of many innocent lives. Napoleon has been said to remark, "Show me a man who has never made a mistake, and I will show you a man who has never done anything. Show me a man who has made the same mistake twice, and I will show you a damned fool." If we paid more attention to our Western history, I believe, we would not so often fall into the latter category—in this and many other of our activities.

This book, of course, deals with deep problems of morality. If we assume that the Indians had prior right to the land and that the Americans were merely conquerors, the question becomes easy. The Americans were entirely in the wrong. But to use this yardstick alone would be to condemn the Sioux, too. They were also comparative newcomers to the plains, having started to arrive there in the late seventeenth century, not long before the Americans, and having taken by force the territory they occupied.

But there are still basic questions of national and personal morality—and immorality—involved in our activities on the plains. The white men's occupation of them was inevitable, as I have tried to point out in this book. All the forces were working against the Indians. But certainly a better adjustment could have been made and might have been except for two important factors: the inability to recognize cultural differences and the greed, either for glory or for money, that marked too many of the characters. If we look around us today, we can find these same forces still playing a similar role. Until we can shake ourselves free of them, the American reality will never measure up to the American dream.

So this is not a book about "Injuns"; it is a book about Americans, Americans of all kinds and of types that are alive today. Perhaps if we can recognize ourselves in those crucial years of our development both as a nation and a people, we can better understand ourselves today.

In writing this book, I am aware that I have lost some impact by not creating a struggle between heroes and villains. Such a book with its attendant sensationalism would, I am sure, have made more exciting reading, but it would simply have added to the legend—on one side or the other. I hope that I have struck a balance that more nearly represents the truth and that I have given a clearer picture of what actually transpired among the men, women, and children of all races that occupied the plains in the nineteenth century.

As to what we can do to rectify the wrongs of the past? Well, that is a subject for a book in itself.

I

The Great Barrier

THE mob descended on Washington—the usual politicians and
self-seekers, and woodsmen from Tennessee, fur traders from the
Rockies, newspaper editors from frontier towns that boasted only a
single street, old soldiers who had wandered west and now hoped to
get a glimpse of—and perhaps a favor from—their onetime commander, keelboat men from the Mississippi and the Ohio Rivers who
had caroused in Natchez Under-the-Hill, mountain men who had
trapped beavers in the Northwest, all making a conglomeration of
riffraff that threatened the city's propriety.

They filled every hotel even though they slept three or four in a bed
and used the billiard tables when no other places remained to lie
down. They swarmed the streets in their muddy boots, drank at the
bars, and went to the entertainments offered at the theaters.

To those who overheard their conversations, much of what they
said was unintelligible. They spoke of strange places like the Belle
Fourche and the Pah Sappa of the Sioux. Many of them had not been
beyond the Mississippi, but a few had floated down the Missouri River
by boat and knew the Cannonball and the Cheyenne. They had talked
with men who had hunted along the valley of the White and were
familiar with the crossings at the South Platte and the strange half-
French, half-Indian language of the Metís. That world was more real
to them than the buildings around them, for they were aliens in their
own capital.

They roamed the city in high spirits, for their moment in history,
they thought, had come, and the voice of the West was at last being

19

heard. As to the future, in March, 1829, they had only one immediate fear: that the capital's supply of whiskey might give out before the celebration was over.

Others, more conservative, were not so confident. John Quincy Adams, the embittered and patrician former President of the United States, announced he would not attend the inaugural. Daniel Webster, the dignified Senator from Massachusetts, wrote his friends that he was torn between hope and fear for the country, but that fear was the stronger emotion. And the Chief Justice of the Supreme Court performed his official duty of administering the oath with open reluctance.

After the inauguration, which was held in the portico of the Capitol, the crowd moved down Pennsylvania Avenue to the reception at the White House. Invited guests had difficulty getting through the door because the uninvited mob was entering, too. In the East Room, they devoured the ice cream and cake that were elegantly waiting on the tables. They broke dishes and glassware and climbed, still wearing their boots, onto the seats of chairs that had cost the government a hundred and fifty dollars each. Some of the formal guests, unable to stand the crush, fled through an open window. The administration of Andrew Jackson, seventh President of the United States, had commenced.

Weary from a lifetime of battling, and grieving over the recent death of his wife, the general had certainly received a mandate from the people during the past election. But a mandate to do what? He himself was not certain, and neither were the people who had gone to the polls and cast their ballots for him. A vast unrest had seized the nation, a resentment at the wide gap between the dream and the reality, and the votes had expressed this. Even the city in which Jackson would govern the nation was only a skeleton of the magnificent plan envisioned by its founders. Like so many people in the United States at the time, Pierre-Charles L'Enfant, the architect, had had unbounded faith in the future, and he had dreamed of a community with great vistas, grand buildings, and spraying fountains—a Versailles of free and democratic men. But the Washington of Jackson's day came nowhere near L'Enfant's dream. Like the country as a whole, it lacked fulfillment.

The Capitol and the White House were imposing structures, and so were the buildings that housed the State, Treasury, War, and Navy Departments. Pennsylvania Avenue, running between the Capitol and the White House, was often filled with quagmires in rainy weather, but at least it was broad and straight. But nowhere else did the city measure up to the plan that L'Enfant had drawn with such care and love. Temporary roads and paths crisscrossed the terrain, and builders placed houses in a hodgepodge wherever they wished. The difference between Washington as it appeared in L'Enfant's drawings and the actual Washington was enormous.

Yet the capital simply mirrored the condition of the country as a whole. Looking at a map, it appeared that Jackson presided over a single nation that stretched unbroken from the Atlantic to the Pacific. Of course, title to Oregon, which then embraced a large, undefined area in the northwest, was shared with Great Britain, but everyone knew that was no bar to settlement. Americans were welcome, and new arrivals could count on assistance from the Hudson's Bay Company, the only effective authority in the region. So, overlooking the legal technicalities, many Americans considered Oregon their own.

With the typical nationalist and expansionist spirit of the time, one leading geographer described the United States by boasting, "This vast region . . . has an outline of 10,000 miles and contains within its vast perimeter nearly 2,300,000 square miles. No government in the world, excepting that of Russia, exercises *territorial jurisdiction* over so large an extent of connected country."

But just as the city of Washington differed so greatly from L'Enfant's paper design, so did the real United States vary from the picture shown on a map. For it was not truly a single nation, but two countries—the East and the West—divided from each other by an almost impenetrable band of territory that ran north and south through the heart of the continent.

The geographer recognized this when he added these words to his glowing remarks on the size of the United States: "More than half of the territory included within these limits contains few or no settlements, and is not formed into states. This immense country has every variety of surface, embracing vast ranges of mountains, and extensive plains and valleys."

The westward travelers, once they had passed the sharp crest of the Appalachian Mountains, found the journey increasingly easy, for as they drew nearer the Mississippi, the lands became flatter and flatter. The absence of trees might trouble them—they needed firewood and building materials—but they could move with comparative comfort.

But when they crossed the Mississippi, all this changed, and they entered a world that was indeed foreign to them. The land spread around them on every side, vast miles of it unbroken by mountains. It seemed to them that the rolling prairies were endless, for most of them had never seen anything like this. The sky was a great inverted bowl placed on top of the flatness, creating a horizon that was almost even on every hand. The rivers were like nothing they had ever known. In the spring, when the snows melted, the water roared through the beds they had carved in the soil, but with the coming of summer they dried up, often turning into bare trickles riddled with quicksand. Even the Missouri, the great river of the Plains, was hardly navigable at some seasons and became a mild and shallow stream.

The trees were few in this great expanse. By the water courses the pioneers might discover some cottonwoods with which to build a fire or create a rude shelter, but they could travel for days and find nothing to burn except buffalo chips, the sun-dried dung left by the great herds of grazing animals, which they learned from the natives to collect and use in their fires.

Even the grass became different from anything they had seen. As they moved west, it became shorter and sparser, for they were entering an area where the rainfall was so scanty that it could support neither farming nor grazing in the manner in which the pioneers had conducted those activities in the East.

When it was hot in that strange land, it was extremely hot. The sun blazed down on the prairies, and there was no relief from it, no place to seek shade. It burned and scorched the skins of the pioneers as no sun had ever done. When it was cold, the small rivers and streams were choked with ice, and the snow was deeply banked, often making it almost impossible for a man or an animal to move, and the cold would bite through the heaviest clothing or the thickest coat of fur. As for the wind, there was nothing like it, because there was nothing to stop it. It swept steadily and relentlessly across the plains, unimpeded by trees or hills or other natural windbreaks. In the East, it was tamed by the mountains and the forests, but on the plains, as on the sea, it became wild and at times vicious.

Washington Irving, telling of the last-minute reluctance of some travelers to continue with their westward-bound parties, described the Plains in words that reflected the pioneer's usual impression. "It was a region," he wrote, "almost as vast and trackless as the ocean, and . . . but little known, excepting through the vague accounts of Indian hunters. A part of their route would lie across an immense tract, stretching north and south for hundreds of miles along the foot of the Rocky

Mountains, and drained by the tributary streams of the Missouri and the Mississippi. This region, which resembles one of the immeasurable steppes of Asia, has not inaptly been termed 'the great American desert.' It spreads forth into undulating and treeless plains, and desolate sandy wastes, wearisome to the eye from their extent and monotony, and which are supposed by geologists to have formed the ancient floor of the ocean, countless ages since, when its primeval waves beat against the granite bases of the Rocky Mountains.

"It is land where no man permanently abides; for, in certain seasons of the year there is no food either for the hunter or his steed. The herbage is parched and withers; the brooks and streams are dried up; the buffalo, the elk, and the deer have wandered to distant parts, keeping within the verge of expiring verdure, and leaving behind them a vast uninhabited solitude, seamed by ravines, the beds of former torrents, but now serving only to tantalize and increase the thirst of the traveller.

"Occasionally the monotony of this vast wilderness is interrupted by mountainous belts of sand and limestone, broken into confused masses; with precipitous cliffs and yawning ravines, looking like the ruins of the world, or is traversed by lofty and barren ridges of rock, almost impassable, like those denominated the Black Hills. Beyond these rise the stern barriers of the Rocky Mountains, the limits, as it were, of the Atlantic world. The rugged defiles and deep valleys of this vast chain form sheltering places for restless and ferocious bands of savages, many remnants of tribes once inhabitants of the prairies, but broken up by war and violence, and who carry into their mountain haunts the fierce passions and reckless habits of desperadoes.

"Such," Irving continued, "is the nature of this immense wilderness of the far West; which apparently defies cultivation, and the habitation of civilized life. Some portions of it along the rivers may partially be subdued by agriculture, others may form vast pastoral tracts, like those of the East; but it is to be feared that a great part of it will form a lawless interval between the abodes of civilized men, like the wastes of the ocean or the deserts of Arabia; and, like them, be subject to the depredations of the marauder."

Washington Irving, who had himself taken the overland route to Oregon, wanted his readers to know that a man could not be accused of cowardice for not wanting to cross the prairies. There were so many enemies there: the monotony induced by the sight of the endless Plains, the lack of water and timber, and the ferocity of the weather, which swung from one extreme to the other. Added to these were the Indians who thrived in this area, such as the Arapahoes, the Pawnees, the Comanches, the Kiowas, the Cheyennes—all those tribes that had learned to adapt to life on the prairies and found there happiness. Most of them were fighters, because fighting was a condition of their lives, and as a result they became superb warriors with military skills admirably suited to the terrain over which they battled. From early childhood, their boys were taught to endure the climate, to find food in the apparent wasteland, to locate water in the seeming desert, and to wage relentless war against their enemies. To the pioneers crossing the plains, the threat they presented was even greater than that of the inhospitable land, and the greatest threat of all came from the Sioux.

*　　*　　*

Because they were far from Washington and the crowds streaming through the capital, the Sioux remained unaware of the inauguration of Andrew Jackson or of the restless mood of the country. During the following summer, when the buffalos concentrated in large herds, their bands joined together for communal hunting and for the celebration of the Sun Dance. In the fall, before the first frosts touched the Great Plains and the rivers began to take on a coating of ice, they staged their last hunts, getting in the meat they hoped would last them during the winter months. Then they went into their winter camps, the only semipermanent homes they knew, raising their tepees in the shelter of some wooded area along a river bottom or in a valley of the Black Hills.

There were seven divisions of the Western Sioux, those Sioux living beyond the Missouri—the Oglalas, who roamed in what is now eastern Wyoming and western South Dakota and Nebraska; the Brulés, who occupied the eastern portion of the last two states; the Miniconjous and the Two Kettle Sioux to the north of them; and three smaller divisions, the Sans Arcs, the Hunkpapas or Those Who Camp by the Entrance, and the Blackfeet Sioux, the latter not to be confused with the Blackfeet Indians, who lived farther west and with whom they occasionally fought. The three smaller divisions largely lived in what is now North Dakota and eastern Wyoming and Montana. Each of these divisions, although they spoke the same language and shared the same customs, remained independent of the others, free to do what its members chose. But they counseled together on problems of common interest and often visited each other to exchange news, recounting the raids they had made on their enemies, the battles in which they had fought, and the births and deaths that had occurred in their bands.

Most of these events would have seemed as inconsequential to the white men in the East as the invention of the plow and the reaper would have appeared to the Indians. What did it matter if the Oglalas had raided the Crows again? Or that the Brulés had had an unusually successful buffalo hunt that summer? Or that in 1831, during Jackson's first term as President, a Hunkpapa named Returns-Again became a father? This was a cause for joy within his own lodge and perhaps his own band, but the addition of one more Hunkpapa child hardly affected the white men.

Returns-Again was a great warrior—his name meant that he returned to fight again—but even he saw nothing especially remarkable about the son who would become one of the greatest of the Sioux warriors, famed throughout the United States as Sitting Bull. Therefore the family gave the child the name Slow until he could earn a better one for himself. This was the Sioux custom.

Slow's childhood was like that of most Sioux boys. When he was still an infant, he spent most of his time with his mother and other female relatives, because his father was busy hunting, fighting, and stealing horses from some of the neighboring tribes like the Crows. When she carried him, she strapped him onto his cradleboard, which left her hands free; and at night, if it was cold, she wrapped him in buffalo robes, caring for him with the devotion that Sioux mothers show for their children.

When Slow grew older, she allowed him to play with the other boys and girls in the band to which his father belonged. His childhood was a happy one, for there were almost no restrictions placed on his conduct. No Sioux father or mother liked to see their children weeping and would go to extreme lengths to prevent their tears. The discipline the Sioux eventually learned was imposed on by the rigors of their existence or resulted from their admiration for the Sioux way of life.

Most of the games Slow played while a child were reflections of the activities of his elders. He and his friends imitated their fathers and mothers in hunting, going on raids, or making and breaking camp, sometimes using miniature tepees constructed for this purpose by their parents. The real ones were much too large for children to play with. It required seven buffalo hides to make even a small one; large ones took as many as twelve to eighteen. To raise or lower these large structures demanded considerable skill, but the Sioux were able to break camp in about fifteen minutes. This speed was necessary, not only to flee from an approaching enemy, but also because the Sioux were constantly on the move.

This had not always been the Sioux's way of life. In a strange paradox, they owed their current prosperity and their strength to the arrival of their ultimate enemy—the white man. Originally they had lived in the forests much farther to the east. A strong and numerous tribe, they were able to hold their own against the surrounding Indians until the appearance of the French traders in Canada. These exchanged guns for beaver skins with the Sioux's traditional enemies, the Crees, and the balance of power was upset. Armed with their new weapons, the Crees invaded the Sioux's lands and created havoc among them. At long range, bows and arrows were simply no match for the new weapons. In desperation, many of the Sioux began migrating westward to the edge of the plains to escape from their lethal and uncompromising foes.

It was an alien world the Sioux timidly approached in the late seventeenth century. They were accustomed to the shelter of great forests with giant branches arching over their heads and giant trunks behind which they could hide. Now they were in the open with a vast expanse of sky overhead and the endless prairie rolling away into the distance in every direction. At first it was as strange to them as it later was to the white men who followed them. But gradually they ventured into this land and found that by stalking the buffalos on foot they could supply themselves with sufficient food and hides to live well.

Then came an unintended gift from white men. Wild horses, descendants of some of the animals brought over by the Spanish, had remained in the south; but about the time the Sioux entered the plains, they began moving north, tossing their manes and roaming over the expanse of grass. The Sioux learned to catch and ride and use them to carry their possessions when they were moving from one campground to another. With horses, the Sioux could kill even more buffalos than before and obtain more meat and hides. Soon the number of horses a man owned, or could afford to give away, became a certain indicator of his wealth. For a good horse meant speed while hunting and also speed while fighting, an obvious advantage over a less well-mounted warrior. So for the second time the Sioux benefited from the arrival of the white men. The guns sold by the French to the Crees had driven them out to the plains, where the opportunity for wealth was greater, and the horses lost by the Spaniards gave them the means for realizing that wealth.

But guns, which could make their lives even better, did not come with the horses. The Spanish were conquerors, not traders, and although they lost some of their horses to the Indians, they were careful to prevent their getting hold of guns. Spanish law prohibited all traffic in either firearms or ammunition with the natives. But gradually, as time passed, guns began to come from the east; and with them, the Sioux began to climb to the pinnacle of their power. The warrior who gained possession of a firearm, no matter how old the model or how worn the parts, had a distinct advantage both as a hunter and a fighter.

As a small boy, Slow saw the few muzzle-loaders around the camp and watched the warriors go out hunting or on a raid for horses or take the warpath against their enemies. Like every youth, he faced a choice. He could either become a warrior himself or a *winkte*. These were men, found in many camps, who turned from the rigors of the warriors' lives and adopted the ways of women. They dressed as women and performed women's work. Among the Sioux, their position was a curious one. Their tepees were pitched on the outskirts of the camps, and they were regarded with scorn by most of the Sioux. Yet they were reputed to possess magical powers and were often consulted on matters of importance, and their skill at tanning and decorating with porcupine quills was considered superior to that of most women. These were two arts highly prized by the Sioux and brought respect to the outcasts.

But Slow had no desire to become a *winkte*. He was at heart a fighter and wanted to be a warrior like his father. There would be plenty of fighting for him to do, far more than his ancestors had known. For the forces were already in motion that would make the white men's invasion of his land inevitable and bring to his country an enemy far more powerful and determined than any his people had ever faced before.

*   *   *

While Slow was still playing the childish games of a young Sioux boy, events were conspiring to bring about bloody conflict between the Americans and the Indians of the plains. In his first message to Congress, given in December 1829, Andrew Jackson had dealt with many issues, and his opinion on some of them was at variance with large segments of the electorate. In spite of the controversy that surrounded many of his first acts as President, there was one issue on which he found himself in almost unanimous accord with the vast majority of the electorate. That was in his attitude toward the Indians. Reversing the federal policies established earlier, he supported Georgia in its efforts to expel by force the southeastern Indians with whom the government had made treaties. He agreed with the state's contention that promises could be broken and replaced with new agreements at the whim of the white men. Because no one else at that time particularly wanted the Great Plains, the southeastern Indians could have a part of them instead of their own more desirable native lands. Indian Territory, which is now the state of Oklahoma, was considered almost worthless and therefore a fit place for "them varmints" to live, and with the army Jackson provided the force to make them move.

The evaluation of the Great Plains as a desolate, useless wasteland served as a protection for the Sioux, as effective a protection as their bows and arrows and the small number of guns they had been able to collect. Nobody wanted the area over which they roamed, so they could have it. But soon that poor opinion of the value of the plains would change, for two men were working on the tools that would help convert it from the "great American desert" into rich agricultural lands capable of feeding millions of people.

One of these was a Virginian, Cyrus McCormick. In the spring of 1831, the year that Slow was born, he decided to carry on his father's unsuccessful attempts to develop a mechanical reaper; and with the help of a black, named Jo Anderson, he developed a practical machine before harvesttime. In the following years, he made many improvements in his original invention and sold his reapers commercially. Orders came to him from various parts of the country, but those that interested him most were from the West. In 1844, he traveled through Iowa, Missouri, and other states that constituted the West and wrote home that although reapers might be a luxury in Virginia, they were a necessity on the flat, level lands he had just seen. His view of the future was accurate. Men never could have reaped the vast acres of the plains with cradle scythes, but they could with McCormick's machine. His invention brought war with the Sioux closer.

The other man was John Deere, who arrived in Grand Detour, Illinois, in 1836 and set up a blacksmith shop. The farmers, he found, were so discouraged that many of them were thinking of returning East. With their cast-iron plows, they could penetrate the earth and break it up on the first pass. But thereafter the dirt clung tenaciously to the bottom. After a few steps, the farmer would have to stop his horse and pull the dirt off by hand. This made plowing too slow and too much work to be profitable. It was as though nature had laid a shield over the face of the earth, and the farther west the settlers went, the tougher that shield became. Farmland? Men could not farm where they could not even plow. That was land for Indians and perhaps cattlemen, but not for farmers.

But John Deere redesigned the moldboard and the share—the point that digs into the earth—and made plows out of polished steel. They cut through the soil of the West as a sharp ax cuts through a soft tree. Suddenly millions of acres of wilderness and buffalo range became potential farms. A man could turn the sod with Deere's plow, and when the grain was ripe, he could reap it with McCormick's machine. These two peaceful men had created the two most deadly weapons the Sioux would ever face.

Three other men, who were missionaries, were also playing a decisive, although indirect, role in shaping Slow's future. At the time of his birth, the name Oregon was used to designate a large area in the northwest, including part of what is now Canada. Although it was the source of a profitable fur trade, not many Americans lived there. It was too remote, too unknown, and the joint control of Great Britain and the United States over the land made titles meaningless. But there were those who were concerned not about the fur trade but about the souls of the Indians. In 1834, Jason Lee of the Methodist Church established the Oregon Mission in the Willamette Valley, and two years later, Marcus Whitman and Henry Spaulding founded the American Board Mission. Interest in their activities and in the reports they sent home began to stimulate interest in Oregon itself. Slowly a trickle of settlers began to move across the plains, seeking new homes. The interest grew, and so did the trickle. By 1842, large numbers of people were beginning to follow the Oregon Trail from Independence, Missouri, across the Platte River, on to Independence Rock, and from there to the Willamette Valley, the goal of most of the travelers. The ruts became deeper as the wagon wheels ground into the dirt; and when they became too deep to make travel possible, the wagons moved to one side and broadened the trail. The Great Plains had now gained additional meaning to the Americans, for they offered the route to a new land.

In the south, the Americans were also moving farther into the plains. By the time Slow was born, at least twenty thousand of them had moved into the Mexican territory that later became Texas. As the years passed, they became more aggressive and less responsive to Mexican traditions and to the Mexican laws they had sworn to obey as a condition of their settlement. As a result, the government passed a new law that imposed a stiff tariff on trade with the United States and prohibited further immigration.

The troops sent to enforce this law were inadequate to their assignment and only succeeded in increasing the resentment of the American settlers. General Santa Anna, dictator of Mexico, then took to the field, made martyrs of the defenders of the Alamo, suffered defeat at San Jacinto, and reluctantly gave the Republic of Texas its independence.

Although in the Adams-Onís Treaty, signed in 1819, the United States had promised never to attempt the annexation of Texas, it was obvious that that treaty eventually would be as little honored as the treaties with the southeastern Indians. The Americans were moving westward regardless of what they had promised they would, or would not, do.

By the time Slow was in his early teens, an invisible web was being woven around the Sioux, one in which they must inevitably become entangled. The Americans had started encroaching on the Great Plains in the south, were drawing nearer in the north, were crossing the prairie in ever greater numbers, and had invented the agricultural tools needed to farm those flatlands.

A process had been set in motion that could not be reversed.

*   *   *

Neither Returns-Again nor any of the warriors in his band was aware of these events, and even if they had been, they could not have understood their meaning. Not being farmers, they would have been unable to comprehend the significance of the reaper and Deere's plow; not being members of a large race, they could never have conceived of the large masses of people who were approaching the outlying regions of their land or starting to move through it.

They undoubtedly knew that a few more white men were passing over the prairie to the south of the Hunkpapas, for news spread quickly in the Indian world. But these strangers were not yet coming in numbers great enough to worry the Sioux, who were free to lead the life they loved so well. Each winter they gathered in their winter camps, while the snows whirled around their tepees. When the warm winds of spring began to blow across the prairie, they started once more to move with the buffalo herds. And in July, or the Moon of the

Ripening Cherries, they gathered in a large group for the greatest of all Sioux ceremonies, the Sun Dance.

On this occasion, the Sioux placed their tepees in a ceremonial circle, while small boys like Slow looked on in anticipation of the excitement that was to follow. The first four days the Sioux devoted to social activities, visiting each other and exchanging news. During the second four days, the medicine men gave instructions to some of the men who planned to dance in order to become medicine men themselves or to gain prestige among their fellows. (Others danced to thank the gods for favors, such as the recovery of a sick child or an escape from danger during a hard-fought battle.)

The last four days were given over to the dance itself. With great ceremony, a tree was selected to serve as a central pole. It was then cut down and brought to the camp and erected where the dance was to take place. After that, the dancers got ready to perform. There were several orders of the dance, some of them considered as higher and more praiseworthy than others. But they all involved driving skewers through the flesh of the dancers, sometimes through the skin just below their shoulder blades, sometimes through their breasts, and sometimes through both. These skewers were then attached by leather thongs to the central pole. During the course of the dance, the participants slowly freed themselves by pulling against the thongs and letting the skewers tear through their flesh. This self-torture exhilarated them and often led them to have visions, which they regarded as messages direct from the gods.

This was a bloody, painful ceremony, but as one contemporary observer, with considerable insight, commented, "The Indian believes, with many Christians, that self-torture is an act most acceptable to God, and the extent of pleasure that he can give his God is exactly measured by the amount of suffering that he can bear without flinching. There are, therefore, always some warriors who are activated to the self-torture of the 'Hoch-e-a-yum' [sun dance], by motives as pure as ever led a Christian martyr to the stake."

To have danced the Sun Dance at least once was to acquire respect, and some warriors danced it more than once. All their lives their chests and backs bore the dramatic scars resulting from their wounds. As Slow watched the bleeding dancers, he longed for the day when he would become an adult and be able to drive the skewers through his own flesh to demonstrate his faith in the Sioux's way of life.

In many respects, this ceremony epitomized the world in which

Slow was growing up. It was cruel, but life on the prairie was often cruel; and it was mystic, because the Sioux themselves were mystics. Much of their life was dictated by their visions and dreams.

This accounts for the extreme importance that Returns-Again attached to an incident that occurred while he was off on one of his frequent hunting expeditions. He was out on the prairie with three other warriors, hunting buffalos, and they had killed one of the large animals and butchered it. The sun had just dropped over the edge of the horizon when they lighted a fire of buffalo chips and prepared to enjoy their freshly killed meat.

Suddenly they heard the sound of something approaching. In that wild country, the Sioux were always alert for the presence of their enemies, so the four warriors quickly picked up their weapons and prepared to fight. But they soon saw that their visitor was nothing to frighten them, for it was simply a buffalo bull that had become separated from the rest of the herd and was walking slowly toward their campfire. This in itself was not unusual, because often a single bull might wander away from the others.

But this bull was different. As it walked toward the campfire, it seemed to be muttering to itself, and the four warriors were certain that it was talking to them. Standing motionless in the fading light so as not to scare the animal away, the warriors listened carefully, hoping they could understand what it was telling them. This was an important moment, because the Buffalo God in whom they believed might be speaking to them.

Returns-Again, who had occult powers, was occasionally able to understand the language of animals, so he listened especially closely as the bull came nearer. To the others, the sounds remained undecipherable grunts, strange noises made by a wild animal. But Returns-Again was finally able to understand what the buffalo was saying. It was repeating the four phrases used by the Sioux to describe the four ages of man: Sitting Bull, Jumping Bull, Bull-Stands-with-Cow, and Lone Bull—infancy, youth, adulthood, and old age.

This was a momentous occasion for Returns-Again, as momentous as a victory against odds over the strongest enemy. For in the quiet of the prairie evening, the Buffalo God had spoken directly to him and had given him four mystic names that he could bestow on anyone he chose. Because of the circumstances under which Returns-Again had obtained them, they were certain to have special significance for their bearers, affording them protection in battle and good fortune during their lifetimes. The names also took on added meaning because there were four of them, and four warriors had heard the buffalo talking. Among the Sioux, as among some of the other Indian tribes, four was a magical number with powers of its own.

Of the four names, the first one spoken by the buffalo was obviously the most important just because it was the first. Therefore Returns-Again decided to keep it for himself. When he and his hunting companions returned to the main camp, Returns-Again described the wonderful event that had taken place and asked the other Indians henceforth to call him Sitting Bull.

*   *   *

During Slow's childhood, nothing occurred to dampen the expansionist spirit of the United States, and the restlessness of Jackson's day still pervaded the country. In 1844, when Slow was only fourteen years old, James Polk had won the presidency on a platform that specifically called for the annexation of Texas in spite of the pledge the United States had given Mexico never to take over that territory. In December, 1845, a few months after his inauguration, he sent troops south, ostensibly to protect Texas, and at the same time offered to purchase from Mexico much of what is now the Southwest. The Mexicans were understandably insulted, for they had no more intention than the United States of selling vast areas of their country. Polk then moved his troops farther south. The Mexicans retaliated by crossing the Rio Grande. A clash occurred, and the American government had the excuse it wanted to declare war on its weaker neighbor.

Forces under Zachary Taylor moved south from the Rio Grande. Winfield Scott landed at Veracruz and marched from there to Mexico City, and the Army of the West, under Colonel Stephen Kearny, was ordered to go through what are now Arizona and New Mexico and take California. The outcome of the war was inevitable from the start. The Mexicans were no match for the aggressive, determined Americans. Proud as they were, they could not resist the advancing armies, and the United States seized the land it coveted.

Not content with this enormous acquisition of territory, the Americans also focused their attention on the north. More of them had been moving into Oregon, and although the Hudson's Bay Company had originally received many of them in a friendly fashion, they were determined to abrogate the Joint Occupation Treaty, under which Great Britain and the United States had shared the land, and make it entirely their own. Nor were they willing to wait. If Great Britain did not immediately accede to their demands, they were ready to fight, and the threat of war, given the mood of the country, was a real one. Rather than risk hostilities, the British government agreed to set the boundary at the 49th parallel with one slight deviation that permitted Vancouver to remain within Canada. Thus the Pacific Northwest became a territorial part of the United States. The boast made by the geographer in Andrew Jackson's administration was now a reality, and Slow, instead of living on the fringes of an alien nation, was close to the geographic center of it.

Although he was still a young boy, he had left childish things behind him. When he played games, they were imitations of men's activities, for he wanted above all else to become a warrior. His father may not have seen anything remarkable about him when the family named him Slow, but the boy was showing himself an adept learner of the arts of warfare. He could shoot rapidly with his bow, keeping several arrows in the air at the same time, and ride a horse swiftly and surely, dropping to one side of it and using its body as a shield against imaginary bullets of imaginary enemies. But he longed for more than games. He yearned for actual battle, when the Sioux would ride down on their enemies and he would have a chance to demonstrate his bravery.

One day Good-Voiced-Elk, a warrior in the band to which Slow's father belonged, formed a raiding party to steal horses from the Sioux's enemies. This, thought Slow, might be his opportunity. Although he was not really old enough to accompany the men, he thought they might not object if he merely rode along with them. Without discussing his plan with his family, he joined the assembled warriors. They were surprised that one so young wished to go with them, but they admired his courage and did not deny him permission to come.

Slow had brought no weapons with him, but he carried a coup stick, a specially decorated stick, his father had given him. Among the Sioux personal contact with the enemy was more highly prized than even the enemy's death. What counted was not who killed the foe, but who first touched his body, dead or alive, with his coup stick and therefore "counted coup on him." That was the finest honor a warrior could win, and it permitted him to wear a feather in his hair. (Three other warriors could also count coup on the same enemy later, but theirs was a lesser honor.) Thereafter the warrior could tell the story of his heroism at any gathering of the Sioux during which the warriors recounted their feats.

Armed only with his coup stick, Slow rode along with the others, imitating their gestures in boyish fashion and pretending to himself he was truly one of them. His greatest hope was that they would find some enemies and that somehow he could distinguish himself. For many miles, they traveled over the plains, the dust rising from the hooves of their horses, and entered the territory of Indians with whom they were habitually at war. Concealing themselves behind a small hill, they sent one of their members ahead as a scout. In a short time he returned and reported he had seen a group of Indians riding in their direction. So the Sioux remained hidden, for the terrain was well suited for an ambush.

Quietly the men prepared their weapons, removing their leather shields from their covers and adjusting their arms. The horses, long experienced in warfare, sensed the coming excitement and shook their heads, for they were anxious to start the fast dash forward. Slow also felt the tension, but in him it became unbearable. Unable to stand it any longer, he suddenly released his horse's head and struck its flanks with his heels. The surprised warriors saw the horse run forward, carrying its unarmed rider, who was waving his coup stick. To make the ambush more certain, they would have preferred to wait longer before attacking, but Slow's precipitous act destroyed the opportunity. Either they had to charge immediately or let the boy be killed or captured. They charged.

The approaching Indians were startled by the suddenness of the attack. At one moment, they had been riding in peace. At the next, the Sioux had emerged from their hiding place and were racing toward them. Not knowing how many more Sioux might be lurking behind the hill, they turned and fled from their pursuers, urging their horses to go faster.

The Sioux, with Slow in the lead, followed them closely. The sound of their hooves echoed over the plain. One of the enemy, whose horse was slower, lagged behind the others, and Slow singled him out. Urging his horse on, he drew nearer and nearer. The fleeing Indian, hearing the sound of the hoofbeats coming closer, threw himself to the ground and fitted an arrow to his bow. Slow was in such a frenzy of excitement he discarded all caution. Instead of dropping to the side of the horse and wheeling away to safety, he kept on coming straight at his enemy. He moved so quickly that the Indian was unable to release his arrow in time. Slow swept past him and, in the symbolic gesture, struck his arm with the coup stick. At almost the same moment his horse hit the Indian and knocked him to the ground. Before the fallen Indian could rise to his feet, the other Sioux came up and quickly killed him. But Slow was the one who had touched him first, and therefore he was the one who could count coup on him.

The rest of the struggle lasted only briefly. Having been put to flight so quickly, the other Indians could not rally to resist the Sioux. Only those with the fastest horses escaped. The remainder were killed.

When Good-Voiced-Elk led the Sioux with their captured horses and scalps back to the main camp, Slow's father was almost as jubilant as Slow himself. His son had counted coup at an unusually early age, an act that would bring respect not only to himself but to the whole family. Surely this boy of his was a remarkable child, one destined for distinction and deserving of a better name than Slow. After careful thinking, he therefore gave him one of the greatest of his possessions, the first of the four names he had received from the buffalo, the name he had originally taken for himself: Sitting Bull. From that time on it became Slow's own name, and his father took the next of the names given him by the buffalo, Jumping Bull.

But while the Sioux were celebrating this new victory, in the distance John Deere's plows and Cyrus McCormick's reapers were inching their way westward, travel on the Oregon Trail was slowly increasing, and the white men's net was gradually closing around them.

II

Wounded in Battle

LIVING with the Hunkpapas in North Dakota and Montana, Sitting Bull felt little affected by the white men in his youth. The route to Oregon lay farther south in Nebraska and southern Wyoming, nearer the Brulé and Oglala Sioux. He did not need Americans to fight to continue his training as a warrior. As relative newcomers to the plains, the Sioux had had to battle to make a place for themselves among the other Indians. Also they needed horses, and they were not adept at breeding them. So they obtained them by raiding their neighbors, particularly the Crows.

Sometimes their raiding parties were composed of small groups of warriors who would slip into their enemies' camps in the darkness. This was dangerous business, because the better horses—those the Sioux especially wanted—were often tethered in front of their owners' tepees just to prevent their theft. If a horse whinnied in the black night or the thieves tripped over a saddle or a dog barked, the whole camp would waken and take off in pursuit of the marauders. For this reason, the raiding parties were sometimes composed of more men than those needed to do the actual stealing. The main body remained out of sight at a distance. Then if the camp became aroused and followed the thieves, the thieves led them directly toward the main force, and often a pitched battle took place.

Sitting Bull joined as many of these raiding parties as he could. On each one he learned something more about the Sioux's art of warfare and had a chance to put his rapidly growing skills to the test. With each year, he could ride better and shoot more swiftly and accurately;

and he found himself exhilarated by the danger of fighting. He liked that moment in the early hours of the morning, when the plains were covered with darkness and the men crept cautiously toward the enemy camp. He enjoyed the slow and careful movement of shadowy figures among the tepees, the gentle urging of the horses away from their owners' lodge toward the vastness of the plains where the other Sioux were waiting, then the final dash to safety, sometimes with the enemy in hot pursuit, sometimes with the enemy unaware that the raid had taken place until the sun rose and showed the horses were gone.

Renown in war was a driving ambition with Sitting Bull. His name, given to his father by the Buffalo God, and the distinction he had won with his first coup promised an outstanding career as a fighter. But for all his love of combat and the ferocity with which he battled, he was known to the Indians of his own tribe as a kindly and affectionate young man, one who liked children and was considerate of the women. Among his characteristics, they particularly admired his ability to sing. In fact, he was already beginning to make up his own songs rather than merely chanting those composed by others. Yet, friendly as he was in his dealings with the Sioux, even among them he was already showing firmness of mind and determination to do things his own way.

He revealed this one night when the band to which he belonged returned victorious from a battle with the Crows. The warriors brought with them the trophies they had secured, the hand of a Crow warrior, a pair of ears from another, and the genitals of the third. (The Sioux did not necessarily take the scalps of their fallen enemies; almost any part of the anatomy would do as well.) They also brought with them a Crow woman whom they had captured and intended to adopt into the tribe.

Before they celebrated their victory, the Sioux who had lost relatives to the Crows were allowed to touch the trophies and to taunt the memories of their dead owners. While this was going on, some of the others talked to the captive woman. During their conversation with her, they decided she was a *witkowin*, or Crazy Woman, one who was sexually promiscuous. This did not mean she had been a prostitute, for prostitution was rare, if not unknown, among the Sioux. But a *witkowin* was one who had been loose for her own pleasure. Perhaps, for example, she had run away with men several times but had not married any of them. Such a person was despised by the Sioux, and the members of the band certainly did not want to receive her as one of their own.

In their disgust and anger, some of the women tore the captive's clothes from her body and bound her naked to a pine tree. Others scurried around the camp, collecting dry brush which they piled high around the defenseless woman's body. As a punishment for her sins, they intended to burn her alive.

Sitting Bull watched their preparations with dislike. He enjoyed a fight when warrior was facing warrior and the guns smoked and the arrows flew through the air. He had little fear of death and was accustomed to seeing it. But he did not want to watch the captive burned by the angry women, to hear her screams in the prairie night, to see the flames licking against her body, or to smell the sickening odor of burning flesh.

He was, however, too young and too lacking in authority to stop the women, for they would not have heeded the objections of a boy in his teens. But Sitting Bull was determined to prevent this torture. Quietly and unobserved by the others, he drew an arrow, fitted it to his bow, and stood inconspicuously outside the ring of celebrating warriors and women.

The fire was now laid, and the women came forward with torches to light it. Sitting Bull pulled back the string of his bow and aimed his arrow. The women leaned toward the ground to touch the brush with their flames. Just at that moment, Sitting Bull released his arrow. The twang of the bowstring was too soft a noise to be heard by the angry crowd, but the arrow sprang forward and pierced the captive's heart before the flames reached her flesh. In spite of the wishes of the other Sioux, Sitting Bull had defied the band and given her a painless death.

* * *

Although Sitting Bull and his division of the Sioux knew little about the Americans, other Sioux were seeing them more frequently. Markets had grown up for the heavier furs of the plains, such as buffalo and antelope, which now, in spite of their weight, could be transported to the cities by taking them by boat down the Missouri River. Pickled buffalo tongues were also becoming a delicacy, and often an animal was killed—by both Americans and Indians—for this one small piece of meat. After witnessing a buffalo hunt near the Yellowstone River, John James Audubon, the bird painter, commented as early as 1843,

"What a terrible destruction of life, as it were for nothing, or next to it, as the tongues only were brought in, and the flesh of these fine animals were left to beasts and birds of prey, or to rot on the spots where they fell. The prairies are literally *covered* with the skulls of the victims." Long before the Civil War and the coming of the railroads, the herds of the West were being severely depleted, and in parts of the plains, particularly close to the Missouri River, all game was becoming scarce.

Taking advantage of the growing economic opportunities on the plains, two Americans, William Sublette and Robert Campbell, had built a trading post in what is now southeastern Wyoming where the Laramie River flows into the North Platte. Next, in an effort to cut into the business of other traders, they persuaded the Oglala Sioux, who were the Sioux living nearest them, to move farther south and trade with them. The Oglalas prospered under the new arrangement, so the Brulé Sioux, who had lived farther east along the White River in present-day Nebraska and South Dakota, decided to join them. This movement of two divisions of Sioux, brought about by the economic rivalry of the traders, placed them directly on the route that would be increasingly used by emigrants to Oregon and made an eventual conflict almost inevitable.

At first the Indians paid little attention to the traveling white men. Their numbers were too scanty to concern them; but as the wagon trains grew in size, tensions rose, not only over the presence of the white men, but also over the damage they were doing to the country. They often arrived with large herds of stock, which ate the grass needed by the buffalos and the Indians' horses. The emigrants had to have food, so they shot game. Soon the area on either side of the trail became, from the Indians' point of view, almost a desert in which they could not live. Yet the wagon trains kept coming.

On occasion, an individual Indian might warn a group of Americans that they were not wanted; but they limited themselves to only minor harassment. A group of them, for example, might suddenly appear before a wagon train and with threatening gestures demand minor tribute for permission to pass. At other times, when the livestock was not carefully guarded, the Indians would sweep down at night, stampede the herd, and run off with it. These actions, however, did not result in bodily harm to the emigrants or even seriously impede their passage west, but the incidents were annoying and sometimes costly. Consequently, when the travelers reached their destination, they wrote home about the troubles they had had; and the federal government finally felt compelled to take action.

For reasons of economy it was reluctant to establish permanent posts in the Indians' lands, but it ordered Colonel Stephen W. Kearny to march from Fort Leavenworth, Kansas, across the northern plains in a demonstration of American strength. Setting out with five companies of dragoons (mounted infantry), two howitzers, and some rockets with which he hoped to impress the Indians, he reached the trading post on the Laramie River on June 15, 1845.

The following day he addressed an assembly of the Oglala and Brulé Sioux, who lived near the trading post and who had gathered to hear him. He spoke of the government's determination to keep the road open and to give safe conduct to the emigrants, and he said that although the Americans wanted to be the Indians' friends, they would not tolerate any further interference with travelers. At the end of the meeting, he distributed the usual trade goods of cloth, beads, looking glasses, and knives.

Then he put on a show of American power. At his order, the soldiers brought up the howitzer, a small but lethal cannon adapted from a design developed by the French for use in the mountains. Normally it was mounted on its own wheels and pulled by a horse. But if the trail was rough, the barrel, which measured less than three feet, could be dismounted and carried by a pack animal. In spite of their small size and lightness, the howitzers were deadly weapons. The gunners had a choice of three standard projectiles: exploding shells, which were charged with seven ounces of rifle powder; spherical case shot, each of which contained seventy-eight musket balls; and cannisters, which contained a hundred and forty-eight balls. By raising or lowering the barrel, the howitzer had a range varying from about a hundred and fifty yards to slightly more than a thousand.

While the Sioux watched, the soldiers fired it. The loud roar and the cloud of smoke rising from the cannon were astonishing in themselves, but the Sioux especially noted the effectiveness of the projectile. No massed band of warriors, armed only with bows or muzzle-loaders, could stand up against this gun. And unlike the cannons mounted at the forts, the soldiers could take this one with them into the wilderness. As a final touch, in the evening Kearny also fired a rocket.

Content that he had made the Americans' meaning clear and that he had demonstrated they had the power to enforce their will, Kearny marched west to the Continental Divide and returned to Fort Leavenworth. Although some people thought that army posts should be established along the trail for the protection of the emigrants, Kearny disagreed. He thought order could be maintained with a yearly march like the one he had just made.

He was, however, only partially right. Although the Sioux on the whole did not seriously bother the emigrants, some of the other tribes were not so friendly. They robbed and stole from the wagon trains, demanded more and more tribute, and eventually killed several people. In 1849, therefore, the government decided to establish a fort at the juncture of the Laramie and the North Platte in conjunction with Fort Stephen Kearny, located to the east in what is now Nebraska. Because the site of the trading post at the mouth of the Laramie had been so well chosen, the government decided to purchase those buildings rather than construct new ones.

With the establishment of the army post, relations between the Indians and the Americans, at least superficially, continued much as they had been before, but the basic change was great. Earlier, except for the traders, the Americans, whether they were soldiers or emigrants, had all been transients. The Indians' territory was merely a passage through which they went on their way farther west. But now the Americans had placed a permanent installation in the heart of the land occupied by the Oglalas and the Brulés and were there to stay.

As more and more wagon trains followed the Oregon Trail, conditions for the Indians grew worse. The grass grew scanty, and the buffalo became scarcer and scarcer. Some of the travelers carried cholera, a disease unknown to the Indians. Soon the Indians found themselves dying from this mysterious ailment against which their medicine men could not prevail and which they knew had been brought by the white men. Some of the Brulés fled back to the White River, from which they had come, but they carried the disease with them. Later on Indians found their lodges still standing, but no living beings were inside, just dead bodies.

No Indian outbreaks had occurred, but the wiser among the Americans knew one must be imminent. As a result of their warnings, Congress finally appropriated $100,000 for a large conference to be held in 1851 at Fort Laramie, not to purchase land from the Indians, but to buy a right-of-way through their territory and thus ensure the safety of traveling Americans.

Indians and an occasional white man or half-breed who was familiar with the tribes were dispatched across the plains to tell the Indians about the impending conference and to promise presents to all those who came. Word went from tribe to tribe and from band to band that the Americans had something to say and gifts to give away. So groups of Indians began to make their way toward the fort at the mouth of the Laramie River.

Many tribes—some of them traditional enemies—came to the conference, and fighting almost broke out between the Sioux and the Snakes. When the Snakes were riding up to the encampment, a Sioux warrior recognized the chief who had killed his father. Seizing his bow and arrow and leaping on his horse, he dashed toward him. The Snake raised his gun, ready to fire. But a French interpreter, who had been watching the Sioux, followed close behind him, pulled him from his horse to the ground, and stood over him. The Sioux outnumbered the Snakes about five to one, but they had far fewer guns and a fight between the two tribes would have been an unequal one. So peace was restored, and the Snakes set up their lodges near the two hundred dragoons who had been brought to the fort to maintain order.

According to those who were present, it was the largest meeting of Indians that had ever been held. Perhaps ten thousand men, women, and children were camped side by side, their tepees stretching into the distance and their horses eating every available blade of fodder.

Although the Indians had arrived, the supply train carrying the presents had not, and Colonel David D. Mitchell, Commissioner of Indian Affairs and a former fur trader, used one pretext after another to postpone the council. But the Indians had traveled many miles to hear the white men's words and receive their gifts, and they were growing weary of waiting any longer. Finally word reached Fort Laramie that the supply train was approaching, but by this time the thousands of Indian horses had eaten the ground bare around the post. Consequently the council was moved thirty-five miles east to Horse Creek.

While the Indians were waiting, they began to run short of supplies. The army had little to give them, and there was little game left in the vicinity of the encampment. Nevertheless, they made a party out of the occasion. "Notwithstanding the scarcity of provisions felt in the camp before the wagons [of presents and supplies] came," wrote a white Jesuit priest who was present, "the feasts were numerous and well attended. No epoch in Indian annals, probably, shows a greater massacre of the canine race. Among the Indians the flesh of the dog is the most honorable and esteemed of viands, especially in the absence of buffalo and other animals. On the present occasion it was the last resort. I was invited to several of these banquets; and a great chief, in particular, wished to give me a special mark of his friendship and respect for me. He had filled his great kettle with little fat dogs, skins and all. He presented me, on a wooden platter, the fattest, well boiled. I found the meat really delicate, and I can vouch that it is preferable to suckling-pig, which it nearly resembles in taste."

Finally on the morning of Monday, September 8, 1851, as Mitchell could postpone it no longer, he opened the council. Promptly at nine o'clock the cannon sounded, and the Indians took their places at the council ground, the chiefs sitting in front, the warriors behind them, and the women and children forming an outer ring. As Mitchell stood up to address this gathering, he faced the almost impossible task of making the Indians understand the terms of the treaty. To people with a European background, they were rather simple. The Indians were to refrain from attacking the emigrants and each other. They were to agree among themselves on boundary lines for each tribe and then stay inside the designated areas except when they were hunting. They were to assume responsibility for the acts of individuals within their tribes, making restitution for any damage they might do. And they were to give the Americans the right to build roads and army posts within their territory. In return, they were to receive $50,000 worth of articles and provisions annually for fifty years.

To the Indians, however, these terms were not simple. Refrain from attack? But warfare was part of their way of life. Where, for example, would the Sioux obtain horses if they could not raid the Crows' herds? Boundary lines? What were boundary lines to an Indian? Nothing in his tradition had prevented him from going anywhere he wanted unless an enemy was strong enough to keep him out. Assume responsibility for the acts of individuals? But the Indians had no mechanism for doing that. Their form of government was not like the white men's. It was individualistic, and each warrior was responsible for his own behavior. What authority the chiefs might have was extremely limited and certainly did not extend over the behavior of each warrior. Roads and military posts? They could not conceive what these would imply for their future. Their concepts of population were so limited that many of them, after seeing the Oregon Trail, thought the East had already been emptied of people. As to the $50,000 worth of goods and provisions, they did not know what $50,000 was, but it sounded like a lot of money and like a lot of gifts. That much they thought they could understand.

Painstakingly Mitchell went over the treaty line by line with the interpreters to make sure there were no misunderstandings. But how could there be misunderstanding when, in the first place, there was no basis for understanding? No matter how carefully Mitchell explained the actual words, he could never explain the meaning of the document. Two entirely different cultures were trying to bridge the enormous gap between them and accomplish the feat in less than a week.

For several days, the Indians consulted among themselves about the terms offered them. The $50,000 worth of goods and provisions to be delivered to them every year was so appealing that one by one the tribes decided to sign the white men's paper.

Then Mitchell made a request that struck them as truly strange. He wanted each tribe to designate a chief who would be responsible for his tribe's carrying out the treaty's terms. A chief? A single chief? But none of the tribes had a single chief who was supreme above all other chiefs and who could exercise authority over all the tribe. Nevertheless, after some discussion among themselves, they acquiesced to this curious demand—all but the Sioux. They were far too numerous, they said, to be led by a single man. Among them, however, was a Brulé named Brave Bear. In his youth he had been employed by one group of traders to harass their competitors, which he had done effectively by stealing their horses, attempting to burn their houses, and planning to murder them. But as he had grown older, he had come to believe that the survival of his tribe depended on good relations with the white men, and he had made many friends among them. Mitchell was at last able to persuade the Sioux to accept Brave Bear as the one who would be answerable for their conduct, although Brave Bear himself did not want to be signaled out in this fashion. He knew the position carried with it much responsibility and no authority.

At last, on September 17, all the discussion was over, and the formal treaty had been agreed upon and was ready for signature. The chiefs came solemnly forward and made X's beside their names. For this was what the white men wanted, wasn't it?

Still the presents and provisions had not arrived, although word came that they were on their way. The area surrounding even the new encampment was bare of grass, and too many people had been living in one place for too long. Bits of refuse stood everywhere, and the smell became so bad the dragoons moved two miles away to escape it.

On the 20th the wagon train finally appeared. "The safe arrival of this convoy," wrote the Jesuit, "was an occasion of general joy. Many were in absolute destitution. The next day the wagons were unloaded and the presents suitably arranged. The flag of the United States floated from a tall staff before the tent of the superintendent [Mitchell], and a discharge of cannon announced to the Indians that the division of the presents was to take place. Without delay, the occupants of the various camps flocked in,—men, women and children, —in great confusion, and in their gayest costume, daubed with paints of glaring hues and decorated with all the gewgaws they could boast. They took the respective places assigned to each particular band, thus forming an immense circle, covering several acres of land, and the merchandise was assembled in the center. . . .

"The great chiefs of the different nations were served first, and received suits of clothes. You may easily imagine their singular movements on appearing in public, and the admiration which they excited in their comrades, who were never weary of inspecting them. The great chiefs were, for the first time in their lives, pantalooned; each was arrayed in a general's uniform, a gilt sword hanging at his side. Their long, coarse hair floated above the military costume, and the whole was crowned by the burlesque solemnity of their painted faces."

The gift of generals' uniforms to the leading chiefs was in keeping with the whole spirit of the council. From the beginning, the Americans had failed to recognize the great cultural difference between themselves and the Indians. They had started by asking them to sign a treaty, written in the Americans' language and terms, which the Indians could not possibly understand, and had ended it by dressing their chiefs as though they were field grade officers.

Next Mitchell distributed the presents for the various bands. "The conduct of this vast multitude was calm and respectful," wrote the Jesuit. "Not the slightest sign of impatience or jealousy was observed during the distribution; each band appeared indifferent until its portion was received.

"Then, glad or satisfied, but always quiet," he wrote, "they removed from the plain with their families and lodges. They had heard the good news that the bison were numerous on the South Fork of the Platte, three days' march from the plain, and they hastily turned their steps in that direction, resolved to make the buffalo atone for the hunger they had recently suffered on the Great Council plain."

As Mitchell watched them depart, he knew that he had helped bring together one of the largest assemblies of Indians and that enemies had camped beside enemies without fighting. And he thought he had brought peace to the plains. For all the bravery Sitting Bull had shown in striking coup at so early an age, a treaty had been made to eliminate any further fighting in the future.

* * *

The treaty, however, did not remain in effect for many years. With an increasing shortage of grass and buffalos, ever greater numbers of wagon trains, and an unsympathetic attitude on the part of the army, by 1853 the Sioux had become more and more restless and disturbed.

To add to the problems of those who wanted peace, some of the Miniconjou Sioux came south that summer to visit the Oglalas and Brulés. They ordinarily lived north of these tribes and had not attended the council and did not feel in any way bound by the treaty just because they were also Sioux. Let the Oglalas and the Brulés do what they wanted for themselves, but they could not speak for the other divisions of the Sioux. Nor was there any means of controlling them. Mitchell had tried to designate a head chief for each tribe, and Brave Bear had reluctantly accepted that position for the Brulés and the Oglalas, but definitely not for the Miniconjous, and even if he had, they would not have recognized him. He had absolutely no authority over them at all. The Brulés and Oglalas outnumbered their guests many times over and therefore had the physical power to suppress them, but this would have been entirely against Sioux customs and would have had serious repercussions throughout the seven divisions.

Consequently the Miniconjous felt free to harass the emigrants as much as they dared without inviting retaliation. Finally they became so bold they stole the Platte River ferryboat from its owner. On June 15, 1853, a sergeant from the fort came to get it. While he was crossing the river on the boat, a Miniconjou fired at him. Either the Indian had no intention of hitting him or he was a poor shot, for the bullet merely struck the water. But the sergeant was furious, and on his return to the fort he reported the incident to his commanding officer, First Lieutenant Richard B. Garnett.

Garnett was an inexperienced officer with little respect for Indians. Ever since the establishment of Fort Laramie, the government had failed to comprehend what was needed there. It stationed far too few soldiers at the fort to protect it in the event of a real uprising; eventually it withdrew the cavalry, leaving only infantry who could not be truly effective against the mounted warriors; and the officers it assigned to the command were, like Garnett, immature.

One problem faced by the army was the inadequacy of its communications. The nearest telegraph station was many miles away from Fort Laramie, so Garnett could not ask his superiors' advice. Yet he had not been trained to make decisions of the sort that now faced him. He was a soldier, not an ambassador, and it was difficult for him to place the incident in proper perspective. In spite of the sergeant's scare, the event had been unimportant, insulting perhaps, but that was all. The terms of the Treaty of 1851 made clear the procedure that should be followed. The chief of the band should be asked to punish the offending Indian and make reparations. Even though the Miniconjous were not parties to the treaty, they should be handled according to its provisions. Furthermore, as any of the traders around the post could have told Garnett, the Indians did not like outsiders interfering in their affairs.

Essentially this was a problem for police action, but Garnett converted it into a military foray. He ordered Second Lieutenant Hugh Fleming, only a year out of West Point and a brevet officer at that, to form a detachment of twenty-three enlisted men, the post surgeon, and the post interpreter, August Lucien, a hot-tempered man who could speak the Sioux's language but whom they disliked. Fleming was to take this force and march to the Miniconjous' village and capture the Indian who had fired the shot.

The Miniconjous, of course, had thought nothing of the incident, if they had even noticed it, until they saw Fleming marching up to their camp at the head of twenty-five men. This, they could see, was no peaceful visit, and while they watched, Lucien, the interpreter, advanced ahead of the others. Drawing close to the lodges, he demanded the custody of the Indian who had fired the shot at the sergeant. The leader of the band was away, however, and no one else could possibly make the decision to turn the offender over to the Americans. In any case, this was not the way the Sioux handled such disputes.

To force the issue, Fleming ordered his men to march against the camp. The Miniconjous fled to a ravine behind the village. Someone fired a shot, and Fleming charged. It was growing dark, or otherwise the casualties might have been greater, but as it was, Fleming killed three Miniconjous and took two prisoners before marching back to Fort Laramie.

In response to this violence, the Miniconjous showed surprising restraint. A few days later their leader appeared at the fort and asked for presents, the usual Sioux fashion of mending a quarrel and making peace. Garnett did not know this Indian custom and considered the chief's request impudent. But after lecturing him on how to behave in the future, he released the two Miniconjou prisoners.

If the Sioux had had any doubt about the arrogance of some white men, that doubt was now dispelled. Three Miniconjous were dead because of a frightened sergeant, their families in mourning, while the sergeant lived to parade around Fort Laramie. And when their chief had gone to the fort to make peace according to the Indian custom, he had received nothing but a scolding, as though he were a small boy, not an experienced warrior who knew more about warfare than the young lieutenant. Some of the Miniconjous now wanted vengeance, but the older men restrained them. Their unrest, however, spread to the Oglalas and Brulés, who sympathized with them.

Toward the end of the summer, when the Indian agent arrived with the annuity goods, he found the Sioux in an ugly mood. Furthermore, he brought them bad news. When they had gathered at the Americans' bidding at Horseshoe Creek, no one had told them such treaties had to be ratified by the United States Senate, whatever that was. Now it appeared that the Senate, instead of approving the agreement, had reduced the period over which the annuity payments would be made from fifty to fifteen years.

This was a drastic change in the terms that had originally been offered the Indians and which they had accepted. Naturally they were confused and could not understand what had happened. Actually the Americans were doing to the Indians what they complained the Indians did to them. The Americans always looked for one central figure in each tribe with whom they could make an agreement and who then would have the power to enforce it. But they were always frustrated, because such figures did not exist. When they negotiated successfully with an individual chief, they discovered he represented only a small part of the tribe and that his enforcement power was minimal. Chiefs were not chiefs, as the Americans conceived of them.

Neither were government peace commissioners what the Indians thought they were. They came with wagonloads of presents, escorts of troops, and many assurances that they had been sent by the "Great

White Father" personally. But now, the Indians discovered, they had no real authority either. Back in the East was another council of white men who had to be consulted. Without their approval the formal-looking document was just a piece of paper. Nor could the Americans seem to control the actions of their individuals any more than the Sioux could control their own young warriors. The young lieutenant had killed three Miniconjous because the sergeant had been scared. That was not justice. Yet the peace commissioners seemingly did nothing about it. Both sides, Indians and white men, were much closer to each other in their forms of government than they realized. Both practiced democracy but expected absolutism on the part of the other. This misunderstanding was not cleared up.

As to the Senate's amendment, the Sioux had no practical alternative to accepting it. If they did not place their X's on the new paper the white men offered them, they would lose their annuities for the year. Again the chiefs lined up and one by one made their marks. But this time there was no happiness and no celebration.

A cloud hung over the Western plains, a cloud as faint as a daylight moon in a summer sky. The Indians visited at the fort as usual, and Brave Bear, the chief chosen to represent the Brulés and the Oglalas, talked to the commander as he always did. Others made purchases from Gratiot, who operated a trading post for the American Fur Company a few miles down the river, or at James Bordeau's post a few miles farther away. But while friendships continued to exist between individual Indians and individual white men, there was no friendship between the two races. Then the temperature began to drop, the winds became chillier, and the Indians left the North Platte to make their winter camps.

                        *   *   *

As midsummer of 1854 approached, the Indians again began to gather around Fort Laramie, drawn by the lure of the annuities. But the cloud that had last year been so faint was now apparent even to the emigrants and the soldiers at the fort. The Indians were no longer docile but insolent. Their harassment of the emigrants increased, and Cheyennes ran off with two horses belonging to the interpreter, Lucien. Some of the soldiers, those who believed delicate problems could be solved by force, wanted an excuse to take to the field and defeat the Indians. Only forceful actions, they argued, would teach them to leave the white men alone. The garrison, however, had been greatly weakened by the withdrawal of two companies of cavalry, and Second

Lieutenant Fleming, who was now in command of the fort, restrained his men.

The death of the three Miniconjous the previous year and Fleming's refusal to make peace by giving the customary presents still rankled the warriors. By spoonfuls of sugar and coffee exacted from the passing emigrants, all of them frightened when surrounded by scowling Indians, the Indians were taking tribute; and when a cow wandered off from a Mormon emigrant train on August 18, 1854, and entered their camp, a Miniconjou warrior, named High Forehead, saw no reason for not killing it and eating it. It was either sick or lame—otherwise it would not have lagged behind the herd—and therefore it would never have reached Utah anyway.

Later in the day, when the train arrived at the fort, the owner of the cow angrily reported its loss to Fleming. The Indian agent was away, and Fleming thought it best to await his return. This would have provided a few days' delay and an opportunity for tempers to subside. Brave Bear also came to the fort to report what had happened. Conscious of his responsibility under the treaty, he was willing to make some sort of reparation even though the offense had been committed by a Miniconjou.

But the theft of the cow—if it could be called a theft—was the opportunity that another second lieutenant, John L. Grattan, had been waiting for. Fresh out of West Point with a brevet commission and no experience, Grattan had arrived at Fort Laramie convinced he was the best Indian fighter the academy had ever graduated. He often shook his fist at the Indians who visited the fort, and he boasted that with only thirty men he could clear the tribes from the plains. Grattan argued he should be assigned the task of arresting the Miniconjou, just as Fleming himself had done the preceding year. Fleming finally acquiesced, and what he did was as dangerous as thrusting a lighted torch into the fort's powder magazine. Sending the excitable, inexperienced, overconfident Grattan into the camp of the Sioux was not the move of a prudent commander.

On August 19, 1854, Grattan called for volunteers and that afternoon, against the urgent advice of a friendly Oglala, set forth from Fort Laramie with twenty-seven enlisted men, two noncommissioned officers, and the post interpreter, Lucien, whom the Indians disliked and who had been bolstering his courage with a bottle of whisky. Grattan, the interpreter, and a few others were on horseback. The rest of the soldiers rode in a wagon. They also had with them two howitzers. Once again the army had converted a police action into a military expedition.

When they reached Gratiot's trading post, Grattan paused long enough for the men to load their guns. He told them that he was determined to capture the Miniconjou regardless of the cost. If it came to a battle, he said, "you may fire as much as you damned please." Then he added, "I do not expect to be compelled to fire a single gun, but I hope to God we will have a fight." At Gratiot's, Lucien apparently got hold of another bottle of whisky. In any case, both his temper and excitement were reaching new pitches. As they passed the lodges of the Oglalas, his mind festered with the thought of the horses he had lost to the Cheyennes, and he hurled insults at the Sioux, reminding them of what had happened when Fleming had come after them.

That small cloud that had been hanging over the plains since the previous summer was now black and ominous like the forerunner of a tempest. At Bordeau's trading post, Grattan stopped again and ordered his men to prime their muskets and load the howitzers. "I hope to God we will have a fight," he had said, and he meant it. Lucien was riding around, shouting more insults at the Sioux and racing his horse so it would get its second wind, a practice sometimes followed by the Indians before a battle.

Grattan wanted Bordeau to come with him, but Bordeau was no fool. One look at the excited second lieutenant and the drunken interpreter convinced him that he had other business to attend to that afternoon. But he sent a messenger for Brave Bear, and he urged Grattan to silence Lucien. At this point, however, nothing would have quieted him except the forceful application of buckets of ice water.

When Brave Bear arrived, he and some other friendly chiefs who had assembled at Bordeau's all advised Grattan to go no farther. Last year the Miniconjous had accepted their defeat by Fleming, but this year the Indians, still bitter and angry, were likely to fight back.

Brave Bear offered to pay for the cow with ponies, and one of the friendly chiefs volunteered to go to Brave Bear's village, where the Miniconjou was staying, and attempt to persuade him to give himself up. When he returned, he said he had found six Miniconjous loading their guns. They had lost three of their people last year, and this year they were determined to die in their own defense.

The village was shaped like a semicircle with the two ends touching the river. In the rear was a deep ravine filled with heavy brush. As

Grattan now advanced in military formation toward the open space in the center of the village, many of the warriors began to slip away to the ravine. If fighting broke out, they wanted to be ready.

By now Grattan was in the center of the semicircle, his howitzers aimed at the lodges, his interpreter still shouting insults, and the situation completely out of hand. Brave Bear did what he could. He tried to persuade the Miniconjous to surrender, and he tried to calm Grattan, but he succeeded in neither effort. Finally he told Grattan there was nothing more he could do. At that moment, somebody fired. Whether it was an Indian or an American no one knew, but the shot started the battle.

Grattan helped man one of the howitzers on which he so heavily depended. The first of the two went off, quickly followed by the other; but both shots were aimed too high and merely tore at the tops of the tepees. The Sioux retaliated with a volley of arrows and bullets. Grattan and the five soldiers with him died before they could reload the howitzers, and their bodies lay slumped over the now useless weapons.

Among the many mistakes the lieutenant made that afternoon was to allow his men to fire at will. For when the howitzers missed, they had no time to reload their guns before the Sioux charged. Some of them raced for the wagon, jumped on it, and, lashing the horses to their greatest speed, tried to escape. But they were not fast enough to outrun the swift horses of the Sioux. All those men perished.

Those unable to reach the wagon tried to make a stand, but they fired only a few shots before the Sioux eliminated them. Lucien, who had caused part of the difficulty with his outrageous remarks, attempted to reach Bordeau's trading post, but he, too, was killed. Brave Bear, who had tried to make peace, was caught in the first crossfire and mortally wounded. Only one soldier in Grattan's detachment survived the fight, and he died of his wounds before he reached Fort Laramie.

Whipped into a frenzy by the battle, the Sioux appeared at Bordeau's trading post and demanded free goods, which he gave out to placate them. At the American Fur Company, they seized by force the annuity goods stored there, knowing the agent would not now issue them, and they also took some of the company's own goods as well. Although they talked of attacking the fort, which would have had a hard time holding out against so many warriors, they finally decided not to, partly because their chiefs dissuaded them and partly because nightfall had come.

As soon as he heard the news of the disaster, Fleming sent a messenger riding as fast as possible to Fort Leavenworth, the nearest post with a telegraph station, asking for additional troops and suggesting that the army undertake a punitive expedition against the Sioux.

But the Indians did nothing more. Having won their victory over Grattan's men and having collected their loot from the two trading posts, they leisurely broke camp and moved away toward the north without causing any further harm to the white men.

The reaction in Washington, when the news reached the capital, was anger and concern. The army refused to lay any of the blame on Grattan in spite of eyewitness accounts of his behavior and the obvious foolishness of what he did. The following year it raised a punitive force under Brevet Brigadier General William C. Harney, who had fought the Seminoles in Florida and the Mexicans under General Winfield Scott. Harney was recognized as a tough fighter, and the War Department knew he would not be easy on any Sioux he caught.

During the winter and early spring, most of the Sioux who had repulsed Grattan's attack had moved far north out of reach of Harney's expedition. Many of the others had reaffirmed their peace with the authorities at Fort Laramie and had resumed their previous life. When the Indian agent learned about Harney's coming, he was concerned that the peaceful Indians would be killed, not the ones who had been involved in the engagement. He therefore persuaded some of the friendly Sioux to restrict their hunting to the land in the south and sent word to Harney that they should not be molested. One band of Brulés, however, was camped on the North Platte. They refused the agent's invitation to come to Fort Laramie, probably because they had just finished a buffalo hunt and had not had time to dry the meat. This band may have contained some of the Indians who fought Grattan, but it was under the leadership of Little Thunder, a good friend of the Americans and one of the chiefs who had helped restrain the Sioux after Grattan was killed.

Marching up the South Platte, Harney heard about Little Thunder's band and believed reports that they were troublemakers. Therefore he determined to fight them and moved over to the North Platte, where he camped near Ash Hollow. Little Thunder's own camp was nearby on Bluewater Creek, and Harney's scouts soon located the tepees.

Harney's plan of attack was simple. His mounted troops and his artillery, under the command of Colonel Philip St. George Cooke, would leave early in the morning, slip quietly past the village, and take up a hidden position at its rear. Harney would follow later with the infantry. Since he greatly outnumbered the Brulés—this was the largest force launched against the Sioux up to that time—the Indians would fall back toward Cooke, who would then emerge from hiding. Caught between the two groups, the Sioux could be massacred.

When Harney drew near the Sioux village, the Indians sent out a delegation to treat with him; but Harney, confident of an overwhelming victory, refused to talk with them. Then he became unsure of Cooke's exact location and wanted to gain time, so he sent word to Little Thunder that he would negotiate after all. With Harney determined to fight, the Indians could gain nothing from the conversation, but Harney got the delay he needed. While he was talking with Little Thunder, some of the Sioux discovered Cooke's men. The confusion this caused in the camp made Harney realize that Cooke was in position, and he gave the order to charge.

Many of the Sioux tried to escape by climbing the cliff on the west bank of the Bluewater. Most of them were cut off by Cooke's men and forced to retreat back to the Bluewater. As there were many small caves in the cliff, some of the Indians climbed into them and began firing at the soldiers. Others dashed up the bed of the creek. The mounted troops went in pursuit, while the artillery fired at the caves, mostly with small arms.

The battle did not last long. If Grattan's defeat had been called a massacre by the white men, this engagement could have been called an even greater massacre by the Sioux, who lost numerous lives. Although the casualties among the women and children were not listed, observers at the scene said they were many. For the time being at least, the power of Little Thunder's band was broken. That was the price he paid for being friendly with the Americans.

At Fort Laramie, Harney may have investigated the details of Grattan's adventure and learned that the Indians were not entirely in the wrong. In any case, he became more conciliatory with them. At a council, he warned them to be peaceful in their dealings with the Americans and then marched north. He wanted to go in pursuit of the Sioux who had moved to the Black Hills, but those who knew the country well advised him that it was too late in the year. So instead he marched to Fort Pierre on the Missouri.

At the fort, he held another council with the nearby Sioux, including Little Thunder, who had fled in that direction after his defeat. As evidence of their good faith, the Miniconjous brought in the Indian who had killed the Mormon's cow, and one other Sioux specially wanted by Harney. In return, Harney agreed that the army would protect the Sioux from the depredations of the white men and would renew the annuities promised at the earlier council at Fort Laramie. Then, to show his own good faith, he released the prisoners he held.

Peace had returned to the plains, but it was an uneasy peace, based on brutal retaliation for an act of self-defense. Misunderstanding and poor communications had turned the Americans' Indian policy into chaos. Young lieutenants were left to make decisions that required the most experienced and mature judgment. Campaigns were launched by commanders who could not distinguish friends from enemies. The work done by Mitchell had been undone and could not be rebuilt.

*   *   *

Although Sitting Bull remained in the north and did not take part in the struggle around Fort Laramie, he was continuing to gain stature as both a warrior and a hunter. His name had been well bestowed. He was young but marked for distinction; and as a result of his evident bravery he became a member of a select group called the Strong Hearts. These men were considered superior to the others as fighters. As an additional honor, he was made one of the society's two sash-wearers. These men were entitled to wear a special sash. In battle, as the enemies faced each other, they were expected to drive a stake into the ground and tie themselves to it with their sashes. This act symbolized that they would never retreat and preferred to die rather than to run before the foe. This honor showed that among the Sioux, Sitting Bull was rapidly moving upward to a position of leadership.

In 1856, a year after Harney's campaign, the Hunkpapa Sioux engaged as usual in their summer hunt, following the buffalos across the plains and securing as much meat and as many furs as they could. When it was over, they decided they needed more horses, and the customary way to obtain them was to steal them. Consequently they formed a raiding party of approximately a hundred warriors and moved westward into the land of the Crows. Always anxious for a fight, Sitting Bull went with them.

They traveled along the Yellowstone, sending out scouts to look for a Crow village. At first their search proved futile, but after a while a medicine man prophesied they would find one within a day. Soon after he had said this, the scouts reported they had discovered a village north of the Yellowstone and within easy reach of where the Hunkpapas were then camped. The men put on their war regalia, and when night came they moved quietly toward the Crow village. As they approached it, they could see in the dark night the poles of the tepees silhouetted against the sky and the shadowy figures of the horses they had traveled so far to capture. Creeping closer to the village, they managed to avoid detection. In the village there was hardly a movement except the half-sleepy stirring of a horse. Nearer and nearer came the Sioux until they were able to encircle part of the Crows' herd. Then, making only the slightest of noises, they gradually edged the animals away from the village and into the surrounding darkness. Every so often, one of the Sioux would listen carefully, but there was no sound of alarm among the tepees. Nevertheless, they knew that the Crows would discover their loss as soon as the day broke, so they hurried on.

Behind them in the Crow village, the men and women were beginning to awaken. Within minutes, they noticed that a large number of their horses were missing and immediately knew the reason. The warriors rushed for their shields, guns, bows, and lances and mounted their favorite horses among those that remained. Then they set out at a gallop, following the trail left in the dirt by the stolen livestock. The Sioux moved as quickly as they could, but encumbered by the herd and busy holding it together, they could not travel as fast as their pursuers. Therefore a few of the younger and less experienced warriors were assigned to handle the horses, while the main body rode at the rear, ready to fight if the Crows overtook them.

Suddenly they saw their enemy in the distance and catching up with them. Flight was no longer possible, so the Sioux formed a line and prepared to fight. When the Crows saw the Sioux were ready for battle, they paused, and the two groups of men looked at each other, waiting for the other side to make the first move. Then three of the Crow warriors came forward. One of them dashed among the Sioux and counted coup twice before one of the Sioux grabbed the long tail of the warrior's headdress. It came off in his hand, and thereafter the year 1856 was known by this event in the band's winter count.

Another of the three leaders came forward and killed one of the Sioux. Then Sitting Bull rode directly toward the third. He was carrying his shield, for although it offered no protection against bullets, it was still useful against arrows, and few of the Indians as yet had firearms. Sitting Bull, however, had a muzzle-loading gun, and the

Crow leader had a flintlock. Because the Sioux had not gained their later proficiency in shooting from horseback, Sitting Bull dismounted and ran toward his foe on foot.

The other Indian took aim with his flintlock. Sitting Bull dropped to one knee and covered himself with his shield. At the same time, he raised his own gun.

Before he could pull the trigger, however, the Crow shot. The explosion echoed in the air, and the white smoke rose in a cloud from the muzzle. The bullet struck Sitting Bull's shield and penetrated the hard leather. But the Crow's aim was low. Instead of hitting Sitting Bull in the body, the ball entered his left foot. He felt a sharp stab of pain but ignored it, as he took careful aim and squeezed his trigger. The Crow leapt in the air and fell to the ground. Rushing forward, Sitting Bull drew his knife and killed his enemy.

The Crow had been an important chief, and his loss dismayed the others. They reined in their horses and then, instead of continuing the fight, turned back to the camp from which they had come. The Sioux watched them disappear in the distance and did not attempt to pursue them. They still had the horses, and that was what they had wanted.

When they reached their main camp, the Indians first mourned the one Sioux who had been killed. Then they celebrated their new conquest over the Crows and boasted of their power and strength. Although he was in pain from his wound, Sitting Bull was the hero of the celebration, because there was little question that his individual victory had turned the tide.

Although he nursed his foot carefully, it did not heal properly. The skin on the sole contracted, and for the rest of his life Sitting Bull would always walk with a limp. The Crow had lost his life, but he had left his mark on Sitting Bull.

III

The Hanging of
the Warriors

ALTHOUGH Kearny, Harney, and other white men had been
preaching peace to the Indians and attempting to persuade them
to abandon their warlike ways, the Americans themselves were following a different course. Since 1820, the Missouri Compromise, even if
it had not solved the question of slavery, had at least stabilized the
nation. Slavery, although condoned, was restricted, and some of the
strain was removed from the relations between North and South. But
in 1854, the year Grattan was killed, Stephen A. Douglas, the senior
Senator from Illinois, upset the delicate balance that had been achieved.

Only five feet tall, Douglas was nevertheless so full of ideas and
energy that some of his contemporaries referred to him as a "steam
engine in britches." He now decided to throw some of his vast energy
into the debate over the chartering of a transcontinental railroad. Although the need for constructing such a railroad was unquestioned,
Congress, because of the differences between the North and South,
could not agree on a route. Douglas, as a resident of Illinois and a
speculator in western lands, wanted Congress to designate a central
route, for this would most benefit himself and his constituents. First,
however, he knew it would be necessary to create a formal government
in the areas through which he wanted the line to pass. Therefore he
introduced a bill to organize the northern part of the Great Plains as
the Territory of Nebraska. Similar bills had always been defeated
before because of the South's opposition. To gain the South's support,
Douglas included a provision permitting the new territory to decide

itself whether it would eventually become a free or a slave state. Although politically expedient for Douglas's purposes, this provision mocked the Missouri Compromise and provoked months of bitter debate.

Most of the arguments centered on the possible expansion of slavery, but at least one man remembered the Indians who lived in the territory being discussed. That was Sam Houston, the hero of the Texans' war for independence. He pointed out that settlement of the area would violate the treaties made with the Indians, treaties that were supposed to run forever. But he added that he made his remarks "with little hope that any appeal I can make for the Indians will do any good." Unfortunately he was correct. The rights of the Indians were never an important part of the debate.

In the end, Douglas was forced to make a concession. Instead of one territory, the final bill called for two, Nebraska and Kansas. It was thought that the people of Missouri, a slave state, would gain control of the latter and the people of Iowa, a free state, would control the former. With strong support from the leadership of the Democratic Party, the bill passed—Houston was the only Southern Democrat who voted against it—and was signed into law.

The Kansas-Nebraska Act had a profound effect on the United States and on the Indians. Emotions that had been controlled during the past decades boiled over. The North berated the South, and the South berated the North. Senator Charles Sumner of Massachusetts delivered a bitter speech in which he denounced the possible extension of slavery and made a personal attack on Senator Andrew Butler of South Carolina. A few days later, a relative of Butler's made his way to the floor of the Senate, and before Sumner could rise from his desk to defend himself, beat the Senator severely with a heavy cane. When he returned to his native state, Butler's relative was acclaimed a hero.

But such violence was mild compared to the events taking place in Kansas itself, close to the lands of the Sioux. Most of the emigrants moving into the new territory came only in search of land and better opportunities than they could find at home But some of them were zealots on both sides of the slavery issue. When Missourians who hoped to make Kansas a slave state arrived, the Northern abolitionists countered by forming a company to finance antislavery emigrants. The two groups, driven by the fervor of their respective beliefs, soon came into armed conflict. The North sent the antislavery men quantities of breech-loading rifles of the latest make. These were called Beecher's rifles, because the noted abolitionist preacher Henry Ward Beecher, unmindful of the words of Christ, advocated their use.

His advice was followed. Bands of Jayhawkers, as they were called, raided into Missouri, burning and killing. The Missourians naturally retaliated. Groups of them, bent on vengeance, came into Kansas, and they were no kinder to the people they attacked than the Jayhawkers. Both sides had lost any semblance of reason or humanity and behaved worse than they accused Indians of behaving.

The year that Sitting Bull received the wound in his foot, John Brown, who later was hanged for his assault on Harpers Ferry, led a bloody retaliatory attack on a small settlement along the Potawatomi Creek in Franklin County, Kansas. Five Kansans had recently been killed by the proslavery people, and Brown, a fanatic who was driven by his faith in a warlike God, believed he was the instrument of the Lord's revenge. With his followers, he reached the settlement, called out five men who were known to favor slavery, and killed them. Although his action was murder and the identity of the perpetrators was suspected, only one arrest was made, and that case never came to trial. Neither the law nor even the army could bring peace to Kansas, as the battle between the two warring elements continued.

For Sitting Bull and the other Sioux the consequences of the Kansas-Nebraska Act were far-reaching. The eventual settlement of the plains had been inevitable—the expansionist pressures were too great to be resisted—but the passage of the Kansas-Nebraska Act hastened it, encouraging emigrants to take up farms near the area controlled by the Sioux rather than continuing on to the West Coast. Kansas was a white man's beachhead in the Great Plains, a beachhead founded in blood and violence.

* * *

In the lives of the Sioux, tragedy was commonplace. Continually surrounded by danger both from nature and from man, their camps were often filled with the sound of mourning. Men were killed during the buffalo hunts if their horses fell and threw them under the pounding hooves of the frightened herd. They died of cold sometimes, when the blizzards swept over the plains and the snow drifted around them. Disease also took its toll, for the charms of the greatest medicine men were not always sufficient to ward off the evils of sickness. And war added to the list of dead men, women, and children. When a raiding party set out, no one knew who would be missing when it returned, what warrior would have fallen before an enemy lance or arrow. And the breaking of each day always brought with it the threat of an enemy attack, for the enemy often took the initiative. Then in the pale light, still sleepy from their night's rest, the Sioux would find themselves the targets of bullets and arrows and hear the cries of the advancing warriors, intent on a victory.

Although he was a young man, tragedy had already struck Sitting Bull twice. When he became a warrior and therefore eligible to marry, he had selected a woman whom he loved. Then he and the woman's father decided on her worth as a bride, the value being set in horses. (Many factors had to be considered, including the character of the woman and the standing of her family.) When Sitting Bull agreed to pay the price demanded, the ceremony was completed with a feast.

Sitting Bull then set up his own tepee. He was now a man of responsibility, with a wife to support. This made his ability as a hunter and his prowess as a warrior even more important than it had been, for he would be judged by the band on the care he took of his wife. In a short time, a child was born, a son, who, like his father, could be expected to grow up to be a warrior. But sorrow came to the newly established tepee, for both mother and child soon died.

As a widower, however, he was not left to live alone. Among the Sioux, the affection between husband and wife was respected, but the important family unit was the one embracing all the relatives. The bonds between brothers and sisters, for example, always remained strong, as did those of other kinsmen, such as uncles and grandparents. So although Sitting Bull was sad in his heart, his life was not greatly changed, and there were women ready to do the work for him that his wife would have performed. He was left free to continue the life of a Sioux warrior.

In the winter of 1857, while the white men were battling each other in Kansas, he accepted an invitation to go on a raiding party against the Assiniboins. These Indians were related to the Sioux and spoke a language close to one of the Siouan dialects. Years before, however, they had become allied with Crees, the traditional foes of the Sioux in earlier days, and so hostility had sprung up between the tribes. To the Sioux, all Assiniboins were now enemies.

The party that Sitting Bull joined was only a small one, composed of three other warriors; but they thought they might win glory and spoils for themselves even though they could not attack a large village. Shortly after they left the main camp, the weather turned bitter cold. The ground became hard under their horses' hooves, and at night the four men huddled for warmth around their small fire. Following the general course of the Yellowstone River, they came to the Missouri, which was now frozen over.

Across the ice on the other side of the river, they saw a single tepee, belonging to a family of Assiniboins, a man, his wife, a baby, and a small boy. This pitiful, almost defenseless group hardly seemed worth the attention of the raiding party; but in the Sioux's world, a conquest was a conquest, however great the odds might be in favor of the attackers. So the four warriors raced across the ice toward the tepee, becoming strung out in a line as they did so. The Sioux shot all four of their enemy. The man, the woman, and the baby were mortally wounded, but the boy, although he had been struck by an arrow, was still alive. With only his toy bow to defend himself, he was nevertheless determined to fight to the end. One after another, he sent his few tiny arrows flying harmlessly in the direction of the Sioux, and then they struck coup on him. During the race toward the Assiniboins, Sitting Bull had lagged behind the others, so he was the last to touch the boy.

The other warriors, still feeling the excitement of battle, wanted to kill the little Assiniboin. After all, he was one of the enemy, and a fighter as well, for he had shot his arrows at them. Sitting Bull, however, was impressed by the boy's spirit and bravery and wanted to adopt him as a brother. The others argued against this; but Sitting Bull, who commanded more and more influence among his people, secured their agreement to take the captive back to their camp alive.

When they arrived home, the Indians held a celebration even though the four warriors had so outnumbered their foe, and the band rejoiced that the warriors had returned home safely after having harmed the enemy. Then Sitting Bull announced to the listening crowd his intention to adopt the captive as his brother.

This was an announcement of great importance. Not only did it prove Sitting Bull's generosity and kindliness—and these were great —it also had social and philosophical significance that was deeply rooted in the Sioux's culture. Their form of society would have fallen apart if the individual members had been allowed to accumulate vast quantities of wealth. Private fortunes would have destroyed the individualism that was a basic part of their lives, and a village in which the leader hired the others to work for him would not have been the traditionally democratic Sioux village. White men might work for each other for wages, but Sioux did not. Only the medicine men received a fee for their services. Yet the opportunities for gaining individual wealth existed. The better hunters and the better warriors naturally had more hides and horses than the others.

To maintain the equilibrium between the poor and the potentially rich, the Sioux gave prominence to a family not for being wealthy, but for giving its possessions away to those who were less fortunate. Thus the advantage of being rich was the ability to give more and larger presents. Out of this philosophy evolved a number of ceremonies that only the wealthy could afford and that spread their wealth among the band. One of these was the ritual of adopting a younger, less favored male as a brother, the less favored the better, because only a strong, wealthy man could afford to take care of a weak brother. In selecting the Assiniboin captive Sitting Bull had shown extreme astuteness, for no one could be more unfortunate than he, orphaned and alone among his enemy. With the performance of this ceremony, Sitting Bull would further demonstrate his importance.

First, he had to hire a medicine man, who in turn hired a number of assistants and also supervised the erection of a special tepee. When the day came for the ceremony, Sitting Bull and the young captive walked together through the camp, announcing that they were going to become brothers. After that, they entered the tepee in which were gathered the *hunkas*, those members of the band who had previously been adopted in the same ritual. Sitting Bull and the young captive sat down together, and the medicine man hid them from the sight of the others by placing a buffalo robe between them and the audience. Then he tied the young boy and the older man together with thongs, an act that symbolized that thereafter their fortunes would be bound together for life. Whenever necessary, each must come to the other's aid. Then the medicine man performed other rites and ended by painting a red stripe on the young man's face and pronouncing him a *hunka*.

Afterwards Sitting Bull provided a great feast for the members of the band at which he served quantities of food. Then he gave away many presents, including horses, to those who were less wealthy than he. At the conclusion of the ceremony, he was a much poorer man, but he had demonstrated his generosity and his ability to give away so much. He had risen one step higher in the hierarchy of the Sioux and was now not only a sash-wearer, but a warrior who had sponsored a *hunka*.

* * *

A short while after the death of his wife and child, Sitting Bull married again. While the Sioux mourned for their dead and felt deep sorrow at the loss of relatives and friends, they could not afford the luxury of prolonged grief, for the pressures of life were too strong to ignore. What with the buffalo hunts, the constant moving from one campground to another, the raiding parties, and the continuous threat of an enemy attack, no one in a Sioux band could long remain aloof from the busy existences of those around him.

Although Sitting Bull had become a noted warrior, his father, who had taken the name Jumping Bull when he had given his own to his son, was still the head of the family and the man of distinction. Growing old was not pleasant in a society where so much depended on physical activity, but the young Sioux took care of their parents, and the word "grandparents" was used as a term of affection and respect. Jumping Bull was no longer as strong and healthy as he had been, but he was honored by his son and still had a Sioux's hatred of his enemy and love of victory.

In the early summer of 1858, the band to which he belonged was camped in what is now North Dakota. The grass of the prairies was green, and the buffalos were moving across the plains. Winter, with its bleakness and cold, seemed far behind them, for this was the time of year when life was good, with plenty to eat and no need to huddle beside the fires in the tepees. Even the horses shared in the general well-being, their flanks fat again after the poor feeding of the winter season. They, like the warriors, were full of spirit and ready to chase the buffalos or charge against the enemy.

The appearance of two Crows in the vicinity of the camp caused no alarm. Before the warriors could mount and pursue them, they had disappeared somewhere on the vast prairie, and no one thought it worth the time to hunt for them. Probably the Sioux believed they were merely stragglers from some other band who were frightened when they accidentally stumbled on the large camp.

Two days later the Sioux decided to move to new hunting grounds and fresher grass for their horses. They folded the large tepees and lowered the poles. Soon everything was in readiness, for the Sioux knew how to break camp quickly, and they started across the plains. Each family rode together, chatting with one another and driving their own herds of horses. No scouts were out, for the Sioux had no fear of being attacked. With the whole band united, only a large number of enemy would dare to assault them, and except for the two Crows, no Indians had been seen.

Suddenly the quiet of the summer morning was broken by the sound of war whoops. Coming from behind a rise in the ground where they had been hidden from the Sioux came fifty Crow warriors, dressed in their war regalia and charging toward the straggling and unprepared column. Taken completely by surprise, the women and young boys of each family tried to hold their herds together and keep them from stampeding off, while the warriors drew their bows and prepared to fight off the attack. Before they could resist, however, the Crows had cut off two boys who were heading the band and separated them from the rest. So the advantage of inflicting the first casualties fell to the Crows.

But the advantage did not last long. Accustomed as they were to fighting, the Sioux took only seconds to rally and recover from the shock of the surprise. The young men drew the strings of their bows and began a counterattack that forced the Crows into a slow retreat. A few of the Crows tried to hold off the angry Sioux. One of them was knocked from his saddle and killed; another fell to the ground when his horse stumbled. He was soon dead, too. At these losses, the Crows began to flee, and the battle was nearly over.

One Crow, however, refused to retreat with the rest. Riding his horse and holding a rifle in his arms, he shouted taunts at the Sioux and dared them to come on. Because of the gun, the young warriors hesitated and remained at some distance, trying to decide what to do.

Sitting Bull was in another part of the battlefield and did not notice what was happening, but Jumping Bull did. Although not as strong as he once had been, he was ashamed of the hesitation of the younger men and said he would fight the Crow. Fitting an arrow to his bowstring, he moved forward to get within range. But a bow was no match for a gun. Before Jumping Bull could get close enough, the Crow raised his gun, sighted it, and fired. The puff of white smoke rose from the end of the barrel, and Jumping Bull received a severe wound in his shoulder.

With his shoulder bleeding and hurting, he could not use his bow, so he dropped it to the ground. Although he was old and not really fit for hand-to-hand fighting with a much younger man, he kept moving forward toward his enemy, while the others watched him. He had a great reputation as a warrior, and he did not wish to tarnish it by admitting defeat. And as a Sioux, he knew there was no better place for an old warrior to die than on the battlefield in defense of his people. The Crow quickly dismounted and waited for him. Jumping Bull fumbled for his knife, but before he could draw it, the Crow was on him with his own knife in his hand. The blade flashed in the air and struck Jumping Bull. The old man, bleeding from this fresh wound, struggled with all the strength he could muster, but the odds against him were far too great. Again and again the knife pierced his flesh, leaving fresh wounds. Finally the Crow struck him in the head, the blade of the knife broke off, and the unequal fight was over. Jumping Bull lay dead on the ground, and the Crow remounted and rode off to catch up with his companions.

All this while, Sitting Bull had been taking part in the fighting elsewhere and did not know what had happened to his father. As soon as he was told, he went in pursuit of the Crow, pushing his horse to its greatest speed. The hooves pounded against the earth of the prairie, as Sitting Bull leaned forward and urged it on. The Crow saw him coming and tried to escape. But his horse was not as fast as Sitting Bull's. As they raced away from the main body of the Sioux, the gap between them became narrower and narrower. Sitting Bull could feel the flanks of his horse heaving between his legs, but the animal kept on. Finally Sitting Bull was close to the fleeing Crow. Gripping his lance firmly, he made a lunge toward his enemy. The lance pierced him. His arms and legs relaxed. Then his dead body slipped from the back of the horse and fell to the ground.

But death alone was not sufficient revenge for Sitting Bull. Dismounting from his horse, he stood beside the corpse of his father's killer, drew his knife, and mutilated the body as severely as he could as an expression of his anger.

The Sioux were excited now. Having recovered from their first surprise and having routed the enemy, they were eager for more fighting. Some of the warriors went in pursuit of the Crows, following them for many miles but without success. Three Crow women, one with a baby, had been present when the original attack took place. They had tried to flee with the warriors but in the rush had been left behind. Then they attempted to hide in the brush that grew along a nearby creek, but the Sioux saw them, counted coup on them, and took them captive.

Sitting Bull mourned for his father. Then, when the customary period of time had passed, the band celebrated their victory, because once again they had defeated their enemy. Although Jumping Bull was dead, his name was not. For Sitting Bull gave it to his adopted brother, the Assiniboin captive.

Jumping Bull had died honorably, and his son had avenged him. There was nothing more that Sitting Bull could do than continue his own existence. He took, of course, his father's place as head of the family, which made him a more respected leader among the Sioux, because he controlled more people.

When he drew the picture of the event by which he would remember each year, as with most Sioux, the event was usually one of violence. In one case, an enemy Indian grabbed the bridle of his horse. Sitting Bull, however, was able to kill him and took his gun and his bow. This was an important victory, because guns were still relatively scarce. In another, he pictured himself running off with seven Crow horses, a good addition to his herd. The next year, he counted coup on a Crow woman and he captured two animals, one of them a mule branded with the army's *A*. Apparently it had been stolen from the military by the Crows.

So the pattern of raiding and occasional fighting continued. Among his band, Sitting Bull was becoming famous as a stealer of horses. Again and again he entered the enemy's camp just before dawn, picked his way among their tepees, located their best horses, and drove them away. This made him a wealthy man, for horses could not only be traded for other possessions, they also were the key to success in war and on the hunt. The best mounted warriors had a distinct advantage over the others in any battle, and the hunter with the finer horses was likely to kill more buffalo and therefore be more useful to his band.

He was wealthy enough to take more wives, because the only limit on the number a man could have was his ability to support them. And the women, rather than being jealous of each other, were glad to have the additional help in the household and proud to belong to a large and prestigious family. As he added to his herd of horses and to the coups he counted, the men of his band were paying more and more attention to his opinions. Life on the plains was good, and Sitting Bull was enjoying it to the full.

*　　*　　*

Among the white men, however, tensions were continuing to mount, and the people were rushing headlong into tragedy. Dred Scott, a slave whose master had taken him from Missouri onto free soil and then back again, sued for his freedom. His case reached the Supreme Court of the United States, where the Chief Justice and six of his associates ruled against Scott. Their decision, in effect, invalidated the Missouri Compromise and further agitated the slavery issue.

In 1858, the year Sitting Bull's father died, Stephen A. Douglas and Abraham Lincoln campaigned against each other for the Senate. Lincoln pressed Douglas hard on slavery, and at Freeport, Illinois, Douglas replied that slavery could not survive without the support of local police regulations. Since Congress had no means of requiring a territory to initiate such legislation, Douglas's statement reaffirmed the doctrine of popular sovereignty.

John Brown, however, was more interested in action than in debates between candidates. Moving east from Kansas, he gathered a small force of thirteen whites and five blacks and attempted to capture the arsenal at Harpers Ferry and set up a free nation in the mountains. His death at the hands of the hangman roused feelings further.

By the time Lincoln was elected president, compromise was impossible. Even before he was inaugurated, South Carolina seceded and the Confederate government was formed. President James Buchanan was unable to bring the country back together, and federal forts and naval stations in the South began to fall into the hands of the Confederacy. When General Pierre Beauregard demanded the surrender of Fort Sumter, its commanding officer refused, and the Civil War began. For years the Americans had been telling the Indians they should follow the ways of peace, not war. Now they were fighting among themselves on a scale no Indian could have envisioned.

Inevitably, the Indians were affected by the white men's struggle. Although most of the fighting was carried on in the eastern half of the country, the war could not be contained in that area. A Confederate army, composed largely of Texans, moved into New Mexico, hoping to secure the Southwest and, when the war was ended, have control of the overland route to California. Stephen H. Carleton, however, marched from California and regained the territory for the Union. But the fighting and the need to concentrate troops in the East gave the Apaches an opportunity to run wild, and they took advantage of it. For a while it almost looked as if they would win back the lands they had lost to the Americans.

In Indian Territory, the reservation set up in what is now Oklahoma, the Confederacy wooed the loyalty of the tribes by promising them a separate state, equal rights with whites, and the privilege of voting in all national elections as soon as the war was over. As a spokesman, the Confederacy had a half-blood Choctaw, Robert M. Jones, who was reputed to be the richest Indian of his time and who was appointed a delegate to the Congress of the Confederacy by Jefferson Davis. With his assistance, the Cherokee, Stan Watie, gained control of his part of the tribe that favored the Confederacy and rose to become a brigadier general in the Confederate Army. (Among his accomplishments, he once captured a Union wagon train having an estimated worth of a million and a half dollars.)

Farther north, in the area where Sitting Bull was roaming, the effects were less immediately apparent. The Union, of course, had fewer troops than before with which to control the Indians; its resources were strained to the utmost by the fighting to the east. As a consequence, its western defenses were weakened, and the Indians were much freer to do what they wanted without being molested. On the other hand, the federal government was less able to keep its Indian services organized, and the tribes were growing discontented over the manner in which their treaties were being carried out by the white men. Some Indians were even thinking of driving the Americans back and ending their encroachment.

Two events were taking place in Washington, however, that would make that dream even more impossible of accomplishment. In his campaign for the presidency, Lincoln had accepted a platform that promised a quarter of a section of land free to any settler who wanted it; and in 1862, Congress passed the Homestead Act. Although many acres were excluded from the provisions of the act, millions of acres were now open to settlement, and the rush to take them up was bound to come.

The other event was the chartering of the Union and Central Pacific Railroads. With the secession of the Southern states, the choice of a route no longer presented a problem, and Congress quickly passed the enabling legislation. Settlement in the West would soon be easier. Furthermore, the railroads could be counted on to promote the sale of the lands that had been allotted to them by a generous Congress.

Ever since he had been born, the life Sitting Bull loved so well had been threatened by an accumulating force of events. Two more had now been added, while he rode, unconscious of them, across the plains and raided the Crows for horses.

*   *   *

When the Western Sioux, attempting to evade their enemies, had migrated to the plains, the Santee Sioux had remained in Minnesota, and they later had every reason to regret their decision. For as soon as

Minnesota was admitted as a territory in 1849, the settlers began to campaign to secure more of the Indians' lands.

By 1861, when Lincoln became president, conditions among the Santee Sioux had deteriorated badly. Fraudulent dealings had cheated them of some of their lands, mismanagement had taken place on the reservations, efforts to turn them into farmers had failed, and the annuity payments they were to receive were often late or short the full amount due. One of the leaders, Inkpaduta, led a small band that had attacked the white men and taken several prisoners. Although a posse had been sent after him, he remained free, and his example stirred up further unrest.

Under the spoils system, Lincoln removed all the previous federal officeholders on the Santee agencies and replaced them with Republican supporters. One of the missionaries among the Santees, a man with a remarkable understanding of them, wrote, "When President Lincoln's administration commenced, we were glad to welcome a change of Indian agents. But, after a little trial, we found that a Republican administration was quite as likely to make mistakes in the management of Indians as a Democratic one." One of the first errors of the new agent was to placate the Santees with a promise of extra gifts. "By such words," wrote the missionary, "the four thousand Upper Sioux [the Santees were divided into the Upper Sioux, who lived near Lake Traverse, and the Lower Sioux, who lived in southern Minnesota] were encouraged to expect great things. Accordingly the Sissetons [one of the tribes] from Lake Traverse came down in the autumn, when the promised goods should have been there, but low water in the Minnesota and Mississippi delayed their arrival. The Indians waited, and had to be fed by Agent Galbraith. And when the goods came the deep snows had come also, and the season for hunting was past. Moreover, the great gift was only $10,000 worth of goods, or only $2.50 apiece! While they had waited many of the men could have earned from $50 to $100 by hunting. It was a terrible mistake of the government at Washington. The result was that of the Upper Sioux the agent was obliged to feed more than a thousand persons all winter."

This was a bitter time for the Santees. In March, 1862, Henry B. Whipple, the Episcopal bishop of Minnesota, felt driven to write President Lincoln personally. "The sad condition of the Indians of this state . . . ," he said, "compels me to address you on their behalf. I ask only justice for a wronged and neglected race."

Then he went on with an astute analysis of what always occurred when the Americans made a treaty with the Indians. "From the day of the treaty," he wrote, "a rapid deterioration takes place. The Indian has sold the hunting-grounds necessary for his comfort as a wild man; his tribal relations are weakened; his chief's power and influence circumscribed; and he will soon be left a helpless man without a government, a protector, or a friend, unless the solemn treaty is observed.

"The Indian agents," he continued, "who are placed in trust of the honor and faith of the Government are generally selected without reference to their fitness for the place. The Congressional delegation desires to award John Doe for party work, and John Doe desires the place because there is a tradition on the border that an Indian Agent with fifteen hundred dollars a year can retire upon an ample fortune in four years." The opportunities for graft in the awarding of contracts and the distribution of goods were so enormous.

"The Indian Agent," the bishop went on, "appoints his subordinates from the same motive, either to reward his friends' service, or to fulfill the biddings of his Congressional patron. They are often men without any fitness, sometimes a disgrace to a Christian nation; whiskey-sellers, bar-room loungers, debauchers, selected to guide a heathen people. Then follow all the evils of bad example, of inefficiency, and of dishonesty—the [Indian] school a sham, the supplies wasted, the improvement fund squandered by negligence or curtailed by fraudulent contracts. The Indian, bewildered, conscious of wrong, but helpless, has no refuge but to sink into the depth of brutishness. There have been noble instances of men who have tried to do their duty," the bishop acknowledged, "but they have generally been powerless for lack of hearty cooperation of others, or because no man could withstand the corruption which has pervaded every department of Indian affairs."

The bishop also had some positive suggestions to make. "The first thing needed is *honesty*," he wrote. "There has been a marked deterioration in Indian affairs since the office has become one of mere political favoritism. . . . The second step is to frame instructions so that the Indian shall be the ward of the Government. They cannot live without law. We have broken up, in part, their tribal relations, and they must have something in their place." This last point was especially perceptive. When the white men imposed their restrictions on the Indians, they destroyed the old laws and customs of the tribe but failed to develop adequate substitutes. The effects, of course, were demoralizing.

The bishop then pleaded for greater assistance to those Indians who wanted to become civilized and for better schools in which their children could be educated.

He ended his letter by saying, "May God guide you and give you grace to order all things, so that the Government shall deal righteously with the Indian nations in its charge." The letter went to Washington, but Lincoln's attention was occupied by other difficulties. After the disastrous rout at Bull Run the year before, George B. McClellan had taken command of the Army of the Potomac, and he was now preparing for the Peninsula Campaign, which was to be a major attempt to capture Richmond and perhaps end the war. Almost nothing at the time seemed further removed from the center of action than Minnesota and its Indian problems or, for that matter, Indian problems anywhere.

Washington's indifference frustrated the efforts of wiser people to avert the impending crisis. Then word reached Minnesota that the government intended to deduct the cost of last year's "extra" gifts from this year's annuities. The concerned missionary, who shared many of his bishop's insights into the Indian question, was alarmed at the effect of this news on the Sioux. "The knowledge of this planning of bad faith in the government," he later wrote, "greatly exasperated the annuity Indians." At the last minute, the government recognized the injustice it was committing, reversed itself, and decided to send the full amount due in 1862. This, however, required the passage of a new appropriation by Congress and delayed the arrival of the annuity money long after the usual date. Lincoln's administration was beset by many problems, but nowhere was it handling them much worse than in Minnesota.

The local Democrats were quick to take advantage of the situation. Having been thrown out of office in the last election, they were now only too glad to point out to anyone, including the Indians, the faults of the new incumbents. At a moment when the white men should have been supporting each other for their mutual safety they were divided by partisan politics. Furthermore, the Sioux were hearing reports that the North was being defeated, and they saw with their own eyes the heavy enlistments of young men to fight in the faraway battles. This in itself indicated to them that the government was beset.

In the summer of 1862, the Sioux gathered as usual at the agency. "It was the regular time for receiving their annuities, before the corn needed watching," wrote the missionary. "But the annuity money had not come. The agent did not know when it would come. He had not sent for them [the Sioux] and he could not feed them—he had barely enough provisions to keep them while the payment was being made. The truth was, he had used up the provisions on them in the previous winter. So he told them he would give them some flour and pork, and then they must go home until he called them. They took the provisions, but about going home they could not see it that way. It was a hundred miles up to their planting-place, and to trudge up there and back, with little or nothing to eat, and carry their tents and baggage and children on horse-back and on dog-back and on woman-back, was more than they cared to do. Besides, there was nothing for them to eat at home. They must go out on the buffalo hunt, and then they might miss their money. And so they preferred to stay, and beg and steal, or starve.

"But stealing and begging furnished but a very scanty fare, and starving was not pleasant. The young men talked the matter over and concluded that the flour and pork in the warehouse belonged to them [it was part of the annuity that would be paid in goods], and there could not be much wrong in their taking it. And so one day they marched up to the storehouse with axes in hand, and battered down the door. They had commenced to carry out the flour when the lieutenant with ten soldiers turned the howitzer upon them. This led them to desist, for the Dakotas [Sioux] were unarmed. But they were greatly enraged, and threatened to bring their guns and kill the little squad of soldiers. And what made this seem more likely, the Sioux tents were at once struck and the camp moved off several miles."

The Indian agent, who was both stubborn and inexperienced, did not know what to do. Left to his own decision, he probably would have let the crisis develop even further, but more experienced voices prevailed and a compromise was reached. In return for their promise to go home and wait until they were sent for, the Indians received the annuity payments due them in goods.

When the Lower Sioux heard what had happened, they demanded the same treatment. Usually the agent paid out both the cash and goods due the Indians at the same time, and sticking to this shred of protocol, he told them they would have to wait until the arrival of the money. One of the traders contemptuously remarked, in a voice loud enough for the Indians to hear him, that as far as he was concerned, if they were hungry, they could eat grass. This comment infuriated the Indians; but instead of using physical violence and breaking into the warehouse as the Upper Sioux had done, they merely muttered angry threats, and it looked as though the crisis might be over.

But the calm was more illusory than real. The Indians were brooding over the years of grievances they had suffered, the delayed payments, the encroachment of the settlers before the original treaties had been ratified, the many misunderstandings between them and the white men, and the racial insults they had received from the Americans. For all the hatred the Indians now felt for many of the whites, they still had no plan for concerted action; and if the money annuities had not been delayed further, relations might have been restored to normal.

Before the money came, however, a group of four young warriors returned from a hunting expedition and came near the settlement of Acton, Minnesota. Some accounts say they had been drinking; others, that they only asked for liquor and were refused. In any case, they stopped at the house of a settler and challenged him and two of his friends to some target practice. After the first round of shots, the warriors reloaded faster than the white men and had them at their mercy. It was then that the killings began.

The Sioux shot the three white men and also one woman and a girl before they had sated their anger. Even then, under more ordinary circumstances their brutal action might not have had any repercussions, for the other Indians might have ignored them or even have helped the white men catch them.

But when the warriors told the Lower Sioux what they had done, they found that many of the Indians considered them heroes and were ready to go to war. Little Crow, one of the great leaders among the Lower Sioux, at first argued for peace, but no one paid any attention to him. A little earlier, his power had been hotly contested by a rival, and he may have thought that he would lose still more popularity if he pressed for the cause of peace. So he gave in to the others and became one of those who advocated war.

On April 18, 1862, the struggle against the whites began. One of the first targets was the agency of the Lower Sioux. During the attack, the trader who had made the insulting remark about the Indians eating grass was immediately killed. After he was dead, the Sioux stuffed his mouth with hay and left his corpse lying in view as a warning to other white men to treat the Indians with more respect. The death toll was high, but while the Sioux were busy looting the agency's warehouse, some of the whites escaped and made their way to the safety of Fort Ridgely, about fifteen miles downstream on the Minnesota River. As soon as news of the outbreak reached the fort, Captain John S. Marsh set out with almost fifty men to recapture the agency. While he was crossing the Minnesota River, he fell into an ambush in which approximately half his men were killed and he himself was drowned.

News of these victories spread rapidly to the Upper Sioux. Friendly Indians helped many of the whites escape, but the buildings at the agency were looted and burned to the ground. If at this point the Sioux had had a plan and common leadership, they could have driven the whites from Minnesota. Except for the possession of howitzers, almost every advantage lay on their side, for the whites were greatly outnumbered and taken completely by surprise.

Instead of first attacking Fort Ridgely, however, the Sioux, probably tempted by the prospect of loot, assaulted the town of New Ulm. Their first attempt to take the settlement was badly planned, and the town was defended relatively easily. Within a few days they were back again. By this time, New Ulm had received reinforcements, but the Indians were much better organized. They killed more than thirty whites and wounded approximately sixty, and set fire to the town, which had to be evacuated a few days later.

Three attacks were also launched against Fort Ridgely, each more serious than the last. The Indians were able to start fires among some of the fort's buildings and to exert extreme pressure on the garrison. But artillery fire held them at a distance and made it impossible for them to overrun the fort itself.

Meanwhile isolated bands of Sioux were rampaging through southwestern Minnesota. Later many tales were told of the atrocities that had been committed, but these stories were exaggerations. The Indians were no more vicious than the Americans against whom they fought. Driven by the hatreds they had repressed so long and by their sense of grievance, they fought like any angry men. The Americans, in turn, were frightened by this sudden uprising of the people they thought they had put down, and frightened men are rarely kindly ones.

Alexander Ramsey, governor of the Territory of Minnesota, commissioned a former trader, Henry H. Sibley, a colonel, and sent him into the field against the Sioux. His arrival at Fort Ridgely with reinforcements placed that post beyond reach of the Indians. But a reconnoitering party he sent to the Lower Sioux agency fared badly. By selecting a campsite that could be approached under cover, the commanding officer invited an attack. The Indians came close to the soldiers without being observed and opened fire. When the battle was over, the Americans had lost more than ten dead and forty wounded. The Sioux's casualties were light, but this was their last major victory. Although bands of them continued to roam through the territory, inspiring fear in the settlers, they lacked the resources to make another concerted offensive. Too many of the Indians did not want to fight at all, and the Americans were rushing in too many well-armed troops.

At Wood Lake, Minnesota, the Indians prepared to make one final attack, but they were discovered beforehand by a group of soldiers. A battle broke out; and at the end of it, the uprising was over. Little Crow and his followers fled westward and northward toward the lands where Sitting Bull roamed the prairie. Inevitably troops would come after them, so that Sitting Bull would not only have soldiers to the south along the Platte, but they would be approaching from the east as well.

The other Santees remained behind to make peace again. Most Americans in Minnesota and other parts of the North were angry and bitter about the outbreak and wanted revenge, but a few were forgiving. One woman who had been forced to flee for her life from the Upper Agency later described her experiences but ended by saying, ". . . what I have written will excite your indignation against all Dakotas [Sioux,] and I cannot bear that this should be so. It must be remembered that the *church members*, as a whole, have had *no hand in it.*"

Other Americans were not so charitable, however, and demanded that the Indians be punished. Although the majority of those who had been most active against the whites had fled with Little Crow, the army set up a military commission to try the remainder. One observer wrote, ". . . instead of taking individuals for trial, against whom some specific charge could be brought, the plan was adopted to subject all the grown men, with a few exceptions, to an investigation of the commission, trusting that the innocent could make their innocency appear. This was a thing not possible in the case of the majority. . . . So that, of nearly four hundred cases which came before the commission, only about fifty were cleared, twenty were sentenced to imprisonment, and more than three hundred were condemned to be hanged. The greater part of these were condemned on general principles, without any specific charges proved, such as under less exciting and excited conditions society would have been demanded. They were Sioux Indians and belonged to the bands that had been engaged in the rebellion. . . ."

Popular opinion cried for blood. The findings of the commission, however, were sent to Washington for review by the President. Away from the battleground of Minnesota, tempers were cooler. In November, 1862, while the cases were still being reviewed, the Commissioner of Indian Affairs commented in his annual report, "I have already called your attention to the decision of a court-martial . . . to try a large number of warriors engaged in the massacre, who have voluntarily, as I understand, surrendered, by which over three hundred of the number have been condemned to death. I cannot refrain from the expression of an opinion that the execution of this sentence would partake more of the character of revenge than of punishment."

Against the protests of the people of Minnesota, Lincoln reviewed each case individually and reduced the number condemned from more than three hundred to thirty-eight. On December 26, these men were marched from their prison cells to the massive scaffold that had been erected nearby. "On each side was a line of infantry, forming a pathway to the place of execution," wrote an observer, "and as the Indians caught sight of the gallows they hastened their steps and commenced to sing their death song. The officer of the day received them at the gallows. . . . Eight men detailed to assist placed them in position, adjusted the ropes and placed on their heads unbleached muslin caps to hide their faces. All this time their song was continued with a dancing motion of the body. . . .

"To those near the gallows, evidences of fear and nervousness under this trying ordeal were manifest. One Indian managed to work the noose to the back of his neck, and when the drop fell he struggled terribly; others tried to clutch the blankets of those next to them, while with a spirit of defiance one went upon the gallows with a pipe in his mouth. Two clasped hands, and remained in this relation in death when their bodies were cut down. In the fall the rope of one was broken, but the fall broke his neck, and he remained quiet upon the ground, until his body was taken up and hung in place. After the lapse of nearly ten minutes one breathed, but his rope was quickly adjusted and life was soon extinct."

The ceremony was over, but the next day the authorities discovered they had made two mistakes of identity and had hanged the wrong men. No one worried much about it, however. As the missionary had commented, "They were Sioux. . . ."

IV

Unprovoked Attacks

EXCEPT for those Indians who had fled with Little Crow, the Santee Sioux had been defeated, but it had nearly been a disaster for the whites. If the Sioux had been a little better organized or more unified in purpose, they would have swept the Americans from Minnesota before the arrival of the troops. As it was, they were now a beaten, humbled people, and the white men had nothing further to fear. They could return to their small farmhouses, certain that next spring they would be able to plow their fields in peace.

But no one in authority felt that safe about the Western Sioux. At the end of 1862, when the Commissioner of Indian Affairs made his annual report, he said that "they are among the most warlike and powerful tribes of the continent. They abound in everything which constitutes the wealth of wild Indians; have an abundance of horses; are expert riders; and if once engaged in actual hostilities with the whites would be found capable of inflicting an immense amount of damage upon the frontier settlements, and in a country like theirs exceedingly troublesome to subdue.

"The defiant and independent attitude they have assumed during the past season towards the whites and especially towards their agent, warns us that not a moment should be lost in making preparations to prevent, and, if need be, resist and punish any hostile demonstration they may make. They have totally repudiated their treaty obligations, and, in my judgment, there is an abundance of reason to apprehend that they will engage in hostilities next spring. Like the southern rebels, these savage secessionists tolerate no opposition in their unfriendly attitude toward the whites."

The words "savage secessionists" were strange ones to apply to a sovereign people whose relations with the United States were governed by treaties. But the commissioner reflected the ambivalent attitude of most Americans. On the one hand, they drew up formal agreements with the Indians and solemnly ratified them in the Senate. On the other, they regarded the Indians as already absorbed into the United States and occupying one of the lowliest positions in the social structure.

There was, nevertheless, good reason for the commissioner to be worried. That spring some of the Indians had come to St. Pierre to receive from the Indian agent the annuity goods promised them under the Treaty of 1851. But they were not in a happy mood. As the agent later reported, "They stated that they regretted to see me without a military force to protect them from that portion of their several bands who were hostile to the government, and to them who were friends of the white man and desired to live in friendly relations with this government, and fulfill their treaty stipulations; that Gen. Harney, at Pierre, in 1856, had promised them aid; that they were greatly in the minority; that that portion of their people opposed to the government were more hostile than ever before; that they had, year after year, been promised the fulfillment of this pledge; but since none had come, they must now break off their friendly relations and rejoin their respective bands, as they could hold out no longer; that their lives and property were threatened in case they accepted any more goods from the government; that the small amount of annuities given them did not give satisfaction; it created discord rather than harmony nor would it justify them to come so far to receive it; that they had been friends to the government and to all white men; had lived up to their pledges made at Laramie in 1851, as was far as possible under the circumstances, and still desired to do so, but must henceforth be excused, unless their 'Great Father' would aid them. They requested me to bring no more goods under the Fort Laramie treaty, nor would they receive those present."

Confronted with this difficult problem, the Indian agent was not certain what he should do. Because of the demands of the Civil War, he could not offer the friendly Indians military protection; and he had no means of increasing the annuities, because that would require congressional action. Yet if all the Indians refused to accept the goods he had brought with him, that would signify the end of the treaty and loss of any control over a vast territory. American dominance on the plains would be set back at least a decade.

Finally he persuaded one chief reluctantly to accept some of the goods for the band he led. At the time, the chief said the hostile Indians might attack and punish him, and he was quickly proved right. A few days later some Sioux assaulted his camp and drove his followers in every direction. The agent was helpless to come to his aid.

But this situation was being changed by the uprising of the Santees, which had forced the Union to divert some of its energy from the war with the Confederacy and send troops against the Indians. The commander, General John Pope, decided to press the campaign and proceed westward in pursuit of Little Crow and the Santees and, at the same time, attack any other hostile Indians the soldiers might encounter. According to his plan, Sibley, who had been promoted to general as a result of his successes the year before, was to follow a northerly route into what is now North Dakota, while General Alfred Sully was to march up the Missouri River. The Indians would be caught between the two forces and defeated.

Until now, Sitting Bull had avoided the white men, not by design, but by chance. He and the Hunkpapas had remained in country that was out of reach of their expeditions, and so they had never come into conflict. Now chance was suddenly reversing itself. As General Pope was planning his campaign for the summer of 1863, the Hunkpapas, finding the buffalo scarce in their usual territory, were moving east. Since this would be a long hunt, they had their women and children with them, their tepees, and their herds of livestock. Everyone was happy over the prospect of finding enough to eat again, and they joked with each other as they traveled unknowingly toward the area where the Americans intended to campaign.

In one respect, Sibley's campaign was directed against a phantom, for Little Crow was already dead. When he led his band out of Minnesota, they were without horses. As soon as he had safely eluded the troops, he returned with a small group of warriors to the fringe of the settlements with the intention of stealing some horses and then taking his people to Canada. When they reached Minnesota, the warriors scattered, planning to reassemble later. Little Crow was alone with his son, when the two Indians were noticed by a farmer and his boy. The whites, with the memory of the recent uprising still fresh in their minds, fired at them. Although they missed Little Crow's son, they mortally wounded the chief. Instead of waiting to see what they had done, they fled and did not know they had killed Little Crow himself.

With 1,400 infantry and 500 cavalry, Sibley first marched to the James River, north of the present city of Jamestown, North Dakota. There he made a fortified camp and sent out scouts to locate the Indians. One of these scouts found Little Crow's son and heard from him about the chief's fate. The scouts also learned that many of the Upper Santees had fled to Devils Lake in what is now North Dakota and had spent the winter on an island. With the coming of summer, they had moved south to the Missouri River, hoping to hear that the government had relieved them of responsibility for the outbreak. Since many of them had not actively participated in the fighting, they had reason to believe they would be forgiven. When Sibley's scouts reported this to the general, he broke camp and started marching westward. What his scouts did not know was that the Upper Sioux had met Inkpaduta, the Santee leader who had fought the white men before the uprising, and had joined him on a buffalo hunt on the eastern side of the Missouri River. The intermingling of Inkpaduta's band with the Upper Sioux created a critical change, because Inkpaduta, with his warlike ways, had gained the respect of many warriors, especially the younger ones.

Sibley and his men crossed the ridge that divides the drainage basin of the James River from the Missouri and almost immediately came upon the Indians, who were taken completely by surprise at finding so large an army nearby. But instead of fleeing, they listened to one of Sibley's scouts, who told them that Sibley had come only to fight bad Indians. The good ones he would reward. The Sioux were reassured by this statement and also by the presence of a number of Upper Santees among Sibley's forces, so they agreed to hold a council.

Before they could have a meeting, however, one of Sibley's officers foolishly rode out ahead of the troops to a point where he could watch the scouts and the Indians conferring and sat on a knoll, completely exposed. One warrior, probably a member of Inkpaduta's band, could not resist the temptation presented by so fine a target. He shot and killed the officer, and the battle began.

The soldiers were anxious to avenge their dead comrade, and both the infantry and the cavalry charged. The Indians tried to fight a rearguard action to allow their women and children to escape, but the odds were heavily against them. As one cavalry officer wrote later, "In passing over the summit of the hill I looked back and saw our whole cavalry force coming thundering along, company colors flying, with the armor of our men flashing and glittering in the sun, while far back in the rear three or four mounted howitzers and a regiment of infantry were coming up on the double-quick.

"We soon distanced the infantry in our headlong march, passed over the brow of another hill and came in sight of the deserted Indian village . . . while away to the southwest, as far as the eye could see, the prairie was dotted with flying figures. . . . The horses while dragging burdens of three or four hundred pounds were also frequently ridden by the squaws with a child behind and another sitting on top of the pack behind, holding a couple of favorite pups. In this way the caravan . . . dashed along in three parallel lines, while their chiefs and braves rode behind and on either flank, ever ready to defend them from our attack.

"If one of the ponies was unable to keep up and dragged its load the fastenings were cut and the owner would mount the pony and dash away. Thus they were continually dropping their burdens from their overloaded animals until the prairie was dotted over with bundles and packs, which contained a mixed and multiform assortment of the habiliments and trappings and toggery of an Indian's outfit."

The Indians were in rout, but the battle was not over. Although it was now late in the day, the cavalry kept up the pursuit. But this time, as the officer wrote, "The fighting force of the Indians exceeded that of our cavalry [the infantry had long since been left behind], and as we rode up to open fire on them they spread out in a semi-circle in the rear of their moving train to prevent us from flanking them, causing our line of battle at times to become extended for about a half mile in length. The warriors fought like tigers and in their repeated attempts to check us performed many acts of brave and dauntless intrepidity and rash defiance. Their mode of tactics was to concentrate their forces and come galloping forward in a body, whooping and yelling as if about to make a furious charge, but as we were constantly on the alert and rushed up to prevent them from penetrating our line of battle, they would wheel round, discharge their guns and retreat."

The Indians, even though they outnumbered the Americans, could not stop the cavalry's pursuit. One reason was the inferiority of their firearms. "While some of them," the officer wrote, "were armed in primitive style and fought with bows and arrows, the majority carried an inferior lot of shotguns, with an occasional rifle, and judging from the way they held their fire—seldom shooting except when at close range or hard pressed—we concluded that they did not have much ammunition."

The battle was following the trend of many fights between the whites and the Indians. The whites could put numerous troops into the field, but unless they were cavalry, they were almost useless. Except at the beginning of the battle, Sibley's infantry had been ineffective, because they could not keep up with the fast-moving Sioux. The Sioux, on the other hand, were greatly handicapped by their poor firearms and lack of ammunition.

By this time, it was growing dark, and both sides were exhausted. The cavalry had ridden about twelve miles from the site of the initial attack. Because of their small numbers, they could not remain where they were and wait for a fresh attack at dawn. In the darkness, they made their way back to the main body of troops.

Having escaped from the Americans, the Upper Sioux, who had been with Inkpaduta on the buffalo hunt, now broke with him. He and his warriors were so impetuous and so determined to fight that they had nearly brought about the destruction of the entire village. So the Upper Sioux left the more warlike band and hoped that sometime in the future they could mend their relations with the whites. Inkpaduta, however, was still anxious to continue his warfare with them. And he quickly found allies.

Shortly after the battle, some of the Western Sioux, including the Hunkpapas and Sitting Bull, crossed the Missouri in their pursuit of buffalo, and their hunt led them to Inkpaduta. Unlike the Upper Sioux, these new arrivals thought they could drive the invading army out of their country.

The day after the battle, Sibley stayed in camp in order to let his men and horses rest. Then he moved westward across the relatively flat land to Buffalo Lake, which he reached in the early afternoon. Knowing that Indians were nearby and expecting them to resume battle, he had his scouts out; and they reported the presence of a large number of Indians ahead of him. They were Inkpaduta's band, now reinforced by the Western Sioux. Realizing from his experience of two days before that his infantry would be useless against the mounted Indians, he decided to fight from a fixed position and therefore made camp.

When the Sioux saw what he was doing, they surrounded him and charged. But Sibley fired his howitzers, and the Indians could not get inside their range. Again and again they tried, but they always had to retreat. Finally they sat on their horses just out of range and hurled taunts at the soldiers, hoping to draw them out, but the soldiers refused to be lured away from their safe position. Weary and frustrated by the ineffectiveness of their efforts, the Indians withdrew toward the Missouri. Sibley followed them the next day, marching some twenty miles along their trail to Stony Lake, where he made camp. The next morning, just as he was breaking camp and the columns were forming, his scouts warned him that the Indians were approaching.

Sitting Bull, who never avoided an opportunity to fight, had played an active role with the other warriors during the earlier engagement; but he, too, had been prevented from doing the Americans any harm and had been unable to distinguish himself. This day, however, he was determined to win some glory for himself.

As they charged toward Sibley's column, the Sioux spread out in a long battle line. When they came almost within range, they divided in two, one half of the warriors going down one side of the column and one half racing down the other. The hooves of their fast horses beat against the dirt. The warriors shouted their war cries, and the soldiers opened up with heavy fire. The Sioux's purpose was to flank the column and get at the baggage train in the rear. Its capture would provide them with a large amount of supplies and greatly hinder Sibley's further advance. But once again they were frustrated in their efforts, for the soldiers, all shooting as rapidly as possible, kept most of them at a distance.

A few of them, however, were able to get near enough to do some slight damage. One of these was Sitting Bull. The bullets rained around him, but he charged directly at a mule skinner, who was armed with a blacksnake whip. The mule skinners were hardy men—they had to be to do their work—and the long, tapered braid of rawhide was, in their hands, a dangerous weapon, accurate and deadly within its range. But Sitting Bull eluded it, got close enough to strike the mule skinner, thereby counting coup on him but not killing him, and rode off with a saddled army mule. Galloping away with his captured mule, he could be satisfied that in his first battle with the white men he had come off the victor. He already had a fine reputation for stealing horses from the Crows, but this was a much greater accomplishment, and his standing among the Sioux increased.

The battle had again been indecisive. The few supplies that Sibley had lost were not important to his expedition. He had inflicted almost no casualties on the Indians; they later claimed that only one was mortally wounded. But neither had the Sioux been able to gain any sort of advantage. They had wounded only two soldiers, and the wounds were not serious. Nor had they been able to halt Sibley's advance through their lands. He continued on toward the Missouri, reaching it just above Apple Creek, a little way north of the present city of Bismarck.

By the time he arrived, the Sioux had decided it was hopeless to try to stop him. Most of them had already crossed to the other side of the river and taken up positions in the hills. But a few of them lurked along the eastern shore, and whenever a soldier wandered away from the protection of the main group, he was likely to be attacked. But again the Americans suffered only light casualties.

Both sides were stalemated. The slow-moving infantry, just as frontiersmen had been saying for years, could not keep up with the elusive Sioux and force a battle on their own terms. But the Sioux's guns were not good enough to enable them to get within the ring of crippling fire that the Americans could lay down. So each force remained on opposite banks of the river, the Sioux watching the Americans, and the Americans hoping that Sully would come up the Missouri and reinforce them. Perhaps with additional troops, particularly cavalry, they might be able to force the Sioux into a battle they could win. But after waiting two days, during which he fired rockets and howitzers to attract Sully's attention, Sibley decided to return to Minnesota. The soldiers formed their column and started the long march back.

Inkpaduta, now that he had removed the threat of an immediate attack, led his warriors back across the Missouri, where they resumed their buffalo hunt. Having lost so many of their provisions in the rout following Sibley's initial attack, they were anxious, with winter approaching, to kill as many animals as possible. General Sully, however, was on the way. He had attempted to bring his supplies up the Missouri River by boat, and this had delayed him almost a month. But although Sibley was gone and General Pope's planned pincer movement could no longer be executed, he was determined to fight the Indians by himself.

Discovering the general area in which Inkpaduta's band was hunting, he marched after them. Early in September, the Indians, who thought all the soldiers had left, were surprised to find four troops of cavalry advancing on them. These were under the command of Major A. E. House, who had been ordered ahead to search for the Sioux. But the Indians, who greatly outnumbered the white men, quickly flanked them and held the soldiers at their mercy. Unable to retreat, House ordered his men to dismount and prepare to fight, while he sent a messenger to Sully for help.

In all probability, if the Sioux had acted quickly they could have annihilated the cavalry, but instead of pressing their initial advantage, they became overconfident. The white men could not escape, and they were so greatly outnumbered that they could be killed at leisure. The women began fixing a banquet to celebrate the coming victory, and the warriors slowly dressed themselves for the battle, putting on their war paint carefully. Every minute they wasted was potentially helpful to House, because his messenger had gotten past the Indians, and Sully should be on his way.

Before Inkpaduta had finished his preparations, Sully's cavalry appeared over the brow of the hill. This was an event the Sioux had not foreseen. Suddenly the odds had changed against them. The women, who had been cooking, dropped their food and began taking down the tepees as quickly as they could. The children started to round up their families' livestock. And the warriors who had pinned down House suddenly found their positions reversed. They were the ones who were now trapped, caught between the two forces of white men. They made a desperate stand in a ravine, fighting for enough time for the women and children to get away.

After an hour of struggling, they could hold out no longer. It was growing dark, and in the fading light many of them were able to get away. But their casualties had been heavy, and Inkpaduta's power was temporarily broken.

Sitting Bull and the other Hunkpapas had not remained with Inkpaduta after the fight with Sibley, so they fortunately missed the fight with Sully. But they did not consider themselves at peace with the white men. While riding in what is now North Dakota, Sitting Bull discovered a white man dressed in a fringed buckskin jacket and chased him. The man tried to get away, but Sitting Bull's horse was too fast. Spurring his horse on, he came close enough to risk a shot. Raising his gun, he fired; the man fell with a mortal wound in his back. This was the first time that Sitting Bull had killed an American, for he now felt that he was at war with them.

* * *

The year 1863 was a good one for the Union. After being defeated at Chancellorsville, the federal forces under General George G. Meade took a stand at Gettysburg in an attempt to stop General Robert E.

Lee's northward march. After three days of furious fighting, Lee found himself checked, and the decisive battle was over. The next day, Vicksburg surrendered, and control of the Mississippi fell into the Union's hands. Texas, Arkansas, and part of Louisiana were now cut off from the rest of the Confederacy. General Ulysses S. Grant then fought the Confederates at Chattanooga. His victory there forced them from Tennessee and opened the way into Georgia.

As one officer later said about the Confederacy in that year, ". . . its government should have seen that it was impossible to succeed, and should have surrendered, thereby saving the vast destruction of property and life which was ultimately to ensue from the overrunning of its territory by the United States forces.

"All Europe deemed the Confederacy as no longer possible of success. Its recognition by European powers was now out of the question, and the United States was enabled to turn its attention to matters of detail. Among these matters," he continued, "was the question of the Indian nations then on the northwest, west, and southwest."

At the beginning of 1864, however, the plains did not need much attention. Sully's expedition had given a severe blow to Inkpaduta's band, one of the few who were aggressively fighting any white men who came near. Others, like the Hunkpapas, were willing to fight, but for the most part they were remaining in areas where the white men did not yet want to go. Still others, although they were disturbed by the ever-growing numbers of emigrants and by the gold miners and other settlers in Colorado, were not ready to go to war over their grievances.

In April, however, a government contractor in Colorado reported the loss of one hundred and seventy-five head of livestock, which, he said, had been stolen by Indians. Whether this was true or not, no one bothered to determine. Kit Carson, who knew the frontier as well as anyone, later said the contractors often reported stock as stolen when it had merely wandered away. But at the time, the military did not question the contractor's word.

A band of Cheyennes had found the lost oxen and, according to their custom, had taken custody of the strays. The acquisition of this extra meat brought happiness to the camp; but the Indians did not know that Colonel John M. Chivington, a bloodthirsty former Methodist minister who was in command of Colorado, had sent out a detachment under Lieutenant George Eayre with orders to recover the animals. Eayre discovered the Indians' trail and followed it to their village. When the Cheyennes saw the soldiers coming, they wanted to talk with Eayre. Then they noticed how many men he had with him and realized that this was a punitive expedition, not merely an informal scout. So they grew frightened and fled. Eayre took possession of their camp, burned the belongings they had left behind, and went in pursuit of them. He later claimed—or at least so Colonel Chivington reported—that he recovered a hundred head of the contractor's oxen. Because oxen move slowly, this would have been an unusually large herd for the Indians to have driven away. If his statement was true, it corroborated the Indians' claim that they found the animals straying.

Having tasted such easy victory, Eayre began looking for more Indians to conquer. He soon came upon the trail of a smaller band of Cheyennes and followed that, too. Before he reached their camp, some of the Indians noticed him and warned the others that soldiers were arriving. Since the Cheyennes were greatly outnumbered and had no idea what the soldiers' mission might be, they fled. Once again Eayre destroyed the possessions they had been forced to leave behind. Thus in the first weeks of April, 1864, the white men had attacked the Cheyennes twice without any provocation.

Before the month was half over, a third incident occurred. A group of Cheyenne warriors were going north to join a war party against the Crows in an effort to avenge the death of a chief. On their way, they found four stray mules, which they took along with them. A white man visited their camp, claimed the mules as his own, and demanded their return. The Indians agreed to give him the animals if he would provide them with a small present to repay them for their trouble in rounding them up.

The man refused and went to a nearby camp of soldiers, where he reported what had happened. Once again, a lieutenant was sent out on the mission of retrieving the animals, and once again, violence broke out. An official investigation conducted later could not determine who fired the first shots. Colonel Chivington said the Indians did. Others reported that the lieutenant tried forcibly to disarm the Cheyennes and that the battle started when he did so. At the end of it, two soldiers had been mortally wounded.

Having now stirred up the Cheyennes, Colonel Chivington marched to the Arkansas River to forestall a rumored Confederate invasion, leaving Eayre behind to continue pursuing the Cheyennes. Soon he had started another battle, which was stopped only when Black Kettle, a Cheyenne chief who was friendly to the Americans, interceded. But

relations between the Cheyennes and the white men had been undermined by Colonel Chivington's aggressiveness, and distrust was beginning to spread to some of the other tribes.

East of Colorado, the military was trying to be more conciliatory.
Camp Cottonwood (later Fort McPherson), which was located on the
South Platte in present-day Nebraska, about eight miles above the fork
with the North Platte, was the site of a conference with the Sioux with
whom Harney had dealt earlier. The purpose was to persuade them to
remain friendly and to keep them from attacking the emigrants on the
trail.

Mutual suspicion pervaded the meetings. One officer later wrote,
"With great pomp the Indians to the number of about one hundred, all
fully armed and finely mounted, came down towards our camp about
nine o'clock. Then seventeen chiefs threw off their weapons, leaving
them behind with their escort, and came forward to the new sutler-
house [where the meeting was to be held] with great pomp and ceremony. Then all of the officers of the post, coming up to within about
fifty feet of the building, took off their sabres and revolvers and left
them in a pile with a guard. . . .

"The Indians all through this matter seemed to be unusually important, and punctilious. They all had their blankets on, and although
they had ostensibly left their arms behind, every one had probably a
sharp butcher-knife in the folds of his blanket. . . . As a sort of stand-
off, we, who had left our arms behind us, each had a pistol in his hip
pocket so as not to be taken unawares."

The Indians, speaking in turns, recited the injustices they had suffered, the loss of game, the encroachment of the whites, and the introduction of whisky, which was demoralizing their people. The general
who represented the Americans answered each of the speakers and
finally made a remarkable statement in which, probably for the first
time, a high-ranking officer of the United States Army argued in favor
of a socialistic attitude toward property.

"He told the Indians," according to one observer, "that they had no
right to claim all of the land. He told them that the good Manitou,
who put us all on earth, intended that each one should have his share
of the earth, and the Indians had no right to take ten times as much
land per head as they allowed the white people. And he pointed out
that the white people had to live all penned up and in discomfort, so
that the Indian could have ten times the amount of land he ought to
have, and kill the buffalo which belonged to everybody on the earth

alike, but which the Indians claimed the entire ownership of. And that the Indian had kept the white man back, and the latter were so crowded that if the lands which the white man had were divided, each white man would have only a small piece, so small that an Indian could shoot an arrow across it, while the Indian had land he could not see over." The Indians listened with the same indifference as the shareholders of a land-grant railroad would have listened to a similar plea made on behalf of a group of settlers.

Finally the general decided to talk more bluntly. The Indians, he said, were to stay out of the Platte Valley altogether. If they needed more bacon, blankets, or corn, the government would consider increasing the annuities, but they must remain away from the Platte. That, he stated, was an ultimatum.

The Sioux were not pleased by the general's remarks. One of their great chiefs, Spotted Tail, a Brulé, took it upon himself to answer. "The Sioux nation is a great people," he said, "and we do not wish to be dictated to by the whites or anybody else. We do not particularly care about the Platte Valley. But we want to come and trade in the Platte Valley wherever we please. We want places where we can sell our beaver-skins and our buffalo-robes. The Platte Valley is ours, and we do not intend to give it away. We have let the white men have it so he could pass, but he has gone over it so often now that he claims it and thinks he owns it. But it is still ours, and always has been ours. It belonged to our forefathers, and their graves are along the hills overlooking the valley from the Missouri River to the mountains, and we do not expect to give it up. We are not afraid of the white man, nor are we afraid to fight him."

Spotted Tail then complained about the quality and the quantity of the goods the Indians received each year as annuities and about the way the Indian agents cheated them. He ended by saying prophetically, "Beside this, we will not give up the Platte Valley to you until we have a regular treaty, and until we have all agreed to it, and have been paid for it. It will soon be that you will want other roads to the west. If we give you this one you will want another, and if we give you that you will want a third."

The gap between the two peoples was far too great to be crossed in a single meeting. The white men wanted complete control of the Indians' land; the Indians did not want to give up their territory, particularly when the Americans were unwilling to pay the full amounts agreed to. But they were not yet ready to go to war.

That spring and early summer, the Indians of the plains had reason to be bewildered. Chivington's command was harassing them in Colorado, other troops were trying to maintain peaceful relations with them along the Platte River, while still others farther north were repeating the campaign waged by Sully the previous year.

Once again, Sully was in command, and he was in a stern mood. He marched up the Missouri River in the summer of 1864 but found no action until he reached the mouth of the Little Cheyenne River, which flows from the hills to the east. Along with him he had a botanist, for it was not unusual in those days for army expeditions to be accompanied by scientists. Unmindful of the dangers of wandering alone in Indian territory and interested in the plants he could find, the botanist moved away from the main body of troops. Several Indians were hidden in the bushes near the river, and they had no way of knowing that he was not a soldier. The only thing they had in common with the white men was war; and as the unwary scientist presented a fine target, they moved closer and killed him.

As soon as word of this attack reached Sully, he sent a detachment of cavalry in pursuit. The soldiers and the Indians raced against each other for approximately fifteen miles, but in the end the soldiers' horses proved faster. They caught up with the Indians and killed them. Then they decapitated the bodies and mounted the heads on tall poles, where they could be easily seen and taken as a warning not to attack white men. Word of this act quickly spread through the Indian world and increased the fear of this invading army.

Although the plains were now ablaze with war, at least some of the emigrants had not heard about the outbreak of hostilities and continued their trips without taking any special precautions. Whenever they could, the Indians took advantage of the travelers' ignorance. Riding along the trail west of Fort Laramie, some Hunkpapa Sioux noticed a small and lightly guarded group of emigrants, the dust rising from the wheels of their wagons as they headed toward what they thought would be their new home. The Indians charged them and in a short fight inflicted heavy casualties and captured a woman, Fanny Kelly, and her daughter, Mary.

As they were riding away among their captors, Mrs. Kelly urged Mary to drop behind and escape. Then she herself tried to hide, but the Indians noticed her absence and immediately recaptured her. In an effort to save her life, she explained that she had been going back to look for her daughter. The Indians quickly started a search for the missing girl. Although they did not tell Mrs. Kelly the results, she later saw a warrior ride up and recognized among his possessions Mary's shawl and her golden-haired scalp.

Next the Hunkpapas surrounded a detachment of soldiers under Captain James L. Fisk. Because the captain had his wagons corralled, they could not attack successfully. In an effort to get him to move on with his wagons and men strung out in a more vulnerable position, they forced Mrs. Kelly to write him a note professing their friendship. Although they could not read, they told her what words to use and also counted them. Then three of them took the note and, under a flag of truce, stuck a stick into the ground with the note attached to it.

But Mrs. Kelly was not willing to betray her countrymen, and when Captain Fisk read her words, he came to the final two paragraphs which said, "Buy me if you can, and you will be satisfied. They have killed many whites. Help me if you can.

"Hunkpapas (they put words in and I have to obey) they say for the wagons they are fighting for them to go on. But I fear the result of this battle. The Lord have mercy on you. Do not move."

When, as a result of Mrs. Kelly's warning, Captain Fisk kept his wagons corralled, the Hunkpapas told her to write another note. Once again she warned the captain, and he remained where he was until the Indians rode off.

While the Hunkpapas were surrounding Fisk, Sully was establishing Fort Rice on the Missouri River at the mouth of the Cannonball. Then he struck west into the higher and more rugged land, where the Santees with Inkpaduta had fled. After his fighting of the year before, Inkpaduta was short of supplies and not willing to battle with the Americans again. But in the western part of what is now North Dakota, he met with the Western Sioux, including the Hunkpapas and Sitting Bull. These Indians were not well equipped either, because they had been unable to trade with either the Americans or with Canadians to the north. Their guns were poor and old, and they had little ammunition.

Yet there was some safety in their numbers, for altogether they probably had about sixteen hundred warriors. With that many fighting men, perhaps they could do battle with the soldiers—if the soldiers wished to fight—even though the Indians were outnumbered. Because Inkpaduta had had more experience with the Americans than any other chief, the others agreed to let him take charge.

As Sully approached—scouts were watching his movements—Inkpaduta took up a position in the Killdeer Mountains just south of the Little Missouri River in present-day North Dakota. Plenty of water was available for the camp, and some heavy timber and steep ravines would make it difficult, if not impossible, for the cavalry to charge. But in choosing this site, Inkpaduta sacrificed the Western Sioux's greatest tactical advantage—mobility.

The manner in which Inkpaduta chose to resist the Americans and the fashion in which Sully decided to fight precluded the heroics that Sitting Bull would have liked. Although he had stature among his own band, Sitting Bull was not yet generally regarded as an outstanding warrior among the Sioux as a whole, so he could not object to Inkpaduta's plans even if he had wanted to. But it is doubtful that he did, because Inkpaduta had won a reputation as a great fighter against the white men.

Any doubts among the Indians that Sully was looking for them were dispelled when, as the country became more rugged, he left some of his provisions and baggage behind and made a forced march directly toward them. As he came closer to the mountains, he ordered his men to dismount and move forward on foot. It was a large force—about two thousand men—that the Sioux saw drawing near them. Sully had several companies on each of his flanks and his howitzers in the center, and several more companies formed a rear guard.

Being unable to check his advance, the few Indians in the nearby hills retreated; but when he reached the plains at the foot of the mountains, they were able to outflank him on his left. They did not, however, have enough warriors and enough good guns to take advantage of their superior position, and Sully's men were able to drive them back. Another group of Sioux gathered on Sully's other flank and prepared to charge. But once again the Americans were able to drive them off, chasing them to the foot of the mountains and, in doing so, getting far ahead of their own skirmishers. The Sioux quickly saw their opportunity and gathered near this small group, ready to slaughter them and avenge the losses they had suffered so far in the battle. But Sully brought his howitzers into play. There was nothing the Indians could do to silence the guns, no way of fighting back against them with their destructiveness and long range, so they had to disperse and allow the Americans to escape.

But they still had one hope that might bring them victory. A large number of warriors had gone off on a hunting expedition to the east. They were due to return; and if they did, they might surprise Sully and take him in the rear. The warriors did arrive in time to engage in the battle, but they were unable to divert the enemy's assault, for Sully ordered one battery brought to the rear and opened fire on them. The Sioux had to fall back.

In his only other encounter with American soldiers, Sitting Bull had been able to follow his usual tactics, charging down on them on horseback; but this was something entirely different. Horses were of little use, and the sound of the howitzers echoing over the prairie and through the ravines of the mountains was a new experience to him, as it was to many of the other Indians. Their arms and their knowledge of warfare were useless against the heavy shots that were being fired at them. And so they decided to retreat. Hastily the women began breaking camp, taking down the long poles of the tepees and packing their belongings for the flight that would follow, while their husbands, brothers, and fathers tried to hold off the enemy's advance. Soon the Indians were streaming over the Killdeer Mountains, and for the first time that day, Inkpaduta's choice of a site began to pay off. Because of the roughness of the ground, Sully did not want to risk following them. The sun was setting, and he was afraid of the advantage the Indians would enjoy in the darkness and the steep ravines. Consequently he remained where he was and made camp. One group of Indians, hoping to salvage something from the rout, gathered at the top of the mountain; but the Americans saw them and chased them away. Inkpaduta had led his people into failure.

The extent of that failure was later revealed by Mrs. Kelly, who, still a captive, was kept with the women and children. "There seemed to be a great commotion and anxiety in the movements of the Indians," she wrote some years afterward, describing the fight and the subsequent retreat, "and presently I could hear the sound of battle and the echoes, that came back to me from the reports of the guns in the distant hills, warned me of the near approach of my own people, and my heart became a prey to wildly conflicting emotions, as they hurried on in great desperation and even forbid me turning my head and looking in the direction of the battle. Once I broke the rule and was severely punished for it. They kept their eyes upon me and were very cross and unkind.

"Panting for rescue, yet fearing for its accomplishment, I passed the day. The smoke of action now rose over the hills beyond. The Indians now realized their danger, and hurried on in great consternation.

"General Sully's soldiers appeared in close proximity, and I could see them charging on the Indians, who, according to their habits of warfare, skulked behind trees, sending their bullets and arrows vigorously forward into the enemy's ranks. I was kept in advance of the moving column of women and children, who were hurrying on, crying and famishing for water, trying to keep out of the line of firing.

"It was late at night when we stopped our pace, when at length we reached the lofty banks of a noble river, but it was some time before they could find a break in the rocky shores which enabled us to reach the water and enjoy the delicious draught, in which luxury the panting horses gladly participated.

"We had traveled far and fast all day long without cessation, through clouds of smoke and dust, parched by a scorching sun. My face was blistered from the burning rays, as I had been compelled to go with my head uncovered, after the fashion of all Indian women. Had not had a drop of water during the whole day.

"Reluctant to leave the long-desired acquisition, they all lay down under the tall willows, close to the stream, and slept the sleep of the weary. The horses lingered near, nipping the tender blades of grass that sparsely bordered the stream.

"It was not until next morning," she continued, "that I thought of how they should cross the river, which I supposed to have been the Missouri [the Little Missouri, which is a fork that is south of the main stream]. It was not very wide, but confined between steep banks; it seemed to be deep and rapid; but they did not risk swimming at that place, to my joy, but went further down and all plunged in and swam across, leading my horse. I was very much frightened, and cried to heaven for mercy.

"On that morning," she continued, "we entered a gorge, a perfect mass of huge fragments which had fallen from the mountains above; they led my horse and followed each other closely, and with as much speed as possible, as we were still pursued by the troops. During the day some two or three warriors were brought in wounded. I was called to see them and assist in dressing their wounds. This being my first experience of the kind, I was at some loss to know what was best to do; but, seeing in it a good opportunity to rise in their estimation, I endeavored to entrust them with an air of my superior knowledge of surgery, and as nurse, or medicine woman. I felt now, from their motions and meaningful glances, that my life was not safe, since we were so closely pursued over this terrible barren country.

"My feelings, all this time, cannot be described, when I could hear the sound of the big guns, as the Indians term cannon. I felt the soldiers had surely come for me and would overtake us, and my heart bounded with joy at the very thought of deliverance, but sank proportionately, when they came to me, wearing their trophies, reeking scalps, soldiers' uniforms, covered with blood, which told its sad story to my aching heart. One day I might be cheered by a strong hope of approaching relief, then again would have such assurance of my enemy's success as would sink me correspondingly low in despair. For some reason deception seemed to be their peculiar delight; whether they did it to gratify an insatiable thirst for revenge in themselves, or to keep me more reconciled, more willing and patient to abide, was something I could not determine.

"The feelings occasioned by my disappointment in their success can be better imagined than described, but imagination, even in her most extravagant flights, can but barely picture the horrors that met my view during those running flights."

Sully's supplies were being sent to him on the Yellowstone River, so he continued to march in that direction, following the route the Indians had taken. Describing the suffering of the fleeing Indians, Mrs. Kelly wrote, "The terrible scarcity of water and grass urged us forward, and General Sully's army in the rear gave us no rest. The following day or two they [the Indians] were driven so far northward, and became so imminently imperilled by the pursuing forces, that they were obliged to leave all their earthly effects behind them. . . ."

Although the Sioux realized they could not stop Sully, they kept up a series of harassing attacks, the type at which they were so skillful. In engagements such as these, an individual like Sitting Bull had a better opportunity to demonstrate his courage than in the battle fought at the Killdeer Mountains. Once he dashed down on the marching column, hoping to steal some of its horses. The soldiers saw him coming, leaning low over his horse's neck and urging the animal to race faster. They leveled their guns and started firing, but all their shots missed. Coming closer, Sitting Bull was able to cut out a chestnut-colored horse and a buckskin from the soldiers' herd and make off with them. Once more, at the risk of his life, he had enriched himself at the expense of his enemy.

He had another encounter with the Americans before Sully reached the boats. In this instance, he charged an individual soldier and wounded him with an arrow. Although bleeding severely and trying to escape, the soldier turned in his saddle and raised his gun. Sitting Bull kept coming toward him, mindless of the danger he was in. The soldier pulled the trigger, and the bullet shot from the muzzle and struck Sitting Bull. It was a flesh wound, but it bled copiously. Unlike his earlier wound, which had left him lame for life, this was painful but not serious. Nevertheless it was the first time that a white man's bullet had hit him.

In spite of the courage shown by the warriors, they had to move their women and children faster and faster to avoid Sully. "We had left, in our compulsory haste," Mrs. Kelly wrote, "immense quantities of plunder, even lodges standing, which proved of immediate help, but in the end a terrible loss."

When Sully reached the Yellowstone, he broke off the fighting. The casualties he had inflicted had not been severe. The loss of supplies, however, had crippled these bands of Sioux for the remainder of the season, and they were practically destitute. "As soon as we were safe, and General Sully pursued us no longer," Mrs. Kelly wrote, "the warriors returned home, and a scene of terrible mourning over the killed ensued among the women. Their cries are terribly wild and distressing, on such occasions; and the near relations of the deceased indulge in frantic expressions of grief that cannot be described. Sometimes the practice of cutting the flesh is carried to a horrible and barbarous extent. They inflict gashes on their bodies and limbs an inch in length. Some cut off their hair, blacken their faces, and march through the village in procession, torturing their bodies to add vigor to their lamentations.

"Hunger followed on the track of grief; all their food was gone, and there was no game in that portion of the country.

"In our flight they scattered everything, and the country through which we passed for the following two weeks did not yield enough to arrest starvation. The Indians were terribly enraged and threatened me with death almost hourly, and in every form.

"A terrible time ensued, and many dogs, and even horses, died of starvation. Their bodies were eaten immediately; and the slow but constant march was daily kept up, in hope of game and better facilities for fish and fruit.

"Many days in succession I tasted no food, save what I could gather on my way; a few rose leaves and blossoms was all that I could find, except for the grass I would gather and chew, for nourishment. Fear, fatigue, and long-continued abstinence were wearing heavily on my already shattered frame. Women and children were crying for food; it was a painful sight to witness their sufferings with no means of alleviating them, and no hope of relief save by travelling and hunting. We had no shelters save the canopy of heaven, and no alternative but to travel on, and lie down on the cold damp ground, for a resting place."

Fighting the Americans, Sitting Bull was learning, was not like making a raid on the Crows.

* * *

The year 1864 was one of bloodletting in the United States. It was as though the country had been swept by a lust for taking lives. As the soldier had said, the South had lost the war the previous year and had no chance of redeeming its defeats. But for a few additional months of independence, a sorry independence that was already crumbling, it was ready to pay a high price in human beings. Sherman made his famous march, burning and destroying as he went to prove to a proud people that pride alone cannot win a war; and Grant, who had been made commander-in-chief, began his relentless pounding of the forces under Lee. Although he could not quite secure victory, his campaign was grinding to pieces what remained of the Confederate Army.

Out in the West, Sully's march to the Yellowstone River had resolved nothing lasting. Inkpaduta, against whom the offensive had been aimed, remained free and more than ever hateful of the white men. On the other hand, the battle at the Killdeer Mountains had involved Sioux who had wanted nothing more than to be left at peace in their own land. What Sully had done was to create an alliance among bands and tribes that might not otherwise have acted in concert. Sitting Bull had spent his youth and young manhood in the isolated world of the Hunkpapas, remote from the comings and goings of the white men and from many of the other Indians, even many Sioux. Now circumstances were forcing him into a much larger and more complex society, one in which many tribes were concerned and in which leadership of large numbers of warriors was important. A simple raid and the capture of a few horses was no longer a sure road to glory and fame. Much more was required of an ambitious man like Sitting Bull.

Yet even the large group of Sioux who had fought at the Killdeer Mountains did not indicate the full extent of the change that was taking place. Farther south the actions of the white men were driving other tribes to combine in their efforts to throw out, or at least control, the invaders. Between them, Eayre and Chivington with their aggressive tactics and outlook were forcing the Indians together.

An officer on the staff of the commanding general was sent out to make an investigation of what was going on. After looking over the situation, he reported that a bloody war was imminent if the army did not stop using scouting expeditions that did not know the difference between one tribe and another. He predicted that only "a few more murders on our part" would bring the tribes together.

His report, however, was made too late. A series of unprovoked attacks, including several on the Sioux, had destroyed the chances for peace; and particularly along the Platte, the Indians were out in force, attacking wagon trains, emigrants, and small settlements. By August, the route along the South Platte was closed. No stagecoaches or wagon trains dared run along it, and Denver was short of food and other supplies.

The American reaction, as it often is in times of stress, was ambivalent. Some believed peace could be restored, if not with all the Indians, at least with many of them, and the effort should be made. Others subscribed to the crudest of frontier philosophies that the only good Indian was a dead one. As the summer of 1864 wore on and public opinion grew more inflamed, the latter group gained ascendancy among both civilians and the military, and the moderates lost influence, a change that was unknown to the Indians but bound to affect their future.

Earlier in the year, the governor of Colorado had published a circular in which he had advised the Indians who wished to be friends to identify themselves. Otherwise they would be regarded as enemies. Among those who heard about the circular from the white traders and decided to act on it was Black Kettle, a chief of the Cheyennes. Through intermediaries, he and some other leaders arranged for a council at Denver between themselves, the governor, and several other white authorities. The council was held, but Black Kettle misunderstood its meaning. Whereas the authorities thought they had told him he must surrender to the army, Black Kettle thought he had made peace.

As a consequence, he led his band of Cheyennes, numbering several hundred people, to Fort Lyon on the Arkansas River, near the post established by the famous trader William Bent. The officer who had commanded the post had been a moderate man, one who understood the Indians and believed peace could be made with most of them. But before Black Kettle arrived, he had been replaced by another officer, Major Scott Anthony, who had an entirely different attitude. When

Black Kettle appeared at the fort, however, Major Anthony did not know what to do, because he did not think he had enough soldiers to fight a band the size of the Cheyennes. As a result, he told Black Kettle to go and camp at Sand Creek about forty miles away. Unsuspecting, Black Kettle did what he was told.

The major also ordered him to surrender his arms, and so the Cheyennes turned in a number of old guns. In all fairness to the major, they probably did retain their better weapons. Not to have done so would have been foolhardy, for they were dependent on them for food as well as protection. After a short lapse of time, the major returned the guns and told them to go buffalo hunting, as he had no food to give them. These actions further enforced Black Kettle's belief that he was at peace. Nothing indicated hostility between his band and the white soldiers.

Then along came Colonel Chivington, finished with his abortive mission against a Confederate invasion that never occurred. He was still looking for a fight, and Black Kettle's camp seemed to him to offer a good target. After making sure that no alarm could reach the unsuspecting Indians, Chivington and Anthony set out on the night of November 28, 1864, for Sand Creek. They had with them about six hundred men, a third of them soldiers with some experience and the rest of them dressed in odd clothes and obviously new recruits who had signed up for a hundred days. The weather was bitter, and the snow lay on the ground to the depth of two or three feet. Finally the old trapper who was guiding them became so overcome with the cold that they had to enlist the services of a half-breed who was with them. The temper of the men was angry. One of them, a giant, suddenly tapped the butt of his revolver and said to the half-breed, "Jack, I haven't had an Indian to eat for a long time. If you fool with me, and don't lead us to that camp, I'll have you for breakfast."

But the half-breed was true to his assignment. Shortly after daybreak, the soldiers reached the camp. The Indians—there were some Arapahoes camped near the Cheyennes—were just beginning to stir when they saw the Americans. They immediately sent out an envoy to assure the troops they were friendly, and Black Kettle raised an American flag he had been given at one of the many councils. He thought this would demonstrate to the soldiers that he was at peace with the Americans. In addition, he stood in front of his tent, calling out to his people that they had nothing to fear, because they were under the protection of the army.

But these pathetic demonstrations of friendship meant nothing to the Americans, who began firing immediately. The Indians had approximately two hundred warriors; the whites numbered approximately six hundred, all better armed and equipped with howitzers. Completely surprised by this superior force, the Cheyennes had no chance. Their best escape route lay upstream, but some of the soldiers had flanked the camp and now blocked the way. The Indians, therefore, were trapped. Nevertheless they fought as best they could. Some of them dug rifle pits in the bank of the shallow stream and determined to make a last stand, for the Americans obviously would offer them no quarter. Sometimes a single warrior, realizing he was about to die, would charge the troops in the hope that he could take at least one American life before he lost his own. Such bravery, however great, could not create a balance in the uneven odds.

A few Indians managed to escape the heavy fire of the rifles and howitzers, but many of these were pursued and killed. For these Americans had come to kill Indians, and now they had hundreds before them, helpless and almost defenseless. They shot women and children as indiscriminately as they did warriors. A group of men captured three women and five children, but a lieutenant shot and scalped all eight Indians in spite of the screams and protests of the women. A private in one campany saw a major blow out the brains of a child, and a lieutenant scalped two other Indians. With such leadership, the men lost their heads and shot at anything that moved.

When the battle—if such a massacre could be called a battle—was over, the bed of the stream was lined with bodies, some lying in the water and some on the sandy banks. But even then, the Americans could not shake themselves free of their frenzy. Like madmen, they scrambled from one dead body to another, scalping them and mutilating them so badly that many of them were unrecognizable to those persons who knew them well. Even later, the horror of what they had done did not occur to them. When they returned to Denver, they brought with them some one hundred scalps, which they triumphantly exhibited during the intermission of a theatrical performance.

News of the massacre at Sand Creek swept across the nation. The government conducted an investigation, but investigations cannot restore lives. Nor can they restore trust. To many Indians, it now seemed clear that peace with the Americans was impossible.

V

Action in the Powder River Valley

IN the nineteenth century, the period in which these events were
taking place, an author—whether he was writing a novel, a history, a biography, or even a newspaper article—was permitted to
emerge at will from behind the façade he had erected between himself
and his audience and speak to his readers directly. But as we became
more sophisticated in our tastes, stricter conventions were imposed on
him, and he was required to state his ideas implicitly, never explicitly.
This stricture, of course, did not fool any intelligent reader, for the
writer must always have a point of view if he is to create anything
more lively than a blueprint or a dissertation that will be read by no
one except his immediate peers.

In the last chapter, for example, it was clear where my sympathies
lay; and I hope that I left you with a sense of horror over the atrocities
committed by Colonel Chivington. It would have been just as easy—
although, I think, less truthful—to have told the same story from the
point of view of some of the settlers who were attacked by the Indians.
In that case, I would have explained that, in the opinion of many
people on the frontier, the friendliness of Black Kettle was highly
suspect and that Chivington's men mutilated the Indians' bodies, not
out of a frenzy for blood, but because they thought they were imitating
the Indians and teaching them a lesson. You, of course, know that
writers work this way and accept it.

In recent years, however, the convention of seeming impartiality has
become less and less strict. Today articles and books appear that only
a decade ago would not have won acceptance because of the imposi-

tion of the writer's direct opinion and even the frequent use of the once-barred pronoun "I." Whether this rending of the transparent veil that used to lie between the writer and the reader is stylistically good or not is a moot question, but it is the style today. So I will take advantage of the new convention and answer directly some questions that may be on your mind.

You may, for example, have wondered why Sitting Bull himself does not appear more often in the pages you have read. If this is the case, then you have expected me to write a white man's biography of a red man, something that cannot be done. You should remember that Sitting Bull and the Sioux had no written language and therefore no records except their winter counts and the recollections of the older Indians, often set down long after the events and just as unreliable as the recollections of old white men—that is, they are colored by pride, the desire for self-justification, old angers and old loves, and the other emotional paraphernalia that we accumulate during our lifetimes. And of those recollections, few can be corrected or analyzed in the light of contemporary letters, journals, diaries, or other written matter. And so we know very little about Sitting Bull's younger days. No one capable of writing about him realized he even existed until much later in the story.

Then why, you may ask, do you devote so much space to that period of his life? Because, like most of us, Sitting Bull was a product of his own time. If, as one example, Chivington had not massacred the Arapahoes and Cheyennes at Sand Creek, the Indians might not have learned to fight together against the Americans. In such a case, the battle in which Sitting Bull most distinguished himself might never have occurred, at least in the form that it did. For Sitting Bull was created, not merely by the society in which he grew up, but also by the events that were taking place around him. Without knowing what some of those events were, it is impossible to know Sitting Bull.

Regrettably, most Americans are not familiar with much of Indian history. A few outstanding events, like Custer's last stand, stick in their minds; but for the most part, the Indians blur together in a confused picture that does not differentiate between the tribes or their attitudes and actions. The Indian wars of the West are not even taught at West Point, for example; that entire tradition of the army is neglected in favor of other topics more nearly European in nature. The academy is not alone in ignoring much of our Western history, so although many readers are familiar with such events as the opening of the Bozeman Trail, I have to assume that many others are not. And I do not wish them to lose the point of what I am trying to say.

In the course of a book of this length, it would be impossible to trace the entire history of the Sioux. They were numerous people, covering large sections of this country, and their history was complicated. But I have tried to outline those events that eventually affected the central figure in this book. For example, I think it is important to know why Sitting Bull's first experience with the white men was a warlike one, but it is impossible to know this without knowing about the uprising of the Minnesota Sioux and how it occurred. It is also important to know about some of the other tribes, like the Cheyennes, because their activities were interrelated.

Now let me bring down again the veil that lies between writer and reader and return once more to the Great Plains and the tragedy that was playing out its course in that vast, windswept area, where two great cultures were bracing for the inevitable clash between them.

* * *

Chivington's attack on the Indians at Sand Creek was like trying to destroy a wick by touching it with fire when it is attached to a keg of dynamite. He had, indeed, killed many Indian men, women, and children—practically all of them friendly—but he had converted the survivors into furious enemies, determined on revenge. After moving northward out of reach of any further attack by the colonel's forces, they held a council and decided to send messengers to some of the Sioux and Northern Arapahoes, inviting them to make war jointly against the Americans. In the past, bands from various tribes had often gone on the warpath together, but their common anger at Chivington's action provided the greatest cohesive force they had ever known. Probably never before had so many Indians concentrated on a single objective—to drive out the white men.

Their first target was Julesburg, a small settlement on the south branch of the Platte River in Colorado. To avoid Indian attacks, the stage had abandoned the route along the North Platte in favor of a more southerly road; and Julesburg was one of its stopping points. In addition to the station, the settlement consisted of some corrals, a store, a warehouse, and a telegraph station. Nearby was Fort Rankin (later Fort Sedgwick), whose troops were intended to guard the small community, which was a vital link in east-west communications.

The Indians' plan of attack was one they had often used before. The main body hid in some sand hills to the south of the river, while a small group of some seven warriors approached the fort under the cover of night and the protection of a ravine. At daybreak, they saw men outside the stockade and charged toward them. The men noticed the Indians in time and dashed safely into the fort. The commanding officer, hearing that only seven warriors were involved, responded just as the Indians had hoped he would. He emerged from the fort with soldiers and armed civilians and gave pursuit. The warriors did not try to resist the American force, which greatly outnumbered them. Instead they lashed their ponies and turned them toward the sand hills, where the major band of the Indians was restlessly waiting.

Closer and closer came the Indians and their white pursuers, and within a few minutes the trap would have closed. But some of the younger Indians, anxious for individual glory, could not wait. Before the Americans entered the sand hills, they charged, thus revealing the presence of the larger band. This mistake was disastrous to the Indians' plan. For the white men, seeing the additional warriors, reined in their horses and raced back toward the fort as fast as they could.

The entire band now joined the charge, but they were unable to cut the fleeing Americans off from the stockade. American casualties were heavy—probably about eighteen men lost their lives—but the battle was not decisive. The Americans were not strong enough to emerge from the fort and fight, but the Indians could not attack the stockade. Some of them rode around it, waving their guns and bows and shouting insults at the white men inside. Others dashed immediately to the stagecoach station and began looting the warehouse. The soldiers did not dare fire their artillery directly at the plunderers for fear of setting the buildings on fire, but they sent shots over the heads of the Indians in the hope of frightening them away.

The looting continued for hours. From time to time, the soldiers trapped in the fort fired their cannons, and the smoke curled above the stockade, but they were unable to prevent the destruction. The Indians carried away so many goods they had to go back to the village and get more horses. They even captured a paymaster's chest containing the funds to pay the troops in Colorado. Because their annuities had been paid in goods, they did not know the meaning of money and amused themselves by throwing the paper into the air and watching it blow away. At last by nightfall they had taken everything they wanted and disappeared into the north. A first blow had been struck in retaliation for Chivington's massacre.

Black Kettle was satisfied with the revenge that had been taken, but many of the other warriors were not, so the band broke up. Black Kettle departed with those Cheyennes who wanted peace, while the other Indians continued to raid throughout the valley of the South Platte.

This part of the Great Plains was heavily settled for those times. The telegraph followed this route, and the stagecoach operated many stations. In between were numerous ranches and some stores. During the early weeks of 1865, these bore the brunt of the Indian attacks. Raiding parties went out in every direction in which there were white men and came back with more and more plunder, until the camps were full of it.

About a thousand warriors decided to attack Julesburg again. Because their tactics had been so nearly successful the previous time, they used decoys again; but this time the commanding officer, having learned his lesson, refused to be drawn out of the fort. So the Indians returned to the stage station and the warehouse, taking bags of corn and other goods they had been unable to carry away earlier. When they had finished looting, they set fire to the buildings in an effort to lure the troops into leaving the safety of the stockade.

A small detachment of soldiers from Camp Cottonwood was approaching Fort Rankin at the same time. One of the officers later wrote, "I could see Indians scattered everywhere in front of us; they were crossing the river, running around the stage station, blacksmith shop and telegraph office, which were burning. The haystacks of the stage station were also burning. Back on the hills west of the post was a large group of Indians, apparently motionless, while between us and the fort was a body of Indians running around and evidently shouting and yelling and having a good time, although they were so far off I could hear no noise.

"When we got to the stage station," the officer continued, "it was a sight. A lot of the Indians were there before us, and they started away. We saw that a large number of Indians were carrying off corn from the stage station. There were so many of them that they had sanded a road across the ice of the river, and this road was about six feet wide. Their ponies being unshod, they could not carry the corn across the road without the road being sanded; it was too slippery. There were enough of them to sand the entire road, and there was a line of them all around the burning stage station. There were animals killed; a couple of horses; and a cow, that had been grazing around. Chicks were killed. It seemed as if the Indians thought it was a funny thing to shoot an arrow down through a chicken and pin the chick to the ground. We saw chickens still fluttering that were thus pinned to the ground."

Because the Indians were concentrating on their pillaging and because the dense smoke limited visibility, the detachment was able to approach without being seen. Then with the help of howitzer fire directed from the fort, the soldiers were able to make the final mile safely and entered the gates of the stockade without any loss of life.

The Indians camped nearby that night, celebrating their victory with dances, while the soldiers watched from the roof of the fort and wondered whether the attack would recommence the following day. But when morning came, the Indians broke camp and moved north.

But they were still in no mood to make peace. In a few weeks, they disrupted east-west traffic, took many lives and captured thousands of dollars' worth of goods and yet suffered few casualties. Against the swift-moving bands of Indians, the army was practically helpless. It had neither the equipment nor the men to guard every point, and it could not shift its troops to meet each attack.

Then the long straggling line of Indians, driving their freshly captured livestock and with their horses loaded with plunder, moved across the plains in the direction of the Black Hills. Behind them, they left ravaged settlements, burned buildings, and the corpses of many Americans. The white men had paid a heavy price for Colonel Chivington's attack on Black Kettle and the friendly Cheyennes.

*　　　*　　　*

Sitting Bull's slight encounters with the white men had taught him they were dangerous, particularly when they were armed with artillery. Against the big guns with their devastating fire and their long range, the Indians were helpless. All they could do was retreat. But the Americans did not pose a serious threat to Sitting Bull and the other Hunkpapas. If Inkpaduta had not fled west after the Santee uprising, Sitting Bull still might not have seen any white men, much less have fought against them. His country was too isolated for them to wish to enter it.

But the fates were slowly working against him. The discovery of gold in California in 1849 had brought hordes of emigrants across the plains, but they had stayed to the south. So also had the travelers in search of land in Oregon. The later discovery of gold in Colorado increased the numbers of white men moving across the plains, but they, too, stayed to the south of the land favored by the Hunkpapas. Then in 1862 a gold rush started in Idaho. Invariably some of the prospectors went farther afield and ventured into the northern Rocky Mountains. In 1862, a wagon train stopped for the night at a small stream that was so infested with grasshoppers that they called it Grasshopper Creek. The next day the men started looking for gold, and they found the stream was rich in it. The only tools a man needed to become wealthy were his pan and a willingness to work, an ideal situation for those who had no capital to invest in heavy equipment.

Naturally word of the discovery spread, and soon other miners were coming to Montana. By 1863, they were spreading farther out in their search, and several parties were exploring in the area around the Yellowstone River. In one of these parties was a young man named John M. Bozeman, who was looking not for gold, but for a shorter route to the country the prospectors wanted to reach. As it was, they came from the east along the Oregon Trail and then swung north on the west side of the Big Horn Mountains. Bozeman thought that if he could discover a shorter route east of the Big Horns, he could make money taking the emigrants along it. This simple act of business enterprise affected the Sioux, for it established a route through another part of their territory. Gold in Montana and the establishment of what became known as the Bozeman Trail drew the white men closer and closer to the lands occupied by the Hunkpapas and other more remote Sioux. On the east they were now subject to expeditions like those in pursuit of the Santees. On the west was the new road opened by Bozeman. And toward the south was the line of forts guarding the Emigrant Trail. A few battles in which the Hunkpapas had fought had done little to check the white men's advance.

Of immediate consequence to Sitting Bull's future were the raids that had been taking place along the South Platte. Although Sitting Bull had undoubtedly heard about them, he had taken no part in them, remaining in the remote wilderness while they were going on. But the devastation caused by the Indians so alarmed the Americans that General G. M. Dodge of the Department of the Missouri reorganized the command by merging the Districts of Utah, Colorado, and Nebraska into one, the District of the Plains, and placed General Patrick E. Connor in charge.

Connor's orders were specific. "With the force at your disposal," Dodge told him, "you can make vigorous war upon the Indians and punish them so that they will be forced to keep the peace. They should be kept away from our line of travel and made to stand on the defensive."

Connor spent the spring and early summer of 1865 strengthening the already existing forts and making preparations for a campaign that would carry the war to the Powder River country of Montana east of the Big Horn Mountains. This campaign would both punish the Indians for their past raids and make travel safe along the Bozeman Trail or any other shortcut to the rapidly developing gold mines of Montana.

In April, while Connor was organizing his command, Lee finally realized his cause was lost and surrendered to Grant at Appomattox. The painful, bloody conflict between the white men—far surpassing in casualties anything done by the Indians on the Great Plains—came to an end, and the nation settled back to a sorrowful peace and an attempt to heal the festering wounds of the past. The effect on Connor's plans were severalfold. The country could now devote more of its resources to the subjugation of the Indians. On the other hand, many of the enlisted men, now that the major war was over, wanted to return home or try their luck in the goldfields. They were restless and sometimes even mutinous.

Nevertheless Connor continued his preparations. He planned a three-pronged attack against the Indians. Colonel Nelson Cole was to leave from Columbus, Nebraska, and march to a meeting place north of the Black Hills. In considerable detail, Connor instructed him in the making of signal fires and the use of pickets and also gave him these grim instructions. "You will not," Connor ordered, "receive overtures of peace or submission from Indians, but will attack and kill every male Indian over twelve years of age."

Colonel Samuel Walker with approximately six hundred cavalrymen was to leave Fort Laramie and march north near the Black Hills and meet Cole. To Walker, Connor repeated the same order he had given Cole.

When General John Pope at St. Louis read copies of Connor's order he told Dodge, "These instructions are atrocious, and are in direct violation of my repeated orders. You will please take immediate steps to countermand such orders. If any such orders as General Connor's are carried out it will be disgraceful to the government, and will cost him his commission, if not worse. Have it rectified without delay." At least some sense of human decency prevailed at headquarters, and Connor's order was immediately countermanded, but it revealed the spirit in which he was taking to the field.

After many delays in assembling the men and equipment he needed, everything was at last ready; and on August 1, 1865, which was late in the year to start such a campaign, Connor was prepared to cross the North Platte near the mouth of La Bonte Creek, a few miles south of the present town of Douglas, Wyoming. But the spring floods had washed away the crossing, and although the cavalry escort searched for hours, they could not find another. The only alternative seemed to be to march more than a hundred miles out of their way, which would have delayed the expedition even further. One officer, however, took advantage of the time to go antelope hunting. As he was riding alone, he noticed a buffalo trail leading into the river and emerging from the other side. He pushed his horse forward and found the footing firm all the way to the opposite bank. By working all night, the soldiers were able to improve the buffalo trail sufficiently so they were able to make the crossing the next day; and Connor's expedition was on its way.

On August 8, one officer wrote, "We obtained our first view of the Big Horn Mountains, at a distance of eighty-five miles northwest, and it was indeed magnificent. The sun so shone as to fall with full blaze upon the southern and southwestern sides of Cloud Peak, . . . and the whole snow-covered range so clearly blended with the sky as to leave it in doubt whether all was not a mass of bright cloud. Although the day was exceedingly warm, as soon as we struck this ridge we felt the cooling breezes from the snow-clad mountains, which was most gratefully appreciated by man and beast. In front, and a little to the northeast, could be seen the four columns of the Pumpkin Buttes, and fifty miles further east, Bear Butte, and beyond, a faint outline of the Black Hills. The atmosphere was so wonderfully clear and bright that one could imagine that he could see the eagles on the crags of Pumpkin Buttes, full forty miles away."

After a few more days, the expedition reached the Powder River, a rapidly running but muddy stream, flowing through a stretch of heavy timber. Connor halted and sent out scouting parties to look for a site for the fort he intended to build and use as a supply depot. Soon he selected a mesa that rose about a hundred feet above the river, and most of the soldiers and many of the teamsters started the construction work, using as lumber the nearby trees.

When the army sent expeditions into the field, they were usually accompanied by scouts, frontiersmen like Jim Bridger, the famous mountain man, or Indians who were unfriendly with the Indians against whom the particular expedition was directed. These men were invaluable to the commanders because they knew the country, could follow trails left by the enemy, and also understood their habits. Connor had with him some Pawnee scouts under Colonel North; and while the soldiers were busy with their axes building the fort, he sent the scouts out to reconnoiter. They discovered the trail of some Cheyennes and, anxious to fight their hereditary enemies, followed the trail. Although the Pawnees' horses were tired, they overtook the Cheyennes and, in a brisk battle, slaughtered them. More than twenty-five Cheyenne corpses lay on the ground.

The Pawnees then returned to the camp. Although they had been riding and fighting over a thirty-hour period, they were exultant about their victory. They came into camp with the scalps of their enemies tied to sticks; and in the evening, instead of resting, they celebrated their victory. "The war dance," wrote an officer who watched it, "was the most savage scene I had ever witnessed. They formed a circle and danced around a fire, holding up the bloody scalps, brandishing their hatchets and exhibiting the spoils of the fight. They were perfectly frantic with this, their first grand victory over their hereditary foe. During the war dance they kept howling, 'Hoo yah, hoo yah, hoo yah,' accompanying their voices with music (if such it could be called) made by beating upon an instrument somewhat resembling a drum."

At first the officers and men were much amused by this wild celebration, but as the night wore on and they wanted to sleep, their amusement gave way to vexation. Finally, when it was long past midnight, Connor ordered North to make them stop. On several subsequent nights, the dance was repeated until Connor enforced a ten o'clock curfew so his other men could get some rest.

In spite of the many delays in getting the expedition started, Connor was deep in the Indians' territory and had already won his first punishing victory. But the season was growing late, and he needed to win more than one relatively minor battle if he were to subjugate the northern tribes and those from the south who had joined them. So he pushed along the path of the river. The hills on either side were covered with grass, and each valley contained a stream filled with the pure water coming from the melting snows in the mountains. The banks were usually lined with trees, wild cherries and some willows and cottonwoods, mixed with a few other varieties.

The expedition kept traveling in a northerly direction down the Powder River toward the Yellowstone until August 26, when it turned more toward the west and ascended the ridges that separate the basin of the Powder from that of the Tongue River. Jim Bridger was riding in the lead. When they reached the high ground, he saw in the valley below them columns of smoke, indicating the presence of an Indian camp. But none of the other white men could see them, even though Connor used his field glasses. Finally Connor gave the order to march on, but he sent North and some of the Pawnees on a scout in the direction toward which Bridger had pointed. Two days later, two of the scouts returned to say they had located a large Indian village.

Since the fighting along the Platte, many of the Indians had become careless. It did not seem likely to them that the Americans would follow them into this wild and relatively unknown country, where, in spite of the Bozeman Trail, few white men ever came. So this camp, composed mostly of Arapahoes with a few Cheyennes, did not have the slightest knowledge of the whereabouts of the troops, although both the soldiers and the Indians were in the same valley.

Connor took advantage of the opportunity to launch a surprise attack. The scouts had returned in the early evening; and at eight o'clock, when the soldiers had had time to eat supper, he set off with a force of two hundred fifty men and eighty Indian scouts. The night was dark, and travel up the valley of the Tongue River was difficult; but the men struggled through the underbrush and climbed over fallen trees, moving as fast as they could.

The Araphoes were peacefully camped on a large tableland above the ravine through which the river flowed. Their tepees were upstream and the rest of the broad acreage was occupied by their grazing horses. When daylight came, they had their meal and then started breaking camp. Nothing was further from their thoughts than the presence of an enemy nearby, as they began rounding up the horses and taking down the tepees. Suddenly they heard a volley of shots from the river. Looking in that direction, they saw Connor's men, who had fired at the village and were now coming toward them at a charge.

The soldiers on their racing horses had no time to take aim, so their bullets struck men, women, and children indiscriminately. But the warriors, although startled by the sudden assault, ran for their bows and guns, and the casualties were not all on one side. "One of our men," wrote an officer, ". . . a fine looking soldier with as handsome a face as I ever saw on a man, grabbed me by the shoulder and turned me about that I might assist him in withdrawing an arrow from his mouth. The point of the arrow had passed through his open mouth and lodged in the roof of his tongue. Having no surgeon with us higher graded than a hospital steward, it was afterwards within a half hour decided that to get the arrow out from his mouth, the tongue must be, and was, cut out."

The Indians' resistance was futile. The main body fled up a creek running into the Tongue River, trying to escape from the white men who were pursuing them, while the scouts rounded up most of their herd. Connor carried the attack for ten miles, but his men's horses were exhausted from the long ride the night before and began to falter. Finally the general had only about thirteen men capable of keeping up with him, and at that point the Indians counterattacked. The Americans were forced to fall back toward the Tongue River, picking up stragglers as they went and thus increasing in numbers. At last they reached the village, where the scouts were holding the captured horses.

The Arapahoes were desperate to recover their horses, but Connor had a mountain howitzer with him and was able to hold them back. While they watched helplessly, Connor's men systematically destroyed their supplies and belongings, making piles of buffalo robes, tepees, blankets, furs, and dried meat and setting fire to them. When the fires were burning brightly, the soldiers placed the bodies of their own comrades on them, so the Indians could not later mutilate them.

At around two thirty in the afternoon, the work of destruction was completed, and Connor started marching back to his camp. The Arapahoes followed him part of the way, but about midnight the Arapahoes gave up, and the battle ended. Although Connor had been forced to retreat, he had inflicted serious injury on the Indians. He had not killed them all, as he had originally intended when he wrote his infamous order, but he had destroyed their supplies, and winter was approaching.

While he was fighting the Arapahoes, another expedition, sponsored by the Department of the Interior, had started earlier from the east. Its purpose was to lay out a road from the Niobrara River in Nebraska Territory to Virginia City in Montana—one that would be shorter than the Bozeman Trail. It was under the command of a former army colonel, James A. Sawyer, and was composed of about two hundred men, of whom approximately one hundred fifty were cavalry and infantry. Sawyer also had with him five emigrant teams and a private freight train of thirty-six wagons. For several weeks the long column moved west, the dust rising from the wagon wheels and the hooves of the horses and oxen. Advance guides sought out the best route to follow, while the main body built fords and occasionally graded the road where Sawyer thought it necessary.

Toward the end of July, the infantry's shoes began to wear out, and the commanding officer had to send to Fort Laramie, about a hundred miles to the south, for new ones. Nobody was anxious about breaking up the command for this purpose. They had seen few Indians, and the expedition had grown careless. The civilians and soldiers did not act as a unified command and even made separate camps, and at night they kept only a few men on guard duty.

After crossing the North Fork of the Cheyenne River, they headed toward the Powder River, which they hoped to reach within a day. But the terrain proved so rough it took them longer. To add to their difficulties, the land was dry. At the end of the third day, each man had only what remained of the scanty supply in his canteen, and the livestock were desperately thirsty. The only nearby water was a stagnant pool, discovered by the wagon master, but the animals soon roiled it so badly it was undrinkable even for them. Sawyer and the officer in command of the escort decided they should send some of the men to drive the livestock loose to the Powder River, let them drink there, rest, and then return before the expedition could proceed.

One-third of the men were detached for this duty. They left at daybreak and drove the herds over a low range of mountains, where traveling was often so difficult the animals had to go single file, but they reached the Powder River at last, and the thirsty animals drank deeply. While the men rested, the guide made a scouting expedition and discovered a large Indian camp only five miles up the river. At this news, the men decided to return immediately to Sawyer's main camp instead of remaining overnight at the Powder River as they had originally planned.

The Indians, who were Cheyennes, learned of Sawyer's presence just about the time he learned of theirs. The warriors took out their bows and guns and prepared for a fight. Sawyer, when his men returned with the news of the Indian village, realized he could not stay in his present camp. Without water, he would be defeated easily, so he immediately began to retreat back to the North Fork of the Cheyenne. When the Indians caught up with him, his men were already moving, so they stayed out of sight. At noon the white men stopped briefly to eat a meal. Nearby was a clump of trees in which the Indians hid and watched the white men prepare their food and rest in the shade of the wagons. Then they saw a young man who was in charge of the private freight train walk toward them because he thought there might be a pool of water among the trees. The Indians waited quietly as he came nearer. When he was close enough they began shooting, killing him and charging into the herd that had been let loose to graze. The livestock stampeded, and the Cheyennes ran off with many animals. Happy over their victory, they returned to their village, which gave Sawyer a chance to travel a few more miles before making camp.

Instead of immediately resuming the battle the next day, the Cheyennes foolishly permitted Sawyer to reach a place where there was enough water for both animals and men and allowed him time to make a corral out of his wagons, which gave shelter to both men and animals. This was a serious mistake on their part. When they finally started fighting, they shot from long range with small loads of powder, which rendered their shooting largely ineffective. But the Americans could neither move on nor drive them away.

This deadlock continued into the next day, when the Cheyennes thought of a better way of getting some of the expedition's supplies. About noon they put up a white flag to show they wanted to talk to the Americans. They told Sawyer they had at first thought he was leading an army to attack them but they now realized the nature of his expedition was peaceful. As a consequence, they would leave if he would give them some supplies.

Sawyer and the commander of the escort disagreed on what to do. Sawyer was for giving them what they wanted; the commander was against it. In the end, Sawyer's view prevailed, and the Americans drove out a wagon loaded with sugar, coffee, tobacco, and flour. There was also disagreement among the Cheyennes. George Bent, who was with them, had also been in Black Kettle's camp when Chivington attacked it. In fact, he had been wounded and was still angry. He told Sawyer the Indians were strong enough to fight the government and that they would not make any treaties until Chivington had been hanged.

His warlike mood was shared by others, and in spite of the presents, they were not ready to make peace. After the supplies had been distributed, two Americans, thinking the battle was over, carelessly remained alone near the flag of truce. The Indians saw one more chance to avenge the deaths of those Chivington had killed. When the Americans sent out a search party to look for the two missing men, they found one only a short distance off, his chest filled with arrows and a lance pinning him to the dirt. The other man was never found.

Some of the more warlike of the Cheyennes continued to make occasional forays against the expedition, but there were no more full-scale attacks. Nevertheless, both Sawyer and the commander of the escort were relieved to reach Fort Connor. After resting briefly, Sawyer continued in the direction of the Tongue River. Although he knew Connor was somewhere in the wilderness ahead of him, he did not know that he had attacked the Arapahoes and set them on the warpath.

When the Arapahoes, who were now on the alert, noticed Sawyer's expedition approaching, they attacked and killed an advance guard. Sawyer did not heed the warning and regarded the soldier's death as an isolated incident. But the next morning, September 1, when he crossed a fork of the Tongue River, the band of Arapahoes was waiting for him on the other side.

No sooner had the train forded the water and started up again than the Arapahoes swept down on the rear guard and ran off with about thirty head of cattle. Now having an armed escort of only thirty-five soldiers, Sawyer could not pursue them. He thought they might be satisfied with the capture of the animals and leave him alone, but he was mistaken. As soon as the column entered the low hills on the far side of the river, the Indians attacked again. Unfortunately for them, they either used too little powder in their charges or fired from too great a distance. Although the bullets flew among the white men, they caused little damage. Nevertheless the attack forced the Americans to retreat to the river and find a place to make a corral of their wagons.

The next day the Arapahoes decided to change their tactics and instead of fighting Sawyer tried to enlist his help in recovering their horses from Connor. During a conference with them, Sawyer agreed to assign three soldiers to accompany three Indians on a mission to Connor. They had not traveled far, however, when they came upon a detachment of more than twenty-five soldiers marching in their direction. Immediately the Indians' suspicions were aroused. Was this a trap that Sawyer had laid for them? Instead of carrying out their original plan, they returned to their own camp in an angry, hostile temper.

The soldiers, however, were not part of a ruse. They had merely carried mail to Connor and were now returning to the fort. They told Sawyer that his three soldiers had gone on to find Connor and that he could expect reinforcements. After they arrived, he continued safely to the mining camps of Montana. When his journey was ended, another road had been cut through the wilderness, and this one was even closer to the lands in which Sitting Bull liked to roam.

Connor had saved Sawyer's expedition, but he was growing more and more apprehensive about the expeditions under Cole and Walker. The time had come when they had planned to meet, but he could not find them. His worries were well based. From the very first, both men had been plagued by difficulties, which were augmented by their lack of experience. Neither officer knew anything about the plains, and neither one had adequate scouts or guides.

From the first, Walker ran into trouble. After leaving Fort Laramie, he found little forage for his horses and few sources of water. Even when he did find water, it tended to be brackish. After days of futile marching, he finally came across the trail left by the expedition headed by Cole, but instead of following it along the Little Missouri River, he decided to go through the Bad Lands. This decision led him into a nightmarish world, where only the most experienced frontiersmen could exist. He later reported that it was the worst country he had ever seen and that "the whole earth seemed to be one heap of burnt ashes." At each step, the horses sank to their knees, and to add to the horror of the journey, the rivers were filled with quicksand. Each time they crossed one, they lost animals and supplies, neither of which could be spared. Finally the horses became so weak that some of the men had to dismount and walk.

In addition to the suffering Walker and his men endured, they did not find Connor, but at last they located Cole's expedition. Cole had also been having a difficult time. He, too, had had trouble finding water and forage, and he had moved even more laboriously than Walker, because he carried his supplies in wagons instead of using pack animals. Many of his horses were dead, and his men had almost reached the limits of their strength. The two officers did not try to combine their forces, because it was difficult enough for them to find sufficient grass for their horses even when they were alone. But they worked in cooperation with each other in their search for Connor.

Then the Indians discovered them. Walker had come to Cole's camp to discuss their joint plans, when they received a report that the Indians were attacking Cole's herd, which was grazing about a mile away. Cole rushed to the spot and found several hundred Indians driving off most of the herd. He ordered out all his troops except those needed to guard the camp and went in pursuit. The majority of the animals were recovered, but one small detachment of Americans was almost wiped out.

Then the Indians faded away as silently as they had come. If they had kept on attacking, they probably could have destroyed both Cole's and Walker's commands, now that the men were dispirited and in poor condition.

Even without the Indians, however, the climate and the land were exacting a heavy toll. Sometimes it was extremely hot, sometimes extremely cold. The horses and mules were exhausted, and some were starving, because Cole was now afraid to turn them loose to graze. So many died that Cole had to abandon wagons and destroy the equipment they carried to prevent its falling into the hands of the Indians. Neither Walker nor Cole had enough supplies and were forced to place their men on short rations. Later, in his official report, Cole said, "Fatigue and starvation had done its work on both men and animals, in so much they were unfit to pursue with vigor the savage foe that circled around their starving way through this desert whose oases were but inviting delusions, for however pleasing to the wearied eye were the green dresses of the prickly pear and the sage brush, they were bitter mockery to the other senses, for they contain no life-giving essence for man or beast. Certes starving soldiers might well wonder why there was no provision made for such contingencies; why old Indian fighters had not, with their knowledge, planned a more consistent campaign; created depots here and hunted Indians there; not had a command starving here, unfit to cope with the Indians everywhere around them, and the supplies they needed so much away no one knew where. . . ."

But it was too late for laments to do any good. Both officers faced the difficult task of salvaging their two commands, and neither of them had the slightest idea what to do. They kept up their search for Connor, while the Indians—Sioux, Arapahoes, and Cheyennes—continued to press them. If the Indians had been better armed and organized, they probably could have destroyed the Americans, who were completely on the defensive. Even if they had wished to counterattack, they could not have done so because of the sorry condition of such horses as they still had.

During these engagements, Sitting Bull played a minor role. In the pictograph record he kept of his own exploits, he showed himself running off with livestock on several occasions, once under heavy fire from the soldiers. This made him wealthier than he had been before, but it did not affect the outcome. The loss of a few more animals hardly made any difference to the Americans.

Connor finally sent his scouts in search of the two lost columns. The scouts discovered their trail and several hundred dead cavalry horses as well as some of the equipment that Cole had been forced to burn. These signs were all they needed to know that Cole and Walker were in serious trouble. Following the trail, they finally caught up with the men on September 13 on the Powder River. The scouts, under instructions from Connor, offered them one of two choices: They could either march over to the Tongue River and join Connor there, or they could go back up the Powder River to Fort Connor, the existence of which they had been unaware. After talking to the scouts, Cole decided he could not get his wagons over to the Tongue, so they retreated to Fort Connor.

The campaign was over. Sawyer had completed his road, but the Americans were not in control of the country through which it passed. Connor had won a victory over the Arapahoes, but not a decisive one, for they were still in force. Cole and Walker had inflicted some casualties on the Indians—no one was certain how many—but they had not defeated them. If anyone had been defeated, it was they themselves, because they had been compelled to retreat without accomplishing their objectives. As a result, the Department of the Plains was abolished, and Connor was sent to Utah.

That fall, when the first snows touched the buttes with white and the branches of the cottonwoods were bare, the Indians began moving into their winter camps. For them, the year had not been a good one. They could feel a certain amount of satisfaction at having repulsed the invaders, and they undoubtedly thought they had won. But the portents of disaster were there. Sawyer's road provided a new and shorter route to the mine fields, three columns of troops had been able to wander through the country for weeks, and the Indians had not been able to muster the strength to stop them.

VI

Forts in the Wilderness

THE most optimistic white men could not have called Connor's campaign a success. Although the three columns had penetrated deep into the Indians' territory, they had accomplished little or nothing in terms of permanent value. Sawyer's road was shorter even than Bozeman's, but no emigrant could safely use either one. If he wanted to reach the Montana goldfields, he still had to take the long way around the Big Horns, for the plains north of the Platte were just as closed to the ordinary traveler as they had been the year before.

From the beginning, relations between the Americans and the Western Indians had been ambivalent. The Indians had welcomed the first white traders, because they provided a ready source of needed supplies, such as guns and ammunition. Only when the white men came in increasing numbers did some of the tribes sense the growing danger to their way of life. Even then, however, many did not; and the Indians remained divided among themselves, some making peace and some making war.

The Americans were just as inconsistent. Most white men looked down on the Indians and thought of them as a definitely inferior race. Yet they considered them as independent peoples with whom it was necessary to make formal treaties that had to be ratified by the United States Senate. Nor did the inconsistencies stop there. Many Americans believed that the cheapest and most effective way to deal with the tribes was to reach agreements with them, place them on reservations, and then pay for their well-being. Others, however, believed that while such methods might work in the long run, it was first necessary to defeat the Indians decisively and show them that the Americans were the masters.

Many of those who held these divergent opinions did so because they were thinking of the good of the country. In the East, for example, those who advocated peaceful methods of subduing the Indians were motivated by humanitarian beliefs, while many of those in the West who wanted to make war against the tribes were influenced by the proximity of the warriors to their own homes and sometimes by the deaths of their relatives and friends. They may have been blood-thirsty, but they were sincere in what they thought.

Others, however, were motivated by purely mercenary considerations. Enormous profits could be made from supplying either the army or a reservation. Indeed, the federal government was the principal source of wealth for many of the Westerners. A farmer or a freighter with large government contracts could become rich; one who did not have access to the funds coming out of Washington might well remain poor. So this ambivalent attitude, kept alive by the complex interplay of altruism and commercialism, caused American policy to veer from one direction to the next.

Connor's campaign having failed, the Americans began again to think of a peaceful settlement, for they refused to take the Sioux's resistance seriously. Although the Indians had clearly demonstrated their unwillingness to permit the white men to enter the northern Great Plains, many officials, as well as much of the public, still believed that some kind of a solution could be quickly and easily worked out. Consequently, during the winter of 1865–66, plans were made to hold another large council at Fort Laramie.

As usual, invitations were sent out to the leading chiefs, asking them to bring their bands to the meeting. Often in the past, the Americans had failed to deal with the appropriate leaders, sometimes making important treaties with unimportant chiefs who had no power to enforce them. In this case, however, they had correctly identified two of the leading Sioux, Spotted Tail, who had high standing among the Brulés, and Red Cloud, who was the most noted leader among the Oglalas. These were the two divisions of Sioux nearest the Emigrant Trail, and the Oglalas also roamed the country through which the Bozeman Trail ran, so their cooperation was essential also to the safety of the short route to Montana.

The appearance of Spotted Tail at the conference did not come as a surprise. In the past, he had made efforts to be friendly with the Americans, but mistreatment had driven him to join the hostile bands. Now he was ready for peace again, and he brought with him the body of his daughter, who, while she was dying, had asked to be buried near the white men. On learning of this request, the commander at Fort Laramie wisely went out to meet Spotted Tail and welcomed him as a friend of the Americans.

Even more hopeful was the appearance of Red Cloud. Unlike Spotted Tail, the Americans could regard him as an enemy, for he had early foreseen the consequences of the growing numbers of white men and had fought hard against them. But even Red Cloud was now willing to talk about peace. Those who had planned the Fort Laramie council had always been optimistic about the results they might achieve. Now they were doubly so.

While the Sioux were gathering at Fort Laramie—there were some Arapahoes and Cheyennes among them—Colonel Henry B. Carrington was marching from Fort Kearny toward Fort Laramie with a battalion of men and orders to occupy the Bozeman Trail. Even before the treaty had been completed, much less ratified, the army was preparing to take advantage of the terms the government hoped it would provide.

Carrington, who knew little about Indians, was as optimistic as everyone else about the probable outcome at Fort Laramie. On June 13, before he had reached the fort, he issued this order: "The pending treaty between the United States and the Sioux Indians at Fort Laramie renders it the duty of every soldier to treat all Indians with kindness. Every Indian who is wronged will visit his vengeance upon *any* white man he may meet. As soldiers are sent to preserve the peace of the border and prevent warfare, as much as to fight well when warfare becomes indispensable, it will be considered a very gross offense to wrong or insult an Indian." Like most Americans, Carrington regarded the negotiations at Fort Laramie as a foregone success, and he was prepared to treat the Indians accordingly.

Only three days later, when he was camped four miles east of Fort Laramie, he was talking to a friendly chief of the Brulé Sioux. When Carrington told him about the plans to build the forts on the Bozeman Trail, the chief replied, "There is a treaty being made at Laramie with the Sioux that are in the country where you are going. The fighting men in that country have not come to Laramie, and you will have to

fight them. They will not give you the road unless you whip them."
And every other chief whom he met at Laramie treated him coldly as
soon as his mission became known.

Red Cloud, like the others, had come to the fort in good faith.
Although he did not like the Americans and did not want to see them
in the lands occupied by the Oglalas, he thought a possibility of peace
existed and that the fighting along the Platte might be stopped. It had
never occurred to him, after Connor's abortive campaign, that the
Americans would demand entry into the lands north of the river. So
when he heard about Carrington's assignment, he was furious. He had
no intention of permitting the Americans to build forts along the
Bozeman Trail, particularly before they had even talked to him about
their plans. In a rage, he stalked out of the conference and prepared
for war. Although the Americans continued to negotiate with the more
friendly Indians, for the practical purpose of Carrington's mission, the
council was over.

By this time, Carrington sensed that his assignment was going to be
more difficult than he had orginally thought and that he had insufficient supplies and men to carry it out. He wrote to headquarters in
Omaha, "I find at this post a supply of hard bread for only four days
for my command, and in poor condition, not a single utensil for baking flour, and only 1,000 rounds of ammunition, caliber .58. I brought
what I could, and shall find 36,000 rounds at Fort Reno [which was
the new name for Fort Connor], giving me a total of 60,000 rounds,
obviously very inadequate. I find myself greatly in need of officers, but
must wait the arrival of new appointments, or until others are relieved
from recruiting service."

And he wrote again the same day, "The entire supply of .58 caliber
at Laramie being only 1,000 rounds renders many troops almost
powerless in case of delay of supplies and remoteness of base. All the
commissioners [who were negotiating the treaty] agree that I go to
occupy a region which the Indians will only surrender for a great
equivalent; even my arrival has started among them many absurd
rumors, but," he added with ill-founded hope, "I apprehend no serious
difficulty. Patience, forbearance, and common sense in dealing with
the Sioux and Cheyennes will do much with all who really desire
peace, but it is indispensable that ample supplies of ammunition come
promptly."

With some misgivings, but still confident that he could carry out his
assignment, Carrington left Fort Laramie before the council ended and

marched to Fort Reno, the post established by Connor the year before. Just before he reached Bridger's Ferry, some Indians ran off two horses belonging to the man who operated the ferry; aside from that, Carrington saw no traces of Indians. At Fort Reno, life was so quiet that the sutler did not even guard his herd of mules when he turned them loose to graze. But a few days after Carrington's arrival, some Indians, who were identified as Sioux, attacked the herd and ran off with it. Carrington sent soldiers in pursuit. They were unable to recover the mules, but they captured a pony laden with goods that had been issued at Fort Laramie. This was an ominous sign, because it indicated that the Americans had not purchased peace as they had expected to.

Because of the wave of optimism that had swept the country over the prospect of reopening this route, several emigrant trains had already reached Fort Reno and were waiting impatiently for the protection they had been led to believe the army would provide. They were, however, in complete confusion, and one of Carrington's first acts was to try to impose order by issuing precise instructions as to how the travelers were to proceed. Although he did not expect war, he was preparing for it.

And he was right, too. Since leaving Fort Laramie, Red Cloud had collected approximately five hundred warriors who were willing to fight the Americans. They held a Sun Dance and then looked for additional allies. Among those they spoke to was a band of Cheyennes. Red Cloud made it clear to them that he would let the Americans retain Fort Reno but he would oppose any attempt they made to construct new forts. He also told them that they would have to join forces with him, or he would fight against them, too. This terrified the Cheyennes, who did not want war with the Americans and yet were not strong enough to battle with the Oglalas.

At the same time, Red Cloud and the Oglalas were watching Carrington's movements closely. After several days at Fort Reno, they saw him march to Crazy Woman Creek. The temperature soared to 122° in the shade, and a number of his wagons were damaged. He left some soldiers under the command of Brevet Major Haymond to repair them and went to Piney Creek, which flows east from the Bighorn Mountains into Clear Creek, a tributary of the Powder River. His search for a good site for the first of the forts he had been ordered to build then took him on a further seventy-mile reconnaissance trip. He saw no signs of Indians, but on his return, he found a messenger from the Cheyennes waiting for him. They wanted to know whether he wanted peace or war and invited him to hold a parley.

As he wished to avoid hostilities, Carrington sent word to the Cheyennes that he would like to speak to them; and they came to his camp and reported what Red Cloud had told them. The warning did not reach Carrington any too soon. Only a few days later the Sioux successfully attacked the four companies under Major Haymond and ran off with almost two hundred head of livestock. Haymond went in pursuit, hoping to regain his animals, but soon found himself surrounded by Sioux. Fifty mounted men and two companies of infantry went to his rescue. But even with these reinforcements he could not continue the pursuit and returned to camp, having lost two dead and three wounded. Red Cloud had meant it when he had said that he would not permit the Americans to go north of Fort Reno.

Shortly after talking to Carrington, some of the Cheyenne chiefs went to a trader named French Pete. While they were talking, some Sioux came up and interrogated the Cheyennes about their meeting with Carrington. They told him Carrington had said he was determined to press on north. Whereupon the Sioux unstrung their bows and whipped the Cheyennes with the bowstrings, counting coup for each one they struck. This was disgraceful treatment, and it indicated how angry the Sioux had become. After the Sioux left, the Cheyennes advised the trader to seek the soldiers' protection, but before he could reach them, the Sioux struck again. They killed the trader and the five white men who were with him, including a government teamster. The only adult to escape was the trader's wife. She was a Sioux and hid in the bushes with her five children.

The Oglalas had won a series of small victories and demonstrated the extent of their resistance, but they had not yet deterred Carrington. He had chosen the site for the first of his forts, Fort Philip Kearny, at the foot of the Bighorn Mountains near the spot where the North and South Piney Creeks join to form one stream. The creeks provided plenty of water, and being near the mountains, the site was close to a good supply of trees that the soldiers could use for lumber. They began felling them and erecting the fort. The Oglalas were furious, but they were not prepared to attack the main body of troops, so they began a series of harassing raids. On July 22, 1866, the Sioux attacked a wagon train bound from Fort Reno to Fort Laramie, killing one man and wounding another. The same day they raided around Fort Reno and went off with a mule.

The next day an army wagon train reached the crest of the divide that leads into Crazy Woman Creek. "A mile or two further," wrote one of the soldiers who was with it, "and the thin fringe of trees bordering the creek came into view, probably five miles away to the west. Beyond the belt of trees were observed numerous objects which were at once pronounced to be buffalo. The field glasses were brought into requisition, and it was agreed that a couple of officers [lieutenants Daniels and Templeton] should ride on ahead, cross the creek somewhat above the buffalo, and getting on the other side of them turn the herd in toward the creek, so that about the time the wagon train and the command got down into the valley near the timber all could join in the big chase, and several hundred weight of fresh buffalo meat be added to the larder of the command."

The men moved forward, anticipating the excitement of the coming buffalo hunt until they came to the bed of a dry stream. While they were trying to get the wagons through the heavy sand, a volley of bullets and arrows struck them.

"By almost superhuman exertions the wagons and ambulances [light vehicles much used in the army for other purposes as well as carrying the wounded] were brought up out of the dry sandy bed and hurriedly corralled on the little rise between the creeks," wrote the soldier.

"The corral was under a hot fire from the Indians, and really before it had been completed, [Lieutenant Daniels's] horse came tearing into the corral, with the saddle turned under him and a couple of arrows sticking in his neck and two more in his flank. The horse was of course riderless. A second later Lieutenant Templeton appeared riding up out of the dry bed of the creek hatless, two or three arrows in his horse's withers and flanks, and an arrow in his own back. Templeton was bleeding profusely from a wound in his face, and his whole visage was one of extreme terror, and as soon as he reached the corral he reeled and partly fell from his horse. He was lifted from the saddle in a state of complete collapse. He merely uttered, 'Daniels! My God, Indians! They wasn't buffalo.' "

The Americans could not remain where they were, for the Indians were hidden by trees, while the white men were out in the open. "It was thereupon decided," the soldier continued, "that we should bunch the wagons, two in front with the two ambulances next, and the other three to follow behind, and in this way retreat to a high knoll south of us about half a mile away between the two creeks. We would thus get away from the timber that was sheltering the Indians and would stand some show of giving them as good as they sent. . . . We had not more than got started when another of the mules was disabled by a bullet, and it had to be cut out. The rear guard of seven men . . . held the Indians off until the mule was cut out. There being no time to lose, as the Indians were constantly being reinforced, we determined to abandon the cook wagon and make our retreat as rapidly as possible. This was done and then it was a fight for life.

"A party of Indians seeing what we were up to undertook to cut off our retreat and to take possession of the hill we were aiming for.

"The advance guard held their ground like heroes and fought every foot of the way. The teams were kept on the run and then came the charge of twelve men . . . up the hill for its possession. The Indians were poor shooters, and wounded only one man in the charge, and then, the cowards they were, broke and ran from the hill. . . .

"In the meanwhile the rear guard was holding the Indians in check from the creek side, and the wagons and ambulances were safely brought to the hill. A corral was immediately made, with the mules inside the corral. The ambulances were protected by the wagons, and all the stock in fact were sheltered by the corral. . . .

"Rifle pits were dug just outside the corral, and we lay there in the scorching sun, famishing for water. But the Indians were between us and the much desired water, and in fact it seemed as if Indians were everywhere. Off to our left three or four hundred yards was a high sandy ridge, that terminated in a knoll down at the creek. Between the corral and this ridge was a deep narrow cleft in the earth, that led in a crooked course down toward the creek. We did not know of the existence of this ravine until a shower of arrows flew from it toward the corral, which succeeded in wounding three of our men."

A soldier and a chaplain volunteered to charge the ravine and drive the Indians out of it, even though the chaplain was "armed with but an old-fashioned 'pepper-box' seven shooter pistol." The two men charged the hill, and "a moment later we heard a strange volley of shots something like the modern rapid fire guns, and several Indians were observed climbing out of the ravine and making hot haste for the ridge to the west. We hurried their departure with a volley from the rifle pits and saw one of them tumble and roll back down the hill and disappear into the ravine." The soldier and the chaplain returned safely and were able to explain the strange volley of shots. The chaplain "had killed an Indian in the ravine with the 'pepper-box,' it having gone off altogether, thus accounting for the strange volley we had heard.

"The Indians began to get very cautious and were not disposed to take any more chances in the ravine," the soldier continued. "However, parties of them would mount their ponies, and swinging themselves to the off side of them would make a serious dash close to the corral, and fire at us from under their horses' necks. Two more men were wounded by these charges and matters began to look very serious for us. Over half of the detachment were now wounded, several of them seriously, and they were making piteous calls for water.

"The middle of the afternoon wore away, and finally it was determined that a heroic effort should be made to secure water from the creek by way of the ravine at our left. A detail of gallant fellows loaded themselves down with canteens and a couple of buckets and started for the creek. They were covered by a detachment of like number, and further protection was guaranteed them from the wagons.

"The Indians did not seem to catch on to the move, and instead of following the water detail, renewed their attack on the wagons with great vigor. The two ladies [the army was encouraging the wives of officers to accompany their husbands to the frontier posts] were angels of mercy and tenderness and looked after the wounded most heroically and bravely. During the absence of the water detail we suffered no casualties, and the detail returned, having met with unbounded success. The water tremendously refreshed all of us, and the poor thirsty animals were also given a portion.

"The Indians by this time discovered that something had happened to revive our spirits and they determined on a concerted attack to finish us. They made two charges on the corral but were repulsed. We lost, however, one man killed . . . and three more wounded. It was solemnly decided, that in case it came to the worst that we would mercifully kill all the wounded and the two women and then ourselves."

Finally two volunteers, mounted on the best horses the Americans had among them, made a dash through the Indians and set off to Fort Reno with a call for help. Although the horses died of exhaustion as a result of the wild ride, the two men reached the fort safely. But before help could be sent, a detachment of several hundred men happened to come from the north. They were marching from Fort Philip Kearny to Fort Reno on a routine mission and had planned to camp some distance away. But the old scout, Jim Bridger, was with them, and he sensed trouble ahead. So instead of stopping for the night, they kept on marching. At the sight of these reinforcements, the Indians broke off the fighting; and after resting several days, the detachment was able to continue on to its destination.

This battle was typical of an Indian fight on the Great Plains. The Indians had been unable to gather sufficient numbers of warriors to annihilate the well-disciplined Americans and had had to flee when the other soldiers had appeared. But when they attacked an emigrant train that was relatively ignorant in the ways of warfare, the results could be devastating. And such constant harassment stretched Carrington's forces thin. Anywhere along the road, the Indians could strike, but Carrington could not keep his troops everywhere. About the time the Indians attacked the army detachment, they also made an attack on a civilian wagon train. Then, on July 28, they made another raid near Fort Reno, hoping to capture some livestock. This time the Americans were able to recover their animals, but the following day, the Indians attacked another wagon train, killing nine men and wounding one.

Carrington was rightly growing anxious about his position. On July 30, he reported to headquarters in Omaha that "my ammunition has not arrived; neither has my Leavenworth supply train. . . .

"My infantry make poor riders, and, as I can only fight Indians successfully on foot, my horses suffer in pursuit and in fight.

"I am equal to any attack they [the Indians] may make, but have to build quarters, prepare for winter, escort trains, and guarantee the whole road from the Platte to Virginia City with 8 companies of infantry. I have to economize ammunition. . . . I sent 2 officers on recruiting service, under peremptory orders from Washington, leaving me crippled and obliged to intrust too much to non-commissioned officers.

"I telegraphed full, as there is at Laramie and elsewhere a false security, which results in emigrant trains scattering between posts, involving dangers to themselves and others."

That "false security" was blinding the army to Red Cloud's intentions. Because he did not launch a full-scale attack as the white men would have, they did not think he was serious about waging war. It was not the first time, nor was it to be the last, that the army found itself unable to cope with—or even understand—guerrilla warfare.

In spite of the lack of support that he received from headquarters, Carrington tried to complete his mission. He sent another detachment ahead to construct an additional fort, Fort C. F. Smith, as he had been ordered, while progress continued on Fort Philip Kearny.

The wife of one of the officers assigned to Kearny described her arrival there later in the year. "The long-sought fort was in sight," she wrote. "I could have clapped my hands for joy, but that would not have adequately expressed my experience, which was that of a far deeper current of emotion beyond the province of mere words to express. That fort was even more to me than 'the shadow of a rock in a weary land.' That metaphor embodies comfort, quiet, peace. It was all that indeed, but more, as a place of refuge from fatigue and danger in the most literal sense, and none the less did I feel to be under the shadow of the Almighty.

"We came in sight of Pilot Hill [a nearby hill where sentinels were posted] and could see the picket guard waving a signal, a double signal, if we could have interpreted it, and it was well that we did not. The first signal indicated that the wood train had been attacked by Indians just west of the fort, and the second signal gave notice of the appearance of a small party from the eastward, approaching the fort. Detachments had been sent in fevered haste in both directions.

"The small party was ours, and we did not quite comprehend the meaning of our tardy welcome from without the gates. Presently the escort fell in line and we moved toward the stockade, but just before entering a halt was made, and I looked eagerly for the occasion of the delay. It almost took my breath away, for a strange feeling of apprehensions came over me. We had halted to give passage to a wagon, escorted by a guard from the wood train, coming from the opposite direction. In that wagon was the scalped and naked body of one of their comrades, scarcely cold, who had been murdered so near the fort that the signals by the picket, given almost simultaneously, were now fully understood. My whole being seemed to be absorbed in the one desire,—an agonized but un-uttered cry, 'Let me get within the gate.' "

That was the feeling of many travelers coming up the road from Fort Reno. They had set out from the East with a sense of the "false security" of which Carrington had complained and had reached Fort Laramie safely. Then they turned north into the country of Red Cloud, and they faced the reality that Washington and the army ignored: The Indians meant war. Having reached the fort at last, these travelers were glad of its protection and realized more than the government did what Carrington had accomplished.

"At this new post, so excellently built, we found houses for the officers and soldiers' quarters instead of tents," the officer's wife continued. "Here also were warehouses, sutler's store, and a guard-house, either completed or under construction, a fine parade ground, which imparted form, comeliness, and system to the whole, without a flag-staff planted as yet, but one prone on the ground where busy workers were preparing it for that event. The presence of mountain howitzers in proper position was a more reassuring feature, bearing, in case of need, their own distinctive message.

"The incessant labor of chopping, hauling, and hewing wood, with saw-mills in full operation, with ditching and such other varied duty that claimed attention day by day, was the execution of the drawings of Colonel Carrington. . . ."

But in spite of the progress Carrington was making with the con-struction of the fort, he found himself unable to protect the entire road. In September, for example, the Indians attacked a citizen wagon train east of the fort on the morning of the eighth, driving off twenty mules. Two days later, they attacked ten government herders, driving off thirty-three horses and seventy-eight mules; and in this instance, darkness and the poor condition of the soldiers' horses made pursuit hopeless. On the thirteenth, Carrington received word that a civilian hay party, under contract to the army, was being attacked. One man had been killed, a mowing machine and much hay had been burned, and the Indians had run off with two hundred nine head of cattle. That same day the Indians stampeded a government herd near the post and wounded two of the herders. Troops pursued them, but again without success. The next morning the bloody uniform of a private was discovered; his body was never found. Two days later another private got a short distance ahead of the hay party to which he was assigned. Before he could return to it, the Indians cut him off and killed him.

Day after day the Indians continued their war. They had no or-ganized plan, of course, but they were united in their objective—to drive out the white men—and in their tactics—to continue harassment rather than to make a direct assault against the forts. At the same time, Red Cloud was recruiting reinforcements. He visited several of the Siouan tribes who had signed the treaty at Laramie and persuaded them to join. He also visited some of the Cheyennes again. The older men were not willing to go to war, but they had difficulty restraining the younger warriors. Red Cloud's oratory and his cause were finding him new allies.

Carrington learned this when a group of Cheyennes came to Fort Philip Kearny. They told him just what Red Cloud was doing and also that he would only stop molesting the white men if they would withdraw from Fort Philip Kearny and Fort C. F. Smith. Because these Cheyennes wanted to be friends with the Americans, they were in great danger of attack from the Sioux. After talking to Carrington, they made a camp outside the stockade. About midnight, a hundred of the soldiers armed themselves and either climbed over the walls of the stockade or slipped through the wicket at the quartermaster's gate. Once outside they assembled and prepared to attack the unsuspecting Cheyennes. Fortunately, however, they were noticed, and a guard went after them. The men had their guns cocked and were ready to fire when the guard stopped them. On their return to the fort, the officers tried to learn their identity but could not halt them. Carrington finally restored order himself but only by firing his pistol twice.

The men were increasingly anxious for a chance to kill some of the Indians and not merely to stay on the defense. One of these was Captain William J. Fetterman, who, the officer's wife wrote, "recently arrived from recruiting service, with no antecedent experience on the frontier, expressed the opinion that a 'single company of Regulars could whip a thousand Indians, and that a full regiment . . . could whip the entire array of hostile tribes.' . . . Captain Fetterman submitted to the colonel his own plan, which he had carefully devised, as certain of decisive results. His plan was to take a detachment, that very night, to the cottonwood thicket along Big Piney Creek in front of the fort, secrete his men, hobble some mules between the thicket and the fort, as a *live bait*, and decoy the Indians into his hands.

"It was a bright night (moonlight) so that the Indians could see that the mules were unprotected and fully exposed to their attack; but the Indians did not appear. They were not surprised and destroyed; but within three hours of the return of Fetterman they ran off a herd not a mile distant."

As fall gave way to winter and ice formed in the water buckets in the morning, conditions along the Bozeman Trail did not change. When Carrington looked out on the frosty world surrounding him, he knew that his domain ended at the distance his howitzers could fire. Beyond that line, the land was Red Cloud's.

Headquarters did not understand this. In spite of all the reports that Carrington had sent, those in command still believed in the treaty made at Laramie and thought that Carrington was faced only by a handful of renegades who could be put down easily rather than by thousands of warriors led by an able chief. So Carrington remained short of ammunition and short of men. But Red Cloud still did not dare make a direct attack on the fort. First, he knew the danger of approaching within range of the howitzers. Second, he had talked with the Cheyennes who had visited the fort. Carrington and Jim Bridger, the scout, had purposely misled them into thinking it was stronger than it actually was. Their report to Red Cloud was, therefore, discouraging.

But the fort was dependent on its wood-cutting parties, both for the lumber needed in its construction and for fuel. And these parties were subject to constant Indian attack, for Red Cloud hoped he could wear down the garrison's resistance. On December 6, 1866, he almost won a major victory. The Indians again assaulted the wood party, and again the soldiers from the fort came to their rescue. Captain Fetterman was to charge them, while Carrington was to slip around to their rear and cut off their retreat. During the skirmish that followed, however, the cavalry became separated from Fetterman's command, dismounted, and waited for orders. One officer, in his zealousness, got too far ahead of Fetterman and was cut off and killed. Some of Carrington's men failed to keep up with him, and if it had not been for the timely arrival of Fetterman, the colonel could easily have lost his life. Some of the men were privately critical of Carrington's actions during the fight. As it was, the Americans' losses were two killed and five wounded. In return, they had inflicted several casualties on the Indians. But with so small a garrison, Carrington could not afford the loss of a single man.

The location of Fort Philip Kearny had one principal weakness. On the far side of North Piney Creek is a long ridge, called Lodge Pole Ridge, that separates the drainage basins of the Powder and Tongue Rivers. This ridge was higher than any of the land near the fort, so it was impossible for the soldiers to see what was going on behind it. This was one of the elements that had led to the near disaster on December 6. No one could tell how many Indians were hidden under the ridge's shelter, and the troops could not see each other's whereabouts. Having now learned his lesson, Carrington gave strict orders that henceforth no relief forces were to pursue the Indians over the ridge.

The Indians were frustrated over their failure to inflict any real damage on the fort. They knew that they had weakened the force protecting it, and they knew they had caused the American commander much concern and also stopped much of the traffic that would have otherwise taken the Bozeman Trail. But they had not won a victory of any major proportions.

So they fell back on their old tactic of using a few warriors as decoys, while the main body of Indians remained hidden. Lodge Pole Ridge would serve their purpose well.

Behind it was another ridge that was perpendicular to it. The Indians could hide on the east and west slopes of that ridge and be out of sight of the Americans even after they had crossed the top of Lodge Pole Ridge. Then when the decoys had hopefully lured them down the slopes, the Indians could emerge and slaughter them.

The Sioux recruited some Arapahoes and some Cheyennes to join them and then prepared their trap. They selected one of their *winktes* —one of those half men, half women who were thought to be gifted with magic power—to tell them how many of the enemy they would find. He rode up a hill and came back saying that he had ten men, five in each hand. The Sioux told him that was not enough, so he tried again. This time he returned, saying he had twenty men in each hand. Again the Sioux told him that was not enough to warrant the large numbers of warriors they had collected. The next time he came back from the hill, he prophesied that they would meet fifty of their enemies, but they still were not satisfied. Not until he promised a hundred were they content.

After long months of minor skirmishing, the Indians were now looking forward to a major victory, one that would impress the white men and make them realize that the Indians were serious about not giving up the lands of the Bozeman Trail. They did not know, however, that Carrington had issued firm orders not to cross the Lodge Pole Ridge and venture into the unknown that it shielded from the Americans' eyes.

Ten Indians—Cheyennes, Arapahoes, and Sioux—were chosen to serve as the decoys who were intended to lure the soldiers from the fort. One of these was an Oglala Sioux named Crazy Horse, who had already been winning distinction for himself. His father was a respected medicine man but not one of the great leaders of his people. Yet, from boyhood Crazy Horse seemed destined for an unusual career, to be a man apart from the others. Physically, he lacked the high cheekbones of most Indians, and even more striking, he had almost sandy-colored hair and an extremely light complexion. As a boy, he was known as Curly, a strange name to bear among the straight-haired Indians; and when he visited the traders' posts with his family, he was often mistaken for a captive and not a native Indian. In the mystic world of the Sioux, where the gods still gave signs to those who watched and listened, these strange physical traits presaged a life of distinction. Emotionally he was also different from the other Sioux. When the warriors gathered together, they boasted of their deeds, recounting each of their coups in detail. But not Crazy Horse. He was so quiet that he was almost taciturn. The Indians noticed this characteristic of his when he was still a boy, and it continued to set him apart when he was a man. To those versed in the ways of "medicine" this, too, marked him.

His early training was much like that of other Sioux. His father taught him all that he had learned from his father and from life; and Crazy Horse was also under the guidance of another warrior whom he adored, named Hump. When he was old enough, the two men let him participate in a sweat bath; and the hot steam, rising from the heated rocks, drove him into a vision in which he saw a warrior riding into battle with a small hawk on his back and a small brown stone tied behind one of his ears. Arrows and bullets flew toward the visionary warrior, but before they could strike him, they mysteriously disappeared in the air. When Crazy Horse recounted this vision to his father and Hump, the older men told him that the warrior was himself. He was destined, they said, to be a great leader of his people, one who could fight unscathed and win important victories. After that, a hawk and a small brown stone became his talismans. Because of his bravery and other outstanding qualities, he had been chosen as a shirt-wearer at an unusually young age. This was an unusual honor, for the shirt-wearers had the responsibility for carrying out the policies decided upon by the elders of the tribe.

Crazy Horse detested the white men and hoped he could lead many of them—as many as the *winkte* had prophesied—to their deaths. While he and the other decoys prepared to ride out in view of the Americans, the remainder of the warriors hid themselves along the sides of the ridge to the north of Lodge Pole Ridge and looked forward to the great victory they expected to win. As usual, Carrington sent out the wood train on the morning of December 21; and while the Americans were felling trees and preparing to take the wood back to the fort, Crazy Horse and the other decoys attacked. The woodcutting party immediately corralled their wagons, as they had done so many times before, and the pickets on Pilot Hill, seeing what was going on, signaled to the fort for help. Carrington had no difficulty in assembling enough volunteers for a relief force. The men at Fort Philip Kearny, weary of the beleaguered state in which they had lived so long, were anxious to fight back at their enemies. Captain Fetterman, by right of his rank, demanded the privilege of serving as commander. Carrington granted him his request, but, knowing Fetterman's brash nature, specifically ordered him not to go beyond Lodge Pole Ridge. As Carrington later reported to his superiors, "My instructions were . . . peremptory and explicit. I knew the ambition of each to win honor, but being unprepared for large aggressive action through want of force . . . I looked to continuance of timber supplies to prepare for more troops as the one practicable duty. . . .

"Hence my instruction to . . . Fetterman, viz, 'Support the wood train, relieve it, and report to me. Do not engage or pursue Indians at its expense. Under no circumstances pursue over the ridge, viz, Lodge Pole Ridge, as per map in your possession.' "

Carrington was not certain, however, that his men would obey him, for he understood their frustrations and their desire for action against the Indians. So he had his adjutant repeat the order. Not content with this, he stepped to a sentry platform just as the men were leaving and gave his order once again to the cavalry.

The Indians had asked that a hundred Americans be delivered into their hands, and Carrington almost fulfilled their wish. Including several civilians, the force headed by Fetterman numbered more than eighty men, just about the number of men that Fetterman had said he would need to defeat all the Indians. With high hearts, they marched from the fort and disappeared from sight. The sentinel on Pilot Hill was still able to observe their movements, however, and he signaled back to the fort that the wood train had been relieved and was now going about its normal operations. That first skirmish, of course, had been easy, for that is the way Crazy Horse and the other decoys had planned it to be. They did not hope to defeat the Americans or even cause serious damage to the wood train. All they wanted was to lure Fetterman over the top of Lodge Pole Ridge and into the valley below where the others were now massed and waiting.

Instead of returning to the fort or remaining with the wood train, Fetterman fell into the Indians' trap. Having broken up their feint against the wood train, he followed them as they fled up the slope of Lodge Pole Ridge. Here at last, he thought to himself, was a chance to win a decisive victory and to satisfy his personal ambition. He could see nothing from the top of the ridge. Below him the land lay peaceful and deserted except for the small group of Indians whom he had been chasing. So in disobedience of his orders, he led his men down the other side.

The decoys they were pursuing crossed the creek in flight and then suddenly turned around and charged toward the white men. This was the signal for others to attack, for they rushed forward from their hiding places. The infantry took shelter behind some rocks, but in spite of the superiority of their firearms, they could not hold the Indians off. Soon the two groups were fighting hand to hand in a bloody struggle, for neither side showed mercy to the other. But the Americans were quickly overwhelmed by the large force arrayed against them.

In the meanwhile, the cavalry had retreated back up the slope and had taken up a position about four hundred yards from where the infantry had been annihilated. The weather was cold, so cold that the blood from the men's wounds quickly froze, and the slope was slippery with snow and ice. The cavalry hid behind some large rocks. In their rear was a flat barren area that offered no cover to the Indians. Given the circumstances, Fetterman had chosen a strong position, because the Indians could not charge up the slippery ground in front, nor could they get behind him. Once in a while, the Indians would pretend to start charging. This would cause the Americans to stand up, ready to fight, and the Indians would kill a few of them. Meanwhile other Indians were working their way slowly up the slope, effectively using the little cover that it offered. Soon they were upon the cavalry and in the bitter fighting that followed, killed them all.

When the struggle was over, a dog emerged from somewhere and walked across the battlefield. One Indian suggested that he be left alive to carry the news to the fort, but another said, no, nothing living should remain. So they killed the dog, too, and then went back into the valley below.

At the fort, Carrington heard a few shots from beyond the ridge, which "were followed by constant shots, not to be counted," as he later reported. Sensing what had happened, he ordered a relief expedition to go to Fetterman's rescue. But by the time it reached the top of the ridge, the firing had ceased and the short battle was over. The Americans could see the Indians below them and hear their challenges, but there was no sign of Fetterman or any of his command. Advancing slowly and cautiously down the slope, the relief expedition recovered forty-nine bodies, including those of Fetterman and one of his officers. The Indians did not attack because they evidently mistook some wagons the Americans had with them for howitzers, and experience had taught them they could do nothing against heavy guns.

"Nature herself seemed shocked by the awful tragedy of the day," wrote the widow of one of the officers who had been killed, "for that very night the weather became unparalleled in its severity, almost too extreme for man or beast, but the faithful sentinels went their rounds of exacting and dangerous duty, at every risk, and it was from them alone that our ears caught, half hourly, the number of the post, and the cheering words, 'All's well.'

"There was little repose, however, for any one that dreadful night. All ears were expectant of a momentary alarm. Subdued discussion of whether some of the missing ones might not have fallen into the hands of the savages as prisoners, a worse fate than death itself, continued late into the night, as some of the bodies had not been discovered by the party returning from the battle-field, and yet it was somehow borne in upon our minds that all were dead."

The fort was now in serious danger. Carrington had asked for more men, so he could take the offensive against the Indians and patrol the Bozeman Trail. Now he needed them merely to hold the fort, for the loss of Fetterman's command had drastically reduced his garrison, and he might not be able to withstand a concentrated attack. A frontiersman, John Phillips, who worked for the quartermaster, realized the gravity of their situation and volunteered to carry a message to Fort Laramie. As there was little hope that a detachment of soldiers could get through—even if they could have been spared—Carrington accepted Phillips's offer. Phillips imposed only one condition: He wanted the best horse at the fort, which was a thoroughbred belonging to Carrington. This was a small request from a man who planned to ride alone for more than two hundred miles through the Indians' territory, and Carrington gave up his horse willingly. The two men walked together to the sally-port gate. Carrington himself unlocked and opened it, and Phillips passed through it into the black, cold world beyond, carrying with him the hopes of the men and women at Fort Philip Kearny.

The next day Carrington held a council of his remaining officers. Forty-nine bodies had been recovered the day before by the relief expedition, and that left more than thirty additional men unaccounted for. Everyone in the fort was certain they were dead, not captives, and the question was whether they should risk more lives to recover the corpses. Carrington argued that the attempt should be made. If they did not, he said, the Indians would assume they were weaker than they were and might attack.

Leading a detachment of eighty men, Carrington marched cautiously toward the battlefield. He stationed a picket to warn him of an attack in the rear and to maintain communications with the fort. "The scene of action," he later reported, "told its story. The road on the little ridge where the final stand took place was strewn with arrowheads, scalp poles, and broken shafts of spears. The arrows that were spent harmlessly from all directions show that the command was suddenly overwhelmed, surrounded, and cut off while in retreat. Not an officer or man survived."

Fetterman and one other officer each had a revolver shot in their left temples. As the battle had raged on and Fetterman had become aware of the enormity of his error, he and the other officer had chosen suicide rather than the risk of capture. Pressing the muzzle against his forehead, he had brought his own ambitious boasting to an end.

In their fury, the Indians had vented their hatred against the dead bodies. "I was asked to send all the bad news," Carrington later wrote. "I do it so far as I can. I give some of the facts as to my men, whose bodies I found just at dark, resolved to bring all in, viz: Mutilations: Eyes torn out and laid on the rocks; noses cut off; ears cut off; chins hewn off; teeth chopped out; joints of fingers; brains taken out and placed on rocks with other members of the body; entrails taken out and exposed; hands cut off; feet cut off; arms taken out from sockets; private parts severed and indecently placed on the person; eyes, ears, mouth and arms penetrated with spearheads, sticks, and arrows; ribs slashed to separation with knives; skulls severed in every form, from chin to crown; muscles of calves, thighs, stomach, breast, back, arms, and cheek taken out.

"Punctures upon every sensitive part of the body, even to the soles of the feet and palms of the hand.

"All this only approximates the truth."

The mutilated bodies were carried back to the fort, identified, and then placed in two common graves, one for the officers and one for the men, for even in death rank separated them.

After the battle, the winter storms swept across the graves and the beleaguered fort. "The constantly increasing andf drifting snowstorms," wrote an officer's widow, "made it possible for the men to walk over the stockade in some places, and the constant clearing of a ten-foot trench in the snow seemed to be almost a useless task for the overworked garrison, as the next snow would immediately fill the gap. Still, it was absolutely necessary to prevent so easy an access by an insidious foe and the work was kept up under the Colonel's personal supervision by the faithful men who were no longer detailed for cutting timber. Not a soul ventured beyond the limits of the stockade except to bring in wood for which the winter's supply was abundantly adequate. Any antecedent lack of provision in so vital a matter would indeed have added terror to the siege. . . .

"Some would persist that the extraordinary cold and stormy spell of weather that immediately followed the battle would check Indian aggressions and that the hour of danger, if we kept behind the stockade, had passed. Others argued that the Indian loss must have been so severe that the savages would never risk so wild a venture as to attack the stockade with artillery ready to discharge grape-shot and canister from block-house and parade-ground. It was evident, however, to all, that any aggressive action to avenge the loss would be suicidal, while we could not fail to know, or suspect, guarded as the secret was, that not only were the Indians better armed and more numerous, but that there was scarcely small ammunition enough at the Post to maintain an action against a vigorous and bold assault."

If the Indians had taken the initiative, they might have overwhelmed Fort Philip Kearny, but they were not as well armed as the widow's comments might indicate. The fort was almost out of ammunition—Carrington had consistently called for additional supplies—but the Indians had almost no guns at all. The surgeon at the fort had carefully examined the Americans' bodies and had decided that only six of them had been killed by bullets. All the rest had died from wounds made by arrows, knives, and spears. With so few weapons and hindered by the cold and their fear of the fort's guns, the Indians refrained from attacking.

Under the strain of waiting, one of the men, the personal servant of Carrington, became crazy. He began striking his head against the wall of the kitchen, then against the stovepipe, and finally against the stove itself, trying to relieve the tension mounting within him. Carrington finally quieted him but only by drawing his revolver, cocking it, and pressing it against the man's head.

During these anxious times, word arrived that a wagon train was approaching through the snow and was being attacked. Carrington led a detachment to its rescue and learned that it was carrying an official notice for him. Instead of the additional men and ammunition he had requested, the authorities advised him that peace with the Indians had been completed and that he was now free to give them presents. Washington still did not believe what Red Cloud had said at Fort Laramie when he had told the Americans that there would be no peace between his people and them until they abandoned the Bozeman Trail.

But John Phillips was carrying the truth to the outside world. Fighting against the cold and the snow and carefully avoiding the Indians, Phillips arrived safely at Fort Reno. Then mounting his horse again, he pressed on south, finally reaching Fort Laramie with news of the disaster. Although Carrington's dispatch had been brief and to the point, the rumors started flying. The Commissioner of Indian Affairs reported to Congress that the incident had occurred because Carrington had refused to give the Indians guns and ammunition with which to hunt buffalos. "The whole is an exaggeration," he said, "and although I regret the unfortunate death of so many brave soldiers, yet there can be no doubt that it is owing to the foolish and rash management of the officer in command at the Post."

Although many Americans still did not understand the gravity of the situation, the army sent additional soldiers to Fort Philip Kearny and transferred Carrington from its command. On January 23, 1867, in weather so cold that the thermometer broke, Carrington started the painful march south. Fort Philip Kearny still stood, but Red Cloud had carried out his threat to close the Bozeman Trail. No emigrant trains could use that shortcut to Montana.

VII

The Struggle for the Road

THE heavy snows fell along the line of the Bozeman Trail, piling up in drifts that made much of it impassable. Sometimes the peaks of the Bighorn Mountains shone brilliant white in the sunlight; at times they were lost in swirls of mist and snow. Even to those who knew it best, the land became strange and unfamiliar. The once sharp edges of buttes and canyons became rounded and soft-looking; clumps of bushes disappeared entirely and no longer served as landmarks; the trees changed shape, and many of their lower limbs disappeared entirely.

Inside Fort Philip Kearny, the men went about their daily duties in the cold. They brought in quantities of firewood from the stacks outside; they dug trenches around the stockade after every snowstorm; they watered and fed the horses; and they took turns at sentry duty, standing on the sentinel platforms and gazing steadily into the blinding white. Somewhere out there, they knew, Red Cloud and the warriors were waiting in their winter camps for the first sign of weakness.

The Indians' tepees, although cool in summer when the sides could be partly rolled up to permit the breezes to blow through, were warm in winter. A fire burned in the center, the smoke escaping through a vent in the top, and a dew cloth hung inside against the walls to serve as additional insulation against the cold. From time to time, the men went off in small parties in search of deer and elk and other game, but sometimes they ran short of food and were forced to eat acorns, rose berries, and the scraping from hides. Winter was not a pleasant time, as their horses grew gaunt from lack of forage, and they called February the Moon of Sore Eyes because of the prevalence of snowblindness among them. Yet they were familiar with the harsh cold of that country, and the white men were not. The latter felt remote from the life they knew.

Although the order for Carrington's transfer had been issued before Fetterman's defeat, the army permitted the public to gain the impression that Carrington had been removed from his command as a punishment for the disaster and that, therefore, all was now well on the Bozeman Trail. But little had actually changed at Fort Philip Kearny, and its garrison remained isolated, besieged, and almost forgotten. Only the men stationed at Fort C. F. Smith, miles farther northwest on the banks of the Bighorn River, were more isolated.

Following the orders he had received from Carrington, Captain N. C. Kinney had carefully selected the site for the fort. It stood on a plateau above the river's floodplain and about eight hundred yards from the ferry used by the emigrants. Looking southward, the garrison could see the Bighorn Mountains, through which the river had cut a deep canyon, breaking into the freedom of the plains only one or two miles from the fort.

The fort itself was modeled after Fort Philip Kearny and was constructed with logs cut in the mountains. In one corner, an observation tower soared above the plains, giving the sentinels, when the visibility was good, a view in every direction. Cannons were mounted at two corners of the fort in embrasures that permitted the gunners not only to fire into the distance but also to cover the areas under the walls of the fort. Although Kinney was farther removed from the principal bases along the Platte than even the men at Fort Philip Kearny, he enjoyed a somewhat safer position than Carrington, for Fort C. F. Smith was to the west of the territory traditionally occupied by the Sioux. In recent years, however, they had been coming north of the Bighorn Mountains both to hunt and to wage war against the Crows, whose home this land was.

As soon as the Americans established the forts along the Bozeman Trail, the Sioux, like true statesmen, tried to make friends with the Crows, so they could concentrate all their efforts on driving the white men out. Kinney was wise enough to see that he could not fight both tribes at once, so he, too, made efforts to come to friendly terms with the Crows. When they did not appear at the fort, he sent word to them that they were welcome, and during part of the summer and autumn they made their camp on the opposite side of the river. Their friendship served an additional purpose for Kinney, because some of the younger men would visit the Sioux; and on their return, they would tell Kinney what was happening among the enemy. It was from them that he first heard of Fetterman's disastrous defeat.

As winter swept over the two forts, the new commander at Fort Philip Kearny, Lieutenant Colonel Henry W. Wessells, grew increasingly concerned about the fate of the men at Fort C. F. Smith. No word came from them, and although he tried to send messengers through in January, 1867, each time the men were turned back by either the weather or the Indians. In desperation, he tried to persuade some of the frontiersmen to undertake the assignment, but accustomed as they were to the rigors of winter travel, they refused to make the journey. Finally early in February, two sergeants volunteered for the task. Traveling for several days on snowshoes through the bitter weather, they at last reached Fort C. F. Smith safely. The garrison, they learned, was short of supplies, but it was surviving the winter and able to hold out for months longer.

On the way back, the two sergeants were accompanied by a halfbreed guide. This time they were mounted, but they had not gone far when they saw signs of Indians. Trying to escape being noticed, they headed for some nearby hills, but the Indians saw them and came in pursuit. Because of the snow, the horse of one of the sergeants was so exhausted that it could no longer move quickly. Rather than trust his life to the weary animal, he jumped off it and started running on foot. In one of those swift decisions that had to be made so often on the frontier, his two companions, certain that he was doomed and that they could not help him, abandoned him and arrived at Fort Philip Kearny without him.

Shortly after their arrival, the sergeant appeared on foot. His clothes were covered with snow, and he was almost frozen as he staggered through the gates of the stockade. But through a miracle of courage and endurance, he was still alive In his effort to escape, he had run along the edge of a cliff. Suddenly the snow gave way, and he dropped to a small ledge partway down. The overhang above prevented the Indians from seeing him, but they noticed his tracks, and several of them climbed down to kill him. Instead he was able to kill them as they approached, and the others gave up the attempt. When darkness came, he escaped and made his lonely way over the snow and back to the fort.

For all the danger the men had endured, however, the expedition had accomplished no practical results. Wessells's concern over the fate of the other garrison was relieved, but further journeys between the two forts were obviously impossible. Winter was proving a good ally to Red Cloud.

*   *   *

Gradually the days lengthened. The snows still fell, but the men began to notice the signs of returning spring. The storms became less severe, bare pieces of ground began to appear among the whiteness, the streams started to run with meltwater from the mountains, and soon some of the first migrating birds were winging their way overhead. Winter was past, but although the two garrisons were now spared the horrors of the cold, they had to brace themselves for renewed Indian attacks. For with the coming of warmer weather, the Sioux would obviously make fresh assaults.

While the two lonely forts were preparing for renewed warfare, the Indian agent among the Cheyennes, a man who had served as a major general in the volunteers, protested against the futility of the army's campaigns. "It is true," he wrote, "that horses have been stolen, ranches burned, and men killed . . . but in what part of our country have not such crimes been committed? and they are little, if any, more frequent in occurrence in this Indian country than in other places having the same number of people. Holding states, nations, or tribes responsible for the crimes committed, has been abandoned for many years, and there seems no reason for applying that rule in this case."

Here he underlined one of the basic tragedies of the war. The Americans often failed to distinguish among Indians, wreaking their vengeance against any Indian who came their way. And the Indians were just as guilty. When they were angry with the Americans, they did not care which man they killed as long as he was white.

"The whole object sought or desired to be obtained by the government in its dealings with the Indians of the plains," the agent continued, "is supposed to be safety of travel and transportation to and from the mountains. Can this result be secured by war? Reason and observation unite their voices in answering No.

"He who argues that the safety of travel and transportation is secured by war argues that a hostile country is safer for its enemies than a friendly one is for its friends. This is an absurdity. In peace alone does the traveler on the plains find safety. But, some war policy man may say, 'We wage war to secure a permanent peace.' No Indian war has ever thus resulted, and in the nature of things cannot so result; for the Indians have no permanent villages, no base of supplies, and no strategic points.

"That they can be driven from their country and from the plains is true, but only after all animals upon which they subsist were so far destroyed that the Indian can no longer find food; for, adding the reason of man to the instinct of all animals to secure their own safety by all possible means, he will, of course, be the last to be destroyed; and while life lasts, and war continues against him, he will steal the property and take the life of the whites on every favorable occasion.

"War against them is, then, the most absurd, expensive and ridiculous policy. Pursuing them with a command sufficiently large, only one or two can be occasionally seen; while with a small command, they are wont to mass and destroy it. And with a country some thousand or fifteen hundred miles square for them to roam over, unfit for settlement or occupation by civilized men, they cannot, though few in number, be destroyed in many years." The soldiers at Forts Philip Kearny and C. F. Smith, bracing themselves for the coming attacks, would have agreed. Out there in the wilderness with, as the agent had said, "no permanent villages, no base of supplies, and no strategic points," the enemy lurked, waiting for the moment to strike.

One of the first victims that year was John Bozeman himself. While traveling through the country that he had tried to open up, he mistook a band of hostile Blackfeet for friendly Crows, and his error was a fatal one. His death, although it did not materially affect the outcome of Red Cloud's war against the white men, demonstrated once again the danger of traveling on the east and north flanks of the Bighorn Mountains. Red Cloud had threatened to keep these lands closed to the white men, and he was succeeding.

Much of his effort that spring was concentrated on Fort C. F. Smith. Kinney had chosen the site well and had constructed the fort carefully, so it was almost invulnerable to attack. Red Cloud would have needed hundreds of well-organized warriors to have laid siege to it in the European manner. But the fort did have one weak point. Like most frontier posts, it was dependent on a source of hay for its herd, and the best nearby hay was about two and a half miles away. The sutler was under contract to do the actual harvesting, and rather than make the five-mile round trip every day with his mowing machines, he decided to set up a camp. On the banks of Warrior Creek (now Battle Creek), he built a corral that served to hold his animals and also gave him a reasonably strong position in case of attack, particularly when he blocked the opening with the running gear from his wagons, as he did every night. The army, of course, also supplied him with a guard, so it looked certain that he would be able to fulfill his contract and supply the post with sufficient hay to last it through the coming winter.

The Sioux, however, fully understood the importance of the hay to the post and were determined to stop the sutler. They were constantly in the vicinity, watching what was going on, and they engaged the Americans in a number of minor skirmishes. Their principal tactic was to permit the civilian workers to cut the hay unmolested, but when it was dry and ready to be collected, they would attack, drive the soldiers and civilians into the corral, and then set fire to the hay.

The Crows, who had remained friendly with the Americans, kept warning them that these were only minor engagements and that the Sioux were planning a major attack to drive them out. They gave these warnings so often that the white men completely ignored them. On July 31, 1867, a band of Crows again came to the camp and said the Sioux had held a council to decide on the best way to destroy the forts on the Bozeman Trail. Some had argued that they should attack Fort C. F. Smith first, while others held that Fort Philip Kearny should be their primary objective. The argument had become so bitter that the band had divided; some of the warriors with Red Cloud were moving toward Fort Philip Kearny and the others planned to attack the hay party. But still none of the Americans would take them seriously.

Early in the morning of August 1, the Indians encircled the hay-cutting party, remaining out of sight while the unsuspecting white men ate their breakfasts and then went out into the hayfield, just as they always did. There was no point attacking them until they were spread out and unprotected by the walls of the corral. But as soon as they had started work, the Indians charged at them. The Americans saw them coming, lashed their mules, and raced back to the corral with the mowers clanking and bouncing behind them, and the men on foot running as they had never run before. The second lieutenant who was in charge of the military detail apparently hoped to fight from trenches they had earlier dug just outside the corral, but the Indians did not give them time to get into those positions. So the civilians and soldiers —about twenty-five men in all—fled inside the corral, dropped to the ground, and began firing at the Indians. The lieutenant, however, did not believe that was the way an officer should fight, so he stood erect at the southern entrance like a figure in a romantic painting.

The initial rout of the Americans encouraged the Indians and made them think they were about to win another victory. One warrior, carrying a firebrand, dashed out ahead of the others and galloped toward the corral, hoping he could set fire to it. When he was within a few feet of its wooden walls, a bullet struck his horse. The racing animal crumpled up and fell on its side, pinning the Indian's leg beneath its body. It took the warrior several seconds to free himself, and then he ran for safety. But he had not gone many feet before an American bullet struck him, and he, too, fell dead. Another Indian noticed the second lieutenant in his foolish posture at the entrance to the corral. Aiming quickly from his galloping horse, he killed the officer and left the Americans without a leader.

Within the corral, one of the civilians, D. A. Colvin, immediately assumed command. He had been a captain in the Civil War and was an excellent shot and a skillful fighter. He ordered all the men to take cover, and under his leadership they put up such resistance that the Indians withdrew for the time being.

The direct assault having failed, they crept close to the corral, using a nearby willow grove and a bluff as cover. From those positions, they sent fire arrows hurtling toward the corral in the hope that they could start it burning, and they fired at the mules and horses inside it, killing all but a few of the animals.

There was some hay outside the corral, so they also set fire to that. It went up in a blaze of heat and light, and the wind blew the blaze closer and closer to the corral. Because part of the corral was constructed of willow boughs, it was vulnerable to fire, and it looked to the Sioux as though they were going to repeat their triumph over Fetterman. But then the flames suddenly went down, the wind reversed itself, and the black smoke from the embers blew back into the faces of the Indians. Because this attempt had been so nearly successful, the Sioux set fire to the grass. Each time, however, the Americans were able to put the fires out when they reached the corral.

And so the morning passed. Sometimes the Indians sniped at the white men, sometimes they started fires, and several times they charged, but always without success. Meanwhile the men at the corral wondered why no help arrived from the fort. In spite of the broad view from the observation tower, the corral was hidden from sight by a bluff. Nevertheless the men at Fort C. F. Smith could have heard the shooting and known that something serious was taking place. Yet no relief came, and the haymakers and their armed escort were left to their own defense.

Two of the men went almost crazy with fear. One, a civilian, hid himself among some of the gear, wept, and refused to fight. Another, a soldier, was so frightened that he threatened to commit suicide immediately and thus avoid capture by the Indians. Colvin, however, was still able to maintain general order in spite of these two outbursts of hysterics.

At noon, the Indians stopped the fighting and drew back, discouraged by their inability to overrun the corral. Neither flames nor arrows had prevailed against the Americans' guns. Unfortunately they did not leave a guard behind them, for the men in the corral were desperately thirsty. During the lull, a group of them volunteered to run to Warrior Creek with buckets, and because of the absence of the Indians, they returned safely.

In the afternoon, the Indians came back to try again. One leader rode within rifle range, and a shot from the corral killed him. Then the warriors attacked the corral on horseback, charging in from the west. A bullet knocked their leader from his horse, and the charge broke up as the Indians devoted their efforts to rescuing him.

But the battle was not over yet. So far, the Indians had not been able to kill the small group of white men, but they were not through trying. They launched their next attack on the side of the corral that faced toward the creek. They crossed the small body of water on foot, entered the grove of willows, and emerged in the open ground between the trees and the corral. Colvin told the Americans to hold their fire until he himself began shooting. As the Indians came closer, he pulled his trigger, and the others followed his example. A devasting volley burst from the walls of the corral, and the Indians' leader fell. The others kept trying to reach the Americans, but the heavy fire finally turned them back. By now they were ready to give up. Neither the fires they had set, their sniping, nor their direct charges had enabled them to conquer the corral; although the fort had failed to send reinforcements, the Americans had withstood the concerted attack. Finally they turned away and rode off. Only a few of them remained behind and for a short time engaged in desultory sniping.

Colvin now permitted one of the soldiers to ride with a message to Lieutenant Colonel L. P. Bradley, who had replaced Kinney as the commander of Fort C. F. Smith. Some of the Indians saw him and tried to cut him off; but they were too late, for he was then within sight of the fort, and the fort's covering fire protected him. He reached the fort on his sweating horse and learned that Bradley already knew about the battle. Another officer had been on the slopes of the Bighorn Mountains with a wood party. Noticing the disturbance on the plains below, he had watched the battle through his field glasses and had then raced to the fort to tell Bradley what was going on. But Bradley apparently preferred to sacrifice the hay party rather than risk a defeat like Fetterman's. Now that the battle was over, he permitted two companies of soldiers to go to the rescue.

The Indians had definitely lost what later became known as the Hayfield Fight. Greatly outnumbering the Americans, they had failed to overrun the corral, and their losses were certainly heavier than the Americans'. But the Americans, even if they could take pride in their victory, could find no reason for comfort in it. Red Cloud had demonstrated that he was determined to close the Bozeman Trail and destroy the two forts. The snows of winter had not in the least cooled his temper, and he was only waiting for another Fetterman to show himself.

Communications between the two forts were slow and poor, and so the commander at Fort Philip Kearny did not immediately hear about the Hayfield Fight, nor did he learn that the Crows had said Red Cloud himself was planning to attack Kearny. Consequently he took no special precautions. He had more men, more ammunition, and better guns than Carrington had had, so although he could not keep the road open, he felt relatively secure.

Like Carrington before him, he, too, was dependent on woodcutting parties for both lumber and fuel. As was often the case, a contract had been let to a civilian contractor to do the cutting, and the army agreed to provide him with an escort. Most of the wood was being cut on Piney Island in the north fork of Piney Creek, and some of the men camped there rather than travel back and forth each day. On a small plateau on the mainland overlooking the river, the soldiers made a second camp. Here they kept the mules, equipment, and supplies. From there, they could keep a watch over the woodcutting parties, and the camp also served as a staging area for wood trains going to and from Fort Philip Kearny. Because the men did not need the wagon boxes to carry wood—only the bodies were necessary—they had removed them and used them in the construction of their corral.

On August 1, the same day that the fighting was taking place at the hayfield, the Indians were gathering near Fort Philip Kearny. Red Cloud was there, and also Crazy Horse, anxious to repeat the success he had enjoyed when he had lured Fetterman over the ridge. Some of the Indians impetuously ran off a few head of stock from the fort, which was foolish, because it might have warned the Americans of their presence. Fortunately for them, however, the soldiers merely regarded the event as another of the customary minor harassments and took no alarm.

On the morning of August 2, 1867, when the Indians were planning to make their real attack, the Americans were just as unsuspecting as the men had been at Fort C. F. Smith the day before. In fact, two civilians decided to go deer hunting that morning in the mountains. They had just reached the foothills when they saw smoke signals and decided it would be wiser to turn back to the fort. Then they discovered that their return was cut off by Indians, so they raced to the woodcutters' corral. They made it just in time, for the Indians now numbered in the hundreds.

Three pickets and a herder were on the way to where some of the others were cutting wood when the Indians saw them. Seven of the warriors charged toward them, and the four white men had to fight their way to the corral. The three soldiers took turns staying behind, one of them holding the Indians off, then racing to rejoin his comrades while another soldier took his place as the rear guard. Even then they would not have reached the corral if it had not been for a courageous sergeant who left the enclosure and laid down a covering fire that protected them.

The Indians struck in several directions at once. One band on foot tried to drive off the mule herd, and when they were unsuccessful, some mounted warriors took their place and succeeded. Other Indians attacked the woodcutting party, who were out in the open. The men quickly abandoned their wagons and retreated toward the fort. As they fought their way back to Fort Philip Kearny, the mule herders saw them and tried to join them. The Indians would have prevented them from doing so, but Captain James W. Powell, who was in command at the corral, noticed the white men's predicament. He dashed out and briefly attacked the Indians in the rear, creating a sufficient diversion to permit the herders to reach the other Americans. Together they fought their way to the fort, although they lost several men in the process.

The Indians concentrated their main attention on the corral. It seemed vulnerable, because it was defended by only slightly more than thirty men, while the Indians had several hundred warriors. (Some estimates, grossly exaggerated as they often were, ran as high as three thousand.) They charged toward the corral, but as they came close to its fragile walls, they met a withering fire and fell back, leaving dead and wounded warriors behind them. Some of the wounded they were able to rescue in the customary Sioux fashion. Two Sioux would gallop up on either side of the fallen man and, without stopping their horses, lean over, grab him by the arms, and gallop away, holding the warrior between them. Others, however, were too close to the corral to rescue. These the Americans shot, arguing later with some justification that they could not leave dangerous enemies near their small enclosure.

But the charge had failed. On almost every side, the Americans were surrounded by level land that offered no cover for the attacking Indians. On the north, however, the attackers could take advantage of the rim where the plateau dropped off into the river bottom. A number of those who had guns took up positions here. They were about seventy-five yards from the corral and fired steadily at the Americans. Being so close, they killed several of the white men.

The Indians then tried to make a number of charges on foot, but each time they were unable to get near enough to the corral to climb over its walls and take it. They also sent burning arrows into the corral. These eventually set fire to the piles of dried manure that were inside the corral, and the heavy, smelly smoke added to the discomfiture of the white men. As so often happened during fights of this sort, the Americans began to need water. The barrel outside the corral was now so full of holes that the water had leaked out, but the cook had filled two kettles with water which were also outside the corral. Two men slipped out of the corral and retrieved these. In the process, bullets struck one of the kettles and knocked holes in it, but the one full kettle and the remaining water in the other was enough at least to alleviate the men's thirst.

Although the fighting had been intense, neither side was winning. The Indians had made many charges and suffered many casualties, but they had been unable to capture the corral. The Americans, on the other hand, had also lost several men but had been unable to free themselves from the Indians' constant fire. They could not leave the corral and make a dash for the fort—that would have been suicide— and apparently the commander at the fort, like the commander at Fort C. F. Smith, was not prepared to risk his men in a counteroffensive. By now it was midday, and the Indians withdrew to reconsider the problem.

They had reason to be discouraged. In the heat of the August sun, they had battled hard and long against a relative handful of white men and had been unable to win a victory. The mule herders and the woodcutting party had escaped to the fort, and the Americans in the corral were still putting up stiff resistance. This was not going to be a repetition of the triumph over Fetterman, and new tactics were obviously necessary.

Across the face of the plateau on which the corral stood, the rains had cut a defile that ran into the valley below. The defile formed a passage that went close to the corral, so some of the Indians, led by Red Cloud's nephew, thought they could use it as cover for approaching the Americans. They assembled on the river bottom, where they could not be seen, and stripped themselves of their clothing for greater freedom of action. Then on foot, they climbed up the defile and emerged onto the plain about a hundred yards from the corral, racing toward it in the form of a flying wedge. Red Cloud's nephew was killed almost immediately, and the casualties among the others were great, for the Indians were so close together that some of the Americans later said that a bullet that passed through one would hit and wound another. If the mounted Indians had attacked from another side at the same time, they might have captured the corral. They remained at a distance, however, and did not take part in the fight. Some of the attackers came within a few feet of the corral, but they could not get inside it. And so, after losing many dead and wounded, they pulled back, although many individuals made heroic attempts to rescue their wounded.

Actually the commander at the fort had not decided to leave the men to their own fates. When he finally realized the severity of the attack, he formed a rescue party, and the Indians saw about a hundred Americans emerge from the stockade. They were accompanied by a number of wagons and ambulances, and they also had a howitzer. The gun was enough to make the Indians withdraw out of its range, and when the rescue party was about two hundred yards from the corral, the defenders left their flimsy fortification and walked out to meet them. The Wagon Box Fight, as the struggle came to be known, was over.

The rescue party had brought with it a keg of whisky. The men had a drink and then, without wasting any time, loaded the dead and wounded in the ambulances, and headed for the fort. As they reached the top of one of the hills, they looked back and saw the Indians collecting their own dead and wounded and carrying them away. By the next day, not a single Indian body remained on the field.

In the struggle, neither side had won. Just as in the Hayfield Fight, the Indians had been unable to conquer a small group of Americans holding a relatively weak position. This was largely because of the inferiority of their weapons and also, to some extent, their inability to coordinate a mass attack. Their tactics would work against wagon trains of inexperienced emigrants but not against well-armed, well-trained troops. On the other hand, the Americans could not claim a victory. For the fight had demonstrated that they could not even cut wood for their fort with any assurance of safety. Each side was stalemated by the other.

*   *   *

That summer, while the army battled to keep the Bozeman Trail open, much of the country had grown weary of the expensive, prolonged warfare. In July, 1867, the Commissioner of Indian Affairs issued a report that expressed the view of many Americans. "From the facts before me," he wrote, "I conclude . . . that we can have all we want from the Indians, and peace without war, if we so will, with entire security on all our frontiers, and in all our territorial domain, at a cost of less than two days' expense of the existing war, to wit, a quarter of a million dollars, and in less than one hundred days. But how shall a peace be so easily and so soon made? Simply by retracing our wrong steps and by doing right. Pay the northern Cheyennes and Arapahoes and the hostile Sioux for the trespass we have committed upon their recognized rights, and negotiate with them by fair treaty for the privileges of way and military posts on their land so far as we may need them. This is only doing them justice, as our established policy requires, and this makes them our friends at once, renders travel and transportation safe, and garrisons almost useless. Restore to the southern Cheyennes their village [he was referring to the village attacked by Chivington] and their property we so wantonly and foolishly burned and destroyed, or pay them a fair price for it, and they will come back from the war path and resume the avocations of peace.

"It is believed that the destruction by our forces of the Cheyenne village and property, valued at $100,000 in April last has already cost the government more than $5,000,000 in money, one hundred lives of citizens and soldiers, and jeopardized all our material interests and along hundred of miles of our frontier."

He saw the problem not only in economic terms, but in moral ones as well. "We have reached a point in our national history," he wrote, "when it seems to me, there are but two alternatives left us as to what shall be the future of the Indian, namely, swift extermination by the sword, and famine, or preservation by gradual concentration on territorial reserves, and civilization. Our present policy, or rather want of a policy, in this regard, is working out, and must result, if persisted in, in extermination. As now situated, the Indian tribes are in the way of our toiling and enterprising population, and unprotected they will soon be inevitably submerged and buried beneath its confluent surges. Possessing originally the continent, they roamed at will among its mountains, valleys, and broad plains, free and untrammelled, the proprietors and lords of them all. But rapidly our race has relieved them of their vast domain, and the remnants of the ancient red nations, encircled by the pressing millions of our people, maintain a precarious foothold on their last hunting-grounds. These millions will soon crush them out from the face of the earth, unless the humanity and Christian philanthropy of our enlightened statesmen shall interfere and rescue them. The sentiment of our people will not for a moment tolerate the idea of extermination."

The commissioner was wrong in his estimate of the ease with which the Indian wars could be brought to a close. Some Indians would be willing to give up their traditional land and live on reservations in exchange for trade goods, but others would not. For much more was involved than the sale of territory, a point that was difficult for the Americans to comprehend. What they were trying to buy was not territory but a way of life, a whole culture that had existed for many years and that the Indians liked. Once they went on reservations—unless the reservations were enormous by American standards—it would be impossible for many of them to continue their old ways. Indians like the Pueblo Indians, who farmed, might be able to make the transition and retain the form, if not the substance, of their traditions, but nomadic Indians like the Sioux could not. Take away from them the right to ride after the buffalos, and they lost everything they had been trained to become and respect. Gone were their robes, their tepees, their need for herds of fast ponies, their skill with weapons, and all the arts they had learned and nurtured from generation to generation. In place of these, they would have to substitute Levis, white men's houses, and the crafts of the farmer or the small-scale rancher, and many of the Indians were unwilling to make that change.

The commissioner was also wrong about the unwillingness of the

American people to adopt a policy of extermination. To some Americans such a policy would be abhorrent, and they would do everything in their power to prevent it. But others lacked such moral restraint and would have been glad to have seen all the Indians killed.

The commissioner was absolutely correct in his statement that the "Indian tribes are in the way of our toiling and enterprising population, and unprotected they will soon be inevitably submerged and buried beneath its confluent surges." In the long run, the Indians had absolutely no chance of withstanding the Americans. They could defeat Fetterman and harass the haying and woodcutting parties at Forts C. F. Smith and Philip Kearny, but actions such as these could only slow the advance of the people, not check it. The Americans had the urge to expand over the land they thought of as their own, and they had means to do it. They had the guns and men, they had the lure of gold and free land to call them on, and they had the plows and reapers to make use of the land once they obtained physical possession of it. They also had the will. Whatever else they may have been—brutal, inconsiderate, greedy, or unscrupulous—they were determined and courageous in taking what they wanted. Nothing could stop them— snowstorms, icy passes, the searing winds of the plains, the death-dealing heat of the deserts, or even the Indians themselves. The Indians, therefore, had only one choice: to get the highest price they could.

Another chance for this offered itself in 1867. After the outbreaks along the Platte and the vigorous warfare farther north, the United States had wearied of fighting the Indians. In response to the mood of the country, Congress created a new peace commission. Its assignment was broad. It was to negotiate treaties that would provide for the safety of both the settlements and the railroads, and it was to plan for the future of the Indians. The bill establishing the commission gave Congress the authority to appoint four members, and it chose four men who favored peace. As a balance, the President was authorized to appoint four general officers from the army, and he chose men who believed the Americans should fight. Shortly after the Hayfield and Wagon Box Fights, the commission met in St. Louis. They then went by steamboat to Omaha, where they talked with the military and were told about the struggle going on in the Powder River country. Not allowing themselves to be discouraged by this news, they sent messages to the Sioux asking them to come again to Fort Laramie for another council. They then went up the Missouri River and talked with some of the tribes that were already friendly. On their return, they learned that no Sioux were as yet assembling at Fort Laramie, so they went to Fort McPherson (formerly Fort Cottonwood) in Nebraska and met with the Sioux and Cheyennes who lived near there.

Henry Stanley, the journalist who later became famous for finding Dr. Livingstone in Africa, was an observer. The council began in a drizzling rain, he told his readers. "The Indians had been dissipating the night previous. Some reckless white had supplied them with whisky, which had plunged many of them into forgetfulness of the scenes about to be enacted. Two hundred dollars reward was offered for the name of the man who had supplied the liquor. No informer could be found, but martial law was established over the denizens of this town, and each saloon and bar had a guard placed over it, and neither white, red, nor black man could get liquor of any kind. Sherman [the general was a member of the commission] is a man who can act promptly on occasion."

This was an inauspicious start to the conference, but for all their hangovers, the Indians made their feelings perfectly clear. Stanley reported one of them as saying through the interpreters, "You chiefs that are here to-day, and all you soldiers, listen unto me, for there is no fun in what I have to say to you. My Great Father did not send you here for nothing, therefore we will listen unto you. The Great Father has made roads stretching east and west. Those roads are the cause of all the trouble. . . . The country where we live is overrun by whites. All our game is gone. This is the cause of great trouble.

"I have been a friend to the whites, and am now. One of these roads runs by Powder River, the other up the Smoke Hill [route of the Kansas Pacific Railroad just north of the Arkansas River and a hunting ground of the Cheyennes']. I object to those—we all object to them. Let my Great Father know this; you can read and write; be sure and let him know. The country across the river [the Platte] belongs to the whites, this belongs to us [north of the Platte]. When we see game there, we want to have the privilege of going after game. I want those roads stopped just where they are, or turned in some direction. We will then live peacefully together.

"Last spring I told that man [one of the generals attending the council] there was plenty of game in this country yet. The time has not come for us yet to go a-farming. When the game is all gone, I will let him know we are willing.

"If you stop your roads we can get our game. . . . When we make peace we will stick together."

The Indian's speech expressed the frustrations of his people. The Indians did not want to become farmers like the Americans. Instead they wanted to continue living as they had always done, but they could not do so with the Americans passing through their country in increasing numbers and driving away the game or killing it for themselves.

Later General Sherman replied. "We now give you advice," he said. "We know well that the red and white men were not brought up alike. You depend on game for a living, and you get hats and clothes from the whites. All you see white men wear they have to work for. But you see they have plenty to eat, that they have fine houses and fine clothes. You can have the same, and we believe the time has come when you should begin to own these things, and we will give you assistance. You can own herds of cattle and horses. . . . You can have cornfields. . . . You see for yourself that the white men are collecting in all directions, in spite of all that you can do. The white men are taking all the good land. If you don't choose your homes now, it will be too late next year."

Later he went on to explain that "a great many agreements have been made by people gone before us. We propose to stand by them, but I am afraid they did not make allowances for the rapid growth of the white race, and you can see for yourselves that travel across the country has increased so much that the slow ox wagon will not answer the white man. We build iron roads, and you cannot stop the locomotive any more than you can stop the sun or the moon, and you must submit, and do the best you can. . . . Our people in the east hardly think of what you call war here, but if they make up their minds to fight you they will come out thick as a herd of buffalo, and if you continue fighting you will all be killed. We advise you for the best. We now offer you this, choose your own homes, and live like white men, and we will help you all you want." Then he added a reference to the emigrants who were coming in from Europe and who were causing much of the Indians' problems, as they swelled the population of the United States. "We are doing more for you," he said, "than we do for white men coming from over the sea." He ended his speech with a grim reminder that the peace commission was also a war commission, for the bill that created it empowered the President to call out troops if the commission failed to obtain peace.

This council accomplished little more than to let each side air its views, views that were already well known. But the Indians agreed to consider meeting with the commission again at Fort Laramie later in the year. Then the commission moved south to treat with some of the Southern Plains Indians like the Comanches and Kiowas. This council, too, got off to an inauspicious start, because some soldiers from Fort Larned, Kansas, who had accompanied the commission on one pretext or another, began shooting buffalos indiscriminately. The Indians objected strenuously to this destruction of their food supply. As a result, several soldiers and the major commanding the battalion were placed under arrest, and the council at last got under way.

The task facing it was a difficult one. The year before, General Winfield S. Hancock, an officer with presidential aspirations, had tried to treat with the Cheyennes near Fort Larned. Although he had served in the Civil War, he did not know the Indians and disregarded the advice of their agent. By approaching their camp in a military formation, he frightened many of them away. (They remembered Sand Creek well.) This led him to think they were hostile, so he burned their tepees. His action confirmed their fears about his intentions, and they began raiding. Hancock's campaign, which resulted in the death of several Indians, had succeeded only in arousing the Indians, not in preserving the peace.

The commission's purpose was to explain away Hancock's activities and more or less attempt to restore the conditions that had existed before he took to the field. The commission had with it large quantities of presents, hauled in wagons from Fort Larned. In order to obtain these, the Indians were willing to talk, but the council did not resolve any basic problems. When it was over, the fundamental conflict remained. The Americans wanted the land, and the Indians did not wish either to give it up or to surrender their old way of life. Even the presents did little to help them. They consisted of axes, kettles, blankets, and other goods, much of them surplus military property. The Indians carried away what they could, but the useless remainder, left on the ground, was testimony to the folly of the Americans' Indian policy.

From this council, the commission went to Fort Laramie. All they found waiting for them were some Crows—the Sioux had not appeared—but the members of the commission decided they must hold the conference anyway.

One of the commissioners opened the meeting with reassurances of the government's concern for the Indians. "Your Great Father at Washington," he said, "though so far away from you, is well informed of your friendship. He knows your friendship to his white children. He knows, also, of the many proofs of peace you have given to the Government. He knows, also, of some of the difficulties and troubles which beset you. He has sent us to see you in order that we may receive from your own lips how you stand, and that we may take all necessary actions to relieve you of your difficulties, and to make the road smooth with you. We learn that valuable mines have been found in your country, and in some instances taken possession of. We learn, also, that roads have been made through your land; that settlements have been made upon them; that your game is driven away, and is rapidly disappearing. We learn, also, that the white people are taking possession of your valuable lands and occupying them."

So far the commissioner had accurately stated the Indians' grievances, and the Crows showed their approval. But then the commissioner got down to the real business of the meeting. "We desire to set by a part of your country, that your people may live on it forever, upon which the Great Father and the white council will never permit any white man to trespass. We wish you to make out what section would best please you. When you have thus marked this tract out, we wish to buy from you the rest of your land, leaving to you, however, the right to hunt upon it as long as the game lasts. Upon the reservation you may thus select, we intend to build a home for your agent, to build a mill to saw your timber when you wish it, and a mill to grind your corn, a blacksmith's shop, and a home for your farmer, and such other buildings as may be necessary. We also propose to furnish you horses and cattle to enable you to raise for yourself a supply of stock, with which to support your families when the game has disappeared. We also intend to supply you annually with warm clothes and farming implements. We will also send you teachers to educate your children."

As the Indians listened to these words, "contempt and indifference were depicted upon their swarthy countenances," according to Stanley, who had stayed with the commission. This was not what they had wanted to hear. All the commission was telling them was what they had been told so often before: Sell your lands, and abandon your traditional way of life. They had no use for a sawmill or teachers or a home for their agent. They merely wished to continue living as they had always done, and this was the one possibility that the commission was ruling out.

One of the Crow chiefs, after addressing several of the commissioners individually, spoke to the group as a whole. "I am hungry and cold," he said. "Look at me, all of you. I am a man, like each of you. I have limbs, and a head like you; we all look like one and the same people. I want my people and my children to prosper and grow rich."

Then he strode up to two of the commissioners. "Call your young men back from the Big Horn," he said. "It would please me well. Your young men have gone on the path, and have destroyed the fine timber and green grass, and have burnt up the country. Father, your young men have gone on the road, and have killed my game and my buffalo. They did not kill them to eat; they left them to rot where they fell. Father, were I to go to your country to kill your cattle, what would you say? Would not that be wrong, and cause war? Well, the Sioux offered me hundreds of mules and horses to go with them to war. I did not go. . . .

"I have heard that you have sent messengers for the Sioux like you did to us, but the Sioux tell me that they will not come. They say, you have cheated them once.

"The Sioux said to us, 'Ah! the white fathers have called for you; you are going to see them. Ah! they will treat you as they have treated us. Go and see them, and then come back and tell us what you have heard. The white fathers will beguile your ears with soft words and sweet promises, but they will never keep them. Go on and see them, and they will laugh at you.'

"In spite of these words of the Sioux I have come to see you. . . ."

He then told how the older Crow chiefs had always advised them to be friends of the white men because the white men were strong, and he said, "We, their children, have obeyed." Then he related a series of specific incidents in which the Crows had been wronged. Once they had approached a camp of whites on the Yellowstone River to ask for bread. One of the white men deliberately shot one of the Crows. He told how he had gone "to Fort Smith, and found that there were whites there. I went up to shake hands with officers, but they replied by shoving their fists in my face, and knocking me down. That is the way we are treated by your young men.

"Father, you talk about farming, and about raising cattle. I don't want to hear it; I was raised on buffalo, and I love it. Since I was born I was raised, like your chiefs, to be strong, to move my camps when necessary, to roam over the prairie at will."

Another chief referred to the previous treaty made at Laramie and pointed out that they had tried to abide by its terms but the Americans had not paid the annuities due under it. Then he told the commissioners that he intended to live as he had always lived and asked them not to talk about reservations but to give up the forts along the trail. "As he uttered this earnest request," Stanley wrote, "his voice rose to the pitch of passion, his gestures rapid, his eyes flashed with excitement, and his old form trembled under his emotion. As he thundered out his righteous demands his body swayed from side to side. While he seemed struck by some sudden spasm, he frantically gathered his long hair and held it up aloft. Then again, as he described the cheats practiced upon his people by the whites, his voice sunk into whispers, while every gesture was eloquence itself.

"Raising himself to his full height, and elevating his arm, with the air of a hero, he proudly exclaimed, 'But for all this, my heart is rock, and I will not complain.' At times he appeared like some prophet of old about to declare the evil that would surely follow this monstrous robbery of their lands, and again his lips would wreathe with lofty scorn for the underhand work to which the pale-faces stooped, as he said, 'Though I am poor, I shall not die; my arm is strong, and I can hunt the buffalo as my father did.' Suddenly, as if remembering the former insults that they had been compelled to endure, his eyes flashed like living coals of fire—and he almost demanded that the soldiers should be recalled from their country; but finally calming down his wild passion, he implored the Commissioners to take pity on them, and do right for once. After which, shaking hands with each Commissioner, he returned to his seat, and as if brooding over past wrongs, over his nation's utter inability to protect themselves from the whites, he smoked his calumet in silence, with bent head, never lifting his head once."

Their oratory was to no avail. What the Crows wanted, the commissioners were not empowered to give. Yet the Americans and the Crows reached an agreement of sorts, and a paper was signed between them.

Commenting on the outcome of the commission's work, Stanley wrote, "They have visited Fort Laramie, and met there many members of the hostile bands of the North, who agree to go no more on the warpath. They have met a large delegation of chiefs of the Mountain Crow Indians, and sent them home to the borders of Montana, the fast friends of the white man." This was a considerable exaggeration, for the Crows had always been relatively friendly, and the council had not really reinforced their friendship. Then Stanley admitted, "It is true they did not meet Red Cloud, who is the leader and soul of the war on the Powder River Road; but they have assurances from him that he will meet the Commission in a grand peace council at Fort Philip Kearny when the grass grows in the spring.

"The Commission," he went on, "could not reasonably have expected the Northern hostile tribes to come to Fort Laramie. The lateness of the season, the consequent shortness of the grass, and the severity of the weather in that latitude rendered it a difficult undertaking. When it is also remembered that the Commission met at Laramie, Red Cloud and his bands must have been compelled to travel in coming and returning a distance of more than six hundred miles, just in the season of their preparation of winter supplies of meat by the chase. Most readers will agree that a meeting under such circumstances was out of the question."

Actually Red Cloud's presence had not been out of the question. He could have come to Fort Laramie as easily as the Crows, but he had told the Americans the condition on which he would make peace with them: They must first abandon the forts on the Bozeman Trail. Until this was done, he would not deal with them. So winter closed in again on Forts Philip Kearny and C. F. Smith. The cold winds blew down from the mountains, and the snows piled up against the stockades' walls. The sentinels again looked out into a world of drifting white, where their tenacious and forceful foe continued his war. And to the east, Sitting Bull, who had not participated in any of the councils, was as hateful of the white men as ever.

VIII

The Outcome of the Treaties

WHEN the peace commission left for the East, it had little reason
to be pleased. For the most part, it had merely reaffirmed relations with Indians who had already demonstrated their wish to be
friendly, and it had failed even to start negotiations with those who
were truly hostile. The absence of Red Cloud from any of the councils
was particularly conspicuous in spite of what Stanley reported to his
newspaper. And the public realized this. Red Cloud had become one
of the best known of all Indian warriors to the Americans, and without
his signature on the treaty, they knew that peace had not really been
made.

So before the members of the commission got on the train to begin
the journey back across the plains, they instructed the commander at
Fort Laramie to keep on trying to talk with Red Cloud. In some
respects, the assignment seemed hopeless. If the commission with all
its presents, messengers, and publicity had not been able to persuade
the chief to come in, what could an army officer do? But in January,
1868, a group of Indians came to Fort Laramie, and one of them was
a nephew of Red Cloud. He told the Americans that his uncle would
be willing to talk about peace if the army would abandon Forts Philip
Kearny and C. F. Smith.

This was the position he had always taken—there was nothing new
about it—but this time Washington was in a mood to listen. For the
army was overextended. With the troops and supplies given it by
Congress, it could not patrol the vast distances of the plains and keep
every road open against hostile activity. And of more importance than
the old Bozeman Trail was the building of the Union Pacific Railroad.

Since the Civil War had finally permitted Congress to agree on its route, it had been pushing westward, and the government, because of the subsidies it was providing, had a large stake in its success. Also its political influence was enormous. Yet its construction crews were constantly being delayed by Indian harassment. Again and again, as they worked at the end of the line, placing the steel rails across the face of America, they were interrupted by the appearance of bands of Indians. The workmen would lay down their picks and take shelter, the bosses would swear at the army for not guarding them better, and the army would hear from the politicians in Washington. Clearly it was impossible to protect the construction crews and still man the forts along the old Bozeman Trail. To be realistic, the army had to choose between one or the other, and it made its choice in favor of the railroad.

Even aside from the economic and political considerations, there was sound logic behind this decision. Ever since Bozeman had first found the route east of the Bighorn Mountains, it had proved of little practical value to the emigrants because of the Indians' resistance. Even the establishment of the forts had not solved the problem, and most of the emigrants had been forced to take the longer route on the west side of the mountains. On the other hand, if the Union Pacific Railroad pushed farther on, the emigrants to Montana could take the train to the west of the Bighorns, thus reducing the overall time needed for the journey. Furthermore, the Northern Pacific had also been chartered, and once it was completed, it would provide direct access to Montana. Under these circumstances, the effort to keep the old Bozeman Trail open seemed a rather pointless expenditure of the army's limited funds and manpower.

In March, General Ulysses S. Grant advised General William T. Sherman to prepare for the abandonment of the forts. He wanted the army's plans made known to the Indians in an effort to gain their goodwill, and he also wanted the work completed before the Indians started fighting again. If another outbreak occurred, he knew that public opinion would not permit him to desert the forts.

At about the same time, the peace commission prepared a new treaty, the terms of which were far more liberal than those offered the year before. Under its provisions, the Indians would retain the land from the Missouri to the Bighorn Mountains and from the boundary of Nebraska to just north of the present boundary between South and North Dakota. This area included the Black Hills, which the Sioux especially wanted.

Messengers again went out to the Indians, telling them to come to Laramie once more. But when the commissioners arrived at the fort in April, none of the leading chiefs was present. The Indians who appeared were largely those who had already signed treaties and were glad to get some more presents in return for signing another. Red Cloud, however, knew the futility of such negotiations and had no faith in the white men's promises. So he sent word that he would not come until the forts had actually been abandoned.

This was being done slowly, because the army was trying to recover as much as possible of its investment and therefore was trying to sell some of the equipment and supplies, a difficult task since there were not many buyers anxious for goods that would then have to be collected from the heart of the Indians' territory. Since Red Cloud would not appear until this had been accomplished, the commission left Laramie, went to Omaha, and took a steamboat up the Missouri River to Fort Rice, situated at the mouth of the Cannonball River.

One of the men accompanying it was Father Pierre-Jean De Smet, a Jesuit priest who had emigrated to the United States from Flanders years before and who was extremely interested in the Indians. A short, heavily built man with indomitable courage, he had traveled widely throughout the West and had dealt with many of the tribes, who seemed to have unusual faith in him. His greatest ambition was to serve as a missionary among them. Although his order insisted that he serve as a procurator at St. Louis, the government occasionally borrowed his services from the Jesuits. He had attended the council at Laramie in 1851, and in 1859 he had been a chaplain with General William S. Harney's expedition against the Mormons. After that, he had gone with Harney to Fort Vancouver on the West Coast, where an Indian outbreak had occurred. By the time he arrived, the campaign was over. "The task, however, remained of removing the prejudices of the Indians," he wrote, "soothing their inquietude and alarm, and correcting, or rather refuting, the false rumors that are generally spread about after a war, and which otherwise might be the cause of its renewal." Once again he threw himself enthusiastically into his work with the Indians and did much to quiet their fears. Later when General Sully was starting his campaign, he again volunteered to negotiate with the Indians, but he could not agree with the conditions that Sully laid down. In 1867 he had tried once more to bring peace to the plains but without much result. Now in 1868 he accepted the invitation of the peace commission to go to Fort Rice ahead of them and attempt to persuade the hostile Indians to come in for a council.

"Upon arriving at Rice," he wrote, "I had first to pass through a numerous file of Indians, ranged along the shore. In all their fantastic accoutrements, they made a truly picturesque and, for the kind, admirable spectacle; their heads were adorned with feathers and silk ribbons, in which red and blue predominated, and their faces were daubed with the most varied colors. I received a good grip from each one, according to their etiquette and usage; I noticed that those who knew me squeezed my hand much harder than the others. My little baggage was then taken to the lodging that had been prepared for me beforehand, and all the great chiefs of the different tribes were waiting for me there to hear the important news of the Government's intentions towards them."

For the next several days, he performed the rites of the Church among the Indians and the soldiers who were Catholics, and then he turned to the real purpose of his visit. Talking to the Indian leaders, he told them of his plans to visit the hostile bands and invite them to the council. At first, they tried to dissuade him, saying he would only lose his life in such an attempt. But De Smet assured them that his friends at home in St. Louis were burning candles for him and that many white children were praying for his safety and the safety of those who accompanied him. Reassured by these words, the Indians agreed to help him.

As his interpreter, De Smet chose a trader named Charles Galpin, whom he had known for many years. Galpin was married to a Sioux woman, who was a convert to Catholicism, and his daughter was attending a church school in St. Louis, where De Smet lived. De Smet had made an effort to watch out for the child, and the bonds of friendship were close between him and Galpin. About eighty Indians, including many of the leaders at Fort Rice, also agreed to go with him and serve as an escort.

The expedition started out on June 3, 1868. De Smet's plan was to go west, following the general course of the Cannonball River, through the southern portion of what is now North Dakota, and on into eastern Montana, searching for the hostile bands. After the first day, he wrote, "The country in all the region which we traversed is very rolling and covered with a rich carpet of flowers, always so agreeable to the sight. The starlike blossoms of the cactus, yellow, white and red, were specially prevalent." Although he was now sixty-eight years old, an age when most men prefer to remain comfortably at home, and although it rained heavily during the first day, Father De Smet was in good spirits and glad to be back on the plains again.

The small party, with two wagons carrying their supplies, kept moving westward. ". . . the country through which we rode . . . ," De Smet wrote, "is a succession of smiling undulating plains and of immense high plateaus, entirely without timber. The soil, or vegetable earth, is very light throughout and in many places impregnated with saltpetre, making the standing water disagreeable to drink, and unwholesome. In summer especially running water is scarce. The Cannonball River has but a small volume of flow throughout its entire course. . . .

"All through this region there are very high promontories or 'buttes,' which contain the springs where the little streams take their rise, and which tell the traveler which route to follow. . . . The surface of the country is covered with scoria, fragments of lava and petrified and crystallized wood. Evidently there have been violent convulsions here, changing the order of nature completely."

But after six days the expedition had seen no signs of the hostile bands, so they sent out four scouts, carrying tobacco. According to the Indians' custom, they would offer the tobacco as a sign of friendship. If the Sioux accepted it, the act would signify that they were willing to talk to the emissaries. At the time, the Hunkpapas, with Sitting Bull among them, and some Miniconjous and Sans Arcs were camped on the Yellowstone River about four miles above the mouth of the Powder River. They knew nothing about the impending council or the mission of the Black-robe, as they called priests, until the scouts reached their village. When they heard that De Smet was traveling with only an Indian escort and no soldiers, they realized he could not threaten them if he entered their camp. So, interested in knowing what news he might be bringing, they accepted the scouts' tobacco, and several hundred warriors, including Sitting Bull, went out to meet the priest.

About four miles above the mouth of the Powder River, the Sioux saw De Smet and his escort, and as they drew nearer, they noticed with alarm that the priest was raising a standard. This was either a signal they did not understand, or perhaps the scouts had not been truthful when they had said no soldiers were close at hand. So the warriors stopped their horses and consulted among themselves. Finally they decided to send four of the older warriors ahead while the others remained at a distance, ready to attack if necessary.

When they came up to De Smet, the four warriors looked at the flag and knew at once it was nothing they had ever seen before. De Smet, however, explained its meaning to them. On one side was the name of Jesus, and on the other, a picture of the Virgin Mary surrounded by stars. It signified peace. With this assurance, they signaled to the other warriors to come up, too.

"They then formed into a single long line or phalanx," De Smet wrote. "We did the same, and with the flag at our head went to meet them. At the same time the air resounded with shouts and songs of joy on both sides. I was touched even to tears at sight of the reception which these sons of the desert, still in paganism, had prepared for the poor Black-robe. It was the fairest spectacle in which I have ever had the happiness of taking part, and, against all expectation it was filled with manifestations of the profoundest respect. Everything was wild and noisy, but at the same time everything was carried out in admirable order. Upon arriving at a distance of 200 to 300 yards, the two columns halted face to face. All the chiefs came and shook hands with me in sign of friendship, and bade me welcome to their country. Then, surrounded by the chiefs, I shook hands with the warlike cohort. Exchanges of horses, weapons and garments took place at the same time between the two columns."

The countryside where they met was beautiful. "I will say but a word of the lovely landscape which was presented to our sight," he wrote. "Powder River lay before us, its bed wide and sandy, not deep; at a short distance on our right it pays its tribute to the Yellowstone and mingles its waters with those of a great cataract or rapid above its mouth, the dull sound of which is heard from afar, resembling the distant roll of thunder. At this point, the mountainous hills of the Yellowstone, though entirely sterile, are very picturesque and remarkable."

The warriors formed a guard around De Smet and his escort. "Plumes of eagles and other birds adorned their long hair," De Smet wrote, "and even their steeds had them in their manes and tails, mingled with silk ribbons of various colors and scalps captured from the enemy. Each one had his visage daubed according to his own ideas, with black, yellow or blue, streaked and spotted in every imaginable shade." But in spite of their warlike appearance, De Smet continued to have faith in the burning candles and the praying children and was certain he was safe.

When they arrived at the village, all the women and children and older men turned out to see him. Then they took him and Galpin to Sitting Bull's lodge, gave them something to eat, and placed a guard of about twenty warriors around the tepee. De Smet, weary from his long journey, fell asleep, and when he woke, he found Sitting Bull beside him, along with Four Horns, an older chief, Black Moon, who was famous as an orator, and No Neck, who was one of Sitting Bull's principal rivals for a position of leadership among the warriors. Sitting Bull was the first to speak.

He had killed many white men, he said, in retaliation for the wrongs that had been done to his people and he specifically cited the massacre that Chivington had carried out at Sand Creek. But, he assured De Smet, he was ready to make peace. After that, the Sioux talked to De Smet about the preparations they were making for the council the next day.

It was held in an area that De Smet estimated was about a half acre in size, surrounded on every side by tepees. In the center, the Indians placed De Smet's flag with the image of the Holy Virgin on it, and on one side they had made a seat of buffalo robes for the priest.

"The council," he wrote, "was opened with songs and dances, noisy, joyful and very wild. Then Four Horns lighted his calumet of peace; he presented it solemnly to the Great Spirit, imploring his light and favor, and then offered it to the four cardinal points, to the sun and the earth, as witnesses to the action of the council. Then he himself passed the calumet from mouth to mouth. I was the first to receive it, with my interpreter, and every chief was placed according to the rank that he held in the tribe. Each one took a few puffs. When the ceremony of the calumet was finished, the head chief addressed me, saying, 'Speak, Black-robe, my ears are open to hear your words.' "

De Smet started with a prayer, imploring for "light and blessing" on the meeting. Then he spoke for almost an hour, telling them that he had been trying to see them for almost two years and that it was important that they go to Fort Rice and talk with the peace commission. The Americans, he said, were far stronger than the Indians realized, but now the "Great Father desired that all should be forgotten and buried." Only the priest's faith in the future of peace had brought him, an old man, far into the wilderness at the risk of his life to talk with the Sioux, and this faith showed in his voice and his face. He stood there, the only white man except Galpin among hundreds of warriors, pleading with them to come to Fort Rice to seek the peace he so much wanted for them, and the Indians were deeply affected, because they could see his obvious sincerity.

When he was finished, Black Moon offered him the pipe, and after it had been passed from warrior to warrior, he rose to speak. "The Black-robe has made a long journey to come to us," he said. "His presence among us makes me very glad, and with all my heart I wish him welcome to my country. I can understand all the words that the Black-robe has just said to us; they are good and filled with truth. I shall lay them up in my memory.

"Still," he added, "our hearts are sore, they have received deep wounds. These wounds have yet to be healed. A cruel war has desolated and impoverished our country; the desolating torch of war was not kindled by us; it was the Sioux east of us and the Cheyennes south of us who raised the war first, to revenge themselves for the white man's cruelties and injustice. We have been forced to take part, for we too have been the victims of their rapacity and wrongdoing."

He correctly stated that the war had not been of the Hunkpapas' choosing. They had been drawn into it by events occurring in the lands outside those they considered their own—the uprising of the Santee Sioux, the resulting campaign led by Sully, and the fighting along the Platte that had originated as the result of Chivington's deadly attack on Black Kettle's village. As long as the white men had stayed out of their land, they were content not to attack them, but when the moment of warfare had come, they had not been slow to accept the challenge.

Black Moon then went on to recite the grievances of the Indians, the same grievances that other Indians had voiced so many times. But at the end he accepted the tobacco De Smet offered him and agreed to go to Fort Rice.

Sitting Bull also spoke. "Father, you pray to the Great Spirit for us, I thank you," he said. "I have often beseeched the kindness of the Great Spirit, never have I done so more earnestly than this day, and that our words may be heard above and on all the earth. When I first saw you coming my heart beat wildly, and I had evil thoughts caused by the remembrance of the past. I bade it be quiet—it was so! And when on the prairie I shook hands with you and my cousin and sister [he was undoubtedly referring to Galpin and his wife, who was a Hunkpapa, using the relationships of "cousin" and "sister" loosely, as the Indians often did], I felt changed and hardly knew what to say, but my heart was glad and quickly scouted deception."

Speaking with great dignity, he continued, "I am and always have been a fool and a warrior, my people caused me to be so. They have been troubled and confused by the past, they look upon their troubles as coming from the whites and become crazy, and pushed me forward.

For the last five years I have led them in bad deeds; the fault is theirs, not mine. I will now say in their presence, welcome, Father—the messenger of peace. I hope quiet will again be restored to our country. As I am not full of words I will thank you in the hearing of the chiefs and braves for your kindness and willingly accept the tobacco as a token of peace, hoping you will always wish us well.

"I have now told you all. All that can be, has been said. My people will return [to Fort Rice] to meet the chiefs of our Great Father, who wants to make peace with us. I hope it will be done, and whatever is done by others, I will submit to, and for all time to come be a friend of the whites."

He then shook hands with De Smet and Galpin and resumed his seat. Turning to the warriors, he asked them if they had heard his words, and they muttered their assent. Then he rose to his feet again and said there were two additional things he wished to say. He would not trade any of the Sioux's lands to the white men, nor did he wish the Americans to cut down any of the timber. He loved the trees, he said, particularly the oaks, which withstood the winter storms. Then he sat down again.

Other leaders also spoke at the council, and they, too, agreed that at least some of them should go to Fort Rice and hear what the commissioners had to say. Perhaps after all there was hope for peace with the Americans. Then, as the council broke up, the Indians asked De Smet to give them his flag, which he readily agreed to do. He also gave them some crucifixes made of bronze and wood, and Sitting Bull prized the one he received.

De Smet went back to the lodge, where he was surrounded by children and women with their babies. They wanted him to lay his hands on their children. After he had done so, they went away.

Meanwhile, the Sioux chose eight delegates to accompany De Smet to the fort and meet the commissioners. One of them was Gall, another of Sitting Bull's rivals for leadership among the Sioux. Gall had hated the white men ever since he had once been arrested by soldiers in the dead of winter for stealing horses. On the way to the nearest fort, the soldiers had thought he intended to escape—or perhaps they were tired of guarding him—and twice ran him through the body with their bayonets. He fell on the snow and pretended he was dead. But before leaving him, they kicked him several times, thrust a bayonet through his neck, and threw him into a ravine. Then they went on their way. But after they were gone, Gall was still able to walk many miles

—perhaps it was as far as twenty—until he came to the lodge of an Indian who cared for him and carried him back to his village. Since then, he had been a bitter enemy of the Americans, and the Sioux obviously believed he would represent them well.

When De Smet returned to Fort Rice, he had with him the eight delegates and also some thirty families from the Hunkpapas, who were curious to hear what the white men wanted and were perhaps anxious to receive the presents they were sure would be handed out. The commissioners were delighted with what appeared to be the success of De Smet's mission, but the presence of a few Hunkpapas did not affect the outcome of the conference. Once again through the interpreters, the commissioners tried to explain the intricate provisions of the treaty, stated as they were with legalistic formality, and again the Indians signed without really knowing what the Americans meant.

*   *   *

That summer the army continued its attempt to dispose of the goods at Forts Philip Kearny and C. F. Smith, and finally a freighting firm agreed to buy some of them for resale in Montana. In August wagons drove up to the stockade and entered the gates that had once held off the Indians. The freighters loaded the goods, while Red Cloud and his followers remained peacefully in the surrounding country. If the white men were really deserting the fort, there was no point in fighting them.

When the wagons were loaded, the Americans left and made their first camp nearby. Red Cloud wanted to be certain that the fort would never be reoccupied, so he and the warriors with him entered almost as soon as the freighters had left. Holding firebrands, they moved from one building to another, setting fire to them. From a distance, the freighters could see the smoke and flames rising from the former fort, as the Indians destroyed it.

Next Red Cloud led the warriors to Fort Philip Kearny. Entering the deserted stockade where the men had first learned the news of Fetterman's defeat, they once again applied their torches to everything that was burnable. Soon the flames were roaring upward, and the logs that the soldiers had brought in at such a cost in labor and lives were crumbling in the heat. In a short time, nothing remained but the gray ashes and blackened lumber. The work of Colonel Carrington and the men who had died defending the old road to Montana was gone, vanished in the smoke that formed a dark cloud in the air. But the flames carried away more than the walls and buildings of the fort and the original dream of Bozeman and the hopes of the emigrants who looked for a shorter route to the riches of the wealth of the West. They also demolished a myth—the myth of American invincibility.

* * *

Having imposed his terms on the Americans, Red Cloud was in no hurry to sign the formal treaty. Summer was ending and winter was approaching, and before the snows fell he needed meat for his people. In October, the members of the peace commission met at Chicago to consider what to do next. Clearly the commission had failed, for in addition to Red Cloud's unwillingness to sign the treaty, some of the southern Indians were again attacking white settlements. In spite of the commission's work and effort, peace had not come to the plains.

After discussing the problem, the commission adopted several resolutions. One called for a drastic change in American policy. Instead of handling the tribes as separate nations, the government should regard Indians as individuals and consider them subject to the laws of the United States. This at least was more in line with reality. Another recommendation also reflected the commission's disillusionment. All Indians, it said, should go on reservations, and those who did not do so voluntarily should be forced to. In other words, the commission was weary of groping for an illusive peace.

The army immediately organized the plains into two districts, one with jurisdiction over the southern Indians and another with jurisdiction over the northern Indians under General Harney. His headquarters were at Fort Randall on the Missouri River just north of what is now the Nebraska state line. This, of course, was far removed from Red Cloud's normal hunting grounds, but the army apparently did not take that fact into consideration.

Early in November, long after the peace commission had left the plains, the commander at Fort Laramie, Major William Dye, heard that Red Cloud was coming to the post and immediately telegraphed his superiors for instructions. The telegraph line was down, however, and he received no answer.

On the morning of November 4, Red Cloud appeared, bringing with him about one hundred twenty-five warriors, including men from other divisions than the Oglalas. "Red Cloud," according to Dye's report, "affected a great deal of dignity and disinterestedness—while other Chiefs arose, advanced and shook hands with the officers with apparent cordiality, he remained seated and sulkily gave the ends of his fingers to the officers who advanced to shake hands with him." He then complained that none of the peace commissioners were there nor anyone else in authority. Only when he was finally assured that Dye was empowered to deal with him did the council open.

Dye explained the provisions of the treaty to him, "but in answer to whether he wished to hear all the points in regard to the reservations and farming, he answered that he had learned from others all he cared to know about that . . . as they did not wish to leave their present home, abounding in game, to go to a new country. . . ." Clearly Red Cloud did not grasp the meaning of the treaty nor did he understand the significance of the government's Indian policy.

Nevertheless the council continued. What Red Cloud really wanted was ammunition to fight the Crows. They had received good guns from the Americans and had killed several of his tribe. He wanted to fight back. Dye told him that ammunition could not be issued to hostile Indians, and in any case, only General Harney at Fort Randall was authorized to issue supplies.

The council continued along this line for several days. At the end of each session, Dye would tell Red Cloud to think over what he had been told. Finally, according to Dye, Red Cloud said "the cause of war between the whites and northern Indians was the establishing of the Powder River Road without their consent; that he was at Laramie in '66 when a heavy cloud (his talisman) hung in the heavens portending war; and that he left the Post saying that he would not return until the new Road was closed to emigration, and their country inviolate restored to them. The great cause of trouble, he says, is now removed; the clouds hung in the heavens have cleared away (The days he was here were cloudless and pleasant); and he rejoices to again take the white man by the hand, as he and their Fathers did years ago, when the country was filled with traders instead of Military Posts." With these words, "he washed his hands with the dust of the floor" and placed an X beside his name.

But he made it clear that he was going to the Powder River country, not Fort Randall, and that the Indians would "live up to the treaty so long as the white man did" but that they might have difficulty controlling some of the younger warriors. He also said they would confiscate the property of any white man who entered their territory.

Dye gave him provisions for his journey, but it was doubtful if he had the slightest idea what it meant to "live up to the treaty."

* * *

While the peace commission and the army were trying to come to terms with Red Cloud in the north, Major General Philip H. Sheridan, who was in overall command of both departments, was reconsidering the army's strategy against the Cheyennes in the south. He was convinced they had to be punished before they would make peace. The problem was to figure out how to do it.

In August, 1868, one of his officers suggested forming a small group of scouts who could travel quickly. They would pursue the Indians, fighting them much as the Indians themselves fought, by relying more on steady small-scale attrition rather than full-scale battles. The idea seemed sensible to Sheridan, and he authorized the enlistment of a number of frontiersmen. Unfortunately for the Americans, however, the campaign did not work out as they had planned. The small band soon found itself surrounded and outnumbered, and it would have been annihilated if two men had not been able to escape at night and succeed in getting help.

After that experiment, Sheridan decided on a new strategy. Because of the bitter weather on the plains during the winter months and the scarcity of food, the Indians usually ended their fighting in the fall and went into winter camp. That was the time to strike against them, Sheridan thought. They would be unsuspecting, and their horses would be in poor condition because of lack of forage.

Sheridan spent the fall of 1868 assembling his forces, and on November 15 began his campaign. "It would have been difficult to have designed a more disagreeable day," a writer who accompanied him said. "It had rained heavily all night. In the morning the air was filled with a heavy penetrating mist. A strong wind was blowing from the north, adding to the driving moisture and almost freezing temperature." Later in the day, "the storm grew more violent. The mist had turned into a heavy rain and aided by the wind, pelted against the ambulances [in which Sheridan and members of his staff were riding] in a nowise encouraging manner. The trails, considerably cut up by the numerous trains which had passed over them, were heavy and soon exhausted the animals. Our 'team' showed very evident signs of being 'played out.' The art of effective mule driving consists, at all times, of a liberal allowance of raw hide, applied with tornadoes of epithets, given with a variety of expression and accent. These usually totally satisfactory measures were totally inoperative in our case. The driver, a powerful robust man, with an excellent pulmonary development, and a powerful leverage in the whip-hand, gave up in complete despair. He had not only demolished his whip, but also his patience, and by way of peroration gave vent to a soliloquy in denunciation of 'shave-tails,' declaring they were only 'sulky and playing off.' "

Sheridan's party, which had left several hours after the main body had departed, finally caught up with the other men. "Upon reaching the site of the camp," the writer continued, "great difficulty was experienced in pitching the tents. The wind blew even more violently than during the day, and was now accompanied by a heavy fall of snow. Wood was scarce, and what little was gathered it was impossible to ignite.

"Through the entire night the wind howled across the plain, threatening, momentarily, a demolition of our canvas walls. Our situation was decidedly comfortless, and, as introductory to a campaign of indefinite duration, presented anything but the most flattering anticipations of bodily comfort. Our tents had been pitched hastily, and flapped, and groaned, and jerked the live-long night. The ground was wet. The men and animals without shelter were severely tried. There was no sleep in the camp that night."

Many of the soldiers must have thought the Indians were wiser than the white men in not fighting during the winter months, for the weather ahead was going to get generally worse, not better. But the next day dawned clear, and although the wind was still strong, "the air was cold and bracing, and the roads frozen." The troops stopped briefly at Fort Dodge, then followed the Arkansas River for a few miles, and turned south. After crossing the Cimarron River, which was so alkaline that only the animals could drink it, they went on to Beaver Creek.

"The silvery waters of the river, winding in graceful curves, coursed through the valley," the writer reported. "Upon its banks the buffalo, the deer, and the wolf found an undisturbed existence. Along the line of the horizon stretched a range of hills, encircling the valley almost completely, while the intermediate gentle undulations broke the monotony of a rigid plain. The grasses, robbed of their vitality by the biting frosts of autumn, covered the surface with a carpet of somber tinge, intermixed here and there with patches of different varieties and varied tints. A few towering trees or a dense underbrush grew now and then along the stream. The pure blue of the great dome of nature spread in sublime expanse overhead. In the west the sun threw out a parting glare, changing the atmosphere from a colorless waste to a vast ethereal sea of gold. The effect was indescribably grand."

But in spite of the peaceful aspect of the country, they were in the Indians' territory, and that night brought several attacks on the sentinels. The Indians were apparently attempting to slip into the camp, unpicket the horses, and stampede them. The next day the troops moved eastward, following the general direction of Beaver Creek. By nightfall they had reached the area where Beaver and Wolf Creeks join to form the North Fork of the Canadian River. At this point they were at the eastern edge of the panhandle of present-day Oklahoma, which was then Indian Territory. Farther east the Canadian River flowed into the Arkansas and then into the Mississippi. To the south of them was the South Fork of the Canadian River and the headwaters of the Washita River, where many of the Cheyennes were reported to be making their winter camp.

Sheridan had ordered General Sully, who commanded the military district, to go in advance and establish a base for the winter's operations, and this was the site that Sully, with the help of an experienced frontiersman, had chosen. At hand were adequate supplies of water, wood, and forage for the animals, and Sheridan proposed building a post here to be known as Camp Supply.

As he approached the campground, a young officer rode out to greet him. This was Brevet Major General George Armstrong Custer, who had already won considerable notoriety and fame.

*   *   *

Custer had graduated from West Point in 1861 at the bottom of his class with so many demerits on his record that only three more would have meant his automatic dismissal. War had already started between the Union and the Confederacy, but instead of leaving to join in the fighting, as his classmates did, he was forced to stay at West Point, because he was under arrest. Just a few days after graduation, he had been officer of the guard when two new students began fighting each other. Instead of stopping them, Custer had been an interested and enthusiastic spectator. At his court-martial, however, he was let off with only a reprimand, and shortly afterward he was on his way to Washington.

Flamboyant, full of high spirits, and physically courageous to the point of foolhardiness, Custer drew attention to himself wherever he went and began receiving promotions. He was also not above army politics, went out of his way to meet generals and other persons with influence, and quickly learned from his superiors how to put himself in a favorable light when reports were written. As a result of his brilliance and courage, at the age of twenty-three he was made a brevet brigadier general.

Later he served under Sheridan, who took a warm liking to him; and at Appomattox he played a vital role by helping to cut off Lee's retreat. For this he received a promotion to brevet major general. At the end of the war, however, like so many other young men, he was reduced to his rank of captain in the regular army.

In his short life, he had known glory and fame, but nothing similar awaited him in the peacetime world. After considering a commission in the Mexican army, looking for civilian employment in the East, and contemplating a political career, he finally decided to stay in the army and accepted an appointment on the plains. He had been given a promotion since the end of the war to lieutenant colonel, and with this rank he went to Fort Riley, Kansas, where he was to serve with the Seventh Cavalry. When General Hancock made his futile campaign against the southern Indians, Custer and the Seventh Cavalry went with him. After Hancock destroyed the Indian village, he sent Custer in pursuit of its occupants. This was his first independent command on the plains, and he was finding life very different from that on the battlefields of the South. There the enemy fought like the white men they were; here the enemy seemed to dissolve in the vastness of the plains, breaking up into small groups that were difficult to track, only to reassemble later. Custer wanted glory, and he did not find it chasing those Indians, for they eluded him.

While camped on the Republican River, he deliberately disobeyed orders. He had been told to send his wagons north to Fort Sedgwick for supplies, but he wished to see his wife, Elizabeth Custer, whom he adored. So he sent his wagons south to Fort Wallace in the hope that Libbie, in response to a letter from him, would meet the wagons there and join him. The letter, however, did not reach her soon enough. At the same time he was having increasing difficulty with his men. He was accustomed to handling disciplined troops, not soldiers who often looked on the army only as a means of getting to the gold fields. By compelling them to make forced marches, he angered them so much that they began to desert in large numbers. In retaliation he gave the order that men caught deserting should be shot, and several were, one of them subsequently dying as the result of his wound.

After an uneventful campaign, he marched back to Fort Wallace in Kansas for supplies. There he learned that his wife, Libbie, was now at Fort Riley, Kansas, only three hundred miles east of him. The fort, he heard, was suffering from an outbreak of cholera, and Libbie was frightened and wanted to see him. Because Fort Wallace was short of supplies, he decided to disobey orders again and make another forced march with a wagon train to the east, instead of staying on the Republican River or asking for new orders. On the march several men were cut off by Indians during a skirmish, and he failed to turn back and attempt to rescue them. Later he argued that they were probably dead and he did not want to risk any more lives. But he could not prove that they had not died because of his neglect.

When he arrived at Fort Hays, he was proud of his march, because he had brought his men about one hundred fifty miles in something like sixty hours. But both the men and the animals were exhausted. At Fort Hays, he concocted a new plan to see Libbie. While his men rested, he rode ahead to Fort Harker, ordered the supplies he needed, and then before his wagons arrived dashed off without leave to visit his wife.

He had not been with her long, however, before he received a telegram ordering him to return to Fort Harker. There he was placed under arrest, and serious charges were leveled against him. He had left Fort Wallace against orders; he had shown excessive cruelty to his men by shooting the deserters; he had made too many forced marches; and he had abandoned his men. Custer's defense was weak, and he was ordered suspended from the army for a year. In November, 1867, General Grant endorsed the sentence with a comment that the leniency shown Custer must have been because of his previous service.

During Custer's suspension, Sheridan had taken command of the Department of the Missouri and had started using his more aggressive tactics against the Indians. The failure of his band of scouts and their near annihilation made him wish for an officer who liked fighting and had demonstrated his courage. So he applied for Custer's reinstatement. In September, 1868, he telegraphed Custer, telling him what he had done, and asked him to come immediately to take part in the winter campaign.

"The reception of this despatch," Custer later wrote, "was a source of unbounded gratification to me, not only because I saw the opportunity of being actively and usefully employed opened before me, but there were personal considerations inseparable from the proposed manner of my return which in themselves were in the highest degree agreeable; so much so that I felt quite forbearing toward each and every one who, intentionally or not, had been a party to my retirement, and was almost disposed to favor them with a copy of the preceding despatch, accompanied by an expression of my hearty thanks for the unintentional favor they had thrown in my way."

This, then, was the officer who rode out to greet Sheridan when the general approached Camp Supply on Beaver Creek to start the campaign against the Southern Plains Indians. He was of unquestioned physical bravery, but he was also brash, willing to disobey orders, and anxious to redeem himself.

*   *   *

The force that Sheridan had assembled at Camp Supply was a large one, consisting of the cavalry under Custer, a battalion of infantry, and the men who had accompanied Sheridan. Altogether they totaled about eleven hundred persons and required a train of four hundred and fifty wagons to carry their supplies. Sheridan was prepared to wage a massive campaign against the Southern Plains Indians.

The weather turned bad almost immediately after his arrival. "Hardly had the tents at headquarters been pitched," wrote one observer, "than a violent snow-storm set in, lasting, with but trifling intermission, for three days. At one time, fears were entertained that we were destined to a snow blockade, and thus an end, for some weeks, be put upon active operations. Notwithstanding the storm, Sheridan, with characteristic energy, resolved to send out a column at once, in hopes of striking the savages when he knew their vigilance would naturally relax, and it would be impossible for them to offer any determined resistance. Custer, ever ready to undertake a desperate mission, was to be entrusted with the command; the troops designated for the service were the eleven companies of the 7th Cavalry, numbering about seven hundred men.

"The very next day after our arrival at the camp, regardless of snow and wet, a train was made up to convey thirty days' supplies for the expedition. The troops and horses, arms and accoutrements, were inspected. But few tents were allowed. A pair of blankets, strapped to the saddle, and the clothes on their backs constituted the quota of baggage alike for officers and men. By the same night, the command was in condition to move.

"At three o'clock, on the morning of the twenty-third of November, the reveille sounded the trooper from his slumbers. The camp of the 'Seventh' was now a scene of busy preparation. Horses were groomed and saddled, and the men buckled on their weapons to await orders to mount. By six o'clock the bugle called the troopers to 'boots and saddles.' The line was formed, and the train started. 'By fours, right;' 'forward,' was borne along the line. The dark forms of horse and rider broke into column, and, led off by their gallant leader, set out on their hazardous mission.

"The storm was still at its height," the writer continued. "The snow lay upon the ground to a depth of twelve inches; but, with a determination of purpose, the command moved out with cheers and the highest anticipation of inaugurating the campaign by striking a decisive blow.

"It was the gray of dawn. The camp was buried in snow. As the column passed through the long line of tents occupied by the infantry, officers and men turned out to say a last word of cheer, and express a pious wish that 'they might kill plenty of red devils and have a speedy return.'

"The column moved out on the plain, followed by the long train of wagons. Through the falling flakes, the dark mass could be traced forward at a tedious pace, braving the elements overhead, and struggling through the soft snow beneath."

Custer had planned on marching only twelve or fifteen miles during the first day, but the weather was so severe his guides wondered whether they could make even that distance. The snow was coming down so hard that they could not see the landscape around them and were in danger of losing their way for lack of landmarks. By using their compass, however, they were able to find their destination and made camp in the deep snow.

The next day was bright and clear, and the troops continued their journey through the fallen snow toward the Washita River and the Indians reported camped in the shelter of its valley. At the Canadian River, Custer divided his force in two. One group under Major Joel H. Elliot was to go up the Canadian River, looking for Indian trails. The other under Custer was to get the wagons across the river and continue south toward the Washita. To get the wheels through the sand it was often necessary to hitch two teams of mules to a single wagon, but after about three hours the task was done. The last of the wagons had finally crossed the river and climbed the bank, and Custer was just about to resume the march when the men saw a horseman riding toward them.

He was a messenger from Elliot, who had already discovered a fresh Indian trail and was following it as fast as he could. Custer detailed eighty men to guard the wagon train and started out with the others to catch up with Elliot.

About an hour before sunset, they came across the Indians' trail.

"The object now," Custer later wrote, "was to overtake as soon as practicable the party of Elliot, which from the heavy trail we could see in advance of us. The almost level and unbroken character of the country enabled us to see for miles in all directions, and in this way we knew Elliot must be many miles ahead of our party. At the same time I could see that we were gradually descending into a valley, probably of some stream, and far in advance appeared the dim outline of timber, such as usually fringes the banks of many of the western streams. Selecting a few well-mounted troopers and some of the scouts, I directed them to set out at a moderate gallop to overtake Elliot, with orders to the latter to halt at the first favorable point where wood and water could be obtained and await our arrival, informing him at the same time that after allowing the men an hour to prepare a cup of coffee and feed and rest their horses it was my intention to continue the pursuit during the night—a measure to which I felt urged by the slight thawing of the snow that day, which might result in our failure if we permitted the Indians to elude us until the snow disappeared."

At about nine o'clock that night, after following the trail down a valley, they finally caught up with Elliot. After a brief rest during which the men drank some coffee and ate some hardtack, Custer was ready to move on again. The Osage Indian scouts, whom the army had employed and who were accompanying him, wanted to wait until morning, but Custer hoped to catch his enemy by surprise. So they marched down the valley, two Indians in front, the scouts and other Indians following them, and the white men in the rear. The moon, which had then risen, cast soft shadows over the valley. The melting and freezing had caused a crust to form on the snow, and the horses' hooves made a loud noise as they broke through it. For this reason Custer ordered the cavalry to stay well in the rear.

They had gone some distance down the valley when one of the Osages said he smelled smoke. Neither Custer nor any of the white officers could smell it, and Custer, remembering that the Indians had wanted to wait until daylight, thought the Osage might be making the report out of fear. Nevertheless he gave the order to advance more cautiously, and in a short time they came upon the embers of a dying fire. Judging from the number of horse tracks nearby, the scouts and the Osages decided the fire must have been left by a herdsman and that the Indian village should be close.

And indeed it was. It was the village of Black Kettle, whose Cheyennes had been massacred by Chivington and who had tried nevertheless to maintain friendly relations with the Americans. As in any community, he had not been able to control the activities of each individual, and some of the younger men continued to be hostile to the Americans. In spite of the chief's admonitions, they raided against the white men, and the trail that Elliot had picked up belonged to some warriors who were returning from an attack on the Americans. But there is little doubt that Black Kettle himself and the majority of his village wanted peace. With the coming of winter, he had moved his camp to the valley of the Washita River and had established his village upriver from several others. Protected, as he thought, by the heavy snow, and unaware that the activities of a few warriors could bring vengeance on the entire group, he believed that he and his people were safe.

Although Custer did not know it, Black Kettle's village had been warned of his approach but, unfamiliar with the white officer's ways, had failed to take advantage of the knowledge. One of the Indians in the group that Elliot had been trailing had left an exhausted horse behind him to rest. That afternoon he had gone to retrieve the animal and had seen Custer and his men in the distance. He told one of his friends that tomorrow he should bring in his horses, because the soldiers were coming. But neither Indian expected the white men to march all night, and so they lost an opportunity to prepare the village for the coming attack.

Continuing to move cautiously down the line of the valley, the Osage scouts kept in the lead, carefully looking ahead as they came to a rise in the land. Finally one of them returned to report to Custer. There was an Indian village ahead. Custer gave orders for the rest of his men to come up as quietly as possible and then divided them into four groups, so that when daylight came, they could attack the village from every side.

While the other three groups marched off to take up their positions before daybreak, Custer remained with the fourth. "During all those long weary hours of this terribly cold and comfortless night," he later wrote, "each man sat, stood, or lay on the snow by his horse, holding to the rein of the latter. The officers, buttoning their huge overcoats closely about them, collecting in knots of four or five, and, seated or reclining upon the snow's hard crust, discussed the probabilities of the coming battle, for battle we knew it would be, and we could not hope to conquer or kill the warriors of an entire village without suffering in return more or less injury. Some, wrapping their capes about their heads, spread themselves at full length upon the snow and were apparently soon wrapped in deep slumber."

In about an hour Custer woke. The moon sank, and the valley became shrouded in darkness. The men watched as the morning star rose, but the Indians slept on in the quiet night, unaware that their enemies had drawn a net around them.

"The distance to the timber in the valley proved greater than it had appeared to the eye in the darkness of the night," Custer later wrote. "We soon reached the outskirts of the herd of ponies. The latter seemed to recognize us as hostile parties and moved quickly away. The light of day was each minute growing stronger and we feared discovery before we could approach near enough to charge the village. The movement of our horses over the crusted snow produced considerable noise and would doubtless have led to our detection but for the fact that the Indians, if they heard it at all, presumed it was occasioned by their herd of ponies. . . .

"We had approached near enough to the village now to plainly catch a view here and there of the tall white lodges as they stood in irregular order among the trees. From the openings at the top of some of them we could perceive faint columns of smoke ascending, the occupants no doubt having kept up their feeble fires during the entire night. We had approached so near the village that from the dead silence that reigned I feared the lodges were deserted, the Indians having fled before we advanced. I was about to turn in my saddle and direct the signal for attack to be given . . . when a single rifle shot rang sharp and clear on the far side of the village from where we were. Quickly turning to our band leader, I directed him to give us Garry Owen [the tune Custer liked during a charge]. At once the rollicking notes of that familiar marching and fighting air sounded forth through the valley and in a moment were reechoed back from the opposite sides by the loud and continued cheers of the men of the other detachments, who, true to their orders, were there and in readiness to pounce upon the Indians the moment the attack began."

In this way, with their band playing, the Americans charged upon the unprepared village. Custer had told his men to shoot only warriors, but he himself admitted that in a fight of this sort it was impossible not to hit women and children as well. Black Kettle had no time to ask for a parley or to explain either his identity or his intentions. The Americans' bullets cut him down almost immediately, and his wife died beside him.

In spite of the suddenness of the attack, many of the warriors were able to get their guns and fight back. "We had gained the center of the village," Custer wrote, "and were in the midst of the lodges, while on all sides could be heard the sharp crack of the Indian rifles and the heavy responses from the carbines of the troopers. After disposing of the smaller and scattering parties of warriors who had attempted a movement down the valley, and in which some were successful, there was but little opportunity left for the successful employment of mounted troops. As the Indians by this time had taken cover behind logs and trees and under the banks of the stream which flowed through the center of the village, from which stronghold it was impracticable to dislodge them by the use of mounted men, a large portion of the command was at once ordered to fight on foot, and the men were instructed to take advantage of the trees and other natural means of cover and fight the Indians in their own style."

One group of warriors lay down in a small depression in the ground. It was sufficiently deep so the white men could not see them, but they had to raise their hands above the rim of it in order to fire. They fought bravely and caused considerable casualties among the Americans until some sharpshooters picked them off one by one.

Some of the women and children tried to hide in their tepees. As the fighting continued, the soldiers gradually found them, and they were made prisoners. Through the interpreter, Custer attempted to reassure them that they would be treated in a kindly fashion, but they were bewildered and frightened and had difficulty comprehending what he was trying to tell them.

In the bitter fighting not all the atrocities were on the side of the Americans. The soldiers saw a woman escaping with a little white boy whom she held as a captive. They cut her off from the others in an effort to rescue the boy. But when she saw that she could not get free, she took out a knife and killed her prisoner. The soldiers immediately shot her.

Although the weather was freezing cold, many of the women plunged into the Washita and walked downstream under the shelter of its bluffs with several warriors trying to cover their retreat. At one point, where the Washita made a sharp horseshoe bend, the water became so deep that it was over their heads. Here the warriors told them to leave the river and walk across the neck of land. Major Elliot and some of his men were attacking from that side and saw what was happening. They dashed over and tried to block this escape route. The sound of the shooting was echoing through the valley, and warriors from some of the villages down the river heard it and were beginning to come to the rescue of the Cheyennes. Consequently, in spite of the heavy casualties among the Indians, their fighting strength was beginning to increase.

Elliot apparently did not realize this when he tried to take up a position at the horseshoe bend, and at first it looked as though he would be successful in stopping the Indians' retreat. His men killed one of the three Indians who were fighting the rearguard action and took a woman and a child prisoner. Elliot detailed one man to take these prisoners back to the village, but the woman was not going to go willingly. Noticing the other Indians arriving, she battled for time by tearing up some cloth to wrap around the child's feet to protect them from the cold. The soldier let her do this and lost his life as a result. For the delay gave the other Indians a chance to get between him and the village, and they killed him.

Meanwhile, Elliot suddenly found his position reversed. He had been trying to cut off the Indians' retreat; now they had cut off his. Placed on the defensive, he and his men took cover in the long grass and began firing at their attackers. But the grass offered them no protection, and the men started to lose their nerve. Instead of firing carefully, they tried to keep their heads down. This prevented them from taking sure aim, and as a consequence many of their shots went into the air over the Indians' heads. Because of this faulty shooting, the Indians were able to creep closer and closer to the Americans. Finally they charged. Elliot and his command could not repel them, and the white men were killed.

More Indians were now arriving from the downstream villages, and Custer, noticing them riding along the tops of the bluffs, began to realize that his position was serious. Although all the initial advantages of surprise had lain on the Americans' side, he had lost Elliot and his men and was in danger of being surrounded himself. The Cheyennes' herd of horses had been rounded up by one of the scouts. Originally Custer had thought of taking the animals with him, but this was now impossible. So he ordered his captives to select mounts for themselves and then had the rest of the horses shot. This at least prevented the Indians from regaining them.

Fortunately for the Americans, the quartermaster, who had been left behind the night before, sensed that they might need additional ammunition. With a small escort, he brought more rounds and was able to get past the Indians, who were too busy shooting at the Americans in the valley to see him. Custer issued the fresh supply to his men and then took count of his position. He had lost a number of men either killed or wounded, he was burdened with more than fifty prisoners of war, and he was surrounded on every side by the gathering Indians. Furthermore, he was worried about his wagon train, which might appear at any moment and which he would be unable to protect.

"As it was now lacking but an hour of night," Custer later wrote, "we had to make an effort to get rid of the Indians, who still loitered in strong force on the hills within plain view of our position. Our main desire was to draw them off from the direction in which our train might be approaching and thus render it secure from attack until under the protection of the entire command, when we could defy any force our enemies could muster against us. The last lodge having been destroyed and all the ponies except those required for the pursuit having been killed, the command was drawn in and united near the village. Making dispositions to overcome any resistance which might be offered to our advance by throwing out a strong force of skirmishers, we set out down the valley in the direction where the other villages had been reported and toward the hills on which were collected the greatest number of Indians.

"The column moved forward in one body with colors flying and band playing, while our prisoners, all mounted on captured ponies, were under sufficient guard immediately in rear of the advanced troops. For a few moments after our march began the Indians on the hills remained silent spectators, evidently at a loss at first to comprehend our intentions in thus setting out at the hour of the evening and directing our course as if another night march was contemplated; and more than all, in the direction of their villages, where all that they possessed was supposed to be. This aroused them to action, as we could plainly see considerable commotion among them—chiefs riding hither and thither, as if in anxious consultation with each other as to the course to be adopted. Whether the fact that they could not fire upon our advance without endangering their own people who were prisoners in our hands or some other reason prevailed with them, they never offered to fire a shot or retard our movements in any manner, but instead assembled their outlying detachments as rapidly as possible and began a precipitated movement down the valley in advance of us, fully impressed with the idea, no doubt, that our purpose was to overtake their flying people and herds and administer the same treatment to them that the occupants of the upper village had received.

"This was exactly the effect I desired, and our march was conducted with such appearance of determination and rapidity that this conclusion on their part was a most natural one."

The Indians were apparently taken aback by Custer's daring move. If they had attacked or if they could have kept him pinned down in the valley without supplies, they might have defeated him. But they did not understand that he was simply bluffing, for he himself realized he could not attack the villages downstream. But they withdrew and gave him a victory. He marched to the next village, discovered its occupants had fled, and burned it. Then he returned to the remains of Black Kettle's village and began retracing his trail, hoping to find his wagon train before the Indians did. At two o'clock in the morning, he sent one squadron ahead to reinforce the train and let the other men rest. The following day he met his wagon train and began the march back to Camp Supply.

General Sheridan was so pleased by Custer's performance that he left Camp Supply to greet him and review his troops. "Every one was anxious to greet the victors of the Washita," wrote a man who was there, "and it was with considerable impatience that the appearance of the column was looked for. Shortly after the sun had passed meridian, a cluster of dark objects appearing upon the crest of a hill, about a mile distant, accompanied with shouts and the firing of musketry, announced their approach. The mules and horses, grazing in the valleys near by, hearing these unusual sounds, stampeded in great alarm from all directions towards camp. On the summit of the hill the head of the column halted for a few moments. Meanwhile, Sheridan, accompanied by his staff and a number of officers of the garrison, took a position in the valley. All the officers and soldiers, not on duty, assembled in the vicinity of the fort to witness the warlike pageant.

"The troopers now resumed their march, and as they descended the hill, the flashing of sabres and carbines, and the shouts of the men, were in wild counterpart of the dreary surroundings of their departure a week before."

They and their superiors counted themselves as victors. They had marched out into the unknown, met the enemy, and defeated them. After the long months of humiliation along the Bozeman Trail, the army had exacted a revenge of sorts. But even from a military point of view, the victory had not been a great one. Custer had attacked by surprise a village composed largely of friendly Indians, and he had had the advantage of many trees for shelter. Nevertheless he had lost two officers and nineteen enlisted men killed and three officers and eleven enlisted men wounded. He had also nearly led his command into complete destruction by not knowing of the proximity of the other villages. Only his daring, but desperate, march down the valley saved him and his men. Even then, if the Indians had been as numerous as he believed, they probably would have organized themselves and routed him.

Reaction to the "battle"—if it could be called a battle—was strong across the country. The army and many Westerners considered it a great victory. As one scout said when he was asked if they had had a fight, "Weel, we've had suthing; you may call it fittin, but I call it wipin' out the varmints. . . ." But other Americans took a different opinion. Once again, in their minds, the army had desperately hunted for Indians to attack and punish, and once again had attacked a village that was largely made up of Indians friendly to the Americans. This, they thought, was merely a repetition of Chivington's massacre at Sand Creek and the victims were mostly the same Cheyennes. And peace had not yet come to the plains.

IX

An Adopted Brother

IN February, 1869, the damp cold of winter lay over Washington, D.C. In the mornings the fog rose from the surface of the Potomac and veiled both banks of the river. Beyond its shores the country had been restored to unity, and hostile armies no longer looked forward to the day when they could ride their horses into its waters and enter the capital, victorious over their enemies.

Yet in many respects the unity was more superficial than real. The country had suffered grievously from the war, particularly in the South, where the people had given so much to their cause, receiving nothing in return but a shattered economy, a disrupted society, and sad memories of those who had died in battle. Even the blacks, who at least had won their legal freedom, often found that their condition had not basically improved.

The city itself was split by dissension and bitter hatreds. The Radicals had gained control of the Republican Party and of Congress and were intent on pushing through legislation that would punish the Southern states for their rebellion against the Union. Often vicious and bigoted, they had plagued President Andrew Johnson, destroying his programs, frustrating his administration, and finally instituting impeachment proceedings against him. Although he was ably defended and the case against him was without foundation, he was saved only by the votes of seven Republican Senators, whose sense of decency led them to desert their party and sacrifice their political careers.

In the election that followed shortly afterwards, General Grant was the candidate of the Republicans. The campaign was bitter. If the

Republicans won, they envisioned prolonged political supremacy through black suffrage in the South, and this would give them the opportunity to continue their economic policies. The Democrats, already shaken by the Civil War, saw in victory a chance to rebuild their party and reverse the Republican trend toward economic exploitation. When the returns were in, Grant had won the electoral votes of all but eight states and had carried the country by a popular majority of 300,000. But the election had been closer than it might appear. Three Southern states had been excluded, and six others were tightly controlled under the Reconstruction laws. This had helped him in the Electoral College. His popular majority had also included about 700,000 newly enfranchised black votes. Nevertheless, to many people he remained the great hero of the Civil War who had finally reversed a series of defeats, and in February, 1869, they looked forward to his inauguration the following month.

In the same month, in one of the last acts of the Johnson administration, the Senate ratified the treaty concluded with Red Cloud the preceding October. Yet it was already clear that the treaty was unacceptable to the Sioux chief. The headquarters of the new reservation at Fort Randall on the Missouri River was a place only the most conciliatory of the Sioux were willing to go. These included the Indians who used to camp regularly near Fort Laramie and the followers of Spotted Tail, who lived in the valley of the White River. Although many Americans did not realize it, the location of the agency headquarters and the trading posts was just as important to the Indians as the location of the nearest store was to the white men. Although they were nomadic, they did not want to travel hundreds of miles away from their hunting grounds either to collect their annuity goods or do their trading. Such trips worked a real hardship on them, because they not only had to stop their hunting, but they also had to kill additional meat to provide themselves with food for the trip. By cutting off their rations at Fort Laramie and issuing them only at Fort Randall, the Americans were trying to force them to move. But Red Cloud still insisted on trading at Fort Laramie and apparently thought the treaty permitted him to.

In March, the month in which President Grant was inaugurated, Red Cloud appeared on the north bank of the river with about a thousand of his people. If he had been in a hostile frame of mind, he might have been able to capture the fort, but he was not. All he wanted was permission to trade. He was given some provisions and told to go to Fort Randall, but instead he spent the summer in the Wind River country.

He was not alone in wishing to reestablish Fort Laramie as a trading center. Many of the traders also wished for the same. One of these was a man named John Richard, Jr., a half-breed whose father also was a trader. Somehow he obtained documents that permitted him to trade with the Sioux away from Fort Randall (it was later claimed that he obtained them by fraud) and set himself up in business near Laramie. For a while he prospered, for the Indians liked him and were glad to have a nearby trader who could supply them. But in September, 1869, he got into a fight with an army corporal and killed him. Before the authorities could arrest him, he fled for safety to the Indians and took refuge with Red Cloud's band. He had considerable influence over the Sioux leader and fully supported his demands for the right to trade near Laramie, inciting him to resist further any effort to move him to Fort Randall. Wild rumors began to reach the small garrison at Laramie, and during the winter of 1869–70, the white men heard that Red Cloud intended to appear at the fort with a large number of warriors and give the Americans the choice of either trading or fighting. As the days lengthened, the white men waited anxiously for the approaching crisis; but in March, 1870, when Red Cloud did come to the fort, it was only to ask for goods and not to threaten the soldiers.

But even if he appeared unwilling to wage war again, he was equally opposed to moving to Fort Randall. Neither threats nor promises were able to make him change his mind. Finally the authorities decided to send him to Washington, D.C., to meet the Secretary of the Interior and the President. They thought that if he and the other Indians in the delegation saw firsthand the power and might of the United States they would become more subservient and pliable.

After some confusion as to who would be included in the party, the Indians left Fort Laramie in May, 1870. Opinion varied widely over the probable outcome of this experiment. Some were optimistic, some pessimistic, and many persons, especially Western settlers, thought the journey should not be made at all. Spotted Tail was already in the capital, having arrived with a delegation from his agency a few days earlier; and the white men accompanying the chiefs were afraid they would quarrel, because there was much ill-feeling between them. But the two men shook hands, and this obstacle was passed.

Little else was accomplished, however. Red Cloud saw the Secretary of the Interior, but aside from the secretary's promising to send a telegram to Laramie saying the delegation had arrived safely, the meeting produced no results. The Indians were then taken to the Capitol, where they visited the dome and watched the Senators debate a bill, an experience that ordinarily does not prove exciting even to Americans. The next day they were escorted to the Arsenal and the Navy Yard. They watched a fifteen-inch gun—the largest they had ever seen—being fired. The shell went hurtling down the Potomac, and they observed it ricochet from the water some four or five miles away. The Marines at the Navy Yard put on a full-dress parade for them. They also inspected a monitor and could not believe the floating ship was made of metal until they had scratched its surface with their knives.

One evening they went to an elegant reception at the White House. Many dignitaries were there, including representatives from the diplomatic corps, and they were served strawberries and ice cream in the State Dining Room. But such sights and treatment did not affect their judgment. When they met again with the Secretary of the Interior, he tried to impress on them the strength of the United States government as evidenced by what they had seen. But when he had finished speaking, Red Cloud answered him by reiterating the same complaints. He did not want to move to Fort Randall, and he did not want roads through his country. He also complained that the white men were surrounding him and taking away his land. This meeting, too, ended inconclusively.

They met once more with the President. Red Cloud repeated his complaints. President Grant, in turn, repeated the desire of the United States government to treat the Indians well. Then they had another meeting with the Secretary of the Interior. He reminded them of the Fort Laramie Treaty of 1868, and Red Cloud replied that he did not remember any such treaty. This flat statement demonstrated the futility of trying to treat with the Indians on the basis of a European culture. They had no way of going over such treaties article by article and had to rely entirely on the impression they received from what the interpreters told them. This impression might be accurate or inaccurate, and there is certainly reason to believe that more than once American negotiators, anxious to get a treaty signed, left an unduly favorable impression of its terms.

In effect, Red Cloud said that the Americans had abandoned their forts, which was what he had wanted. In return, he had signed the treaty, which was what they wanted. But there were still many details to clear up. One more meeting was held, and in order to prevent the trip to Washington from being a complete failure, the government told Red Cloud he could suggest the names of the men he would like to have as agent and trader and that he could live at the headwaters of the Big Cheyenne River.

This was an important concession, for it resolved the question about moving to Fort Randall. That location, so alien to his people, and so distant from his hunting grounds, had now been struck from the list of places where he would have to live. This had been his most important objective, and he had gained it by his steadfastness. None of the displays of might—such as the firing of the gun—or of elegance—such as the reception at the White House—had awed him. Unsophisticated as he was, he had moved through Washington with dignity and never once had lost sight of his goal: agreement that he did not have to live near the Missouri River. The most skilled statesman could hardly have accomplished more for his people.

On the other hand, there were many questions still to answer, such as the exact location of the agency; and given the indecision of the Americans, who still could not make up their minds what to do about the Indians, these details could protract the negotiations further.

From Washington, Red Cloud and the rest of the delegation were taken to New York for a brief visit. They went on a tour of the city, while the citizens stared at these Indians from the wilderness in the West. The day after his arrival he was scheduled to make a speech at Cooper Institute. The hall was packed. Many had come merely to see the man who had defeated the American army, but also many were there because of a real interest in the Indians and their cause. Red Cloud spoke eloquently of his people's problems, and when he was through, the audience applauded loudly.

After that, he set out for home while the nation debated over the success of the journey. Some thought it had been highly successful and that Red Cloud had been so impressed by what he had seen that he would never again wage war against the Americans. Others were far less certain, and many believed the trip had been a waste of time and money. The only way to settle the question of Indians, they argued, was to fight them. If they were beaten badly enough and made to suffer, they would finally agree to keep the peace. For the most part, these opinions were just about the same as they had been when the journey was first proposed, and the results of the Washington trip had not affected them.

After his return to the West, Red Cloud talked to the Sioux about making a permanent peace with the Americans, and the government agreed to send out yet another peace commission, this one headed by Felix Brunot, chairman of the Board of Indian Commissioners. Brunot was an able man, but the council followed the pattern of so many others. Red Cloud repeated his list of grievances, including the white men's invasion of his people's lands and his desire for an agency on the North Platte. But neither point was negotiable. Brunot could not stem the flood of emigrants, nor did he have authority to permit a trading post where Red Cloud wanted one, for the government was determined to separate the Indians from the passing stream of travelers.

The council went on for several days in the early fall of 1870, the principal chiefs and the American negotiators sitting on the porch of the commander's house, while around them were gathered soldiers, civilians, and Indians, all listening to the endless speeches and words that were getting neither side anywhere. At the end of the council, the commission gave away the usual assortment of gifts and went home.

This long series of fruitless councils was beginning to have an effect on Red Cloud. Before the Treaty of 1868, he had been one of the Sioux's outstanding leaders, capable of organizing them into a fighting force and waging a protracted war. But he had now lost his bargaining position, for, having become a spokesman for peace, he could not suddenly return to being one for war. Yet having forced the Americans to abandon Forts Philip Kearny and C. F. Smith, his dealings with them now were not producing the results he and the other Indians wanted. Although the Americans did not understand it, each month of delay was lowering Red Cloud's standing among the Sioux generally. The Americans considered him a great chief—and he had been—but gradually they had been destroying him.

The argument over the location of the trading post went on throughout 1871 with neither side yielding. Winter came over the plains, the winds piled the snows in drifts, the soldiers felt the cold at Fort Laramie, and the Indians lay in camp in the most sheltered places they could find. But still there was no formal peace. Everything depended entirely on the goodwill of each side, and the settlers were growing restive, for they would never feel safe until the Sioux were on a reservation and reporting regularly to an agent. (A temporary agency had been set up down the river from Fort Laramie, but this did not satisfy either Red Cloud or the government.)

The negotiations continued to drag on, although both sides were beginning to think about settling the Sioux on the White River, which runs east in southern Kansas into the Missouri. Here the Indians thought they would have sufficient water and game, and the officials in charge of them were willing to let them go there. Weary and tired of talking, Red Cloud asked that he be allowed to go to Washington again, and permission was granted him. In May he was back in the capital and saw the President and the Secretary of the Interior once more. They were in a more conciliatory mood. Although Red Cloud had lost much of his former stature among the Indians, he was still an important figure and could be a valuable friend.

President Grant warned Red Cloud that the area he had chosen might soon be settled by the whites, but he had no objection to his living there temporarily. The Secretary of the Interior said much the same thing but agreed to protect the Indians as long as he could.

With this assurance, which Red Cloud probably thought would at least last his lifetime, he returned to the West and began, more strongly than before, to argue the cause of peace. When an Indian agent was going north to talk to some of the other tribes, Red Cloud gave him a message of peace to carry to some of the other leaders. He reminded them that he had once fought a war against the Americans but told them that was now over. The white men were taking care of him and his people, and he saw no reason not to trust them. But the northern Indians like Sitting Bull were not interested in following his lead. They had no sense of the power of the Americans, the vast numbers of people ready to explode out of the East, their belief in the "manifest destiny" that would cause them to sweep over the continent, or of the advanced tools and other equipment that would enable them to do it. Now that Red Cloud had closed the Bozeman Trail, these Indians thought the threat to their land was removed, and they saw no point in exchanging their territory for a ration of trade goods. Nor did they realize the profound effect that Red Cloud's surrender would have on themselves. As the number of resisting Indians dwindled, the army could concentrate its limited resources on those that remained hostile. So Sitting Bull rode across the plains, proud, free, and sure of himself, in spite of the tide of the western expansion creeping closer and closer to him.

Finally in the early fall of 1872, the agent near Laramie was ready to move Red Cloud and the Indians who were with him to the White River. Many of them were willing to go, but some were reluctant. In spite of his earlier agreement with the Americans' plans, Red Cloud joined the latter. Most probably he had lost influence among the Sioux because of his endorsement of peace and was now trying to regain it by being more antagonistic. Nevertheless he, too, finally gave in, and the Red Cloud Agency was established on the White River.

For the Oglala Sioux, this was the end of an era. Obviously their troubles with the white men were not over. President Grant had told them the land they wanted for their reservation was land that the American settlers would also soon want. And when he said this, he implied that—treaty or no treaty—the Americans would take it away from the Indians. This implication was lost on Red Cloud. He thought he had fought his war to an honorable, if not altogether happy, conclusion, preserving the way of life that he and his people had led for so many years. Instead he had taken a step from which he could not retreat, a step toward at least the temporary degradation of his people.

At the sites of burned-out Fort Philip Kearny and Fort C. F. Smith, the rains and snows were dissolving the ashes, and the beetles were eating away at the remains of the wood. Along the edges of the barren ground, the grass and brush were gradually moving inward, covering it with new growth. The traces of Red Cloud's great victory were being lost, and lost, too, were the fruits he had hoped to gain.

*　　*　　*

Although these events had a direct effect on the future of the Hunkpapas and Sitting Bull, he had taken no part in them except for the meeting with Father De Smet. He continued to treasure the brass and wood crucifix he had received from the priest, but the meeting itself was merely an incident to which he attached little importance. The council at Fort Laramie and the resulting Treaty of 1868 also had no real significance in his eyes, and neither did the completion of the Central Pacific Railroad, which joined the Union Pacific in May, 1869, binding the country together with their metal rails and making east-west traffic safer and faster than ever. But at that time the Hunkpapas did not feel threatened by the Americans' invasion. Most of the Americans' activity was taking place far from their territory, and they had the mistaken idea they were equal to any challenge. So instead of fighting the white men, they concentrated on fighting other Indians just as they had done for so many years. And in these battles Sitting Bull continued to gain glory and prestige.

Also, when the rare opportunity offered itself, they liked to attack the white men; and one such chance came in 1869, the year the last spike was driven in the railroad ties and Red Cloud was still trying to interpret the Treaty of 1868. A lonely mail courier, Frank Grouard, was riding up the Milk River in northern Montana from Fort Peck on the Missouri to Fort Hall. It was early in January, and the snow was blowing in his face. To keep himself warm, he had tied a handkerchief around his throat and was wearing leggings, moccasins, and mittens made of buffalo skins. Although Indians had been making attacks at the mouth of the Milk River, where it empties into the Missouri, he was not expecting trouble this far along in his journey.

Between him and his destination lay a deep gulch. In the rainy season, it was filled with water, but it was now covered with snow. Although he had not seen any Indians, they had seen him and were preparing to capture him when he was in the gulch, where they could hide among the big trees that grew in the bottom.

Completely unsuspecting, he rode his horse down the twenty-foot bank, leading another horse that followed closely behind. The Indians waited until he had started to climb the opposite bank. Then they dashed from the shelter of the trees, closed in on him from behind and, striking him on the back, dragged him from the saddle. In the scuffle he dropped his gun, so he was defenseless except for his hands and feet. One of the Indians wanted to kill him and kept aiming a gun at him, but another was more interested in obtaining his heavy coat and grabbed for it. Grouard wrestled with this Indian and tried to keep his body between himself and the Indian with the gun, thus using his enemy as a shield.

The unequal fight could not have lasted long, but while it was going on, Sitting Bull suddenly appeared at the top of the gulch, carrying in his hand a heavy bow. He told the Indian with the gun not to shoot Grouard but to take him prisoner, and when the Indian refused to listen, he dismounted and struck him with the bow, knocking him to the ground. The other Indian, who had been holding Grouard's coat, let him go, and the entire band began to argue among themselves. There were about fourteen Indians altogether, and finally the one who had wanted to kill Grouard walked away in disgust.

Having won the initial argument, Sitting Bull took out his pipe, sat down, and signaled to Grouard that he should sit down, too. Talking to Grouard in sign language, he indicated that he was leaving and that Grouard was to mount a horse and come with him.

For three days, the band of Sioux traveled down the Milk River toward their camp. Sitting Bull rode ahead to tell the others about the captive, and when Grouard arrived, the Indians were waiting to look at him. He did not know their language or their customs and expected that they would torture him and burn him alive. But instead they led him to one of the tepees and told him to dismount and go inside. There was Sitting Bull, waiting for him. Grouard was suffering from exposure to the cold, his body was swollen from the effects of the trip, and he feared the horrors that might lie ahead for him. But Sitting Bull merely motioned to him to sit down on a pile of buffalo robes. Seated on the warm robes, with the fire burning brightly in the center of the tepee, he soon fell asleep.

While Grouard was resting, the Sioux held a council to debate his fate. Some of them still wanted to kill him, but Sitting Bull was determined to adopt him as a brother, just as he had done with the small Assiniboin boy, whom he had named Jumping Bull. Partly he may have been influenced by the color of Grouard's skin, which was unusually swarthy. (At various times Grouard claimed he was the son of a missionary father who had married a girl in the South Pacific; at others he said that he was partly black.) In any case the color of his skin was unusual, and this may have influenced Sitting Bull in his desire to save him, although it is difficult to see how he could have noticed this while Grouard was fighting with the Indians in the snowstorm. More likely he presented a miserable figure, surrounded and disarmed. Since he had not yet been killed in the fight, Sitting Bull saw another opportunity to gain more prestige by adopting a friendless man.

Two of the Sioux leaders, Gall and No Neck, wanted to kill Grouard, and they were men of standing among the warriors. But Sitting Bull was determined to have his way. He must have been an imposing figure as he stood before the council, with his long black hair and large, expressive eyes that moved from one Indian to another.

"The coups of Sitting Bull," he said, "are like the stars, shining and almost numberless. I look; I act; I talk afterwards. That which I will is so. The captive in the Sioux lodge is resting on robes that Sitting Bull has taken with his own hand from the buffalo, and it is my will that the captive shall not die. When Little Assiniboin [Jumping Bull] was taken from his people, it was Sitting Bull who bore him to his lodge and made him his brother. So with the paleface within the lodge of Sitting Bull this night. He is Standing Bear, the brother of Sitting Bull. My will is spoken."

Jumping Bull had made a fine reputation for himself as a warrior and was well liked by the other Indians. Sitting Bull's relatives and friends often spoke of his wisdom in sparing him when he was a boy, and this may have helped sway the council. For the warriors listened to Sitting Bull and finally decided to let him have his wish.

Grouard could not at first speak the Sioux language, so he was unable to take care of himself. Also he was perhaps in danger of being attacked by some of the Indians who had not approved of Sitting Bull's decision, and Sitting Bull may have thought that he might try to escape. So he placed his new brother in the care of his sister, White Cow.

She had raised Jumping Bull, and she was willing to take on Grouard. For many months, the white man found himself a virtual prisoner, and although White Cow was always kind to him, he had no opportunity even to try to flee. Gradually he learned a few words of Sioux, but he could not adjust himself to living only on meat without even salt or pepper. Bread was what he most wanted, and he thought about bread by day and dreamed about it by night. Sometimes he would stir on the buffalo robes that served as a bed and wake up just as he was dreaming that he was about to have a cup of coffee and a piece of bread.

He thought about escaping, but he was never left alone. He even contemplated killing himself, but he had no opportunity to do so. The diet and his own state of mind began to impair his health, and he finally became seriously ill. Later he could never tell how long he had lain semiconscious on his pile of buffalo robes when one day he opened his eyes and saw White Cow working at the fire. To his surprise and delight, she had sensed what he needed and was baking some dough. He looked with amazement as she finally drew the bread from the ashes and was so overcome with pleasure that he could barely bring himself to eat it. Next she took some coffee, placed it in a cloth, and ground it by pounding it. Then she boiled it for him in a can of water. She had procured the ingredients for this meal from some of the agency Indians, who, after they received their annual supplies, would trade some of the goods at extraordinarily high prices to the Indians who did not live on a reservation.

From that day on, Grouard began to take a greater interest in his surroundings and to adapt himself to his new way of life. White Cow gradually weaned him from his taste for white men's food, and he began to learn to speak to the Sioux, first by using sign language and then becoming familiar with their words. He also acquired a nickname among the Indians. When Sitting Bull had first seen him, dressed in his heavy clothing and struggling with the Indians in the gulch, he had thought that Grouard was a bear. Consequently he had given him the name Standing Bear. Because bears will often reach out and seize their victims in a "bear hug," the Indians often referred to them as "grabbers," and Grouard became known as the Grabber.

The months wore on, but Sitting Bull still did not entirely trust his adopted brother. Although summer had come and the camp was constantly on the move, Grouard was almost always under guard. Wherever he went, either Jumping Bull or White Eagle, a cousin of Sitting Bull, went with him. Nevertheless Sitting Bull decided to give his adopted brother a gun, an old flintlock he owned and which was so inaccurate as to be barely usable. Grouard was delighted with the gift. Regardless of the condition of the gun, he was pleased to have a firearm in his hands again after so long a time without one.

One day in the early fall, when the village was on one of its last buffalo hunts of the season, some of the warriors gathered for one of their many gambling games. Before playing, they laid their guns and arrows to one side, and so they were unprepared when a large deer came running over the top of a nearby hill. Grouard, however, had his flintlock, which he had cleaned and oiled as best he could. While the others watched, he raised the barrel toward the deer and held his fire until the animal had come within the maximum range of the old gun. Then, squeezing the trigger, he fired. To everyone's surprise, the deer fell down dead.

It was a good shot, if perhaps a lucky one, and the Sioux admired Grouard for it. Sitting Bull gave him a more modern gun, and many of the men asked him to accompany them when they went hunting. In this way, he became a useful and valued member of the band, and Sitting Bull could congratulate himself that he was repeating the success he had had when he adopted Jumping Bull.

While Grouard was living with the Sioux, Sitting Bull once again had a chance to prove his bravery. It was winter, and the Indians, as usual, had gone into camp. Food, however, was running low, so Sitting Bull led a group of warriors on a hunt for game. Somehow the Crows, their traditional enemies, learned they were absent and decided to raid the village and steal some of the horses. Fortunately Sitting Bull's group came across the Crows' trail and immediately guessed what they were planning. So they raced back to the village and drove the Crows away. As the Crows fled to the west, the Sioux, anxious to kill as many of the enemy as possible, followed. But the Crows found an ideal place to make a stand and took up a position on a rocky knoll that amounted almost to a fortress. It rose high enough above the surrounding ground to dominate it in every direction, and in many places the rock of which it was composed presented a sheer face to any attackers.

The Sioux rode around the knoll, hoping they could get some shots at their enemy, but the Crows were too well sheltered by the rock. No matter what the Sioux did, they could not draw the Crows out into the open, and it looked as though the Sioux might have to let them go. But before doing so, they decided to hold a council. During the meeting, Sitting Bull said they should not let the band escape now that they had them cornered, but he agreed that the only way to dislodge them was to charge the knoll. This meant certain death for some of the Sioux, but he was willing to take the chance and would lead them.

Mounting their horses, they prepared for the desperate charge. Sitting Bull raced ahead of the others, reached the foot of the knoll, jumped off his horse, and began to work his way through the rocks. Climbing from one to another and managing to avoid the Crows' fire, he was the first to reach the top. The others followed as quickly as they could and soon joined him.

The scene was a bloody one. There were about thirty Crows and an equal number of Sioux, but the Sioux had the advantage of the initiative. There was no way the Crows could escape, because to leave the knoll was to leave all cover and stand exposed to the arrows and bullets of the Sioux. Soon the struggle was over. The rocks were covered with the bodies of the dead and wounded, and the Sioux were in command of the knoll. After scalping their dead enemies, they returned to their village.

Although they had suffered many casualties, they considered it a great victory and celebrated it by having one of the greatest scalp dances that Grouard ever saw during the years he spent with them, and they also marked it down in their winter count. During the fighting, Sitting Bull had counted several coups and emerged from it a greater hero than ever before.

The encroachment of the Americans on the Indians' territories was putting pressure on all the tribes. Those who tried to stay free found increasing competition among themselves for the hunting lands that still remained. The Sioux had already had to fight to make a niche for themselves on the plains when they were first driven west. Now they had to fight to retain it, as other tribes were pushed back by the

Americans into the small area that was still relatively wild and free. Among these were the Flatheads, who were coming in from the west, and the Hunkpapa Sioux decided to go on the warpath against them. After riding for several days, they sent scouts ahead to look for a village. While they were waiting, the warriors asked Sitting Bull to prophesy what was going to happen, for he had a reputation as a medicine man. He finally foretold a battle within a short time and that he himself would be wounded.

In a little while, the scouts returned with the news that they had found a Flathead camp. After talking among themselves, the warriors decided to adopt their traditional strategy of sending a few warriors ahead as decoys, while the main body remained behind in an ambush. A few of the younger warriors therefore rode out ahead until they could see the Flatheads' camp.

One of the Flatheads was driving his horses out to graze, and the Sioux rode hard toward him. Finding himself so greatly outnumbered, the Flathead deserted his herd and raced back to the camp to give the alarm. The Sioux rounded up the horses and started back toward the ambush, while the Flathead village, now fully aroused, mounted their horses and came in pursuit.

So far the strategy was working well, just as it had so many times before. But to demonstrate his bravery, one of the Sioux turned back and charged the Flatheads by himself. After he had done this several times, the other Sioux could no longer resist the temptation to win glory for themselves also, so instead of leading the Flatheads to the ambush, they turned around and began fighting.

This rash action, of course, destroyed the overall strategy. Realizing the decoys were no longer serving as decoys and not wishing to be left out of the fight, the other warriors galloped out of their hiding place and joined in the battle. Soon the Flatheads were in full retreat toward their camp.

Although the Sioux were winning, one of their leaders decided that both sides had suffered sufficient losses and that, instead of attacking the Flatheads' camp, the Sioux should stop the fighting. Most of the warriors agreed with him, but Sitting Bull and several others did not. They remained on the battlefield, hoping the Flatheads would return. Soon some of them did come back to recover their dead, and Sitting Bull and the warriors with him began the fighting over again. Once more they routed the Flatheads, who again retreated toward their camp with the small group of Sioux warriors chasing them.

Just before they reached the camp, one of the Flatheads suddenly dropped from his horse and, turning around to face Sitting Bull, put an arrow to his bow. Sitting Bull came charging on, his horse's hooves beating against the ground. Seeing the Flathead's intentions, he threw up one arm to shield himself. And he was just in time. The arrow flew through the air, but instead of striking Sitting Bull in the body, it pierced his arm.

No longer able to fight, Sitting Bull quickly swung his horse around and raced back to the main body of Sioux warriors. The Flathead undoubtedly sent another arrow after him, but this time he missed his mark, and Sitting Bull escaped without further injury. The wound in his arm was serious, but the Indians cut off the head of the arrow and drew out the shaft, and in time the wound healed.

As Grouard later commented, "Some men who have written of Sitting Bull, claiming that he was a medicine man and not a warrior, are unacquainted with the circumstances surrounding his life among the Indians themselves. No man in the Sioux nation was braver in battle than Sitting Bull, and he asked none of his warriors to take any chances that he was not willing at all times to share. I could recall a hundred different instances coming under my own observation to prove Sitting Bull's bravery, and in the first great Sun Dance that I ever witnessed after my capture by the Sioux, I heard Sitting Bull recount his 'coups in action.' They numbered sixty-three, most of them being victories over Indian enemies."

*　　*　　*

Bravery was the quality that the Sioux respected most, and although Sitting Bull had many times demonstrated his courage, his adopted brother, Grouard, had not. Some day, Grouard was certain, he would have to undergo some form of torture. "I did not know what to expect," he later wrote, "and while I dreaded what I knew was inevitable, I found myself wishing they would make the test and free my mind of the suspense I suffered. I knew very well they would invent some means of making the test as excruciatingly painful as possible."

The test came early in 1872. The Indians were camped near the Yellowstone and were preparing for their religious ceremonies. In these the sweat bath played an important part; and so with willow bows, the Sioux constructed a dome-shape frame over which they placed robes, making it almost airtight. In the center, they dug a small hollow in the earth in which they placed heated stones. Outside they collected firewood to use in building the necessary fire. When the time arrived, the participants entered the structure and engaged in the ceremonial rites such as smoking the sacred pipe. Then one of the medicine men poured water on the stones, and the steam rose in the air. It was so hot that the men could feel their skin was being seared, but they chewed sage and spat it on the parts of their flesh that seemed to be burning. This cooled it and brought relief from the pain.

Before Grouard was allowed to enter the hut for the sweat bath, he had to undergo another religious ceremony of extreme importance that was sometimes performed before the Sun Dance. The Sioux believed the flesh represented ignorance, and so to propitiate the spirits, they would offer pieces of it, taken from their own bodies. This was the rite that Grouard was called upon to perform.

"I had no idea," he later wrote, "what torment and suffering I would be forced to undergo but was not kept long in doubt. I made up my mind, however, that if it was possible, no groans should escape my lips during the period of torture. The first thing done was to select four braves to operate upon me. They took positions upon each side of my body and, with needles, raised up the flesh between the shoulder and the elbow on each arm and cut out pieces each about the size of a pea. . . . I did not mind it much at first, the cutting out, or off, of these pieces causing little pain. But the savages took the flesh off in five rows on each arm, and before they had finished the job, I was suffering the agonies of the damned. The pain became so intense that it seemed to dart in streaks from the point where the small particles of flesh were cut off to every portion of my body until at last a stream of untold agony was pouring back and forth from my arms to my heart. I managed to bear the pain, however, without a murmur, great to the delight of Sitting Bull and his faction.

"The next operation," Grouard continued, "consisted of pulling out, one at a time, my eyebrows, eyelashes, and the hairs on my upper lip. After this came the test of fire. They had prepared by previous burning several little cone-shaped blocks of pith from the stalk of sunflower. These blocks were about half an inch in length and very much resembled the pieces of punk the small boy uses on the Fourth of July with which to light his firecracker. I know they hold fire a long while, at any rate. Well, they placed four of these blocks half an inch apart on my right wrist and ignited them, and I lay there while the cruel fire burned down into my flesh without giving any sign of the torture I was enduring. When the fire had burned itself out—when the little blocks had been consumed—I was raised to my feet and shortly afterward put

through the sweat, the Indians being satisfied that I was 'good medicine' and would pass through any ordeal unflinchingly."

But, he added, "Five great ridges rose on my arm, and for a
couple of months I could not bear the softest kind of fur to touch the
half-raw spots. The ceremonies attending my tortures lasted four
hours, but it seemed to me like a year."

When he had recovered from the wounds inflicted on him, Grouard
was regarded by the other Indians as a full-fledged member of the
band. He had already proved his ability as a marksman and hunter,
but now he had performed one of the ceremonies that brought prestige
among the Sioux and was a credit both to himself and to Sitting
Bull.

In the Indians' world, danger and hardship lurked in every direction, and it did not always come from man. Once when Grouard had
been sent out with two other Indians to scout for a buffalo herd, they
came across a bull and a cow. Ordinarily on an expedition like this,
they were not expected to kill any animals themselves, but they were
hungry for meat and decided they could kill one of these without
frightening the main herd, which was some distance away. Because
Grouard was the best shot of the three men, he was chosen to shoot
one. The animals were out of range, so he crawled into a hiding place
at a point he thought they would pass. When they approached, he shot
and downed the cow. But instead of walking on, the bull began to sniff
the blood; and as it did so, it began bellowing and pawing the dirt.

Grouard was lying flat on the ground, and he knew that if he
moved, the bull would see him and charge. So he stayed still, but
finally after about an hour of waiting, he tried to put powder into his
gun. The bull saw him and, with its head lowered, it ran toward him.
Just behind Grouard was a small gully about three feet deep. He
rolled over into it just in time to escape the animal's horns. Although it was unable to reach him, it stood looking into the gully and
pawing the earth.

After what seemed like a long time, it finally lost interest and returned to the dead cow. Once again Grouard tried to load his gun, and
once again the bull saw him and came racing back. This time Grouard
was able to work himself further into the gully, so he was safer, but
he was still a helpless prisoner of the angry animal. As the buffalo
would not leave, he lay there trapped until darkness fell, when finally
the bull walked off, and Grouard was able to rejoin his hunting companions, who had been watching but had been unable to help him.

On another buffalo hunt, the Indians were near the Yellowstone River when they came across a herd. During the hunting, Grouard had gotten ahead of the others and had dismounted to skin the animals he had shot, when he noticed his horse running around in half-circles. The buffalo pony he was using had been given him by an Indian, who had told him that the horse was especially useful, because it would always warn of danger. Grouard had attached little significance to the remark, but he untied the horse and rode to the top of a nearby hill and looked around. Seeing nothing, he returned to the carcasses he had been skinning.

But the horse would not be quieted, so Grouard finally became concerned, mounted it, and started riding back to the place where they had left the pack horses. He had gone about two miles when he heard the sound of gunfire. Looking back, he saw a band of Crow warriors attacking the hunters. He tried to give the alarm, but before the Sioux could organize a counterattack, the Crows had killed several men. Such warfare was part of the Indians' way of life on the plains, and they waged it incessantly. No village was safe from attack by its enemies.

In addition to the dangers of buffalo hunting and enemy ambushes, Grouard learned about the other hardships of the Indians' existence, one of which was hunger. During the summer, when the buffalo were fat and the herds large, the Indians lived well. There was plenty of meat for everyone, and no one went hungry. But at other seasons, when the herds were thin or the hunting poor, the Indians were often hungry. As Grouard said later, "The one great problem among the Indians was the securing of food. All other matters were of secondary importance."

Once when they were camped along the Missouri, they were so low on supplies that it looked as though the band might face a period of starvation. On the opposite bank, however, they saw two buffalos. The weather being cold, the river was filled with pieces of ice that made it difficult to cross. But the need for food was so great that Grouard and several Indians decided to take the risk. Tying their ammunition pouches to their heads and their guns to logs, they plunged into the river. The water drove the sharp pieces of ice against their bodies, lacerating them badly, but they kept on swimming. When they reached the other side, all of them were covered with bloody wounds, but they shot the two buffalos, butchered them, and then made a raft on which they carried the meat back to a grateful village.

At another time, Grouard, as many Indians had done, almost starved to death. The band's supply of ammunition was running dangerously low, but they were expecting a party of reservation Indians, who were bringing them more. Off in the distance they saw what looked like a smoke signal, and Grouard and two Indians were to meet the Indians and lead them into camp. Because they did not expect to travel far, they took with them only a day's rations.

The distance was farther than they thought it would be, and they ran out of food. Grouard shot twice at game, but this time he missed, so they were left with nothing. When they reached the point from which the smoke signal might have been sent, they found the remains of a fire but no trace of a village. Apparently the fire had been started accidentally, not as a signal. So they could not obtain food from their friends.

"On the way back to the village," Grouard later wrote, "all three of us became nearly insane from hunger, having been eight days without a particle of food. We were very weak. When we were within twenty miles of the village, I managed to kill three prairie chickens with my bow and arrow. I tried to induce my companions to eat as sparingly of the meat as possible, but they were so ravenously hungry that I could do nothing with them. I saved the necks of the chickens for myself, which I roasted and thus got the benefit of the juice from the meat, which satisfied me until my arrival in camp. My two companions ate every particle of the bodies of the chickens raw. They were taken sick very shortly afterwards and did not live long enough after reaching the village to enjoy another meal. We were ten days making the trip."

Even when he arrived at the camp, Grouard could not satisfy his hunger because he was so easily nauseated by food. Gradually, however, he became stronger, but the memory of those ten days remained with him all his life.

The fire that had sent them on this long and dreadful trip had been an act of fate, but sometimes fate behaved more kindly. One winter they ran so short of food that they even killed and ate all their dogs, and there seemed to be no hope for the band. Around them lay the snow, and no living thing moved through the white except their horses. And these they were reluctant to kill, because to destroy their horses in that country was the equivalent of committing suicide.

One night as he lay in a tepee, Grouard began to dream of deer ribs and became so hungry that he decided to go hunting regardless of the lateness of the hour. Mounting his mule, he rode to a good hunting ground and made his camp. The next morning he was up early and soon discovered the tracks of a herd of elk. Leaving his mule behind, he raced about three miles to get ahead of the herd and hid himself where the elk would walk past him. This would give him a chance to pick out the fattest one. As the elk moved by, he made his choice and fired. The elk fell dead, but the rest of the herd, instead of stampeding as they ordinarily would have done, began milling in a bunch. This time fortune was smiling on Grouard and the Indians, and he took advantage of it. Shooting as quickly as he could, he killed thirty-one of the animals.

After butchering the elk, he loaded his mule with as much meat as it could carry and started back to camp. Someone saw him coming and told the others, and so the women came out to meet him. Hungry and worried about their families, they stripped the meat from the mule's load before he even reached the village; and when he told them there was more meat waiting for them, they were overjoyed. The next morning they all rode out to the hunting ground, and the camp was well stocked with food until they found some buffalo.

That was the existence of the Sioux, the existence that Sitting Bull loved so much. At one time they might be eating well and making merry. At another they might be mourning their dead. They lived in the present, not the future, taking each day as it came and accepting its gladness or its sorrows with little thought—and no fear—for the day after. Time was an endless pattern of seasons, of snows or heat, droughts or rains, each with its own feasting or famine.

And always they lived in the presence of danger. Noises in the night might mean the enemy had entered the camp on a raiding party, ready to strip them of their horses. Noises in the daytime might be the sound of gunfire signaling a battle between tribes. There was also the danger inherent in the buffalo hunts when a horse tripping over a stone or a bull maddened by the smell of blood could mean death by hooves or horns. And the specter of starvation always loomed large. A shortage of buffalos or a shortage of ammunition could quickly spell hunger, not the hunger of a person who has missed a few meals but the hunger of the weak and dying.

Nor was everything peaceful even among themselves. Sitting Bull, Grouard observed, led one faction of the Hunkpapas; and No Neck and Gall led the others. Often they struggled against each other for power as they had done over Grouard himself. It had been Gall and No Neck who had argued for his death, and Sitting Bull who had wished to adopt him as a brother. In the battle of wills, Sitting Bull had won, but this did not mean he always had his way. Although he was a man of standing among the Indians, they did not always agree with him or even do what he wanted.

Sometimes the struggles between the Sioux became violent. Once when the Hunkpapas were visiting with the Miniconjou Sioux, a great dance was held. During the ceremonies, a warrior mounted his horse and rode around the camp several times. Then he stopped in front of a young man who was beating a drum, removed a bow and arrow that he had held hidden under his blanket, and shot him. Immediately fighting broke out in the camp, as the members of the victim's faction attacked the others. Finally one side was driven from the village, but only after the loss of several lives.

As soon as the struggle started, Sitting Bull went back to his own camp, for he refused to be drawn into an internal struggle among the Miniconjous. But when the battle was over—and a battle it really was—he rounded up some of his horses and took them as a present to the family of the original victim. Then, using his considerable powers of persuasion, he talked to both sides and argued them into making peace. Such an act, of course, further increased his reputation for wisdom and enhanced his prestige among the Sioux.

As long as there were buffalo and as long as he could get enough ammunition to shoot them, he had no other worries. In his limited world, he had risen far and had been a credit to his family. And because he lived at such a distance from the Platte, he had no concern about the white men. Other Sioux could go on reservations, but he assumed the Americans would not come into his land; and if they did, he was equally certain he could defeat them.

X

Surveyors in the North

SITTING BULL had certainly never heard of the Philadelphia financier Jay Cooke, and it is doubtful if Cooke had ever heard of Sitting Bull. Between the two men lay thousands of miles of land— the Appalachians, the broad Mississippi, and the wide plains that were Sitting Bull's home. But the geographical distance between the two was not nearly as great as the intellectual and cultural differences that divided them. Sitting Bull was occupied with hunting the buffalos, raiding the Crows, and finding safe shelter during the winter. In such a world, Cooke would have been a weakling, dependent on the others for survival. But in his own world, the world of finance, he was a giant; and although his dignified banking house in Philadelphia, with the clerks entering the figures in his accounts, seemed far removed from the turbulent camps of the Sioux, he was the most dangerous enemy Sitting Bull had yet encountered, far more dangerous than any major accompanied by a squadron of cavalry.

A handsome man, who inspired confidence in those who met him, Cooke had established an excellent reputation for himself during the Civil War. The Union, unable to finance its armies with taxation and normal borrowing, had resorted to the issuance of paper money with no security behind it and to the sale of bonds. Because there was no ready market for the latter, it turned to Jay Cooke. A master salesman, Cooke used posters, popular songs, inspired newspaper articles, and a host of subagents and was so successful that one issue, which the banks would not touch, was oversubscribed.

Therefore in 1865, Josiah Perham, president of the Northern Pacific Railroad, asked Cooke's help. Perham and his associates did not have sufficient capital to finance the railroad they wished to build, but they were certain that Cooke, with his great skill at raising money, could find the funds they needed. Cooke, however, was not interested and turned them down.

But in 1869, the year after the treaty had been signed at Fort Laramie, he changed his mind. With his usual enthusiasm he plunged into this new effort and gave the company the impetus it had lacked before. So in 1871, while Grouard was living with the Sioux, two surveying parties set out from the east and the west. One left Fort Ellis in Montana and went along the Yellowstone River, turning back before reaching the Bighorn, and the other went as far as the Yellowstone in eastern Montana, cutting a temporary line across the top of the territory that Sitting Bull considered his own. Until then, the Americans had approached him on the south, east, and west, but he still had free access to the plains of Canada without passing a barrier of white settlements. Now this flank, too, was being threatened; and although the two expeditions did not meet and although their reports were inconclusive, the publicity generated by Cooke meant that it was only a question of time before the survey was completed and work on the railroad started.

Having refused to make peace with the Americans, Sitting Bull could not personally visit the trading posts set up on either the Red Cloud or the Spotted Tail agencies. Therefore for most of his supplies —the most important being ammunition—he had to rely on the Indians who did trade with the white men. This was better than nothing, but it was an uncertain source, and he began to look for one that would be more steady and reliable.

To the north of him in Manitoba lived the Metís, the half-breed descendants of French traders. These were almost a race in themselves, suspicious and distrustful of Indian and English-speaking Canadians alike. Near Fort Garry, which later became Winnipeg, they had their own settlement, St. Boniface, on one side of the Red River, while the English-speaking Canadians lived on the other. In 1869, when Jay Cooke agreed to accept responsibility for raising the capital needed by the Northern Pacific, the Hudson's Bay Company ceded its title to this land (it had come from a grant under Charles II) to the Canadian government. The Metís were so disturbed by this change in status and so fearful that their own customs and rights would not be respected that they captured Fort Garry. One of their leaders, Louis

Riel, set himself up as president and arrested the government's representative, Lord Strathcona, when he came to negotiate. Riel became so extreme that he summarily executed a young man from Ottawa for using defiant language, and the government then sent out a military force that compelled him to flee. But many of the Metís remained behind, and it was to them that Sitting Bull looked for help.

In the fall of 1871, he traveled to Manitoba with the hope of making a trading treaty with them. He was gone about a month, and when he came back he was pleased with what he had accomplished, for the Metís agreed to come to the camp later in the year and bring him all the supplies he needed. This agreement, he thought, made him independent of the Americans.

True to their word, about two months later after the snows had fallen, the Metís arrived at the village. But the five sleighs they brought with them did not contain the supplies Sitting Bull had ordered. Instead they were filled with whisky. Having had long experience trading with Indians, the Metís knew exactly what they were doing. The Indians would pay a far higher price for the whisky than they would for the articles they actually needed.

The drinking started almost immediately, and it was not confined to the warriors, for the women drank just as much and got just as drunk. Inevitably fights sprang up between friends as well as enemies. Those who disliked Sitting Bull made their feelings known, and so the camp was torn into factions. Grouard simply mounted his horse and left for the hills, where he stayed until the trouble was over, but Sitting Bull remained.

The warriors in his faction stayed loyal to him and protected him, so he was not hurt; but pandemonium reigned in the village. Drunken Indians roamed over the packed snow, all of them in an ugly temper. Some of them recklessly slit the tepees, destroying in minutes the work of days. Others merely knocked the tepees over, taking pleasure at seeing the poles collapse and the great structures fall to the ground. Yet others, losing all sense of responsibility, began shooting into the herds, killing the horses and mules on which the Indians were so dependent.

But worst of all were the fights among the Indians themselves. Old antagonisms were fueled by the whisky, and all restraint vanished. The resulting fights were vicious, and several Indians were killed, thus increasing the bitterness that was already ripping the village apart. Friends of the dead ones sought out the killers in order to exact vengeance, and so the fighting spread. It might have engulfed the camp and destroyed it if the Metís, taking the remainder of their whisky with them, had not left as soon as they had secured the goods they wanted.

Grouard remained in the hills for three days. When he returned, all that he saw was desolation and despair. For the next three or four days, the Indians walked around in a stunned state, gathering up their belongings and preparing to depart. When they did so, they left in small groups of close relatives. Tradition demanded that they avenge their dead relatives, but this was no time to follow tradition, for that would have only led to endless bloodletting. So the camp dispersed until the Indians had had time to collect their thoughts and reestablish social order.

The event was no credit to Sitting Bull, and the horrors of it made a deep impression on Grouard. The Yankton Sioux, who were not as warlike as the Hunkpapas, had an agency at Fort Peck on the Missouri River in Montana. The following spring, when the snows were melting and a touch of green was coming to the plains, a Yankton Sioux visited the camp. He had been sent by the trader at the agency who wanted to obtain Sitting Bull's business. But although he brought tobacco as a present, he could not persuade Sitting Bull either to come to the trader's or enter into an agreement with him. Sitting Bull argued he already had a treaty with the Metís and must abide by it, although more likely the affair had now become a matter of pride with him. Stubbornly, he wanted to prove he had been right in spite of the disaster he had brought to the Hunkpapas.

In any case, he refused to negotiate with the Indian courier. But Grouard, at great risk to himself, saw a chance to prevent a repetition of the same error. Unknown to Sitting Bull, he gave the Indian a note to take back to the trader, telling him what had happened and asking him if the Metís could be stopped. In a few weeks, the Yankton Sioux returned, bringing with him some of the leaders of his band, for they wanted to make a treaty with Sitting Bull. They also carried with them a letter from the agent asking Grouard to persuade Sitting Bull to come to Fort Peck or, if he could not do that, to come by himself anyway. The Indians, of course, held a council, as they always did when they had an important question to discuss, and Sitting Bull promised to go, although he expressed no interest in making an agreement with any Americans.

With him on the journey he took Grouard, Jumping Bull, and a number of the other Hunkpapas. After a two-day trip, they reached the south bank of the Missouri, and the agent sent rowboats out to ferry them across. It was too late at night to start negotiations, but Grouard had an opportunity to speak to the agent alone and was able to tell him everything that had happened. The agent said that the army was organizing a party to punish the Metís, and he would like Grouard to return and go with it, for he could be helpful in identifying the individual Metís who had brought the whisky.

The following day the Americans held a council with Sitting Bull, but he was not moved by their arguments. Proud and independent, he flatly refused to sign any treaty with them, and the next morning he set out again for the Hunkpapas' village, and Grouard went with him.

Grouard now had to find some excuse for leaving the camp and returning to Fort Peck without Sitting Bull's knowing either his purpose or his destination. Casting around for an excuse, he told Sitting Bull he was going alone on a raid to see if he could steal some horses. Apparently Sitting Bull was pleased that his adopted brother should act so much like a true Indian. He only asked Grouard where he was going; and when Grouard told him that he planned to raid along the Missouri River, Sitting Bull was completely satisfied.

Leaving the camp after dark, Grouard rode hard toward the north, hoping that none of the Indians—and particularly Sitting Bull—would become suspicious and follow him. By noon the following day, he reached Fort Peck, where the agent told him the troops assigned to punish the Metís were waiting at Frenchman's Creek, a tributary of the Milk River. As trading whisky with the Indians was against the American law and as the Metís were camped south of the Canadian border, the army had the legal right to arrest them. Its difficulty was identifying the individuals who had actually sold the liquor to Sitting Bull's band. But Grouard, if he joined them, could do that.

Frenchman's Creek was a considerable distance from Fort Peck, and Grouard covered the miles as rapidly as he could, for he did not want to be away from the Indian village too long. Later he estimated that there were about a thousand of the half-breeds living on Frenchman's Creek. Among them were some Santee Sioux, who recognized Grouard as Sitting Bull's adopted brother. Grouard could do nothing to hide his identity. Working with the soldiers, he pointed out the men who had brought the whisky to Sitting Bull's camp, and the soldiers arrested them as well as some others. They also searched the camp for liquor and destroyed all that they found. In addition, they confiscated the horses belonging to the arrested men.

Because he needed to substantiate the alibi he had given Sitting Bull, Grouard asked for three of the horses to take back to the village with him as evidence he had actually been on a raiding journey. The commanding officer readily agreed, for this was a small price for Grouard's services. Grouard rode quickly back to the village, because he was afraid some of the Metís might pursue him and kill him. But he reached the camp safely. Sitting Bull was pleased at the apparent prowess shown by his adopted brother and even more pleased when Grouard gave him one of the animals and presented the other two to his mother and sister.

But the truth could not be hidden for long. In about ten days, some of the Santee Sioux who had been with the Metís came to the camp, and they told Sitting Bull what had happened. Sitting Bull, of course, was furious. Not only had he been duped, but his prestige suffered from the misbehavior of his adopted brother. He questioned Grouard closely and asked him if he was still friendly to the Americans, and if Grouard had not been in the lodge of Sitting Bull's sister, Sitting Bull would probably have killed him at once. As it was, only a fragile truce stood between the two men. The faction of Gall and No Nose were obviously happy over what had happened, because it lowered Sitting Bull in the esteem of the other Indians and therefore raised the standing of their own leaders. They invited Grouard to come and live in their part of the camp, but Sitting Bull's mother told him not to go. Her son, she was certain, would get over his anger. Nevertheless Sitting Bull and Grouard tried to avoid each other, and when the camp moved, they rode on opposite sides of it.

*   *   *

That year two more surveying expeditions were sent out in the north. Although the previous surveyors had not been disturbed by hostile Indians, the authorities decided to increase the size of the guard. General David S. Stanley left Fort Rice on the Missouri with almost five hundred men, and Major E. M. Baker left Fort Ellis on the Yellowstone with almost four hundred. The large numbers of soldiers and armed civilians were intended as a deterrent to the Indians, but the herds of horses and pack animals they brought along with them also served as a temptation.

On August 13, Baker made camp at Pryor Creek, which is west of the Little Bighorn River. A band of Indians was watching him and hoped to run off with some horses. During the night they crept close to the camp and might have attacked it successfully except for a mistake made by one of the warriors. A civilian who was sleeping at the outer edge of the camp had placed his gun against a tree. The Indian saw it and thought he could steal it, but the civilian was awake and noticed his movements in the darkness. Drawing his revolver, the civilian shot him in the head. The noise aroused the camp, and the Americans began firing at anything that looked like an Indian. In the fighting that followed, the Indians were forced to retreat. Both sides suffered some casualties, and the Indians escaped with some livestock. But by that afternoon, the surveyors were at work again. Their enthusiasm was considerably dampened, however, and a few days later they refused to continue, pleading that the troops were unable to guard them closely enough. And so they returned to Fort Ellis.

General Stanley's party also ran into trouble. In August, it reached the Powder River, but Gall, the leader of the faction opposing Sitting Bull, had noticed it. When one engineer strayed away from the main body, Gall pursued and almost captured him. Gall then indicated to Stanley he would like to talk to him. He wanted to know what the Americans were doing and how much they would pay him. But nothing came of the parley, desultory fighting broke out, and Gall left the area. Altogether several lives were lost that year in making the survey, but neither side had accomplished what it wanted. The Indians had failed to expel the Americans, but the Americans had not completed their survey.

While the expeditions were pushing into the wilderness during the summer of 1872, the Secretary of the Interior, still hopeful that he could bring an end to the fighting, appointed another delegation, composed of an assistant secretary and two commissioners. They were to go to Fort Peck, meet with the northern Indians, and try to make a final peace with them. One of their specific assignments was to see Sitting Bull, whose name was becoming more generally known to the white men.

Sitting Bull, however, had no interest in negotiating with them. So far, he had seen no need for treating with the Americans, and nothing had occurred to make him change his mind. Frustrated in their efforts to talk to him personally, the commissioners tried at least to learn everything they could about him from the Indians and white men they met. Some officials had accused him of having been a participant in the Minnesota uprising, but the commission, on the basis of what they heard, dismissed this rumor with the comment that his band "have committed crime enough, without being charged of any of which they may be innocent." Some of the chiefs from the more southern agencies, they went on to report, "affect to consider Sitting Bull as a mean-spirited sort of fellow, with but little or no influence, and a very small following." But other Indians, they continued, "consider him the leading man of their people, and their speeches at the council sufficiently indicated their fear of and respect for him. When he had visited the post [on his trip with Grouard] his control of his braves is said to have been more complete than is usual among Indians. . . . In order to fully understand the situation with regard to Sitting Bull, it may be well to state the fact that he has in his company a Sandwich Islander, called Frank [Grouard claimed that he was born in the Sandwich Islands], who appears to exercise great control in the Indian councils, and who excels the Indians in their bitter hatred to the whites.

"We have had no opportunity," the commission continued, "of forming an accurate or even an approximate idea of Sitting Bull's followers prior to the secession therefrom of those now in the immediate neighborhood of Fort Peck. Their numbers have been variously estimated, as you know, at from fifteen hundred to three thousand lodges, but, from the data we have been able to collect, we are of the opinion that one-half the smaller number is nearer the true estimate of his present force, if it not be really in excess of the truth."

At least the commission was more realistic than some of the settlers in guessing at the size of Sitting Bull's following, but it could obtain no real information about him. To the Americans, he remained an indistinct but dangerous threat, lurking in the wilderness, unapproachable and unfriendly.

In the early fall of 1872, the Superintendent of Indian Affairs for Montana Territory wrote his official report, which reflected his frustration and his fear for the future safety of the men working on the railroad. "Repeated efforts have been made," he said, "to get Sitting Bull into Fort Peck to hold council with agent Simmons, but without success. He once visited the fort, promising to call again and arrange terms of peace; but it has not been found possible to get further interviews with him. I am satisfied, however, that further desertions from his leadership will take place this winter among his followers, when they discover (as they must) that previous seceders have found it to their advantage to accept the aid and protection of the Government."

He then looked ahead and described the policy he would pursue with regard to Sitting Bull and the other Indians that remained hostile.

"In dealing with these Sioux," he wrote, "it has been my aim to have licensed traders exercise great care in their dealings with them, and every precaution has been exercised, with regard to trading them arms and ammunition, the respective agents being held responsible for any carelessness or negligence in this respect. Their trading with the Red River half-breeds of the North [the Metís], in the British Possessions is beyond my control, and it is from these people that the Sioux have procured most of their firearms and ammunition.

"I have my doubts," he continued, "as to whether it is prudent to have any trader for these Indians. I have had serious thoughts of revoking the trading-license at Fort Peck, and on the first suspicion that any trouble may arise shall certainly do so."

His first efforts, therefore, were directed toward closing off Sitting Bull's sources of supplies. But "should these wandering Sioux under Sitting Bull (in connection with the hostile bands of Arapahoes and Cheyennes, with whom they co-operate) persist in their efforts to molest and interfere with the progress of the Northern Pacific Railroad, I sincerely trust that a sufficient military force will be sent against them to severely and sufficiently punish them, even to annihilation, should the same be unfortunately necessary. They have had fair promises [he was writing, of course, from a white man's point of view], which have in every particular been carried out when any of them would accept the bounty of the Government. They know just exactly what the Department is willing to do for them; they have the evidence of three-fifths of their original numbers that the promises made are ready to be fulfilled, and a continued warfare on their part must be taken as an evidence that they wish to die fighting, and are on no terms willing to live at peace with the white race. These are the only Indians in the Northwest from whom any serious trouble may be entertained, and in the event of their continuing hostile, the interests of civilization and common humanity demand that they should be made powerless."

The superintendent expressed the sentiments of many people, especially in the West. They considered the terms offered the Indians as generous, overlooking the point that the Indians were the original possessors of the land and that they might not want to trade their freedom for the dubious "bounty of the Government." He was also in accord with the prevailing feeling that Jay Cooke's Northern Pacific Railroad must go through. If it was necessary to annihilate the Indians in order to complete it, that was part of the cost of advancing "the interests of civilization and common humanity." But even if Sitting Bull had known the superintendent's thoughts, he would not have been concerned. He was too busy laying in the winter's supply of meat and too sure he could maintain his independence against the Americans.

*   *   *

After his attack on Black Kettle's village and his return to Camp Supply, Custer accompanied Sheridan on a march down the Washita River, during which they persuaded the Kiowas under their leader, Santana, to return to their agency. They accomplished this by first trying peaceful means. When these failed, they held Santana and another leader captive and threatened to kill them if the other Indians did not come in.

During the winter, Custer made two more campaigns. While on the second, he located a Cheyenne camp that contained two captive white girls. Although he was determined to rescue them, he did not dare attack the camp for fear the girls would be immediately killed. So he rode up to the Indians, professed his friendship, and asked them to suggest a campground for his men. They showed him a place some distance away and out of sight of their village. Custer, however, had the foresight to post lookouts where they could keep the Indians' village under constant observation.

That afternoon about a hundred or a hundred and fifty warriors visited the Americans' camp and said that later some of the young men would come to play their musical instruments, which were made of reeds. Custer suspected this performance was a ruse to divert the attention of the soldiers while the rest of the camp slipped away, and the reports he received from his lookouts confirmed his suspicions. They could see the Indians bringing in the herds and preparing to take down the lodges.

Custer quietly told some of his officers to pick out about a hundred of their best men, see that they were armed, and have them intermingle with the visiting Indians. He then waited until the musicians and the crowd had started to dwindle. "Of the forty or more Indians in the group," he later wrote, "there were but few chiefs, the majority being young men or boys. My attention was devoted to the chiefs, and acting upon the principle that for the purposes desired half a dozen would be as valuable as half a hundred, I determined to seize the principal chiefs then present and permit the others to depart. To do this without taking or losing life now became the problem.

"Indicating in a quiet manner to some of my men who were nearest to me to be ready to prevent the escape of three or four of the Indians whom I had pointed out, I then directed Romeo [his nickname for the interpreter] to command silence on the part of the Indians and to inform them that I was about to communicate something of great importance to them. This was sufficient to attract their undivided attention. I then rose from a seat near the fire and unbuckling my revolver from my waist asked the Indians to observe that I threw my weapons upon the ground as an evidence that in what I was about to do I did not desire or propose to shed blood unless forced to do so. I then asked the chiefs to look around them and count the armed men whom I had posted among and around them, completely cutting off every avenue of escape."

He explained to them that they had tried to trick him by secretly moving their camp but that they were now in his power, and he told them to remain calm until they had listened to his requests. As soon as Custer had referred to his own armed men, the Indians had sprung to their feet and taken up their own weapons. "A single shot fired," Custer wrote, "an indiscreet word uttered, would have been the signal to commence. My men behaved admirably, taking their positions in such a manner that each Indian was confronted by at least two men."

The Indians, of course, prepared to fight. One of them kept fingering his revolver, and another began taking out the arrows for his bow. "Suddenly a rush was made," Custer wrote. "But for the fact that my men were ordered not to fire, the attempt for the Indians would have been unsuccessful. I, as well as the other officers near me, called upon the men not to fire. The result was that all but four broke the lines and made their escape. The four detained, however, were those desired, being chiefs and warriors of prominence."

By using his hostages with skill and remaining calm and patient, Custer was able to negotiate the return of the two young white captives and to persuade the Cheyennes to go back to their reservation. But although Custer accomplished this mission without bloodshed, the episode nevertheless ended in tragedy. At Fort Hays, the commander decided to transfer the Indian hostages from tents pitched inside the stockade to some rooms inside the guardhouse. The post had no interpreter, so the guards tried to explain their intentions to the hostages in crude sign language. When the hostages failed to understand what was expected of them, the guards attempted to move them by force. The hostages had knives hidden under their blankets and, fearing they were being attacked, resisted. Shots were fired. One hostage fell dead, one received a mortal bayonet wound, and another was knocked senseless with a musket butt. The Americans' diplomacy had again left death in its wake.

In spite of this tragedy, life at Fort Hays was pleasant. The commander, General Nelson A. Miles, liked Custer and his wife, and his favor made the Custers' existence all the more enjoyable. Custer amused himself by hunting and writing articles for a number of magazines. That winter the troops moved to Fort Leavenworth, but Custer was growing impatient with the routine of army life—service at Fort Hays in the summer and at Fort Leavenworth in the winter. So he asked for and received an extended leave to go East. But he could not find anything there to satisfy his restless temperament and returned to the army. In the fall of 1871 he was assigned to Elizabethtown, Kentucky.

The only break in the monotony came in 1872, the year that Grouard led the soldiers against the Metís. Grand Duke Alexis, the son of the czar, was in the United States and wanted to participate in a buffalo hunt. The government arranged a gala expedition for him with "Buffalo Bill" Cody as guide, and Sheridan assigned Custer to help escort the visitor. After the hunt was over, Custer and his wife joined the duke in a trip down the Mississippi. Then they returned to Elizabethtown and resumed the relatively quiet and unadventurous life they led there.

In Philadelphia, Jay Cooke continued to struggle with the financial problems of the Northern Pacific Railroad, which were growing worse and worse. Like most railroads at the time, it was in serious financial trouble; by the winter of 1872–73, Cooke was desperate. He had done everything he could to end the inefficiencies he had discovered when he became involved in the road's management, and he had searched everywhere, including Europe, for additional funds, selling stocks and bonds to anyone who would buy them at almost any price they would pay.

But he was unable to repeat the success he had had with the obligations of the United States government and found that this time he had exhausted the capital markets. To keep the railroad solvent, he had to advance money from his own firm in increasingly large amounts, and the drain was beginning to tell. By the winter of 1872–73, many investors thought that construction work might be halted the following year. If it had, the pressure on Sitting Bull might have been relieved, because there would no longer have been reason to send surveying parties into the territory he claimed as his own.

But Cooke was not yet ready to give up. He was so deeply committed that he attempted to salvage what remained by forming a syndicate. Its purpose was a final effort to sell even more bonds by offering purchasers a fifty percent bonus in stock. Although money was tight and the United States was tottering on the verge of a depression, his action breathed enough life into the troubled railroad to continue work during the summer of 1873.

As a consequence, the road asked the government to provide another escort for the expedition that would try to complete the survey. Alarmed by the attacks made on the surveyors in 1872 and knowing that the party would penetrate still deeper into the Indians' territory, the army decided to have a much larger escort and one that was supported by cavalry. Accordingly, the Seventh Cavalry was reassembled, and Custer was ordered to report to Fort Rice on the Missouri.

Once more General Stanley commanded the escort, and General Thomas L. Rosser, a veteran of the Confederate Army and a cadet when Custer was at West Point, was again in charge of the surveyors. They met at Fort Rice and marched from there to the Yellowstone River, reaching it about a hundred miles from its mouth. There they were joined by a steamboat sent to bring them fresh supplies and to ferry them across the river. After that, Custer later wrote, "Our course for several days carried us up that stream; our tents at night being usually pitched on or near the river bank. The country to be surveyed, however, soon became so rough and broken in places that we encountered serious delays at times in finding a practicable route for our long and heavily laden wagon trains, over rocks and through cañons hitherto unexplored by white men. So serious did these embarrassments become, and so much time was lost in accomplishing our daily marches, that I suggested to General Stanley that I should take with me each day a couple of companies of cavalry and a few of the Indian scouts, and seek out and prepare a practicable road in advance, thereby preventing detention of the main command."

This change in marching procedure probably helped the expedition, but it also served a private purpose of Custer's. Although he remained respectful to General Stanley in public print, saying he was "an officer whose well-known ability and long experience on the Plains and with the Indians amply qualified him for the exercise of so important a command," he had taken a hearty dislike to him. Writing home, he told his wife that Stanley was drinking heavily and that he feared he was going to have official trouble with the general. Stanley had just as low an opinion of Custer. When he wrote his family, he told them that Custer was a cold-blooded, unprincipled man. By riding ahead of the main command, Custer was able to avoid seeing so much of Stanley, and obtained a measure of the freedom he always enjoyed.

But as he had done before, he took advantage of the liberty given him. When they were crossing one of the many rivers, he was four miles in advance, but instead of returning to help his own wagon train over the river, he kept on going. When he was about fifteen miles away, he sent word back to Stanley that he wanted forage and rations delivered to him. Stanley curtly ordered him to return, which, of course, he had to do. After he had seen his train across the river, Stanley permitted him to move out ahead again.

The escort was approximately three times as large as the one the year before, and the Indians quickly learned of its presence and began following the advance under Custer. Although they did not have the strength to overcome Stanley's main command, they thought they might defeat the ninety or so men with Custer's advance party and began to make their plans. As they had done so many times before, they decided to use decoys to draw Custer on.

On August 4, the soldiers broke camp at five o'clock in the morning, and Custer went ahead as usual. He made it a custom always to look for signs of nearby Indians, and that morning his Indian scout, Bloody Knife, discovered that Indians had been prowling around the camp during the night. "The hostile party of whose presence we had become aware," Custer later wrote, "numbered nineteen; our party numbered over ninety. So, sending intelligence back to General Stanley of the circumstances of the discovery, we continued our march, keeping up if possible a sharper lookout than before, now that we were assured of the proximity of Indians in our neighborhood.

"Over rock-ribbed hills, down timbered dells, and across open, grassy plains, we wended our way without unusual interest, except at intervals of a few miles to discover the trail of the nineteen prowling visitors of the previous night, showing that our course, which was intended to lead us again to the Yellowstone, was in the same direction as theirs. Bloody Knife interpreted this as indicating that the village from which the nineteen had probably been sent to reconnoitre and report our movements, was located somewhere above us in the

Yellowstone valley." So far, the Indians' tactics were working well, for Custer was moving confidently forward, unaware that he was near a large village, not a small one.

At ten o'clock, he and his command had reached the top of the bluffs overlooking the Yellowstone near the mouth of the Tongue River, and he ordered a halt. "Here and there," he wrote, "the channel of the river was dotted with beautiful islands covered with verdure and shaded by groves of stately forest trees, while along the banks on either side could be seen for miles and miles clumps of trees varying in size from the familiar cottonwood to the waving osier, and covering a space in some instances no larger than a gentleman's garden, in others embracing thousands of acres."

After admiring the view, Custer led his men down the bluffs and toward a particularly inviting cluster of trees about two miles away. When they reached it, he wrote, "We found it all that a more distant view had pictured it. An abundance of rich, luxuriant grass offered itself to satisfy the craving appetite of our traveled steeds, while the dense foliage of the forest trees provided us with a protecting shade which exposure to the hot rays of an August sun rendered more than welcome. First allowing our thirsty horses to drink from the clear, crystal water of the Yellowstone, which ran murmuring by in its long tortuous course to the Missouri, we then picketed them out to graze."

At this point, the valley was about two miles wide and almost flat with some deep washes running through it. Except for the clump in which the soldiers had stopped, there were no trees for about a mile in every direction, so Custer believed there was little chance of being surprised. He posted six pickets around the grove and told his men they could rest. Most of them lay down in the soft grass and quickly fell asleep. Custer himself made a pillow out of his saddle and buckskin coat, took off his boots, unbuttoned his collar, and was soon asleep like the others.

This was the opportunity for which the Indians had been waiting. Custer was separated from the rest of Stanley's command, and except for his pickets, his men were off their guard. About six Indians were chosen to make the first attack. They were to ride down on Custer and his men, perhaps get away with some of the horses, and lure the soldiers into following them—the same tactic that had worked so often before.

"How long we slept," Custer wrote, "I scarcely know—perhaps an hour, when the cry of 'Indians! Indians!' quickly followed by the sharp ringing crack of the pickets' carbines, aroused and brought us—officers, men and horses—to our feet. There was neither time nor occasion for questions to be asked or answered. Catching up my rifle, and without waiting to don hat or boots, I glanced through the grove of trees to the open plain or valley beyond, and saw a small party of Indians bearing down toward us as fast as their ponies could carry them.

" 'Run to your horses, men! Run to your horses!' I fairly yelled as I saw that the first move of the Indians was intended to stampede our animals and leave us to be attended to afterward."

The Indians kept galloping forward as if they planned to ride down the party of ninety men. As they did so, they fired their guns at the Americans, hoping to draw them forth. Custer had now been fighting long enough on the plains to be aware that this attack was probably a ruse and that so small a band of Indians would not normally attack so many of the enemy in the open. While the pickets, joined by some of the other soldiers, kept firing in an effort to prevent the Indians from overrunning the temporary resting place, the other men rushed for their horses and guns and prepared for the battle.

"A few moments found us in our saddles," Custer wrote, "and sallying forth from the timber to try conclusions with the daring intruders. We could only see half a dozen Sioux warriors galloping up and down in our front, boldly challenging us by their manner to attempt their capture or death."

As the Americans began pouring out of the grove of trees, the Indian decoys began a slow retreat toward the main body. "Of course," Custer wrote, "it was an easy matter to drive them away, but as we advanced it became noticeable that they retired, and when we halted or diminished our speed they did likewise. It was apparent from the first that the Indians were resorting to a strategem to accomplish that which they could not do by an open, direct attack."

Growing impatient with the game the Indians were playing with him, Custer took twenty troopers and told the rest to remain behind but within a supporting distance. But the Sioux were no more fooled by Custer's trick than he had been by theirs. Instead of attacking the smaller number of soldiers, they continued to lure the Americans up the valley, and as their horses were extremely fast, Custer could not overtake them. Finally he decided to carry his own ruse a step further. "Thinking to tempt them within our grasp," he wrote, "I being mounted on a Kentucky thoroughbred in whose speed and endurance I had confidence, directed Colonel Custer [his brother, Thomas, a brevet colonel who was assigned to his command] to allow me to approach the Indians accompanied only by my orderly, who was also well mounted; at the same time to follow us cautiously at a distance of a couple of hundred yards. The wily redskins were not to be caught by any such artifice. They were perfectly willing that my orderly and myself should approach them, but at the same time they carefully watched the advance of the cavalry following me, and permitted no advantage."

The Indians were well pleased by what was taking place. About two miles up the valley from the point where Custer had allowed his men to rest, a heavy stand of trees grew at the edge of the river, heavy enough to provide cover for several hundred warriors. Here were hidden most of the fighting men from the large camp. Their guns were loaded, and those who did not have guns had taken out their arrows. From behind the willows 'and cottonwoods, they watched the decoys draw Custer closer and closer.

"The route taken by the Indians, and which they evidently intended us to follow, led past this timber, but not through it," Custer wrote. "When we had arrived almost opposite the nearest point, I signalled to the cavalry to halt, which was no sooner done than the Indians also came to a halt. I then made a sign to the latter for a parley, which was done simply by riding my horse in a circle. To this the savages only responded by looking on in silence for a few moments, then turning their ponies and moving off slowly, as if to say, 'Catch us if you can.' My suspicions were more than ever aroused, and I sent my orderly back to tell Colonel Custer to keep a sharp eye upon the heavy bushes on our left and scarcely three hundred yards distant from where I sat on my horse. The orderly had delivered his message, and had almost rejoined me, when, judging from our halt that we intended to pursue no further, the real design and purpose of the savages was made evident."

Seeing Custer stop, the decoys decided that they had drawn him as close to the wood as possible, so, as a signal to the hidden warriors, they turned their horses around and began to advance toward Custer. "I could scarcely credit my eyes," he wrote, "but my astonishment had only begun when turning to the wood on my left I beheld bursting from their concealment between three and four hundred Sioux warriors mounted and caparisoned with all the flaming adornments of paint and feathers which go to make up the Indian war costume. When

I first obtained a glimpse of them—and a single glance was sufficient —they were dashing from the timber at full speed, yelling and whooping as only Indians can. At the same time they moved in perfect line, and with as seeming good order and alignment as the best drilled cavalry."

At this critical moment, Colonel Thomas Custer was about three or four hundred yards behind Custer, and the charging Sioux were about the same distance off on their flank. Custer's first thought was to get back to his brother and his twenty men before they were either surrounded or cut off. The larger body of troops under Captain Myles Moylan was now too far behind to be of any immediate assistance.

"Wheeling my horse suddenly around," Custer wrote later, "and driving the spurs into his sides, I rode as only a man rides whose life is the prize. . . ." As he galloped toward his brother, Custer kept calling out, "Dismount your men! Dismount your men!" This was a standard maneuver, in which three out of four troopers dismounted. This gave them a firmer position from which to fire and relieved them of the hindrance of managing their horses. The fourth trooper in each group remained mounted and held the reins of his companions' horses.

Thomas Custer could not hear his brother calling to him, but he could see there was almost no chance of retreating toward Moylan. His men would have been cut to pieces if he had attempted to. So on his own he gave the order to dismount. Fifteen troopers jumped from their horses, moved in front of them, and dropped to one or both knees in the low grass, their carbines loaded and ready.

The Sioux kept charging. They hoped to cut Custer off from his men and then overrun the others, and their numbers were so great compared to the Americans' that certain victory seemed to be in sight. That night there would be great singing and rejoicing in the village. The air was filled with the sound of their shouting and the pounding of their horses' hooves. Closer and closer they came, but they failed to get between Custer and his brother. That, however, they felt was of no real consequence, because they would kill him as soon as they reached the small band of dismounted cavalrymen.

"The victory was almost within the grasp of the redskins," Custer wrote. "It seemed that but a moment more, and they would be trampling the kneeling troopers beneath the feet of their fleet-limbed ponies; when 'Now, men, let them have it!' was the signal for a well-directed volley, as fifteen cavalry carbines poured their contents into the ranks of the shrieking savages. Before the latter could recover from the surprise and confusion which followed, the carbines—thanks to the invention of breech-loaders—were almost instantly loaded, and a second discharge went whistling on its deadly errand. Several warriors were seen to reel in their saddles, and were only saved from falling by the quickly extended arms of their fellows. Ponies were tumbled over like butchered bullocks, their riders glad to find themselves escaping with less serious injuries. The effect of the rapid firing of the troopers, and their firm, determined stand, showing that they thought neither of flight nor surrender, was to compel the savages first to slacken their speed, then to lose their daring and confidence in their ability to trample down the little group of defenders in the front. Death to many of their number stared them in the face. Besides, if the small number of troopers in the front was able to oppose such plucky and destructive resistance to their attacks, what might not be expected should the main party under Moylan, now swiftly approaching to the rescue, also take part in the struggle."

Once again, superior arms defeated the Indians. Custer's men were certainly brave and calm under attack, standing off as they did such a large number of warriors. But they also had by far the better guns, and the speed with which they could fire their breechloaders was a surprise to the Indians. The year before the commission that visited Fort Peck had reported that the Indians there "are very poor, indifferently mounted, and armed for the most part with bows and arrows. There are some old-pattern muzzle-loading guns and pistols, but probably not more than ten or a dozen improved breech-loading arms among them, while the latter are almost useless because of the impossibility of their procuring ammunition to suit them." These were the types of weapons with which the Sioux were trying to destroy Custer's command, and it was difficult for them to comprehend the speed and accuracy of the Americans' fire.

They faltered, then turned their horses back. The troopers, encouraged by the results of their first two volleys, quickly reloaded again and fired for a third time. The bullets struck the retreating Indians and their horses, as they spurred the animals on and disappeared temporarily into the wooded area they had used for their ambush. Almost at the same time, Moylan arrived with the rest of the command, and the first part of the battle was over.

Custer, however, could not remain where he was. He needed to be nearer the river and find a place where he could either shelter his horses or conceal them. Consequently he began moving back to the grove of trees where they had stopped only a short time before. Three-fourths of the men were on foot and deployed in a circular skirmish line with the horses in the center. As they retraced their steps, the Indians began to attack them, dashing along their flanks. "That the fire of their rifles should be effective under these circumstances," Custer commented, "could hardly be expected. Neither could the most careful aim of the cavalrymen produce much better results. It forced the savages to keep at a respectful distance, however, and enabled us to make our retrograde movement." During this short march, several of Custer's horses were wounded, but none fatally, and one of the troopers was seriously wounded in the arm. But in spite of the constant fire from the Indians, the soldiers were able to reach the clump of trees.

Because the horses were now sheltered, Custer could reduce the guard from one soldier for every four horses to one for every eight. This gave him more fighting men, which he sorely needed. Then, "taking advantage of a natural terrace or embankment extending almost like a semicircle in front of the little grove in which we had taken refuge, and at a distance of but a few hundred yards from the latter," Custer wrote, "I determined by driving the Indians beyond to adopt it as our breastwork or line of defense. This was soon accomplished, and we found ourselves deployed behind a natural parapet or bulwark from which the troopers could deliver a carefully directed fire upon their enemies, and at the same time be protected largely from the bullets of the latter." And at their rear was the Yellowstone River, which at that point had a bank about twenty to thirty feet high. This protected them from a mounted charge in that direction.

The Sioux had now lost their greatest opportunity. In the beginning, they had been able to fight the battle under conditions that were favorable for their tactics. But the failure of their first charge and their inability to prevent Custer's retreat to the grove of trees turned the tide against them. The Americans now had a fixed position, which made their superior firepower an even greater advantage. The Indians made repeated attempts to dislodge the soldiers. Several of them tried creeping through the grass in an attempt to get close to the embankment, but the soldiers always saw them and sent bullets flying in their direction, thus driving them back. Others engaged in their traditional custom of riding back and forth in plain view, presenting themselves as targets. Their purpose was two-fold: to demonstrate their own individual bravery and to make the enemy waste his ammunition. The soldiers, of course, could not resist shooting at the flying figures of the

Indians and their horses, and Custer finally had to tell his men to hold their fire.

One Indian in particular drew the white men's attention. He rode closer to the embankment than any of the others, coming within almost two hundred yards of it. But although the troopers repeatedly fired at him, they always missed. "Encouraged by his success perhaps," Custer wrote, "he concluded to taunt us again, and at the same time exhibit his own daring, by riding along the lines at full speed, but nearer than before. We saw him coming. Bloody Knife [Custer's scout], with his Henry rifle poised gracefully in his hands, watched his coming, saying he intended to make this his enemy's last ride. He would send him to the happy hunting ground. I told the interpreter to tell Bloody Knife that at the moment the warrior reached a designated point directly opposite to us, he, Bloody Knife, should fire at the rider and I at the same instant would fire at the pony.

"A smile of approval passed over the swarthy features of the friendly scout as he nodded assent," Custer continued. "I held in my hand my well-tried Remington. Resting on one knee and glancing along the barrel, at the same time seeing that Bloody Knife was also squatting low in the deep grass with rifle leveled, I awaited the approach of the warrior to the designated point. On he came, brandishing his weapons and flaunting his shield [many of the Sioux still carried rawhide shields, which protected them from arrows but not from bullets] in our faces, defying us by his taunts to come out and fight like men. Swiftly sped the gallant little steed that bore him, scarcely needing the guiding rein. Nearer and nearer both horse and rider approached the fatal spot, when sharp and clear, and so simultaneous as to sound as one, rang forth the reports of the two rifles. The distance was less than two hundred yards. The Indian was seen to throw up his arms and reel in his saddle, while the pony made one final leap, and both fell to the earth."

Displays like these, which the Sioux so highly esteemed and which were part of their culture, were costly when fighting men of a different culture. In the old days, one of the enemy might have taken up the challenge, emerged from behind the embankment, and fought the warrior individually and with equal chances on both sides. But that was not the way with the Americans. Their sole purpose was to defeat the Sioux, and they were willing to shoot from behind the natural breastwork that protected them. In their battles against the white men, the Sioux lost many of their bravest warriors in this fashion.

Custer was still holding out, but, as he later wrote, "Many of the men who had been firing incessantly now began to complain that their stock of ammunition was well-nigh exhausted. They were cautioned to use the few remaining rounds as sparingly as possible. At the same time I sent a couple of non-commissioned officers quickly into the timber, instructing them to obtain every round remaining in the cartridge-boxes of the horse-holders and the wounded. This gave us quite a number of rounds, as this supply had not been touched during the fight."

The Indians were now losing the battle. The day was wearing on, and with each hour that passed, Stanley and the main body of troops were coming closer. Once they arrived the fight would be over. So finding their tactics were not working, some of the Indians decided to concentrate on stealing the Americans' horses. By following a ravine that led from the woods in which they were first hidden, they could reach the river unseen and then move downstream under the cover of the large bank. In this way, they hoped to get in among the horses before the troops noticed them.

One of them rode above the bank and, serving as a lookout, could advise the others if the Americans took any unusual action or changed the pattern of their defense. Unfortunately for the Indians, Custer noticed him. "While the greatest activity was maintained in our front by our enemies, my attention was called to a single warrior who, mounted on his pony, had deliberately, and as I thought rashly, passed around our left flank—our diminished numbers preventing us from extending our line close to the river—and was then in the rear of our skirmishers, riding along the crest of the high bank with as apparent unconcern as if in the midst of his friends instead of being almost in the power of his enemies. I imagined that his object was to get nearer the grove in which our horses were concealed, and toward which he was moving slowly, to reconnoitre and ascertain how much force we held in reserve. At the time, as I never can see an Indian engaged in an unexplained act without conceiving treachery or stratagem at the bottom of it [those last words reflected Custer's attitude toward Indians and the attitude of many other white men as well], I called to Lieutenant [Charles A.] Varnum, who commanded on the left, to take a few men and endeavor to cut the wiley interloper off. This might have been accomplished but for the excessive zeal of some of Varnum's men, who acted with lack of caution and enabled the Indian to discover their approach and make his escape by a hurried gallop up the river."

The Indians, who were following the course of the river at the base of the bank, saw their lookout suddenly turn and gallop off. This made them believe the Americans had discovered their whereabouts. Although they had already covered about two-thirds of the distance, they thought they could not go forward, because the edge of the river was a pebble-covered beach with no shelter behind which they could hide. If the Americans started shooting at them from the top of the bank, they would be in a dangerous position. So they turned their horses and rode away.

After the battle was over, Custer learned what had happened, and he wryly commented, "Had they been willing, as white men would have been, to assume greater risks, their success would have been assured. But they feared we might discover their movements and catch them while strung out along the narrow beach, with no opportunity to escape." The Sioux were brave, but their bravery was individual, and they had no line of command for carrying out intricate maneuvers.

In a final effort to dislodge the Americans and force them into the open, some of the Indians gathered in small groups in front of the Americans' line, dismounted, and then crept toward them through the grass. When they were as close as they could get, they built fires, hoping that these would spread and create a series of grass fires that could sweep down on the white men and force them to run into the open. But the grass was not dry enough, and the fires merely smoked instead of burning.

Suddenly the Indians saw a large column of dust rising beyond the hills to Custer's right. They guessed it meant the arrival of more troops and started withdrawing to the other side. Soon four squadrons of cavalry appeared in the distance, galloping toward them. Without waiting for them to arrive, Custer ordered his men into the saddle and charged against the Indians. But, he wrote later, "the only satisfaction we had was to drive at full speed for several miles a force outnumbering us two to one."

The next day Stanley decided that with the Indians so close at hand, he would pursue them. The trail went along the north bank of the Yellowstone River, but by August 8, the soldiers had not caught up with the fast-moving Indians. So Stanley permitted Custer to go on ahead with four squadrons of cavalry and to march at night when the moon was bright enough to see the trail. On the evening of August 10, having paused only twice to rest, the cavalry came to the edge of the river and discovered that the Indians had crossed it.

Since night was coming and the stream was swift, Custer made camp. He was much closer to the Indians than he realized, for nearby at the mouth of the Bighorn was a large encampment, composed of Oglalas who had not followed Red Cloud onto the reservation, as well as some Sans Arcs, Miniconjous, and Cheyennes.

The next day, "at early dawn," Custer later reported, "the entire command forded the river to an island located about the middle of the channel; but our difficulties in the way of crossing here began, as the volume of water and the entire force of the current were to be encountered between the island and the opposite bank—the current here rushes by at a velocity of about seven miles an hour, while the depth of the water was such that a horse attempting to cross would be forced to swim several hundred yards. Still, as we knew the Indians had not discovered our pursuit, and were probably located within easy striking distance of the river, it was desirable that a crossing be effected."

A lieutenant with three good swimmers tried to cross on a log raft, taking with them a cable made out of lariats. But the current carried them two miles down the river until they abandoned the raft and swam back to shore. Again and again the lieutenant tried to get across the river with the cable but failed.

"Almost the entire day was spent in these unsuccessful efforts," Custer reported, "until finally a crossing in this manner had to be abandoned. I then caused some cattle to be killed, and by stretching the hides over a kind of basket-frame prepared by the Crow guide, made what are known among the Indians as bull-boats; with these I hoped to be able to connect a cable with the opposite bank at daylight next morning. . . ."

The delay at the river cost Custer the advantage of surprise, because that evening several Indians came to water their horses and saw his camp. They went back to the village and the Indians prepared for a fight the next day. At dawn they moved their women and children up into the hills on the south side of the Yellowstone, where they could safely watch the coming battle. About this time, they also received reinforcements, for Sitting Bull and others of the Hunkpapas, along with Grouard, arrived at the village.

The battle began when the Indians started shooting from the opposite bank at the soldiers. Custer's men quickly grabbed their rifles and began returning the fire. But because of the rapid flow of the river, they could not charge over to the other side and launch a counterattack. So the fighting became a shooting contest between sharpshooters. From the distance, the Indians would try to pick off the white men. The Americans would wait to fire back until they saw the telltale puff of white smoke that revealed the presence of an Indian who had just pulled the trigger of his gun. This was not the mode of fighting that Custer enjoyed, pinned down under the enemy's fire with no opportunity to advance and no purpose in retreating. The mobility of his cavalry, which was its greatest asset, was in this case no asset at all.

The fighting continued in this fashion until the Indians decided to press their attack more vigorously. Although the Americans were not able to cross the river, this was not a problem for the Indians, because both riders and horses were familiar with the waters. Moving away from the battlefield so the Americans could not see them, they urged their small, light ponies into the water and made it safely to the other side. Once they were on the north of the Yellowstone River, they rode onto the bluffs that stood above Custer's position. They now had him surrounded, and the shooting became more intense. The bullets were flying among the Americans, and one struck Custer's horse. The animal fell, carrying Custer with it, but he rose and calmly took another mount.

Many of the Sioux were again giving demonstrations of their individual courage, riding out where they could be seen and taunting the Americans. Several of the younger men had received charms from one of the medicine men that were guaranteed to protect them from all bullets. During the fighting, the medicine man persuaded them to test it by riding out in front of the Americans' lines and exposing themselves.

A number of them were wounded, one quite seriously, but they continued to believe in the charm's efficacy because they were not killed; and the medicine man kept exhorting them to show themselves and to get as close as possible to the white men's guns. Sitting Bull had built up much of his reputation among the Indians by feats of bravado, but he thought this one needless. The young warriors had already shown their courage, and there was no point in having them all killed. So he remonstrated with their leader for encouraging them any further. After some argument, he persuaded them to stop, but the medicine man then cast some aspersions on Sitting Bull's own courage.

In the society of the Sioux, a warrior who wanted to stand well among the Indians could not afford to ignore such remarks. So Sitting Bull laid down his weapons, took out his pipe and tobacco, walked out in the open, sat down on the ground, and, with his flint and steel, lighted the pipe. Then he called back to the other Indians and invited them to join him. The bullets were striking the ground around him, but two Sioux and two Cheyennes accepted his challenge. In the midst of the battle, the five Indians sat there together, targets for the enemy's guns, and quietly smoked Sitting Bull's pipe. The act, of course, did nothing toward bringing the Indians victory, for it did not endanger a single American soldier. But it reminded the Sioux of the bravery of their tribe—and of Sitting Bull—and may have helped to raise their morale.

Although the other four Indians had joined Sitting Bull in his dangerous feat, they were worried about their safety and wanted to withdraw as quickly as possible. But Sitting Bull refused to be hurried and smoked his pipe as leisurely as though he had been sitting in a council. Only when he had finished the tobacco and scraped out the bowl was he willing to walk back to the main body of Indians.

Custer was planning a charge against the Indians on his side of the river. "Everything being in readiness for a general advance," he wrote in his report, "the charge was ordered, and the squadrons took the gallop to the tune of 'Garry Owen,' the band being posted immediately in the rear of the skirmish line. The Indians had evidently come out prepared to do their best, and with no misgivings as to their success, as the mounds and high bluffs beyond the river were covered with groups of old men, squaws, and children, who had collected there to witness our destruction. In this instance the proverbial power of music to soothe the savage breast utterly failed, for no sooner did the band strike up the cheery notes of 'Garry Owen,' and the squadrons advance to the charge, than the Indians exhibited unmistakable signs of commotion, and their resistance became more feeble, until finally satisfied with the earnestness of our attack they turned their ponies' heads and began a disorderly flight. The cavalry put spurs to their horses and dashed forward in pursuit, the various troop and squadron commanders vying with each other as to who should head the advance."

Grouard was with the women and children on the opposite bank during the fighting and heard the band play "Garry Owen." As the hot August sun beat down, he became thirsty and went to the river to get a drink. Several soldiers noticed him and started shooting at him, but although he did not have time to remount his mule, he ran safely on foot to the shelter of a nearby clump of trees.

Shortly after Custer started his charge, Stanley arrived. His appearance meant that Custer could pull in his skirmishers and concentrate all his men on the charge. The Indians retreated before the onrushing cavalry, racing to get back across the river that seemed to offer them safety, and soon Custer was in command of the northern banks.

Neither side could truly claim a victory. The Indians had been unable to drive the Americans out of their country, but neither had Custer been able to inflict serious damage on them. His official report, however, had a jubilant tone. "The losses of the Indians in ponies," he told his superiors, "were particularly heavy, while we know their losses in killed and wounded were beyond all proportion to that which they were enabled to inflict on us. . . ." In the early stages of the fighting, his scouts had talked with the Indians across the river, and he learned their identity, so he included this sentence in his report. "The Indians," he wrote, "were made up of different bands of Sioux, principally Hunkpapas, the whole under the command of 'Sitting Bull,' who participated in . . . the fight, and who for once had been taught a lesson he will not soon forget." Both statements were gross exaggerations.

The survey went on as planned without any further incidents except once when some Indians shot at soldiers who were bathing in a river. The soldiers had to scamper naked to safety, and the affair seems to have been more of a joke than an attack.

The season was now getting late, and the air was turning colder. Overhead the sky was marked by the flying V's of the Canada geese, and the sound of their wild honking broke the stillness of the nights. High in the mountains ice was forming in the pools of water, and the first snowstorms of the winter were beginning to threaten. It was time for the surveying expedition to turn back east. On the way, Custer, who had grown even more weary of serving under Stanley, asked permission to take his cavalry across a shortcut back to the point on the Yellowstone where the expedition was to meet the steamboat, and Stanley, probably just as weary of having Custer under his command, let him go.

Making one of the forced marches that he liked so well, Custer traveled about a hundred and fifty miles in five days and reached the Yellowstone safely, although his horses were worn out and he had run short of forage for them. But he enjoyed pitting his physical strength against the country, and the troopers under him—who usually either liked him or heartily detested him—had to follow his orders. Assignment to the Seventh Cavalry was no sinecure for the enlisted men.

Stanley, who brought the infantry back to the steamboat, took a longer but less difficult route. Then the soldiers headed back to civilization and their winter quarters. Custer had been given command of Fort Abraham Lincoln, which had been established the previous year near Bismarck, North Dakota. There he was joined by his wife and was to stay until the next campaign or expedition was organized and he would be needed again in the field.

The Sioux made no effort to continue to fight the Americans, for that was not their way. Winter was approaching, and as Sheridan had noted, they never fought in the winter. The snow was too deep for them to move easily, and they did not like to leave the refuge of their winter camps. So Sitting Bull and the Hunkpapas took the buffalo meat they had collected during the warmer months and found a sheltered place to spend the winter. If there was to be any more fighting, it would have to wait until the following spring when the snow melted from the prairie's surface and the grass was again green.

A temporary lull had come to the plains, but in Washington the Commissioner of Indian Affairs was not satisfied with what had happened. He recognized that the reservation policy was not working as it should have and that cooperation between the War Department and the Department of the Interior was not good. Writing his official report, he said, "The actual depredations committed by the Sioux have been comparatively few, but a portion of the tribe have assumed a hostile attitude toward the Government by attacking the surveying expedition on the Northern Pacific Railroad. According to the best information of this office, the greater number of Indians engaged in these hostilities were a band of Northern Sioux, who have hitherto declined to treat with the Government, and with them a large re-inforcement from different agencies along the Missouri River, as also from Spotted Tail's and Red Cloud's camps. There is no doubt that the majority of the Indians whom General Stanley encountered in Dakota have been at different times in the year on reservations, and have drawn rations from the Government, some occasionally and some regularly. It is to be regretted that these hostiles could not have been met and defeated by military force. Their actual punishment, in the loss of four or five warriors, was so slight that they seem to regard it as at least a drawn fight, if not a victory on their side. The Sioux at Red Cloud and Spotted Tail agencies have also assumed impudent manners and made hostile threats, which have prevented the proper administration of agency affairs." The attacks of Sitting Bull and the continued hostility of many of the northern Indians was spreading discontent among them all, and the commissioner was growing concerned.

"Hitherto," he continued in a less optimistic tone than commissioners had sometimes used in the past, "the military have refrained from going on this reservation [in this instance the commissioner considered the various agencies as one] because of the express terms of the treaty with the Sioux, in which it is agreed that no military force shall be brought over the line. I respectfully recommend that provision be made at once for placing at each of the Sioux reservations a military force sufficient to enable the agents to enforce respect for their authority, and to conduct agency affairs in an orderly manner. Also, that all Sioux Indians be required to remain on the Sioux reservation, and that any found off, or refusing to come in and treat with the Government, be forced in and brought to obedience by the military. I am confident that steady progress towards civilization is being made at the different agencies of the Sioux, and, if the turbulent element of this nation can be subdued, the question whether they can be induced to live quietly and to adopt the habits of civilization, so as to become self-supporting, will be only one of time and patience."

And in Philadelphia early that fall, the banking house of Jay Cooke was forced to recognize the failure of its syndicate and closed its doors. Any concern about future surveying expeditions was at the moment purely hypothetical. With the demise of Cooke's firm, work on the Northern Pacific Railroad came to a halt. For the time being at least, Sitting Bull and the northern Sioux seemed to be safe from further organized invasion of their lands.

XI

A Search for Gold

THE hopes of the Commissioner of Indian Affairs that the Sioux could be easily managed once they were upon reservations were hardly justified by the reports presented by the Indian agents in 1873. Taken together, they showed the difficulty of trying to impose a European culture on the Indians so quickly.

From Devils Lake in Dakota, the agent reported that the Sioux are still "wedded to their traditions and are superstitiously afraid of innovations. The 'medicine dances' and 'singing doctors' keep their superstitions alive through fear of sickness and death if disobedient, and the belief in the power of these medicine-men to have punished back-sliders from their teaching, [together] with the practice of polygamy, are deplorable obstacles in the way of Christianizing this generation."

An epidemic of measles—a disease introduced by the white men— had struck the agency at Lake Traverse, although the agent noted that "through a kind providence the number of deaths have been less than usual among so many so much exposed." From the Standing Rock agency, the agent reported, "The land was planted by them in corn, pumpkins, squash, and melons, but, receiving very little cultivation, was overrun by weeds, and, as a consequence, the crops have amounted to little or nothing as a means of subsistence beyond a little fresh garden-truck, which was mostly consumed before properly matured."

From Crow Creek, Dakota, where the Upper Missouri Sioux agency was located, came this comment: "I would respectfully call the attention of the Department to the fact that these Indians are now being subsisted in accordance with the 10th article of the treaty concluded April 29, 1868, between the Government and different tribes of Sioux Indians, and which expires with the close of the present fiscal year, at which time these Indians will be thrown entirely upon their own resources so far as subsisting themselves is concerned. This they are wholly incapable of doing at the present time, owing to their limited experience in agricultural pursuits, and the scarcity of game. Without further aid they will probably make forays upon the settlers and farmers of the frontier for the necessities of life, and which would soon lead to serious trouble." He asked the government to pass legislation permitting him to continue to issue rations.

The report from the Yankton agency was no more optimistic. "There is a universal feeling of uneasiness among the Yanktons [another of the Sioux tribes] with regard to the prospect of future subsistence," the agent wrote. "They have been informed that this year may end their rations. The general expression is of utter hopelessness. They say, 'In that case we may as well make up our minds to die.' I would give it here as my judgment, that if now all further aid in rations is withheld, very serious consequences will follow as far as the Yanktons are concerned. The greater part of the young men will leave the reservation and join the wild Indians. . . . Others will scatter among neighboring white settlements and towns, and become outcasts of the lowest order."

As the reports came into Washington, they took on a monotonous, gray tone. Every once in a while, an agent reported some ray of light—after all, their jobs were at stake—consisting of a sawmill built or the establishment of a missionary. But the cold fact remained that the government's reservation policy was failing. It was impossible, even if it had been desirable, to destroy the Indians' culture in the space of five years and replace it with the Americans'. The Sioux were horsemen and hunters, not farmers; they were nomads, not settlers; they were sun-dancers, not Christians. Many of them had made a degree of adjustment to the white men's way of life. They preferred metal kettles to pots and baskets; they found that the Americans' guns made hunting easier, particularly now that game was getting scarce; they enjoyed the white men's food, such as bacon and flour, and some of them had developed a taste for sugar and coffee; and, of course, almost all of them liked the white men's whisky and were willing to do anything to obtain it. Some of them were content to hang around the agencies, doing as little work as possible but maintaining friendly relations with the Americans, in order to get these goods. But they had neither the skill nor the inclination to make their own living in the white men's manner, and their position was one of dependency.

Others, although they liked the supplies they could get at the agencies, refused to live on the reservations. They came and went, sometimes appearing and asking for rations, at others disappearing into the plains, where they resumed their old way of life. Without a much larger military force than the depression-striken United States wanted to support, there was no way of controlling their movements. Others, like Sitting Bull and most of the Hunkpapas, were still openly hostile and ready to fight at the sight of a soldier. Even the entreaties of the agent at Fort Peck, who was notoriously lax in imposing conditions on the Indians, could not induce them to come in and talk.

Nor could the government even ensure the physical safety of those living on reservations. On September 22, 1873, shortly after Sitting Bull had fought with Custer along the Yellowstone, the agent at the Red Cloud agency sent off this brief but alarming telegram: "Please notify the Ponca agent that a war-party of one hundred Sioux left this agency 18th instant, to attack the Poncas."

The agent was away at the time, so his wife had to organize the resistance, a duty, he later argued, that was outside anything that should be required of her. As he wearily told Washington, "Attacks from war-parties in small or large numbers have been frequent, and made during the day and in the night season [sic]. Every reasonable precaution which suggested itself to my best judgment has been, and will be taken for the safety and comfort of the people and their property. . . . There are no cowards in camp, except it be the young women and children; the old women, when they are not permitted to fight, urge on the lagging and make the most excellent camp followers, and in the last battle . . . when no other way was left, an old Ponca woman, to contribute to the defense of the village, while brandishing a long knife she carried to quiet opposition, caught and made ready for the affray, the Indian ponies of the village, and riding around until she found a footman, gave him the horse, if his face were toward the fighting ground."

Under such conditions, it was no wonder that many Indians, including many Sioux, refused to go on the reservations. The government's policy had little to offer them. If they surrendered their freedom and their right to pursue their old customs, they received in return little hope of financial independence in the future and could not even count on their own personal safety.

But while the Indians, driven onto reservations or roaming the few remaining areas where the army had not been able to establish control, were suffering heavily, their ranks ravaged by disease and war, the white men were prospering. Anyone living in the United States in 1873, while Sitting Bull was fighting Custer on the Yellowstone, could read the story by picking up a copy of the latest United States Census and looking at the columns of figures.

Iowa, one of the states west of the Mississippi, was one of only thirteen out of a total of thirty-eight that had a population of more than a million persons. It was bigger than all but five of the original thirteen colonies, almost as big as the heavily populated state of Massachusetts, with its factory towns and the emigrants disembarking at its ports.

Nebraska, only admitted to the union in 1867, six years before, had a population of 122,993, not large by today's standards, but at the time only about three thousand short of the population of the much older state of Delaware. On its plains, the white men were grazing 47,000 horses and 73,000 oxen and other cattle, many more than in the states of Delaware and Rhode Island combined.

Minnesota, where the Santee Sioux had staged their futile uprising just a few years ago, now produced multimillion-dollar crops of wheat, as well as large harvests of oats. Kansas produced far more corn than all of the New England states taken together and fed more hogs than either South Carolina, New Jersey, or Kentucky.

These figures, arranged by the government's statisticians in dull-looking rows, revealed the westward shift of the nation's energies and forecast the fate of the Indians. The soldiers whom they feared and hated were not the real enemy, for most of them would have welcomed orders calling them back to the more comfortable posts of the East, where the danger and hardship were so much less. The real foe was the swelling population of the nation, which had more than doubled since Sitting Bull's birth: thirty-eight million restless men, women, and children, most of them with a stake in the development of the West. They owned bonds in Western railroads, they invested in the stock of corporations with Western interests, they worked in businesses that expanded when the West expanded. Even if they did not come West themselves, driving their wagons across the plains or riding more comfortably and swiftly behind the smoking locomotives, they were convinced the future greatness of their country lay in the West, and they were determined to gain control of those lands that were still occupied by the Indians. Sitting Bull was misled by the handful of troops under Custer that had faced him at the Yellowstone. In spite of their fine guns and precision tactics, these soldiers could be checked, but not the force behind them. If Sitting Bull smoked his pipe a thousand times under enemy fire, the westward movement would not be stopped.

*   *   *

Among the Sioux who shared Sitting Bull's unfounded faith in the future—his belief that the Americans could eventually be defeated—was Crazy Horse, the Oglala who had led the decoys when Fetterman was killed and who had taken part in the attack on the Wagon Box Corral at Fort Philip Kearny.

Early in life, Crazy Horse had been marked as a man apart, and all his actions confirmed the prophecies of his father and the older warrior Hump. He was distinguished by his hostility toward the white men—unlike many Oglalas, he did not follow Red Cloud onto the reservation—and the story of his love for Black Buffalo Woman and the disgrace she ultimately brought him was well known among the Sioux. Black Buffalo Woman had been courted by many warriors, including one named No Face. Crazy Horse had often visited her tepee, but strangely he had never offered to marry her. Then one day the Sioux were going on a raid. No Face, pleading that he was sick with a toothache, remained behind. When the warriors returned, Black Buffalo Woman had gone to live in his lodge. But instead of choosing another young woman—the village contained many—Crazy Horse remained alone. He was indeed different.

Later in their many travels over the plains, No Face's band again made their camp near Crazy Horse's, and Crazy Horse went to visit his rival's village and gave a great feast for them. When the party was over, Black Buffalo Woman gave her three children to her relatives to care for and rode back to Crazy Horse's village with him. Such wife-stealing was permitted by the Sioux's customs, for the women were allowed to choose the man they wanted even if they were already married, and Crazy Horse had performed his act openly and according to tradition.

But No Face was not willing to let go of his woman so easily. He tracked her and Crazy Horse and entered their tepee while they were eating. In his hand he had a revolver, and in his eyes vengeance. Crazy Horse grabbed for his knife, but to prevent bloodshed among the

Sioux, another Indian who was in the lodge seized Crazy Horse's arm. No feelings of gallantry stirred No Face, however, and an unarmed victim to him was merely an easier one. He fired his revolver. In the narrow confines of the tepee the shot sounded louder than a blast of thunder. At such close range, he could not miss. The bullet struck Crazy Horse in the face, and he fell to the ground. No Face turned and left the tepee.

In the village, he announced to those who had heard the shot that he had killed Crazy Horse. Then he mounted his horse and rode away before the friends of Crazy Horse could arm themselves and attack him. Black Buffalo Woman, thoroughly frightened by the anger shown by her former husband, ran to her relatives for protection; but No Face had exacted all the revenge he wanted and did not try to harm her.

Although he was seriously wounded, Crazy Horse was not dead. His followers, of course, wanted immediately to avenge him, to trade No Face's blood for his, and it looked as though there might be fighting between the two bands. But Crazy Horse did not want an internecine struggle, one that would weaken the Sioux and cost them many lives. Neither did his closest friends, so they kept him hidden from the younger warriors for fear that the sight of his sorry condition would anger them further and make them take their weapons and search for No Face.

In his own camp, No Face was rebuked by the older warriors. Crazy Horse had been well within his rights to persuade Black Buffalo Woman to leave her husband, and custom did not permit No Face to resort to violence. To prevent an outbreak of warfare between the two bands, he was required to send a gift of horses to Crazy Horse's village. The present was accepted, and peace made.

But these were evil days for Crazy Horse, and the gods who had marked him apart seemed to plot for him a destiny of grief and trouble. His younger brother, Little Hawk, went on a raiding party to the south. On the journey they met a party of white men, and in the fight that ensued, Little Hawk was killed. His death not only brought sadness to Crazy Horse's heart, it also intensified his already deep hatred of the Americans.

And his troubles with No Face were not over. By accident, he met his rival, and his anger was still so great that he tried to kill the warrior, who escaped only by dashing into a nearby river. This was a serious violation of the Sioux's code, for once the gift of horses had been accepted by Crazy Horse's camp, the feud was ended, and he had no right to renew it. As a punishment, he was removed from his office as a shirt-wearer.

This was a grave dishonor. The shirt-wearers were warriors chosen to carry out the decisions of the older leaders and were important officials. In spite of the disgrace, he continued to have a following of his own, and his word was still taken seriously by the warriors sitting in council. Among the Oglalas who did not join Red Cloud on the agency, he was a man of importance.

Because of the increasing numbers of white men along the Platte and the pressure brought by the government, he and his people spent more of their time in the north than they had done before; and as a consequence he was in the Yellowstone country during the summer of 1873 and joined in the gathering of tribes shortly after the fight with Custer.

The animosity between Sitting Bull and Grouard was causing concern among the Sioux because it might lead to greater ill-feeling between the two factions of the Hunkpapas. It was not wise, some of the older men thought, to allow the two enemies to live in the same camp no matter how careful they were to avoid each other. Crazy Horse's uncle, Little Hawk (the Sioux often repeated the same name in the same family), as one of the leaders, sent for Grouard and asked him how the trouble had started. When he learned the story, he told Grouard he should leave the Hunkpapas and come and live with the Oglalas.

Grouard took his advice. "I never went back to Sitting Bull's camp," he later wrote, describing the end of his friendship in those few words. From then on, if he was a follower of anyone, he was a follower of Crazy Horse, that strange, ill-fated Oglala.

*   *   *

As the year 1874 opened, the United States was in a somber mood. Greed and overexpansion had shaken the country. In Congress, an investigation had exposed the extraordinary manipulations of the Crédit Mobilier, a company formed specifically to milk the Union Pacific not only of its profits but of much of the capital with which Congress had intended to endow it. By charging exorbitant prices for doing the construction work, its stockholders enriched themselves and left the railroad a financial shell, all with the connivance of the Union Pacific officials.

Other scandals were about to break. Whisky manufacturers in St. Louis were avoiding federal taxes with the apparent assistance of officials of the Treasury Department. Secretary of War William W. Belknap, as a later investigation revealed, made a custom of charging for Indian traderships. Secretary of the Navy George M. Robeson gathered a fortune while he was in office as a result of selling Navy contracts. The American minister to Brazil defrauded Brazil of a hundred thousand dollars and was forced to flee the country while the taxpayers of the United States picked up his debt.

Almost everywhere the story was the same. The officials of the Federal Customs House in New York were thriving on corruption, and in Washington even the President's personal secretary had discovered ways to make extra dollars from his position by putting out his hand at the right time. Nor was the corruption limited to the federal government, for it extended into every corner of the land. In state capitals across the country, politicians manipulated the voters' mandates for personal gain; in the boardrooms of many corporations, the directors plotted wealth for themselves at the expense of other stockholders.

Partly as a result of this expensive and far-reaching corruption and partly because of international financial conditions, the United States had fallen into a depression. Jay Cooke's banking house had been only one of the most notable victims. Other firms were stricken, too, and the twins of bankruptcy and unemployment wrapped their tentacles around the nation. Not only was the Northern Pacific Railroad dead; no one was around with the funds to revive it. If Sitting Bull could have understood this, he would have given a sigh of relief, for economics and corrupt politics had done what he and the Sioux warriors had not been able to accomplish by themselves: They had stopped the intrusion of the Americans into the lands along the upper Missouri and the Yellowstone. A government that was unable to redeem its paper money with specie was not likely to spend funds surveying a route for a railroad that might never be built.

Yet any sigh of relief would have been premature. Although racked by graft and shaken by depression, the American people had not lost their vast energy or their spirit of expansionism. They were just as determined as ever to advance into the lands of the Indians, and one area they wanted was the Pah Sappa, the mysterious Black Hills of the Sioux.

All sorts of rumors surrounded those mountains rising along the western boundary of the present state of South Dakota and spilling over into Wyoming. They were regarded by some as a fortress to which the Indians regularly retreated, a stronghold from which they could launch attacks on white settlers. This alone would probably have not caused their invasion, but there were other rumors, too, and these rumors dealt with gold. Although unsubstantiated, word spread among the settlements that there were vast deposits in the Black Hills, and since the Indians would never mine it, why should not the white men?

There were two obstacles. One was posed by the Treaty of 1868, in which the United States government had recognized the right of the Indians to the mountains. (Mountains they are, rather than hills; Harney Peak is the highest point east of the Rockies.) The second was presented by their unusual geography, which discouraged exploration and caused travelers to circumvent them rather than cross over or through them. Originally they had been a great dome of sandstone and granite bulging from the earth's surface. Then as the centuries passed, the infinite chisel of the elements had cut away some of the sandstone, leaving the harder rocks as the bones of mountains. In the process, this formation was ringed by several "hogbacks," or steep narrow ridges. The largest of these, the Dakota Ridge, rises several hundred feet and serves as an enclosing wall. It was as if nature had intended to bar all trespassers.

The only practical way of penetrating this ridge, particularly with a wagon train, was to follow one of the narrow canyons that the water inside had cut in its attempt to escape to the drainage basin of the Missouri. As events proved, this was not difficult. But psychologically the sight of that strange wall surrounding those weird, pine-covered mountains—and they also sheltered numerous hostile Indians, the settlers were sure—was a deterrent even to the braver frontiersmen. Only a few wandered into the mountains, and the stories told by the survivors were vague and incoherent, the mutterings of untutored men explaining something they could not understand. Yet if the mountains contained gold, it was the duty of the government, the people thought, to extinguish the Indians' title and open them up to white prospectors. Only the army had the physical power necessary to do that.

The generals were conscious of the increasing pressure at least to explore the Black Hills, and they were also weighing the possibility of establishing a post in the area, so the soldiers could better monitor the Indians' movements. Before doing so, however, General Sheridan proposed an exploratory expedition through the Black Hills to determine what they contained. Although the Indians undoubtedly did not realize it, the army believed it could legally do this under the Treaty of 1868, because in the long text was a provision that permitted the government to send its officials onto the reservation.

At first, Sheridan thought of starting the expedition from Fort Laramie, which was only about a hundred miles away; but two trips to the fort convinced him that the Indians near there were in such a hostile state of mind that the sight of the marching column might provoke them into warfare. Casting around for another starting point, he finally selected Fort Abraham Lincoln on the Missouri, where Custer was stationed with part of the Seventh Cavalry, four companies being at Fort Rice, a little farther down the river.

Custer, of course, was delighted with the assignment, which in his opinion was far better than spending the summer in hot, mosquito-infested Fort Abraham Lincoln, and set about making his preparations. The Indians, of course, quickly learned what was going on, for they talked with the soldiers and traders. As a result, they sent several delegations to Fort Abraham Lincoln to protest against the expedition, but Custer went ahead with his plans undeterred.

Finally his force was assembled. It consisted of almost a thousand soldiers and teamsters, several journalists, some private miners, and numerous military aides, including President Grant's son, who was a lieutenant in the army. In spite of the presence of the miners and some geologists on the scientific staff, the army adamantly maintained that it was not searching for gold. But the West still looked on with interest. If gold should be discovered, there would be riches for many, and if enough gold were discovered, people believed the depression might be broken.

On the morning of July 2, 1874, the expedition started out. The wagons formed four long lines parallel to each other, with the cavalry riding in columns on either side. At the front was Custer, riding one of his favorite horses, a bay, and behind were a battery of artillery and the band, which was playing "The Girl I Left Behind Me."

Custer planned short marches for the first several days to give the men a chance to get into condition, and it is lucky he did. As he wrote Libbie Custer on the following morning, "Yesterday was a hard day on the trains. The recent rains had so softened the ground that the heavily-loaded wagons sunk to the hubs, and instead of getting into camp by noon as we expected, one battalion did not get in until after dark. . . . I am making a late start to give the mules a chance to graze." But in spite of the leisurely way they broke camp that morning, one of the soldiers forgot to bring along the three boards that Custer usually placed under his mattress to keep it dry. From then on, he had to lay it on the ground, wet or dry, just like the enlisted men.

The column moved in a southwesterly direction over alkali flats, where the feet of the infantry and the cavalry horses churned the dust into the air until the men choked on it, through grassy country where antelope abounded and some of the officers and men went hunting, and across the Grand River, whose tributaries had cut deep gullies into the ground. For two days, the column hunted for possible crossings and built bridges where necessary, but it finally emerged into an area with good water and grass.

Crossing the southeastern corner of Montana, they continued along the eastern border of what is now Wyoming; and in a dispatch dated August 2, Custer described entering the Black Hills. "On the 20th, we crossed the Belle Fourche [River]," he wrote, "and began, as it were, skirmishing into the Black Hills. We began by feeling our way carefully along the outlying ranges of hills, seeking a weak point through which we might take our way to the interior. We continued from the time we ascended from the valley of the Belle Fourche to move through a very superior country, covered with the best of grazing and an abundance of timber, principally pine, poplar, and several varieties of oak. As we advanced, the country skirting the Black Hills to the southward became each day more beautiful."

They had now passed through the hogback of the Dakota Ridge and started to climb into the area that formed the Black Hills proper. On July 25, they came into a magnificent valley, and Custer wrote, "This valley, in one respect, presented the most wonderful as well as beautiful aspect. Its equal I have never seen; and such, too, was the testimony of all who beheld it. In no private or public park have I ever seen such a profuse display of flowers. Every step of our march that day was amid flowers of the most exquisite colors and perfume. So luxuriant in growth were they that men plucked them without dismounting from the saddle. Some belong to new or unclassified species. It was a strange sight to glance back at the advancing column of cavalry, and behold the men with beautiful bouquets in their hands, while the head-gear of the horses was decorated with wreathes of flowers fit to crown a queen of May."

Although the Indians did not congregate in the Black Hills in the numbers that the Americans had suspected nor use it as a stronghold from which they launched attacks, they went there for game or to take shelter from the winter storms. So while Custer was leading his small army up what he named the Floral Valley, a group of about twenty-five Oglala Sioux composed of five lodges was camped nearby. Their leader was named One Stab and, not suspecting the presence of white men, he had gone off to a salt lick with three of the warriors to hunt for deer, leaving the camp in charge of another warrior, Slow Bull.

Custer had now crossed over the divide that separated Floral Valley from the next stream and had entered the valley where the Sioux were camped. Strange limestone formations had eroded into forms that looked like weird castles, which caused Custer to name it Castle Valley. "Having preceded the main column as usual . . . ," Custer wrote, "I came upon an Indian camp-fire still burning, and which, with other indications, showed that a small party of Indians had encamped there the previous night, and had evidently left that morning in ignorance of our close proximity. Believing that they would not move far, and that a collision might take place at any time unless a friendly understanding was arrived at, I sent my head scout, 'Bloody Knife,' and twenty of his braves to advance a few miles and reconnoiter the valley. This party had been gone but a few minutes when two of Bloody Knife's young men came galloping back and informed me that they had discovered five Indian lodges a few miles down the valley and that Bloody Knife, as directed, had concealed his party in a wooded ravine where they awaited further orders. Taking a company with me, which was afterward reinforced by the remainder of the scouts, and Colonel Hart's [company], I proceeded to the ravine where Bloody Knife and his party lay concealed, and from the crest beyond obtained a full view of the five Indian lodges, about which a considerable number of ponies were grazing. I was enabled to place my command still nearer to the lodges undiscovered. I then dispatched a guard, the interpreter, with a flag of truce, accompanied by two of our Sioux scouts, to acquaint the occupants of the lodge that we were friendly disposed and desired to communicate with them. To prevent either treachery or flight on their part, I galloped the remaining portion of my advance and surrounded the lodges."

The Sioux were startled to find American soldiers and their scouts on every side of the village, and the women and children were frightened. But Slow Bull was reassured by the interpreter's words and even more so by the sight of Custer dismounting and walking forward to shake the Indians' hands. At least, he thought, the soldiers did not intend to attack the village immediately. And after talking to Custer, he agreed to send some of the children in search of One Stab.

When the village's leader appeared, Custer told him he would like to have the Indians camp with him for several days and give him information about the Black Hills. In return for this service, he would give them flour, bacon, sugar, and coffee out of his supplies. One Stab accepted Custer's offer—he could not have done otherwise—but he was suspicious of so many soldiers and hoped he could make his escape. After Custer left and the warriors had a chance to talk among themselves, they agreed upon a plan. The village was to move away as quickly as possible, while four of them remained behind to collect the promised rations and to talk again with Custer, thus delaying as long as possible his discovery of their flight.

In the afternoon they appeared at Custer's camp, asked for the supplies, and told him they would join his force on the following morning. This was agreeable to Custer. While the Indians were talking, Custer noticed they showed signs of anxiety and thought they might be afraid the soldiers would attack them during the night. Consequently he offered to send a guard of fifteen men to protect their village. This, of course, upset them even more, because the detail would find the campground deserted. Two of the warriors therefore slipped away while Custer and One Stab were talking, and One Stab and the remaining warriors galloped off before the guard could saddle up.

It was now Custer's turn to be suspicious. He sent some of his scouts after the Indians to ask them to return. When they did not reappear, he sent more scouts, instructing them this time to seize the Sioux's bridles, if necessary, but, as he said, "to offer no violence." The Sioux, however, did not know what his orders were. When the scouts grabbed their reins, one of the Sioux seized the scout's gun, and in the ensuing struggle, the gun went off. The Sioux escaped, but, as Custer noted, "from blood discovered afterward, it was very evident that either the Indian or his pony was wounded."

One Stab was captured, and Custer kept him prisoner for several days in order to learn from him what he could about the Black Hills. This was not a peaceful act, but Custer, like many white men, expected the Indians to do what he wanted; and when they did not, he used force to effect his wishes.

So far, the expedition had accomplished much of its intended purpose. The white men had penetrated the Black Hills and dispelled

much of their mystery. No longer were they a dark, unexplored emi-
nence rising above the surrounding land, but a place that Americans
had visited and in which they had camped. Nor were they, as the
expedition had discovered, a hiding place for unnumbered Indians.
Yet the question on everyone's mind was still unanswered. Did they
contain gold? Every time the troops stopped long enough, the miners
searched for traces of it but found nothing.

On July 30, however, when they were about ten miles from Harney's Peak, one of the miners was panning in the stream. As he poured
out the water, he noticed some tiny particles of gold remaining in the
bottom, not many particles and not large ones, but enough to show the
metal existed in the hills. The next day they found richer sources and
estimated their value at ten cents a pan, a sum well worth the small
amount of labor entailed in panning it. This was not a fabulous find by
any means, but it substantiated the earlier rumors that the Black Hills
contained gold.

Before leaving, Custer had planned on sending mail and dispatches
back from the expedition. This seemed an opportune time, so he notified the troops that the messenger would leave the next day. Those
who were not on duty or engaged in looking for gold wrote letters
home, staying within the strict weight limits that formed the allotment
of ounces permitted each company.

In his own official report, Custer wrote glowingly of what he had
seen. "The country through which we have passed since leaving the
Belle Fourche River," he wrote, "has been generally open and extremely fertile. The main portion of that passed over since entering the
unexplored portion of the Black Hills consists of beautiful parks and
valleys, through which flows a stream of clear, cold water, perfectly
free from alkali, while bounding these parks or valleys is invariably
found unlimited supplies of timber, much of it capable of being made
into good lumber. In no portion of the United States, not excepting the
famous blue-grass region of Kentucky, have I ever seen grazing superior to that found growing wild in this hitherto unknown region.

"I know of no portion of our country where nature has done so
much to prepare homes for husbandmen, and left so little for the latter
to do, as here," he continued. "The open and timbered places are so
divided that a partly-prepared farm of almost any dimensions, of an
acre and upward, can be found here. Not only is the land cleared
and timber, both for fuel and building, conveniently located, with
streams of pure water flowing through its length and breadth, but

nature ofttimes seems to have gone further and placed beautiful shrub-
bery and evergreens in the most desirable locations for building-sites.
. . . Everything indicates an abundance of moisture within the space
enclosed by the Black Hills. The soil is that of a rich garden, and
composed of a dark mold of exceedingly fine grain."

After talking about the profusion of wild berries they had seen—
strawberries, currants, and gooseberries—and the ease with which cattle could winter there, he came to the point everyone wanted to hear
about. "As there are scientists accompanying the expedition who are
examining into the mineral resources of this region, the result of whose
researches will accompany my detailed report," he wrote, "I omit all
present reference to that portion of our explorations until the return of
the expedition, except to state, what will appear in any event in the
public prints, that gold had been found in paying quantities.

"I have upon my table," he wrote, "forty or fifty small particles of
pure gold, in size averaging that of a small pin-head, and most of it
obtained to-day from one panful of earth."

He then explained that they had never remained in one camp long
enough "to make a satisfactory examination in regard to deposits of
valuable minerals," but he hinted at the presence of silver deposits
also. Then he added with a touch of caution, "Until further examination is made regarding the richness of the gold, no opinion should be
formed."

Of course, his cautious warning—and those of others—was ignored. Many foresaw a new gold rush, and one journalist even prophesied that the national debt could be paid off as a result of the discovery. In any case, with the filing of his dispatch, Custer had made
the ultimate invasion of the Black Hills inevitable. Even if he had not
found the gold, his description of the agricultural richness of the
country was enough to stimulate the desire of the Americans to take
possession of it. That piece of paper, sent by a messenger across the
plains along with the letters of the soldiers, was more destructive of
the hopes of the Sioux than a battery of howitzers would have been. It
unleashed new forces against the Indians.

Custer may not have been fully conscious of what he had done. By
his warning to be cautious in appraising the extent of the gold, he
carefully stayed within the limits of an objective observer, a role imposed on him by his capacity as the official head of a government
expedition. On the other hand, he certainly knew that word of the gold
would flash across the telegraph wires of the nation and that his name

would appear in newspaper after newspaper, as indeed it did. And Custer was not averse to publicity for himself.

On August 15, the work of the expedition was done, and Custer prepared to leave the Black Hills. Writing in his dispatch book, he said, ". . . we pitched our tents for the last time in the Black Hills; nearly everyone being loathe to leave a region which had been so delightful in almost every respect. Behind us the grass and foliage were clothed in green of the freshest of May. In front of us, as we cast our eyes over the plains below, we saw nothing but a comparatively parched, dried surface, the sun-burnt pasturage of which offered a most uninviting prospect both to horse and rider, when remembering the rich abundance we were leaving behind us."

And he also added a few more words about gold, inflammatory words but still with enough caution to safeguard his position as an officer. "I referred in a former dispatch to the discovery of gold," he wrote. "Subsequent examinations at numerous points confirm and strengthen the fact of the existence of gold in the Black Hills. On some of the water-courses almost every panful of earth produced gold in small, yet paying, quantities. Our brief halts and rapid marching prevented anything but a very hasty examination of the country in this respect; but in one place and the only one done within my knowledge where so great a depth was reached, a hole was dug eight (8) feet in depth. The miners report that they found gold among the roots of the grass, and, from that point to the lowest point reached, gold was found in paying quantities. It has not required an expert to find gold in the Black Hills, as men without former experience in mining discovered it at the expense of but little time or labor."

Like the journey out, the trip back to Fort Abraham Lincoln contained its hardships. In the interest of further exploration, Custer chose a new route home, thus abandoning the trail he now knew in favor of the unfamiliar. Marching across the plains, some of the horses became so worn out that they could no longer be ridden, and several of them had to be shot. During one day, the men marched for thirty-five miles over a portion of the prairie that had been burned by a grass fire, set either by lightning or Indians and leaving no pasturage in its wake. Several men fell ill, one died, and the sick lists grew. But on August 30, the expedition arrived back at the fort.

"When we could take time to look everyone over," Libbie Custer later wrote, "they were all amusing enough. Some wives did not know their husbands, and looked indignant enough when caught in an embrace by an apparent stranger. Many, like the general [Custer], had grown heavy beards. All were sun-burnt, their hair faded, and their clothes so patched that the original blue of the uniform was scarcely visible. Of course there had been nothing on the expedition save pieces of white canvas with which to reinforce the riding-breeches, put new elbows on sleeves, and replace the worn knees.

"The boots were out at the toes, and the clothing of some were so beyond repairing that the officers wanted to escape observation by slipping, with their tattered rags, into the kitchen-door. The instruments of the band were jammed and tarnished, but they still produced enough music for us to recognize the old tune of 'Garry Owen,' to which the regiment always returned."

Custer was back, and the notes of his favorite tune were echoing across the prairie. But the words of his dispatch were echoing even farther. "It has not required an expert to find gold in the Black Hills, as men without former experience in mining discovered it at the expense of but little time or labor."

". . . at the expense of but little time or labor"—that was what America wanted. Easy riches even for the inexperienced. And that is what Custer invited them to find in the Black Hills.

XII

Victory at the Powder River

CHARLES COLLINS, editor of the Sioux City, Iowa, *Daily Tribune*, was as expansion-minded as almost any American. In 1869 he had joined an effort to encourage the establishment of Irish-American colonies along the Missouri River. His purpose was not to develop a few more frontier settlements but to add western Canada to the territorial possessions of the United States. Although his plan may have seemed farfetched, it was eminently practical and based on sound reasoning. These Irish-American settlers, he believed, would tend to drift north. Then if Ireland and England started fighting, they would march into Canada and seize Britain's western territory. In 1871 approximately sixty men did cross the border and captured a post belonging to the Hudson's Bay Company, but the federal government intervened and put a stop to Collins's plot.

He then turned his attention to the Black Hills and printed as many articles about them as he could find frontiersmen to interview, and in 1873 he produced a circular to promote an expedition to explore them. Only two adventurous souls responded, however, and General Harney announced he would use all the troops at his disposal to prevent any such invasion of the Indians' lands.

Although rebuffed in carrying out this idea, Collins read with interest the dispatches sent by Custer and the later reports of the individuals who had been with him on the expedition. As he read, his impatience mounted. With a friend, Captain Thomas H. Russell, he opened a recruiting office in Chicago to enlist members for a private expedition into the Black Hills in search of gold. But General Sheridan, as

259

soon as he heard what was going on, reiterated Harney's announcement of a few years before. This time, however, Collins did not give
up.

Publicly he said the expedition had been called off, but after returning to Sioux City, he remained in secret correspondence with the people whom his campaign had attracted. In October, 1874, only a short
time after Custer's return, almost thirty recruits, including a woman,
Annie D. Tallent, had gathered at Sioux City, ready to go to the Black
Hills. Russell was to be the active leader of the expedition, and Collins
was to remain behind to attend to its business.

The purported destination of the travelers was O'Neill, a small
settlement on the Elkhorn River in Nebraska, which had been founded
by a friend of Collins, and they painted the name on the cover of one
of their wagons. But they passed O'Neill, crossed the Niobrara, and
began looking for Custer's trail. When one of their members decided
to turn back, they held a council and decided it was too dangerous to
let him go. So far they had "by sagacity and shrewd management,"
according to a resolution they passed, "succeeded in eluding the
vigilance of the powers that be," and they did not want to risk the
chance that the army might learn their true destination. Therefore they
would permit no desertions and would use force, if necessary, to de-
tain anyone who tried to leave.

Early in December, they came upon Custer's trail, and by Christmas
Eve they had reached his former campground near Harney Peak. Here
they built a stockade and prepared to settle in for the long, rigorous
winter. The army, however, had now discovered the real purpose of
their trip and sent a troop of cavalry and some infantry to find them
and send them away. Late in December, the soldiers left Fort Robinson, but bitter weather had already set in. On New Year's Eve the
thermometer dropped to forty degrees below zero, and the snow was
blowing around them. Under those conditions, the commanding officer
saw little hope of finding the illegal settlers and gave the order to
return to the post. If he had not done so, he would probably have lost
some of his command, for the men were suffering severely from the
cold.

During the winter, the men at the small settlement hunted game and
mined between the frequent snowstorms. In February, 1875, two of
them returned to Sioux City to tell Collins there was indeed gold in the
Black Hills, and later two others were permitted to go to Fort Laramie, as the expedition relaxed its rules against desertions. But the

remainder stayed through the winter until one April night when, just as they were closing the gate of the stockade, an army captain and several soldiers rode up. They were in advance of a detachment that had been ordered to evict the settlers. Within twenty-four hours, the men and the woman who had weathered the winter in the Dakota wilderness were on their way back to civilization.

But the ejection of one party of miners did not solve the problem. The words of Custer that gold could be obtained "at the expense of but little time on labor" stimulated the imaginations of hundreds of adventurers, and they began to converge on the Black Hills. Public pressure for opening the area mounted, and the government's resistance to it weakened. In the spring of 1875, President Grant authorized another official expedition to explore the mountains, this one headed by a professor of mining, Walter P. Jenney. Its purpose was to make a more accurate survey of the region and a more scientific evaluation of its mineral resources. If gold was really there, perhaps the government should make an effort to buy the Black Hills from the Indians and open them up to settlement.

Jenney's official report left no doubt that the miners were not waiting for a formal revision of the Treaty of 1868 before they started prospecting, and it reflected the ineffectiveness of the army's patrol of the Black Hills. "When (June 16) I reached French Creek," Jenney wrote, "about fifteen miners were found camped four miles above the stockade [the one built by Russell's party], where they had been at work for several weeks, and had staked off claims, built small dams, and were digging ditches preparatory to commencing the sluicing on the bars along the banks of the stream. These miners were very enthusiastic in regard to the mineral wealth of the gulch. . . ."

The fever quickly spread to the military and civilian personnel who were accompanying him. "The fact of the existence of gold caused considerable excitement among the soldiers and teamsters of the escort," he reported, "and quite a number were busily engaged in prospecting along the creek, sinking holes to the bed-rock whenever there was the slightest indication of a deposit of gravel, or cleaning out old prospecting-shafts dug by the miners the preceding winter, and panning the pay-gravel which had been reported to be so rich in gold." The first results were so discouraging, however, "that after a few days they abandoned the search for the precious metal and did not resume it for more than two weeks, until a very encouraging prospect on a bar near the stockade caused a renewal of the excitement. . . ."

About five miles upstream from the stockade, Jenney discovered other miners had put a small sluice. "Unfortunately," he wrote, "the work on this bar was stopped by the stampede to the new discoveries in Spring and Castle Creeks, before it could be thoroughly tested and the richness of the deposit proved to be constant and regular."

At Spring Creek, the deposits were no richer, but the flow of water was better, making it possible to extract the gold with less labor. "While I am writing," Jenney said, "hundreds of miners are hard at work, prospecting this region, and the valuable deposits, wherever they exist, will soon be found and made to give up the gold they contain and have held useless locked up for ages."

Farther on in his report, Jenney wrote, "In July, while I was engaged with my assistants in testing the value of the placers on Spring Creek, a party of miners discovered gold in paying quantities on Castle Creek, below the north bend, and quite a stampede took place to the new diggings. When, three weeks afterward, I visited the new discovery, I found nearly one hundred and fifty miners camped along the valley, prospecting the claims they had taken. Most of them were old Montana miners, and, working together in companies, had done a surprising amount of work for so short a time. Nearly every claim had been prospected enough to prove its value, and preparations were being made to enable them to work with sluices on a large scale."

Article 2 of the Treaty of 1868, entered into by commissioners appointed with Congressional authorization, ratified by the Senate, and signed by the President of the United States, unequivocally stated that this land "is set apart for the absolute and undisturbed use and occupation of the Indians herein named . . . and the United States now solemnly agrees that no persons except those herein designated and authorized to do so . . . shall ever be permitted to pass over, settle upon, or reside in the territory described in this article. . . ."

Read that, you American Legionaires who, after a tour of desk duty in the latest war, thump your chests and don your uniforms on the Fourth of July and imagine you are kin to some of the real partriots this nation has produced.

Read that, you members of Congress, particularly those of you who sit on the military affairs committees and whose offices are adorned with self-congratulatory photographs of yourselves shaking hands with the world's famous, read that and ponder some of the statements you make about America's honor, an honor for which you encourage others to die.

Read that, you officers of the Air Force, including generals, who have deliberately lied to the President and the public, and realize you are part of a long heritage and are not the first to debase the pledge of your government.

Read that, you Presidents who prate about "peace with honor" at the cost of thousands of lives, as though "honor" was the same as American apple pie.

Read that, too, you who are the nation's true patriots, the millions of quiet men and women who provide the basic decency of this country and whose hearts are saddened by the antics of the summer patriots, the flag wavers, and the orators. Read that, you honest, good people, whose hearts yearn for a smaller gap between the vision and the truth, and know that once again you were disgraced.

". . . and the United States now solemnly agrees that no person. . . ."

". . . about fifteen miners were found camped four miles above the stockade. . . ."

". . . quite a number were busily engaged prospecting along the creek. . . ."

". . . I found nearly one hundred and fifty miners camped along the valley, prospecting the claims they had taken. . . ."

". . . work on this bar was stopped by the stampede to the new discoveries. . . ."

". . . and the United States now solemnly agrees. . . ."

*   *   *

The Jenney expedition made no pretense of measuring political or moral values. These were outside its mandate. Its sole purpose was to determine the potential utility of the Black Hills to the white men. This, it found, was great. "The Black Hills," Jenney reported, "are an oasis of verdure among the open and level plains. A luxuriant growth of grass spreads over the whole region; even on the rocky hillsides grass is found growing in the crevices in the rocks wherever there is a particle of soil for its support. A heavy forest covers the greater portion of this area, the trees growing thickly together and attaining full size, not only on the rich bottom-lands of the valleys but on the tops of the level limestone 'mesas;' and the steep rocky ridges are clothed with pine of good size to their very crests. . . .

"Even a casual examination shows that the soil of the valleys, the broad swales of the parks, and the bottom-lands along the creeks is exceedingly rich. . . . Often in sinking prospecting-pits along the valleys in search of gold, the soil would be found to be a black peaty loam from 2 to 3 feet in thickness, and frequently in the bottom-lands the soil was 4 feet in depth, resting on a gravelly subsoil."

As for gold? "In conclusion," Jenney wrote, "in reviewing the gold placers in the Black Hills, it should be noted that at best the gold-field has been but partly prospected, and it is extremely difficult to predict, even approximately, the value of any particular gulch or district until the gravel deposits have been completely opened and nearly worked out. . . .

"The deposits of auriferous [gold-bearing] gravel in the Black Hills may generally be said to be favorably situated for working, and that the gold can be very cheaply extracted with the expenditure of but comparatively little time or capital in opening the deposits. . . .

"Compared with the world-renowned districts in California and Australia, the placers at present discovered are not remarkably rich, yet there are claims already opened and worked which are yielding a very good return for the labor employed.

"At Cheyenne [Wyoming], the railroad is not more than two hundred and fifty miles from the gold-fields; the roads over which machinery and supplies are transported are excellent, the grades usually easy and the drives not long between water.

"The climate of the Black Hills," he continued, "is wonderfully healthy and invigorating; wood, water, and grass are everywhere abundant and of the best quality.

"There is gold enough," he said, "to thoroughly settle and develop the country, and, after the placers are exhausted, stock-raising will be the great business of the inhabitants, who have a world of wealth in the splendid grazing of this region."

Jenney wrote as though the United States already owned the Black Hills. He spoke casually of the roads leading into them, roads that went where no roads were supposed to go, of their inhabitants, people living where no one was to reside, and of the claims the miners were staking out, claims that were not registered with the Indians. But if the United States did not already possess this area, Jenney's report made pressure for its acquisition overwhelming.

First, however, the government felt compelled to go through motions of legality. The commander of the Department of the Platte that spring was General George Crook, who had just been transferred from Arizona, where he had been waging war successfully against the Apaches. Crook was an extremely modest man, who rarely even wore his uniform. The story is told that once when he was having an official picture taken, he arrived at the photographer's studio with his uniform under his arm. He put it on for the picture and then promptly took it off again. He was also known as a tenacious, but fair, fighter. In Arizona, for example, he always took pains to make no promises to the Indians that he could not keep, but he also pursued them more vigorously than any general had done.

But the task of driving the miners out of the Black Hills was too much even for him. In July he entered the mountains with troops, but he realized it was hopeless to try to drive the miners away by force. The sentiment of much of the country was on their side, and if they resisted, the position of the army would be untenable. So Crook, having little backing from Washington, resorted to diplomacy. He issued a proclamation, asking the miners to assemble at Camp Harney near the stockade built by Russell's party and draw up resolutions that would "secure to each, when the country shall have been opened, the benefit of his discovery and the labor he has already expended."

The implication of those words was clear. Crook definitely expected the United States to take possession of the Black Hills, at which time the miners could come back. In the meantime, the claims they had already made would be protected. The miners accepted Crook's proposal, but as fast as some left, others came. The army stopped one party of miners headed for the Black Hills, burned their wagons, and demanded that each of them give his word not to try to reenter them. One of the prospective miners, however, refused to sign his parole and hired a lawyer. The government's attorney, by bending the law to fit the public will, failed to uphold the army's position, thus greatly hindering the effort to keep the Americans out of the Indians' lands.

The Indians, of course, knew what was going on and were greatly disturbed, for the white men had again violated their word. Yet some of the Indians who had previously stayed away from the agencies were driven to them by the lack of game and the need for supplies and began to show up. The agent at Standing Rock noted "the success recently had in inducing a number of chiefs and headmen from the hostile camp on the Yellowstone to come in and be enrolled. . . .

"The Indians of which this hostile camp are composed are from all the different bands of the great Sioux family, but the great majority are said to be Hunkpapa Sioux. Their principal chief is Sitting Bull, a Hunkpapa Sioux, who is described to me as a man about 45 years old, and possessed of more than ordinary intelligence and ability for an Indian. [The implication that Indians were inferior is obvious.] He is said to wield great influence and authority over his followers. The other chiefs of note that are recognized at this camp, and who take rank in the order named, are Four Horn, Iron Dog, Slave, Little Knife, Gall [the leader of the faction opposed to Sitting Bull], and Red Horn.

"The four latter have come to this agency and enrolled themselves and a portion of their followers," the agent continued. "Slave and Little Knife came in some time ago, and are become entirely reconciled to their present condition. Gall and his followers, owing to more recently availing themselves of the privileges and advantages of the treaty of 1868, are yet restless, and Red Horn, whose first appearance here was in May last, with his followers, together with other chiefs and headmen of smaller bands and lesser note, principal among whom is a chief named Long Dog, enrolled in June last, are wild, demonstrative, and insolent, and very difficult to manage; yet they all of them manifest a desire to cultivate friendly relations with the Government and its agents, and with all the white people except soldiers, for whom they manifest great antipathy. They attribute the encroachments upon their country and the loss of friends and relatives killed in battle and otherwise to the presence of soldiers among them, and believe they are paid for killing them and robbing them of their country."

The agent had been at Standing Rock only since May 1, and his unfamiliarity with the Sioux under his charge could have accounted for his optimism. The agent at the Spotted Tail agency reported that "a less number of Northern Indians have visited this agency than during the previous year, and more of ours have remained near the agency than formerly, for the reasons that they did not go south to the hunting-grounds this season and the excitement about the Black Hills has kept them together." The agent had noted two important points about the Indians. The shortage of game was making them more dependent on the agencies—not a desire for peace—and they were aroused over the invasion of the Black Hills.

The agent at Red Cloud agency also commented on the effect of diminishing game. As a result of the Indians' "roving habits," he reported, "and proximity of the hunting region of the Black Hills, Bighorn, and Powder River countries, the number of Indians at the agency at different times is variable. This constitutes one of the chief difficulties in making an accurate distribution of food, and in making estimates of the quantity required for a year's supply. The rapid destruction of the game caused last year a larger number to remain permanently at the agency, rendering an increase in the amount of supplies necessary. As there are no means of ascertaining the facts regarding the amount of game, or the exact number of Indians remaining in the hunting regions, estimates must of necessity be but approximate. And this will continue to be the case until the hostile bands are broken up."

The hunters were accomplishing what the army could not. Custer could fight Sitting Bull at the Yellowstone and leave the battlefield thinking he had taught the Hunkpapas a lesson, but he had done far less to damage the Indians than the men who shot the buffalos and smaller animals. A profusion of game was absolutely necessary to the Indians' way of life, and the growing lack of it had brought more Hunkpapas and other northern Indians to the agencies than the military campaigns had done.

But their physical presence did not mean they were adjusting to the white men's ways. They made no effort to become the farmers the Americans wished them to be. They had little interest in the churches and teachings of the missionaries sent among them, nor did they want to put their children in schools. In every way, they resisted the attempts to convert them to a different civilization, and yet they could not retain one of the underlying features of their own, its independence. At the agencies, they haggled over the allotment of the rations they had come to need and supplemented them with short hunting trips and trade with the hostile Indians. But they were not free men, and they were not friends of the Americans. Men conquered by hunger rarely are. Although they had been driven to the agencies by the threat of starvation and consequently forced to submit to the white men's will, they saw no reason for parting with their lands to gratify the miners.

The agent at Standing Rock, in spite of his optimism about the future, recognized this. "The expedition to the Black Hills by the military," he said, "and the subsequent invasion of that country by parties in search of the precious metals, caused much dissatisfaction and bad feeling among the Indians. They emphatically expressed their belief that the Government was trifling with their rights in permitting the treaty to be violated, and asked the pertinent question, 'How can the Great Father expect us to observe our obligations under treaty stipulations when he permits his white children to break it by coming into our country to remain without our consent?' The lawless invasion of the Black Hills by white men, in violation of the intercourse laws of the United States and treaty stipulations with the Indians, and the apparent tardiness or inability of the Government in removing them, caused great distrust and lack of confidence among the Indians toward all white men and the white man's Government."

But the government had a way of remedying this, one it had often used in the past. If a treaty did not work in favor of the Americans, then relace it with another one that would. And so in 1875 a new commission was appointed for the purpose of negotiating a new agreement with the Indians that would include the purchase of the Black Hills. Then everything would be legal, and the miners could dig for gold.

Looked at one way, the decision was not utterly immoral. The Americans, as the Indians at Standing Rock had complained, had not been able to control their individuals, but neither had the Indians. Both sides had continued skirmishing after the treaty had been signed. The Americans had not provided an adequate life for the Indians on the reservations, but neither had many Indians tried to provide one for themselves. Large numbers of them refused to take up farming, which was their principal hope for survival. Even in accepting the "bounty of the government," as some officials called it, the Indians were not cooperative, refusing to be counted so that the agents could neither equitably distribute the supplies they had nor even order the proper amounts. Now, after the expiration of the four-year period during which they were to receive subsistence, they were still unable to support themselves.

This was a matter of grave concern to many of the agents. In their reports to Washington, they had again and again pointed out that regardless of the original provisions of the Treaty of 1868, the government would have to continue feeding the Indians for some years to come. Otherwise mass starvation would take place.

The specter of indefinite charity lay ahead, and this provided a moral excuse for another treaty. In his instructions to the new commission, the Commissioner of Indian Affairs emphasized this point. "The attention of the commission is invited to the tenth article of the treaty of 1868, in which provision is made for an appropriation for clothing and other beneficial purposes for the Sioux, for thirty years from the date of the treaty, and also for subsistence of meat and flour, for a period of four years. [This was the critical issue.] This latter provision has expired by treaty limitation, leaving the Sioux Nation dependent for the necessaries of life upon the annual charity of Congress. The appropriations for the last few years for this purpose of subsistence vary from $1,200,000 to $1,500,000 annually, and if it should be denied by Congress in any of the annual appropriation bills, these Indians must be left to great hardships, and to hunger verging upon starvation, unless they attempt to supply their wants by marauding among the settlers, which attempt would inevitably lead to a conflict with the military. . . .

"The best interests of these Indians will require that any compensation made to them shall include this provision for subsistence in some form, and that in no case shall it take the form of a cash annuity. . . .

"The outlook for this tribe," he continued, "is by no means encouraging. They cannot live by the chase; they cannot be supported in idleness by the Government."

The answer, then, was to make a new treaty that would give the Indians a longer period in which to adjust to the way of life the white men planned for them. Since this would require considerable additional expense not envisioned by the Treaty of 1868, the Indians could pay for it by ceding the Black Hills. What could be fairer? The Indians would receive the food they needed, and the Americans would obtain the land they wanted.

Some people, however, saw the inherent injustice in this line of reasoning. The Indians were not wards of the government because they wanted to be. They were wards because the game was gone and because they were subject to military attacks if they resumed their old life. Rather than dependents, they were almost like prisoners of war. Those who looked at the proposed treaty in this light, however, were too few and their voices too faint to influence the government's policy. The dominant will of the country demanded the acquisition of the Black Hills.

The commission was originally instructed to hold the council at Fort Sully as soon as possible, but it finally decided to meet at the Red Cloud agency on September 1. Three members went ahead to notify the Indians at the other agencies, and the reaction was what might have been expected. The agent at Standing Rock wrote, "When asked to go to the grand council at Red Cloud to participate in treating for the sale of the Black Hills, they very intelligently reviewed the whole condition of affairs, and finally refused to go, saying it was no use making agreements when the Great Father would either let white men break them or had not the power to prevent them from doing so. Notwithstanding that these Indians promised the commissioners who visited them here in August last that they would attend, yet when the time arrived for their departure they refused to go. . . . I finally succeeded, however, in prevailing upon all of the principal chiefs and headmen, with a number of their head soldiers, to go."

This was typical of the reluctant participants being assembled at the Red Cloud agency. But these were the more peaceful Indians. The council also wanted to meet with the bands who had not come to the agencies and were camped on the Yellowstone. The problem was how to find them. The year before, Frank Grouard had been thinking of leaving the Indians and had made a visit to the Red Cloud agency in the fall. Then in the spring, he returned to the agency and remained there until the arrival of the commissioners. He knew where the Indians were and was on friendly terms with some of them, and he needed money badly. So he accepted the commissioners' offer to serve as their messenger. With Louis Richard, a trader, and about a hundred warriors who were committed to agency life, he started out for the camp.

Although he was well supplied with tobacco to offer as a sign of his friendly intentions, the mission was dangerous. He had enemies as well as friends among the Indians, and the news he was bringing was nothing any of them wanted to hear. He found the camp on the Tongue River, near the present town of Dayton, Wyoming. "They received us in a very hostile manner," he later wrote. "They were just on the point of going on the warpath. I went out to Crazy Horse's lodge as soon as I got in and told him what we had come for. His father went out and harangued the camp and told them it was best to listen to what we had to say. Crazy Horse told me himself that all who wanted to go in and make this treaty could go, but he said, 'I don't want to go.' He said that whatever the headmen of the tribe concluded to do after hearing our plan, they could and would do."

The day after the messengers arrived, Sitting Bull sent word that he wanted to see Grouard. This was a critical moment. The camp was in an ugly, restless mood, and Grouard had not seen Sitting Bull for many months. If the Hunkpapa still harbored his anger against Grouard, he could easily kill him. As a precaution, Grouard took Crazy Horse with him when he visited Sitting Bull's tepee, but their meeting passed peacefully. Grouard tried to persuade his former friend it would be best if he went to the council at Red Cloud, but Sitting Bull refused to commit himself, saying he would speak out only when the warriors assembled the next morning.

When the meeting began, Grouard later wrote, "All the buck Indians, about one thousand, made a big circle in the center of the camp. Big Breast was the first to make a speech. He got up and refused flatly to come and told me his reason why. He didn't want to sell the land, but he said: 'All those that are in favor of selling their land from their children, let them go.'

"He spoke for a long time, but to that effect.

"Sitting Bull then got up and made a long speech," Grouard continued. "It had the same purport. He said he would not sell his land. He said he had never been to an agency and was not going in. He was no agency Indian. He told me to go out and tell the white men at Red Cloud that he declared open war and would fight them wherever he met them from that time on."

At that moment, the council at Red Cloud was doomed to be a failure. No matter what the Indians at the agency agreed to do, the northern Indians were not going to give up the Black Hills without a struggle. Sitting Bull's "entire harangue was an open declaration of war," Grouard wrote.

Little Hawk got up and spoke on behalf of Crazy Horse's band. He said, according to Grouard, "My friends, the other tribes have concluded not to go in, and I will have to say the same thing."

Altogether about one hundred warriors spoke, expressing their opinions, while the Indians from the Red Cloud agency tried to explain the advantages of their coming in to talk. At the end of the council, the northern Indians asked Grouard's party how long they expected to remain and were told three days. The arrangement was made that any Indians who wanted to go to Red Cloud would move over to the other side of the Tongue River. They would then all travel together.

That night a number of the more hostile Indians decided to massacre the messengers, but Crazy Horse learned what was happening. He called the leaders together and berated them for violating the Sioux's tradition. Once the messengers had arrived and their tobacco had been accepted, custom demanded that they be fed and allowed to depart safely. "That cooled everything down and stopped it right off, and there was no more said about it," Grouard later remarked.

When the time came to leave, a considerable number of Indians had moved to the other side of the Tongue River, but the majority would not even discuss selling the Black Hills. Nevertheless, when Grouard returned to the Red Cloud agency, the commissioners were pleased with what he had done. "I got quite a little sum of money—about

$500—" . . . for the trip, Grouard said. "That was the first money I had received or handled since I had been captured by the Indians. It gave me the means to buy what clothing I wanted, and I needed clothes badly. I was dressed in regular Indian costume. I had long hair. I stayed at the agency quite a while. I was getting familiar with the English language again. It was two or three months," he added, "before I could talk English without getting the Indian mixed up with it."

The council at the Red Cloud agency was supposed to convene on September 1, but the commission did not get there until September 4. Even then the meeting could not begin, because the Indians from the Spotted Tail agency thought it should convene at a point halfway between the two places. Finally a compromise was reached, and the council opened on the White River about eight miles from the Red Cloud agency. But this argument had consumed thirteen days.

The commissioners were also divided among themselves. A majority believed they should negotiate only for the mining rights in the Black Hills, "as it seemed clear . . . that the Indians would not make an absolute sale upon any terms that would be acceptable to the commission." Furthermore, it would be impossible to get three-fourths of the adult population to sign for the sale of the Black Hills, as required by the Treaty of 1868. The minority thought it would be possible to get full title to the mountains at the same cost as the mining rights and "that in the end it would become necessary to divest the Indians of all title to the hills." Probably they were right. Certainly the Indians would have regarded the mining rights "and such other rights as are incidental and necessary thereto" as an outright sale of the land, and the minority commissioners were correct in believing the Americans would eventually want to take complete title to the lands. The majority opinion, however, prevailed.

When the council finally opened on September 20, the chairman explained that the government only wanted the mining rights and "when the gold or other valuable minerals are taken away, the country will again be yours to dispose of in any manner you wish." He then said, "The great object we have in making this agreement is to have a lasting peace with you. It will be hard for our Government to keep the whites out of the Hills. To try to do so will give you and our Government great trouble, because the whites that may wish to go there are very numerous." This at least was a frank admission that the government was impotent to enforce the terms of the Treaty of 1868 as they applied to the Americans, but it most certainly must have left the Indians doubting the ability of the government to enforce a new treaty either.

Then the chairman explained, "If you will give us the rights we ask we will give you in return a fair equivalent, and in such a way as to do you good and improve your condition. We do not wish to take from you any right or property you have without making a fair return for it. We are asked by our Great Father, and it is our own wish, to consider the interests of both parties as far as we can." The basic trouble, however, was that the interests of both parties did not coincide. This was not a transaction between a willing buyer and a willing seller simply bargaining over the price. The buyer was willing enough, so willing that if it could not get the land by purchase, it would probably take it by force. But the seller was far from willing, so unwilling, indeed, that the council could not have been held without the threats of starvation and war.

Then the chairman added another point: The United States wanted not only the Black Hills, but much of the Bighorn country, too. But the commissioners soon dropped this issue. They could see they were going to have enough difficulty in getting the Black Hills, if they acquired them at all. "The Indians," they later reported, "seemed to be divided into two parties, the larger willing to part with the Hills if a large price could be obtained; a smaller portion, more resolute, because composed chiefly of the young men, were opposed to parting with the Hills for any consideration whatever."

"These differences," the commission explained in its report, "delayed a second meeting until the 23rd. . . ." On that day, the commissioners went out to the council ground; and about noon, some two hundred warriors came galloping up to the tent where the commissioners were waiting and circled around it, firing their guns. Soon other bands followed the example of the first, and the commission found itself surrounded by angry warriors dressed in their war regalia. When Red Cloud and the other chiefs arrived, none of them dared offer to sell the Black Hills, regardless of the price, in the presence of such opposition. As a consequence, they spent an hour conferring among themselves, trying to decide on their next step.

Suddenly a single warrior broke through the crowd and rode directly toward the comissioners, shouting that he was going to kill them. Some of the other Indians intercepted him and took him away, but the crowd was now even more excited. The warriors began dashing back and forth on their horses, a practice they often followed before a battle to make the animals get their second winds. They yelled insults and taunts and called for a charge against the commissioners and the relative handful of troops guarding them. The interpreter, knowing what they were saying, believed that an attack was imminent. To the horror of the commissioners, a band of Sioux now dashed toward them, but these were not hostile. Rather they were Sioux who believed in preserving the Indians' custom of not killing men with whom they were holding council. By threatening to fight if necessary, their leader gradually persuaded the crowd to disperse, and the commissioners went back to the agency under escort.

Even the commission knew they had clearly failed. Half of the Indians took down their tepees and departed. "It was plain from the proceedings of that day," the commission reported, "that no agreement could be made; yet the members of the commission were anxious to continue their efforts at least long enough to secure an open and public expression of the view of the Indians." As a result, they sent for twenty of the leading chiefs and talked to them at the agency for three days.

But the chiefs made it clear they would not part with the Black Hills on easy terms. Red Cloud was one of the speakers. "These hills out here to the northwest," he said, "we look upon as the head chief of the land. My intention was that my children should depend on these hills for the future. I had hoped that we should live that way always hereafter." He was willing to sell the lands, but he wanted enough money so that the interest would support his people in the years to come. He also asked for houses, steers, furniture, food, tobacco, and equipment. What he wanted was far more than the commission could possibly offer him.

Another chief, who was also willing to sell the Black Hills for a high enough price, took the opportunity to complain about the cattle issued to the Indians. "The beef-cattle that the Great Father has issued to me, no doubt each steer was weighted twice and called two." He also demanded payment for "that road." When a commissioner asked him what road he meant, he scornfully replied, "that thieves' road." He was referring to the route taken by Custer.

Another opened his comments by saying, "I never call anybody our Great Father but God," thus deriding the paternalistic and condescending term the Americans used for their President when they were talking to Indians. But for convenience he employed the words and continued, "You white people have brought word from the Great Father. You have brought tidings, and it is not a very small thing. It seems as though you take the head from my shoulders; that is just the way I feel. . . . Our Great Father has asked me to give up the heart of this land where I was born and raised, and the heart of this land is big and good, and I have camped all around it and watched and looked after it." He then went on to demand rations for the Indians, not for seven generations as many of the others had done, but for the entire future existence of his race.

On September 29, at the request of Spotted Tail, the Brulé, the commissioners agreed to place their best offer in writing. They were willing to pay $400,000 a year for the mining rights or $6,000,000 for the outright purchase of the Black Hills. This was far less than the Indians wanted, so the council came to an end.

"We do not believe their temper or spirit can or will be changed," the commission reported, "until they feel the power as well as the magnanimity of the Government; and inasmuch as Congress is required by existing law to approve of any agreement before it is made binding on either party, the commission are unanimously of the opinion that Congress should take the initiative and by law settle for itself what shall be done upon the whole subject, and then notify the Sioux Nation of its conclusion. If they assent to the terms proposed," the commission continued in the same high-handed manner, "let them be carried out by the Government; if they do not consent the Government should withhold all supplies not required by the treaty of 1868. If the Government will interpose its power and authority, they are not in a condition to resist. This authority should be exercised mildly but firmly, and should be directed mainly to provisions looking to the ultimate civilization of the Indians. They can never be civilized except by the mild exercise, at least, of force in the beginning."

That was the conclusion of the commission, and it was a conclusion that could only lead to war. The commission assumed the Indians would submit to force, but this assumption was unwarranted. Their mood at the council had not been submissive, and up at the Yellowstone were those who had refused even to talk. Grouard had reported that Sitting Bull's "entire harangue was an open declaration of war," and Louis Richard, the trader, had carried this message from Crazy Horse: "Are you the Great God that made me, or was it the Great God that made me who sent you? If He asks me to come see him, I will go, but the Big Chief of the white men must come to see me. I will not go to the reservation. I have no land to sell. There is plenty of game here for us. We have enough ammunition. We don't want any white men here." Those were not the words of Indians who would surrender to "the mild exercise" of force.

The inability of the commission to persuade the Indians to sign the new treaty did not stop the flow of white men into the Black Hills. The lure of gold called them, and they responded. As one army officer noted, "During the closing hours of the year 1875 the miners kept going into the Black Hills, and the Indians kept annoying all wagon-trails and small parties found on the roads. There were some killed and others wounded and a number of wagons destroyed, but hostilities did not reach a dangerous state, and were confined almost entirely to the country claimed by the Indians as their own. It was evident, how-ever, to the most obtuse that a very serious state of affairs would develop with the coming of grass in the spring."

*   *   *

A new crisis was brewing on the plains, but Washington did not understand its dimensions. In the fall of 1875, Indian Inspector E. C. Watkins, after returning from an inspection trip, filed a report with the Commissioner of Indian Affairs. "I have the honor to address you," he wrote, "in relation to the attitude and condition of certain wild and hostile bands of Sioux Indians in Dakota and Montana that came under my observation during my recent tours through their country. I refer to Sitting Bull's band and other bands of the Sioux Nation under chiefs or 'headmen' of less note, but no less untamable and hostile. . . . From their central position they strike to the East, North and West, steal horses, and plunder from all the surrounding tribes, as well as frontier settlers and luckless white hunters or emigrants wherever found unarmed."

After reviewing their character, he came up with his recommenda-tion for action. "The true policy, in my judgment," he wrote, "is to send troops against them in the winter, the sooner the better, and whip them into subjection. They richly merit punishment for their incessant warfare, and their numerous murders of white settlers and their fami-lies, or white men wherever found unarmed."

Following this recommendation, the government embarked on a program that was unrealistic on several counts. In December, the Secretary of the Interior ordered all Indians to report to the agencies by January 31, 1876, or face the threat of force. But the winter was unusually severe, and the messengers had difficulty even reaching the scattered bands. The Indians could not have been expected to travel through the snow-covered wilderness with their women and children to gratify the Americans' wish. Second, there was barely enough food at the agencies to feed the Indians who were already there. The arrival of more would merely have aggravated a serious problem. From the Americans' point of view, however, the gravest miscomprehension was the estimate of the number of Indians who were away from the agencies. The Commissioner of Indian Affairs believed there were about three thousand in all and that they could not muster more than six to eight hundred warriors, a gross miscalculation. As the Secretary of War later admitted, "The force estimated as necessary to whip them was one thousand men."

On February 1, 1876, the Secretary of the Interior notified the Secretary of War that "the time given him [Sitting Bull] in which to return to an agency having expired and the advices received at the Indian Office being to the effect that Sitting Bull still refuses to comply with the directions of the Commissioner, the said Indians are hereby turned over to the War Department for such action on the part of the Army as you may deem proper under the circumstances."

The action the army deemed proper was to send Crook into the field, using Fort Fetterman as the point of departure for what the government believed would be a short and decisive campaign. Fort Fetterman was on the North Platte west of Fort Laramie at the point where the old Bozeman Trail began.

Receiving a report that there was an Indian encampment on the Powder River, Crook headed north on March 1, 1876. He had with him ten companies of cavalry, two companies of infantry, a wagon train with forage for the horses, and a pack train consisting of four hundred mules. He also had a large number of capable scouts whom he had recruited. These included Frank Grouard, who had now definitely decided to side with the white men.

"The march from Fort Fetterman to old Fort Reno, a distance of ninety miles," wrote Captain John G. Bourke, who had fought with Crook against the Apaches in Arizona and accompanied him now, "led through a country of which the less said the better; it is suited for grazing and may appeal to the eye of a cow-boy, but for the ordinary observer, especially during the winter season, it presents nothing to charm any sense; the landscape is monotonous and uninviting, and the vision is bounded by swell after swell of rolling prairie, yellow with a thick growth of winter-killed buffalo or bunch grass, with a liberal sprinkling of the most uninteresting of all vegetation—the sage-brush. The water is uniformly and consistently bad—being both brackish and alkaline, and when it freezes into ice the ice is nearly always rotten and dangerous. Wood is not to be had for the first fifty miles, and has to be carried along in wagons for commands of any size. Across this charming expanse the wind howled and did its best to freeze us all to death. . . ."

In spite of Bourke's gloomy words, he and the rest of the soldiers were in good spirits. Crook, who was an eminently practical man, let his soldiers wear what they wished as long as they were warm, so although the column presented a nondescript appearance, the men were comfortable. The Indians quickly learned about the column and tried to run off the herd the first night; and during the daytime, small groups would appear on the flanks. But Crook ordered his men not to pursue them, because he was quite certain they were decoys, and he refused to fall into that often-used trap.

After several days of marching, they came to the ruins of old Fort Reno, which the army had abandoned at the same time that it gave up Forts Philip Kearny and C. F. Smith. "Nothing remained," wrote Bourke, "except a few chimneys, a part of the bake-house, and some fragments of the adobe walls of the quarters or offices. The grave-yard had a half dozen or dozen of broken, dilapidated head-boards to mark the last resting-places of brave soldiers who had fallen in desperate wars that civilization might extend her boundaries."

A short distance from Fort Reno, Crook made camp and called his officers together. While fighting the Apaches, Crook had learned the importance of traveling light when attacking the Indians. Soldiers encumbered with wagon trains and the army's usual paraphernalia could not move fast enough to outmaneuver them. At this point, therefore, he intended to send the wagon train back to the site of Fort Reno under guard of the infantry. The rest of the men would then move forward with the smallest amount of supplies compatible with the bitter cold. No one was allowed to carry more clothing than he could wear on his back, and their bedding was severely limited. Even the food was cut to half rations.

On the night of March 7, the column began to move north in the moonlight. "At first the country had the undulating contour of that near old Fort Reno, but the prairie 'swells' were soon superseded by bluffs of bolder and bolder outline until, as we approached the summit of the 'divide' where 'Clear Fork' heads, we found ourselves in a region deserving the title mountainous. In the bright light of the moon and stars, our column of cavalry wound up the steep hill-sides like an enormous snake, whose scales were glittering revolvers and carbines. The view was certainly very exhilarating, backed as it was by the majestic landscape of moonlight on the Big Horn Mountains. . . . Above the frozen apex of 'Cloud Peak' the evening star cast its declining rays. Other prominences rivaling this one in altitude thrust themselves out against the midnight sky. Exclamations of admiration and surprise were extorted from the most stolid as the horses rapidly passed from bluff to bluff, pausing at times to give every one an opportunity to study some of Nature's noble handiwork."

Early that morning the weary men made camp on Clear Creek, a fork of the Powder River, and quickly fell asleep. At eight o'clock, they woke up to find themselves in a blinding snowstorm with the flakes whirling from every direction, so there was no escaping them. "Our situation was not enviable," Bourke wrote. "It is true we experienced nothing we could call privation or hardship, but we had to endure much positive discomfort. The storm continued all day, the wind blowing with keenness and at intervals with much power. Being without tents, there was nothing to do but grin and bear it. Some of our people stretched blankets to the branches of trees, others found a questionable shelter under the bluffs, one or two constructed nondescript habitations of twigs and grass, while General Crook and Colonel [Thaddeus H.] Stanton seized upon the abandoned den of a family of beavers which a sudden change in the bed of the stream had deprived of their home."

As the men marched on, the weather grew even colder. One morning the thermometer did not register. It was built to go down to twenty-two degrees below zero, but the mercury lay congealed in the bulb. Day after day when the soldiers saddled up, they first had to put the bits in hot water or draw them through warm ashes to prevent damage to the horses' mouths; and before the cook could fry the bacon, he had to cut it into pieces with an ax. To add to their troubles, the trail was frozen and slippery, and often the horses or mules fell down.

For several days they saw no signs of Indians, but then the scouts reported discovering the sites of former villages. Yet there was no evidence of any large occupied camp. As Crook pointed out, his men were in no danger of starvation, because they had so many mules with them. But he had taken rations for only fifteen days, and either he had to find the Indians soon or turn back.

Most of the scouts thought they would be camped on the Yellowstone, but Grouard was certain they would be on the Powder River. With Crook's consent, he went ahead to reconnoiter. After seven hours of riding, he saw two Indians who were tracking game. Although the other scouts had been ordered to remain with the command, several of them came riding along the hillsides in full view. The Indians noticed them and fled in the direction of the Powder River.

The camp, as Grouard rightly surmised, was on the bank of the Powder. The band was headed by a Sioux, named He Dog, who usually was a follower of Crazy Horse. He Dog later said he had heard about the Americans' ultimatum and had decided to go to the agency. On the way, he had been joined by Two Moon and a band of Cheyennes who were coming from the Red Cloud agency to trade with the Sioux. So they were well supplied with powder and lead, and the lodges were filled with meat. As soon as the snows melted, they would again worry about war, but the bitter cold made winter a time for peace. Even the report of the Indians who saw the scouts did not alarm them, for they apparently mistook them for a small band of Crows.

Among the officers in Crook's command was Colonel J. J. Reynolds, who held a brevet rank as a general. While serving in the Department of Texas, he had been reprimanded and relieved of his command, but Crook liked him and now offered him a chance to redeem his reputation by leading the attack on He Dog's village. He was to go ahead with Grouard, and if they found a village, he was to burn the tepees but keep the horses and the dried meat. He was also to send a courier back to Crook, who would then come up with the four companies he retained under his own command. If they did not find the village, they were to meet at a designated point on the Powder River.

Reynolds seized the opportunity Crook offered him. He did not, however, entirely trust Grouard. The scout had lived with the Indians so long he might well be a traitor who planned to lead them into an ambush. This thought was shared by some of the other officers, and the poison of suspicion tainted the expedition.

Grouard went ahead in the dark, following the trail of the Indians he had seen. At daylight, he was on a hill overlooking the Powder River. A deep fog covered the valley, so all he could see was mist, but he could hear the bells on the Indians' horses. One other scout was with him, and Grouard sent him back to notify Reynolds he had found the camp. While he waited, he moved down the slope until he was below the blanket of fog and could see the village.

The Indians were camped in the circle of an old riverbed in the shelter of a bank. Above the bank was a mesa covered with sage brush. Their horses were grazing at the northern end of this mesa. Also to the north was a row of hills. From his hiding place, Grouard could overhear an Indian announcing to the camp that they had sent out several warriors to locate and identify the scouts they had seen the previous day. But from what he said, Grouard realized they had taken a trail different from the one he had followed, so they were still unaware of the presence of the soldiers.

When Reynolds arrived and prepared to attack, he divided his force into three groups. The first was to cut off the Indians' herd and charge the village. The second was to follow the first, occupy the village, and burn the tepees. The third was to move north and prevent the Indians from escaping through the hills.

To spare their horses, the Americans advanced at a trot. The first Indian to notice them was a boy who was about fifteen. He was driving his horses down a small ravine that separated the Americans from the village. When they entered it, he let out a cry of warning that echoed against the bluffs. Then, as they neared the village, the Americans spurred their horses to a gallop and emerged from a grove of cottonwoods. A woman looked out the door of her tepee, saw them coming, and shouted. The Indians grabbed their guns and ran for the hills, but as they ran, they turned around to shoot. Earlier Grouard had recognized some of the horses and mistakenly thought this was Crazy Horse's village, so he yelled taunts at his old friend and protector. At the meeting at the Yellowstone, Crazy Horse had said he would rather fight than sign the Black Hills treaty. Now was his chance, Grouard shouted, because the camp was surrounded. But there was no answer except the bullets of the fleeing Indians.

So far, everything had gone according to Reynolds's plan. The charge on the village had been successful, and the horses had been rounded up. But the Americans had suffered three men wounded, six horses had been killed, and three more wounded. Therefore out of the original detachment of about forty-seven men, one-quarter were either wounded or dismounted, and the Indians were counterattacking.

The second group, who were supposed to reinforce the first, now appeared and began to burn the tepees, as they had been ordered to do. Many of the lodges contained kegs of powder that began to go off with loud explosions and sent the lodge poles whirling into the air. Although the Americans had had the advantage of complete surprise, they were now in trouble. The village was under control, and they had captured the Indians' herd, but the third group of white men who were supposed to have been in the hills seemed to have disappeared, and instead of cutting off the Indians from the rear, the Cheyennes and Sioux were free to concentrate their fire on the white men in the village. When the third detachment finally did make its appearance, it was in the wrong position, and some of its bullets fell among the Americans.

Nevertheless the victory would have gone to the white men except that Colonel Reynolds inexplicably went to pieces. Perhaps his nerves gave away, or perhaps his lingering suspicion about Grouard's faithfulness made him think he had been lured into a trap. In any case, he preserved none of the Indians' supplies, even though he knew the troops were desperately short of rations, and instead of sending a courier to Crook, telling him to come up with the other four companies, he abruptly ordered a retreat. He withdrew so quickly that he left his dead behind him and, according to an ugly rumor, one man who was merely wounded.

He moved as fast as possible back to the mouth of Lodge Pole Creek, where, Bourke said, "the bivouac . . . was especially dreary and forlorn; the men named it 'Camp Inhospitality': there was a sufficiency of water—or ice—enough wood, but very little grass for the animals. There was nothing to eat; not even for the wounded men, of whom we had six. . . . Here and there would be found a soldier, or officer, who had carried a handful of crumbs in his saddle-bags, another who had had the good sense to pick up a piece of buffalo meat in the village, or a third who could produce a spoonful of coffee. . . . A small slice of buffalo meat, roasted in the ashes, went around among five or six; and a cup of coffee would be sipped like the pipe of peace at an Indian council."

That night, although Grouard begged him to, Reynolds failed even to place a guard around the Indians' herd of horses. As a result, the Cheyennes and Sioux raided the camp and recovered almost all the animals they had lost. Grouard chased them in the night, but there were too many Indians for him to defeat with the small number of scouts who volunteered to go with him.

Because no courier had come from Reynolds, Crook supposed he had failed to find the village, and so he went directly toward the meeting place at Lodge Pole Creek. During his march, he came upon some of the Indians who had recovered the herd and was able to recapture about a hundred of the horses. But that and the burned tepees were the extent of the victory.

As Bourke later wrote, "There was nothing to do but abandon the expedition, and return to the forts, and reorganize for a summer campaign. . . . We were out of supplies, although we had destroyed enough to last a regiment for a couple of months; we were encumbered with sick, wounded, and cripples with frozen limbs, because we had not had sense enough to save the furs and robes in the village; and the enemy was thoroughly aroused, and would be on the *qui vive* for all that we did. To old Fort Reno [where the wagon train was waiting], by way of the valley of the Powder, was not quite ninety miles. The march was uneventful, and there was nothing to note beyond the storms of snow and wind, which lasted, with some spasmodic intermissions, throughout the journey. The wind blew from the south, and there was a softening of the ground, which aggravated the disagreeable features by adding mud to our other troubles."

The Indians had not given up the battle, however. Although they would not launch a campaign against the Americans during the winter months, some of them followed the retreat and harassed the soldiers' camp at night in an effort to get back the hundred horses Crook had recaptured. Finally Crook ordered the animals killed. When the listening Indians heard the sounds of the dying horses whose throats were being cut, they let out a yell of defiance, fired a final volley at the Americans, and left. The hungry soldiers cut the dead animals into steaks and ate them.

For the Indian village, the loss had been severe. They had recovered most of their horses, but they were short of food and short of ammunition, and it was the dead of winter. Their best hope was to find a village with supplies to spare, so they returned to Crazy Horse, whose band shared their belongings with them.

But the Americans had also been beaten. Out of kindness Crook had given Reynolds a chance to reestablish his reputation, but Reynolds had failed his trust. After gathering the facts, Crook relieved him of his command and ordered him held for a court-martial. If Reynolds had properly carried out his orders, held the village, sent for Crook, and preserved the supplies that might have been captured, Crook could have continued his winter campaign, and Sitting Bull's camp was not far away. As it was, the Indians had won a major victory, for they had repulsed one of the strongest forces ever sent against them, a force that was under one of the ablest Indian fighters in the army. Any thought that this would be a short, easily-waged campaign was dissipated on the banks of the Powder River in the winter of 1876.

XIII

The Greatest Victory

IN the spring of 1876, the forces that for decades had been mounting against the Sioux and Cheyennes continued to gain in strength and momentum, and no man alive could now have checked them. Although the Indians did not know it, Sitting Bull and Crazy Horse, oiling their worn-out guns as the smoke curled from the fires in their tepees, were leading them in a hopeless fight. Outside the winds piled the snow in drifts, and the prairies were empty and peaceful, but this was an interlude granted only by the severity of the weather. Even the few white men who still preached fairness to the Indians and spoke of the sanctity of solemn pledges could not stop the tide.

Although the attention of both the American public and the Indians was focused on the Black Hills, the gold in the Pah Sappa, those once-mysterious mountains, was not the real issue. The thousands of miners who wished to wrest the metal from the placer sands could generate pressure to deprive the Indians of their treaty rights, but they were transients with no lasting desire to hold the land. Once they had built their sluices and despoiled the earth, they would move on to wherever gold had next been discovered. Like the locusts that sometimes swept the Great Plains, emerging in clouds out of nowhere, the miners, too, would eventually disappear.

The enticement of a 160-acre homestead in return for minor filing fees was a greater lure than gold and a greater threat to the Indians. Between 1862, when the Homestead Act was passed, and 1880, almost 150,000 homesteads were established in Minnesota, Kansas,

Nebraska, and Dakota Territory, the recent hunting grounds of the Sioux. Unlike the miners, these white men intended to stay. They plowed their land, planted their crops, and harvested them; and although many of them faced incredible hardships, they were determined not to be driven out by droughts or locusts or the prairie fires that sometimes swept down upon them and destroyed their possessions. Other thousands who had more capital bought farms, and they, too, sank their plows into the prairie sod and were resolved to make homes for themselves and their children.

Sometimes the advancing line faltered, slowed by bad weather and poor agricultural prices, but even when the farmers had to be sustained by public and private relief funds, which happened several times, the line did not recede. Then in the period when the Sioux were struggling to retain the Black Hills, even greater interest developed in the acquisition of farmlands on the plains. The impetus came, curiously enough, from Jay Cooke's defunct Northern Pacific Railroad, which rose like a ghost from its grave of bankruptcy to haunt Sitting Bull and the Sioux again. Among the railroad's assets was the land granted to it by the generous government—the government did not demand it back in spite of the railroad's failure to complete its agreement—and it sold this land at an average price of slightly more than five dollars an acre. That was relatively expensive as against homesteading or even buying land direct from the federal government, although much of it was better than many of the lands retained in the public domain. (The railroads usually had acquired the prize property.) But as they often do, knowledgeable investors soon found a means of cutting this price. Instead of paying cash, they purchased it with the railroad's own depreciated bonds and preferred stock. This brought the average price down to between fifty cents and a dollar, making it one of the greatest agricultural bargains the United States had to offer.

Small investors were just as eligible as large ones to participate in this bonanza, but large ones were more likely to know how to take advantage of it. Between the early fall of 1873 and 1875, the railroad disposed of almost 500,000 acres, of which more than 300,000 acres were purchased by just twenty-three people. Cass, who had served as the railroad's president, picked up more than four thousand acres, and some buyers acquired more than 28,000 each. Most of this land was located in the valley of the Red River, the valley down which the Metís had come to trade with the Americans, and which included six counties in Minnesota and nine counties of what later became North Dakota.

These farms—if holdings so large could be called farms—were mammoth operations, sometimes employing as many as a thousand men each in the harvest season. John Deere's plows broke the sod for them, and Cyrus McCormick's reapers cut the ripened wheat. (Those two inventions remained Sitting Bull's greatest enemies, but how does a warrior fight a piece of agricultural machinery?) In the end, many of the giant farms proved economically impractical, but the profits they reported at first were enormous. Capital flowed in from the East. Two brothers from Pennsylvania purchased more than sixty thousand acres, and the directors of the Maine Savings Bank in Portland, Maine, conservative New Englanders no doubt, sat around the table in their boardroom and voted to buy more than seventeen thousand acres on behalf of their depositors.

The miners were, for the most part, a wild lot, gamblers and adventurers, but these new investors were solid citizens, who went to church on Sundays and knew their Congressmen. Although the lands they acquired had already been relinquished by the Indians, they formed an advancing bulwark that the Indians could never again penetrate. Land that was planted in wheat was lost forever to the grazing buffalos and to the Indians who pursued them. Where the Indians had once butchered the fallen animals and prepared their winter's supply of food, the white men now followed somewhat the same routine, but their work was performed with a reaper instead of a knife and their harvest was stored in grain elevators instead of tepees. But the resemblance ended there. One civilization had been irrevocably replaced by another in a vast area of the Indians' former range. Aside from entrenching themselves in the land and casting an aura of respectability over Western farming, these large-scale farmers generated publicity. The small farmers, who might have doubted the glowing claims of the railroads' agents and the local officials who were paid to encourage settlement, could hardly question the wisdom of those important investors who were putting their fortunes into Western land. That was where the future lay, and so the small followed the big. The movement had power and influence, and it also had votes.

If some Solomon had arisen in the spring of 1876 with a solution to the conflict between the Indians and the miners, he could at best have bought the Indians only a year or two of grace, perhaps a truce but not a peace. For the miners were only the tip of the proverbial iceberg.

Underlying them was a force even greater and more irresistible. Thousands of additional arrows and bullets and the best of guns in the hands of the Indians might have made the conflict bloodier, but at best they would only have postponed the outcome. Even the gods of the Indians, talking through the medicine men, spoke with hollow voices. Everything but the details was foredoomed by the spring of 1876.

Even the officials in Washington, who had had such difficulty facing the realities of existence on the plains, recognized that the ultimate showdown was coming and made their preparations. Crook's campaign during the past winter had demonstrated that a single column pressing into the Indians' territory was insufficient to win total victory. It might force an occasional battle or take a village by surprise and destroy it, but it could not fight the war to an end against an elusive foe who had many square miles of wilderness in which to maneuver.

The Department of Dakota had not been involved in Crook's campaign, its soldiers having remained inactive. Now Sheridan planned a three-pronged attack in which Crook, marching up the old Bozeman Trail again, would be one. The other two would come from the east and the west, and all three would converge on the Indians' stronghold.

On March 17, the Montana Column left Fort Shaw and headed east toward Fort Ellis near the city of Bozeman, Montana. The weather was cold and the snow heavy underfoot. The column was under the command of Colonel John Gibbon and consisted of 450 men from the Second Cavalry and the Seventh Infantry. The air was so clear and the sun so bright that many of the men became afflicted with snow-blindness. "The loss of sight," wrote one of the sufferers, "comes on with a feeling such as is created by smoke in the eyes, that, if the case is a severe one, soon increases into the most intense burning pain. The eyes cannot bear the light, and the eyeballs seem to roll in liquid fire with a grating feeling as though in contact with particles of sand." But in spite of this sickness and a number of desertions, the column reached Fort Ellis safely.

On May 17, the Dakota Column left Fort Abraham Lincoln and marched west. It was under the command of General Alfred H. Terry and was composed of about 925 men, including the Seventh Cavalry under Custer. Libbie Custer rode with her husband on the first day's march and later wrote, "From the hour of breaking camp, before the sun was up, a mist had enveloped everything. Soon the bright sun began to penetrate this veil and dispel the haze, and a scene of wonder and beauty appeared. The cavalry and infantry in the order named, the scouts, pack-mules, and artillery, and behind all the long line of white-covered wagons, made a column altogether some two miles in length. As the sun broke through the mist a mirage appeared, which took up half of the line of cavalry, and thenceforth for a little distance it marched, equally plain to the sight on the earth and in the sky.

"The future of the heroic band, whose days were even then numbered, seemed to be revealed, and already there seemed a premonition in the supernatural translation as their forms were reflected from the opaque mist of the early dawn."

Custer himself was in good spirits and glad to be with his regiment. "The sun, mounting higher and higher as we advanced," Libbie wrote, "took every little bit of burnished steel on the arms and equipments along the line of horsemen, and turned them into glittering flashes of radiating light. The yellow, indicative of cavalry, outlined the accoutrements, the trappings of the saddle, and sometimes a narrow thread of that effective tint followed the outlines even up to the head-stall of the bridle. At every bend in the road, as the column wound its way round and round the low hills, my husband glanced back to admire his men, and could not refrain from constantly calling my attention to their grand appearance." The day may have been a difficult one for Libbie, but Custer was happy. "The general," she wrote, "could scarcely restrain his recurring joy at being . . . with his regiment. . . . His buoyant spirits at the prospect of the activity and field-life that he so loved made him like a boy."

According to Sheridan's plan, Crook, too, was to march again from the south, using every available mounted man in the Department of the Platte. (Their regular duties were to be assumed by infantry drawn in from relatively faraway posts.) "May 29," Bourke wrote, "saw the column moving out from its camp in front of Fort Fetterman; the long black line of mounted men stretched for more than a mile with nothing to break the somberness of color save the flashing of the sun's rays from carbines and bridles. An undulating streak of white told where the wagons were already under way, and a puff of dust just in front indicated the line of march of the infantry battalion."

Sheridan's three columns were now in the field, and he was confident of success. Each one of them, he thought, would be capable of defeating any band of Sioux they might find, and together they could scour the country and prevent the Indians from retreating. His assessment of the situation was a gross miscalculation and represented a complete breakdown of American intelligence. For Sheridan had unquestioningly accepted the estimate that only seven or eight hundred warriors had remained away from the agencies. By increasing his own forces, therefore, he thought he could force a victory. But he overlooked the capacity of the Indians to increase theirs.

While the white men were preparing for their spring campaign, the Indians had not been idle. In their camps that winter, they held many councils and agreed that the demands of the white men were incessant. If they gave up the Black Hills, what would be next? Always in the past, when they had ceded land or a right, they had bought peace for only a short period of time, for as the white men became stronger on the plains, they always asked for more. They also agreed they needed more strength in the battlefield than ever before, and this could only be attained by abandoning some of their old independence. Henceforth, instead of operating in relatively small bands, they would have to work together more closely. This was a change in strategy of which Sheridan was unaware.

The center of activity became the camp in which Sitting Bull resided. This was no longer, as it had once been, a village of Hunkpapas. It was now composed of a conglomeration of Sioux—Hunkpapas, of course, but also Sans Arcs, Brulés, Oglalas, Two Kettles, Miniconjous, and Blackfeet Sioux. Nor were the inhabitants limited only to Sioux. Any Indian who hated the white men and who was willing to fight them would find a warm welcome and a place to set up his tepee, whether he was a Sioux or a Cheyenne or belonged to some other tribe. On the other hand, those who did not want to fight were free to leave, and some of them did. They foresaw the uselessness of trying to match their strength against the Americans, and so they made the trip to the agencies. What is remarkable is the ignorance of the Indian agents. A major shift in population was taking place under their eyes, and they seem for the most part to have been unaware of it. Indians were obeying the government's earlier proclamation and were coming in, but even larger numbers were going out. Because counting the agency Indians was so difficult—they had always objected to being counted—it is not surprising that the agents had not measured the actual numbers. But it is surprising that their communications were so poor that some of the friendly Indians did not tell them what was going on, or if they did, their warnings were ignored.

So the camp in which Sitting Bull lived grew larger and larger, as the number of warriors increased, traveling through the snow to join the others in what they, like the white men, hoped would be the final battle. Two Moon and He Dog, after the attack by Crook, joined the camp, adding more Sioux and Cheyennes to the total fighting force, and Indians came also from the agencies, slipping away and preparing for war. Guns and ammunition were, of course, a problem and in short supply, but the agency Indians brought some, and other agency Indians, although not willing to fight themselves, were glad to trade and helped add to the supply. There were also the Metís, the friends of neither Indians nor white men, but always willing to do business. They brought weapons down from Canada.

Sitting Bull was not the leader of the camp—there was no single leader—but he was a figure of great importance. Broad-shouldered and with his dark eyes flashing with anger, he walked through the village, exhorting the Indians to fight and predicting a victory. Because of his feats in war and his renown as a medicine man, his words gave encouragement to the younger warriors who listened to him. Gall was there, too, the rival of Sitting Bull; and if fame was to be won in the coming struggle, he wanted his share of it. Crazy Horse, of course, was there, along with many other fine warriors. It was the largest group of independent Indians—proud and determined to fight for their lands— that had ever set up their lodges side by side. And Sheridan did not know about it. His three columns were blindly marching into the wilderness against a force many times greater than they thought it was.

Spring was coming to the prairies. The snow, which had once covered the ground with endless white, was now like the torn and tattered garment of a beggar, and the brown of the fresh earth appeared and began to turn green with the promise of a new year. But the future it was bringing was not a good one for either the red men or the whites.

*   *   *

By June 1, Crook's column had again come within sight of the Bighorn Mountains. The weather turned cold, and the men found themselves caught in a heavy snowstorm, sweeping down on them from the mountains. But it was followed by clear and warmer weather. "We were now getting quite close to Cloud Peak, the loftiest point in the Bighorn range," Bourke wrote. "Its massy dome towered high in the sky, white with a mantle of snow; here and there a streak of darkness betrayed the attempts of tall pine trees on the summit to penetrate the open air above them. Heavy belts of forest covered the sides of the range below the snow line, and extended along the skirts of the foot-hills well out into the plains below. The singing of meadowlarks, and the chirping of thousands of grasshoppers, enlivened the morning air; and save these no sound broke the stillness, except the rumbling of wagons slowly creeping along the road."

The first intimation that all was not as they thought it would be came to the column when they met a group of Montana miners, who were traveling from the Black Hills back to the Yellowstone. They reported they had been under constant attack from the Indians. Even more serious, they had seen many horse tracks headed north but few of the marks left by the dragging of lodge poles. This could only mean the warriors were leaving the agencies without their families to join the independent camp. A little later, Crook received dispatches officially confirming this news and advising him that the Fifth Cavalry had been ordered up from Kansas to join him.

The Indians had now discovered the approaching column and prepared to attack it. On June 9, Crook made camp on the Tongue River and placed his pickets on the nearby hilltops. The attacking Indians were able to drive the pickets back and hide behind rocks from which they could fire into the camp. Then they made a mistake. Instead of firing at the soldiers, they spent much of their ammunition shooting into the tents, which were largely unoccupied. The bullets tore the canvas, broke the stovepipes, and split the tent poles. But only two Americans were wounded, and these not seriously. Several companies of cavalry charged the attackers and drove them away.

This was only a skirmish in the war. Before they were ready really to fight, the Sioux held another Sun Dance to ensure their complete victory over the Americans in the coming struggle. Once again, as they had so many many times in past years, they cut down the pole and erected it where the dance was to take place. Sitting Bull had said he would offer his flesh to the spirits, as well as take part in the dance itself. So he subjected himself to the same torture Grouard had undergone several years previously. He sat down on the ground, and Jumping Bull, his adopted brother, raised the flesh a little and with his knife cut away the first small portion of it. The pain was not bad at first, but soon Sitting Bull's arm was covered with blood, and each additional slicing added to the total torment. One after another, Jumping Bull removed bits of flesh, each of them an offering for the sake of victory. When one arm was a mass of blood and tortured flesh, he began on the other and repeated everything he had done before. According to what the Indians said later, he took a hundred pieces of flesh from the arms of Sitting Bull.

Then the Sun Dance began. With the help of his friends, Sitting Bull drove the sharp skewers into his already bloody body, and the thongs were attached to the pole. Then he and the other dancers started to circle it, gradually letting the weight of their bodies work the skewers free by tearing the flesh. Around and around the pole they danced, sweating and bleeding under the June sun, while the onlookers watched them. Surely in view of the ardor with which they performed this ceremony, the Sioux would be granted the victory they so much desired. One of the last to finally free themselves was Sitting Bull, and he fell to the ground unconscious. When he regained his senses, he had had a vision. He had seen many soldiers coming, but they were riding in a distorted fashion, which indicated they would be killed. Clearly the Sioux were to enjoy a great victory. All of the Indians regarded this as a propitious sign, for the prophecies of Sitting Bull were known to come true.

Crook had moved his camp from the Tongue River to the confluence of the two forks of Goose Creek, one of the tributaries of the Tongue, where the grass was better. Here he made his preparations for the final stage of the campaign. As he had done before, he proposed leaving the wagon train behind to permit him to move more rapidly. With some Shoshones, Crows, and Snakes, all traditional enemies of the Sioux and willing to fight alongside him, and with every mounted man in his command, he intended to move forward with only four days' rations of hard bread, coffee, and bacon, each man carrying his own supplies in his saddlebags. To increase his force even further, he asked for volunteers among the infantry, provided they were willing to ride the mules from the pack trains. This time his plan was somewhat different from the last. If they found a village and conquered it, the men were to be careful to save the supplies it contained. These would then be used by the command, and instead of returning to the wagon train, it would continue to advance until it met either Colonel Gibbon's column or the one under General Terry.

Their destination was the Rosebud, one of the tributaries of the Yellowstone and in the heart of the Indians' stronghold. By June 16, they had reached the headwaters of the Rosebud, "which was at that point," according to Bourke, "a feeble rivulet of snow water, sweet and palatable enough when the muddy ooze was not stirred up from the bottom. Wood was found in plenty for the slight wants of the command, which made small fires for a few moments to boil coffee, while the animals, pretty well tired out by the day's rough march of nearly forty miles, rolled and rolled again in the matted branches of succulent pasturage growing at their feet."

The Sioux's scouts had been watching the advancing column, and Crazy Horse with many warriors went out to meet them. This time they were not going to wait in camp, where their fighting would be encumbered by their women and children and the need to protect their supplies and other possessions.

On the morning of June 17, 1876, Crook's soldiers rose, saddled their horses, and started to follow the stream bed of the Rosebud. "At about eight o'clock," wrote John Finerty, a correspondent for the Chicago *Times*, "we halted in a valley, very similar in formation to the one in which we had pitched our camp the preceding night. Rosebud Stream, indicated by the thick growth of wild roses, or sweet brier, from which its name is derived, flowed sluggishly through it, dividing it from south to north into two almost equal parts. The hills seemed to rise from every side, and we were within easy musket shot of those most remote."

The horses were tired from the long march of the previous day, and at eight o'clock in the morning Crook gave orders to unsaddle them and let them rest. During that brief respite, some of the men lay down, using their saddles as pillows. They occupied the flatland on both sides of the river and presented a peaceful scene. And it was there that Crazy Horse found them.

Unlike so many times when the Indians had relied either on a direct charge to overwhelm the soldiers or on the old ruse of sending out a few decoys to lure them into a single trap, Crazy Horse had thought out several alternatives. He concealed the major portion of the warriors in the bluffs and hills, where the Americans could not see them. Then with hundreds of men, he planned to attack Crook from various points and draw detachments of soldiers in pursuit. These he would cut to pieces once they reached the hills. If this plan failed, he hoped to draw Crook down into the canyon of the Rosebud, where the vertical walls would make escape impossible and where a natural dam of fallen trees and other debris had raised the water level to about ten feet. This would seal off a further advance—or retreat—and permit the Sioux and Cheyennes to slaughter the Americans at their will.

The Crow scouts were in the hills, because Crook had sent them to search for the village, so they were the first of the enemies that the Sioux and Cheyennes fought. The skirmish was brief, for the Crows were greatly outnumbered and raced back to the valley and the protection of the troops. The Sioux and Cheyennes followed, charging from different sides against the soldiers. They "were extremely bold and fierce," Bourke wrote, "and showed a disposition to come up and have it out hand to hand; in all this they were gratified by our troops, both red and white, who were fully as anxious to meet them face to face and see which were the better men. . . . As the hostiles advanced at a full run, they saw nothing in their front, and imagined that it would be an easy thing for them to sweep down through the long ravine leading into the amphitheater [cut by the river], where they could see numbers of our cavalry horses clumped together. They advanced in excellent style, yelling and whooping, and glad of the opportunity of wiping us off the face of the earth." The shattering fire of the Americans drove them back, however, but they stopped and reformed not much farther than three hundred yards away. When they charged again, the Americans with the Shoshones countercharged and forced them back some distance. But the Americans did not press this attack, because they were having difficulty distinguishing between the Sioux and Cheyennes and their own allies, the Crows.

Some of the highest land was on Crook's right, and he ordered Colonel William B. Royall to take it. This led to desperate fighting, and the Sioux were almost able to cut him off from the remainder of the soldiers. But he gained the heights and, with active support from the rear, was able to retain them. This gave Crook an advantage, because his men could then see what was going on over a wide area.

But he could not drive the enemy away. His men made charge after charge, and the Indians would retreat. Yet each time they came to a new ridge—and there were many of them extending from the banks of the river—they would turn again. They were fighting differently than they usually did. Not only had they massed an unusual number of warriors, but they were battling with less heroics and more intent to kill Americans. When they charged, they were not so interested in counting coup, as was their usual custom, as they were in shooting or clubbing the soldiers. They also had Crook at a disadvantage, for every time they retreated to the hills and his men followed them, Crook's line became too extended, particularly since he was not sure how many Indians were facing him. So he would then have to call his soldiers back, and the battle would start anew. Crazy Horse and the Cheyennes and Sioux who were with him were fighting brilliantly, and Crook was concerned. This was no minor skirmish with an inferior number of Indians or an attack on a relatively immobile village, the two contingencies that Sheridan had foreseen when he planned the campaign; this was a battle against a superior force that was working according to a coordinated plan.

Crook then made a desperate move that might have cost him the battle. In order to relieve the pressure on his flanks, he ordered Captain Anson Mills to make a demonstration on the right and then start downstream. He then intended to follow with the remainder of his men in a feint toward the location of the Indians' village. In this way he hoped to put them on the defensive. This, of course, was what Crazy Horse wanted, for it meant that Crook was on the verge of falling into the second trap that Crazy Horse had planned for him.

The Indians pulled back just out of range of the Americans' guns, although they still continued to press Colonel Royall, who occupied the heights. "I went with Mills . . . ," Bourke later wrote, "and can recall how deeply impressed we all were by what we then took to be trails made by buffaloes going down stream, but which we afterwards learned had been made by the thousands of ponies belonging to the immense force of the enemy here assembled. We descended into a measly-looking place: a cañon with straight walls of sandstone, having on projecting knobs an occasional scrub pine or cedar."

This was a dangerous route for the Americans to take. As Finerty, the reporter, wrote, "The bluffs on both sides of the ravine were thickly covered with rocks and fir trees, thus affording ample protection to an enemy and making it impossible for our cavalry to act as flankers. Colonel [a brevet rank] Mills ordered a section of the battalion moving on the east side of the cañon to cover their comrades on the west side, if fired upon, and vice versa. This was good advice and good strategy in the position in which we were placed. We began to think our force rather weak for so venturous an enterprise, but Lieutenant Bourke informed the Colonel that the five troops of the 2nd. Cavalry under Major H. E. Noyes were marching behind us. A slight rise in the valley enabled us to see the dust stirred up by the supporting column some distance in the rear.

"The day had become absolutely perfect, and we all felt elated, exhilarated as we were by our morning's experience. Nevertheless, some of the more thoughtful officers had their misgivings, because the cañon was certainly a dangerous defile where all the advantage would be on the side of the savages."

Each step was taking the Americans toward almost certain death, for the Indians were massing in order to close the trap that Crazy

Horse had prepared. But Crook then changed his mind. Several of the groups of soldiers remaining near the original battlefield were being hard pressed, and Colonel Royall, occupying the heights, was in danger of being overwhelmed. So Crook sent a staff officer dashing after the advance with orders to get out of the defile in any way they could and go to the relief of Royall as fast as possible.

"Crook's order was instantly obeyed," Finerty wrote, "and we were fortunate enough to find a comparatively easy way out of the elongated trap into which duty had led us. We defiled, as nearly as possible, by the heads of companies in parallel columns so as to carry out the order with greater celerity. We were soon clear of Dead Cañon, although we had to lead our horses carefully over and among the boulders and fallen timber.

"The crest of the side of the ravine proved to be sort of a plateau, and there we could hear quite plainly the noise of the attack on Royall's front. We got out from among the loose rocks and scraggy trees that fringed the rim of the gulf and found ourselves in quite open country. 'Prepare to mount—mount!' shouted the officers, and we were again in the saddle. Then we urged our animals to their best pace and speedily came in view of the contending parties. The Indians had their ponies, guarded mostly by mere boys, in the rear of the low, rocky crest which they occupied. The position held by Royall rose somewhat higher, and both lines could be seen at a glance. There was very heavy firing and the Sioux were evidently preparing to make an attack in force, as they were riding in by the score, especially from a point abandoned by Mills' battalion in its movement down the cañon, and which was partially held thereafter by the friendly Indians, a few infantry, and a body of sturdy mule packers. . . . Suddenly the Sioux lookouts observed our unexpected approach, and gave the alarm to their friends. We dashed forward at a wild gallop, cheering as we went. . . . But the cunning savages did not wait for us. They picked up their wounded, all but thirteen of their dead, and broke away to the northwest on their fleet ponies, leaving us only the thirteen scalps, 150 dead horses and ponies, and a few old blankets and war bonnets as trophies of the fray."

Crook's unexpected change of plans just as the Americans were marching down the canyon and the sudden relief of Royall's men upset Crazy Horse's strategy. His first attack had failed in its objective of either pinning down the white men or drawing them off into the hills where they could have been slaughtered, and his reserve plan had failed when Crook countermanded his own orders. The Indians now had to decide between continuing a battle in which they were not destroying the Americans or breaking off the fighting, and they chose the latter.

Crook had repulsed the Sioux and Cheyennes, but he had not won a victory. "The General was dissatisfied with the result of the encounter," Finerty wrote, "because the Indians had clearly accomplished the main object of their offensive movement—the safe retreat of their village. Yet he could not justly blame the troops who, both officers and men, did all that could be done under the circumstances. We had driven the Indians about five miles from the point where the fight began [but had been unable to hold that gain] and the General decided to return there in order that we might be nearer water. The troops had nearly used up their rations and had fired about 25,000 rounds of ammunition. . . .

"Our wounded were placed on extemporized travois, or mule litters, and our dead were carried on the backs of horses to our camp of the morning, where they received honorable burial. Nearly all had turned black from the heat, and one soldier . . . had not less than a dozen Indian arrows sticking in his body. This resulted from the fact that he was killed nearer to the Indian position and the young warriors had time to indulge their barbarity before the corpse was rescued. . . .

"We went into camp at about 4 o'clock and were formed in a circle around our horses and pack train, as on the previous night. The hospital was established under the trees down by the sluggish creek, and there the surgeons exercised their skill with marvelous rapidity. Most of the injured men bore their sufferings stoically enough, but an occasional groan or half-smothered shriek would tell where the knife, or the probe, had struck an exposed nerve. The Indian wounded [Crook's scouts]—some of them desperate cases—gave no indication of feeling, but submitted to be operated upon with the grim stolidity of their race.

"General Crook decided that evening to retire on his base of supplies —the wagon train—with his wounded, in view of the fact that his rations were almost used up and his ammunition had run pretty low. He was also convinced that all chance of surprising the Sioux camp was over for the present, and perhaps he felt that even if it could be surprised his small force would be unequal to the task of carrying it by storm. The Indians had shown themselves good fighters, and he shrewdly calculated that his men had been opposed to only a part of the well-armed warriors actually in the field."

On July 19, Crook was back at his wagon train. Two days later, he sent a detachment to Fort Fetterman to take in the wounded and to obtain more supplies. Then he waited. He waited for the return of his detachment. He waited for news from Terry. He waited for further orders. He really waited to recover from the shock. He was a brave man and an aggressive general, but he had run headlong into the unexpected. He had thought there were six hundred, perhaps even eight hundred warriors in the enemy village. There were apparently thousands. He had expected to take the offensive against them, surprising them in their winter camp. Instead they had taken the offensive against him and surprised him in that natural amphitheater in the valley of the Rosebud. This was a turn of events no one had foreseen, not the generals in Washington, not Sheridan at headquarters, not Crook in the field. And Crook was obviously dazed by the experience.

The night after the battle, the Indians did not, as was their usual habit, return to the field and engage in sniping at their enemy. Instead they went back to their camp, a bewildered group of men, for they had failed to annihilate Crook's command, as they had expected to do. In the darkness of the Montana evening, when the wind swept over the prairie and the tired horses browsed and slept, there was rejoicing in the Indian camp over the casualties inflicted on the Americans and mourning for those who had died. They had won a victory, one of the greatest they had ever achieved. For this battle had not been a raid on an isolated settlement or undermanned fort or an attack on a wagon train or a single company of cavalry. This had been an encounter between two major forces, and the Indians, thanks to their new tactics and massed warriors, had compelled the Americans to retreat without attaining their objective. Such a triumph deserved celebrating, and yet it accomplished little. That was the tragedy. Nothing the Sioux could do would stop the usurpation of their lands. Those warriors who died at the Rosebud—and those soldiers, too, like the private with a dozen arrows sticking into his body—might just as well have stayed alive. Human blood could not deflect the course of history.

But the Sioux saw only that they must fight on. The buffalos moved over the prairie, the waters of the Rosebud flowed slowly toward those of the Missouri, and the light of each dawn struck the slopes of the Bighorn Mountains, tinting them with color, while the Sioux and

Cheyennes talked about the victory promised them in Sitting Bull's vision.

*   *   *

As early as April, General Terry began to have second thoughts about his role in Sheridan's campaign. The Montana Column was then camped on the bank of the Yellowstone at the site of Fort Pease, a post the army had abandoned the previous February. On April 21, the column received dispatches from Terry announcing that Reynolds's attack on the village had not been a success after all and that Crook had not yet taken to the field again. As a consequence, Terry was worried and thought the Indians might join forces and defeat his men. Therefore, they were to remain at Fort Pease until further orders.

After several weeks of sitting in camp, he ordered the column to march down the Yellowstone to join the forces leaving Fort Abraham Lincoln. On the way, it came across a Sioux trail, and the men were certain a village was nearby. Colonel Gibbon decided to move against it. "It was two months to the day since we had left Fort Shaw for the purpose of cleaning out the Sioux nation," one of the officers wrote in his journal, "and during that time we had done nothing but march, march, and rest in camp; but now the enemy had been found and we were going over [the river] to whip them. The accumulated satisfaction of the sixty blessed ["blessed" used in its derogatory sense] days that had preceded, if combined in a single lump, could not have equaled that with which this order was received. Not that there were no soreheads who were personified gloom and despondency and whispered of dire overthrow and dreadful disaster; but the great majority were hopeful, jubilant, and full of the fire of battle. Everybody fell to with a will, and there was more real good feeling and enthusiasm in the camp than I had witnessed in a body of men for a long time."

But the difficulty of getting his men and horses across the river and the appearance of a band of Sioux on the other side discouraged Gibbon, and he gave up his plan. So they continued down the Yellowstone, noticing frequent signs of the Indians, who were gathering in ever increasing numbers. If at this time one of the warriors had organized an attack such as the one Crazy Horse led against Crook on the Rosebud, they might have destroyed Gibbon's command before it joined Terry. But the Indians were more busy moving to the camp where Sitting Bull lived than in conducting their usual sporadic warfare, so they remained on one side of the river while Gibbon prudently stayed on the other.

General Terry was also advancing with caution, although he was determined to carry the fight to the Sioux and Cheyennes when the time came. But first he had to discover the location of their camp. So when he reached the Tongue River, he divided the Seventh Cavalry into two groups. One, directly under Custer, was to go up the south bank of the Yellowstone as far as the mouth of the Rosebud. The other, under Major Marcus A. Reno, was to scout the headwaters of the Tongue and the Powder.

The Indians, who had to move from time to time to provide grazing for their horses, were congregating on the Little Bighorn River; and Reno, during his scout, came across a broad trail that might have been made by more than three hundred lodges. He followed it for a distance to be sure of the direction in which the Indians were going and then sent word to Terry of his discovery. The fates had been working against the Indians, who, for all the loss of many brave warriors, had not been able to check the white men; but on May 17, 1876, they for once worked against the Americans, even if in only a small way. On that day, Reno decided he knew where the village was and decided to return to Terry. At the very moment, he was only a short distance from Crook, who was fighting desperately on the Rosebud to free himself from Crazy Horse's attack. If Reno had known where Crook was and had joined him, Crook might have won.

When Terry, a lawyer who had earned his commission in the Civil War, received Reno's report, he moved up the Yellowstone to the mouth of the Rosebud to meet Reno on his return. "The particulars [of Reno's discovery] were not fully known," wrote one of the officers with Terry. "The camp was full of rumors; credulity was raised to the highest pitch, and we were filled with anxiety and curiosity until we reached Reno's command [at the Rosebud] and learned the details of their discoveries. They had found a large trail on the Tongue River, and had followed it up the Rosebud about forty miles. The number of lodges in the deserted villages was estimated by the number of camp-fires remaining to be about three hundred and fifty. The indications were that the trail was about three weeks old. No Indians had been seen nor any recent signs. It is not probable that Reno's movements were known to the Indians, for on the very day Reno reached his furthest point up the Rosebud, the battle of the Rosebud, between General Crook's forces and the Indians, was fought."

Not everyone agreed with this last opinion. Custer wrote Libby a letter in which he complained that Reno, by not following the trail and attacking the Indians, had given them "an intimation of our presence." This criticism was hardly justified. If Reno had advanced with the comparatively small number of men under his command, he would have been slaughtered; and in any case, he had not alarmed the Indians, who were already aware of the concentration of troops on the Yellowstone. But the remarks reflected Custer's keen wish to fight and destroy the enemy.

The first part of this wish was soon to be granted. At a conference aboard the *Far West*, the steamer that supplied the Dakota Column, Terry laid out his plan. Custer, with all the fast-moving Seventh Cavalry, was to march up the Rosebud until he came to the trail discovered by Reno. If, as Terry expected, he found that it turned toward the Little Bighorn, he was to continue south on the Rosebud before moving west. This should bring him to the south of the camp. Meanwhile Colonel Gibbon and his column would be approaching it from the north. In this fashion, the village would be caught between the two columns and destroyed.

Terry was confident. The possibility he foresaw was not defeat but the chance that the Indians might escape. He stressed this point in his written orders to Custer, advising him to constantly search his left flank in the event the Indians might slip by him. His plan was explicit and so were his instructions. But like a wise general, he knew that action on a battlefield does not always take place as headquarters believes it will. His orders said, "He [Terry] will . . . indicate to you his own views of what your action should be, and he desires that you should conform to them unless you see sufficient reason for departing from them." These orders, signed by the assistant acting adjutant general, made it clear what Custer was to do but gave him some latitude to use his own judgment.

With his usual fervor, Custer threw himself into the task of preparing for his expedition. The men were to travel light, with no tents and sleeping equipment; they could use their overcoats and saddle blankets. Their sabers were to be left behind, and they were to take rations for fifteen days, for he planned to follow the Indians that length of time even if the pursuit carried him far from his base of supplies. He also turned down Terry's offer of the Gatling guns that were with the column. These guns, with their revolving barrels, could fire fast and were effective weapons. But they were also bulky and would have slowed down the cavalry. He did, however, take several of the best Crow scouts from Gibbon's command.

On the morning of June 22, he set out up the Rosebud. His departure was marred only by his pack train. Usually the Seventh Cavalry carried its supplies in wagons, but for this campaign Custer was using pack animals, because they could move faster and over more rugged terrain. But being unaccustomed to them, the men had not tied the packs properly and some of them fell off; also, some of the men were unable to control their animals. Much to Custer's embarrassment, this performance brought a mild rebuke from Terry.

But in spite of this incident as he left camp, few people had any doubts about what would happen. They saw the possibility of the Indians escaping, but if Custer could contain them, he was certain to defeat them. One of Gibbon's officers wryly commented, ". . . it is understood that if Custer arrives first, he is at liberty to attack at once if he deems prudent. We have little hope of being in at the death, as Custer will undoubtedly exert himself to the utmost to get there first and win all the laurels for himself and his regiment."

After defeating Crook, the Indians allowed themselves to be overcome by a false sense of security. Having turned back one general, they did not seem to feel the need for being on guard against another. Their camp on the Little Bighorn was enormous, so enormous that they themselves did not know how many people it contained. Perhaps there were ten to twelve thousand, with twenty-five hundred to four thousand warriors to protect them. All the western Sioux were represented and some of the eastern Sioux as well, along with many Cheyennes. Such numbers, they believed, afforded security against any possible attack on the camp, and under normal circumstances they would have been right. The usual small command, consisting of a company or two, would have been unable to assault them. But just as the Indians had congregated the largest force they had ever done, so had the white men.

At the place where the Indians had established their camp, the Little Bighorn runs approximately northeast, so slowly that at several points it had cut large meanders. The Indians occupied the left bank at one of these points, with the Cheyennes to the north and the Sioux to the south. Although the lodges were placed in circles according to the various tribes, there was much visiting back and forth. In spite of their common anger at the white men, the Indians were in a happy frame of mind. There was plenty of grass and water for their horses, the buffalos would soon be getting fat and worth the hunting, and it seemed as though the old days were here again and the threat of the Americans remote. But as they relaxed in their village, Custer was marching toward them, eager for battle and for the glory he hoped to win.

The first day's march was a short one, but then he began pressing his men somewhat harder, for he was fearful the Indians might escape or that Gibbon would get there in time to take part in the battle. Soon they came across a large Indian trail, larger than anything they had expected to find. The scouts warned Custer to be careful, but previous experience had taught him scouts were sometimes overcautious. So in his eagerness to reach the village, Custer now made a decision from which there was later little chance to retreat. Instead of continuing south and coming up on the village from the opposite direction from Gibbon—a maneuver that would also have allowed Gibbon time to arrive—he exercised to the full the discretionary power Terry had given him and started up the divide that separates the Rosebud from the Little Bighorn, moving directly toward the village.

On the night of June 24, correctly believing he was near the village, he ordered his men to keep marching in an attempt to surprise the Indians. But he had trouble in the darkness with his pack train. Some of the supplies dropped off, so in the morning he ordered a detachment to go back over the trail and recover what they could. These soldiers discovered several Indians breaking into a container of hard bread and fired at them. This may have influenced Custer's subsequent action, because he had reason now to believe the village was aware of his presence. Curiously enough, however, either the Indians did not report what had happened, or, if they did, the others paid no attention to them.

By this time, Custer had reached the point where his past actions really made his decision for him. Instead of going south of the village, as he had been instructed to, he had gotten close to it; he thought his soldiers had been discovered; and furthermore, he did not agree with his scouts on the size of the village and was more obsessed with the fear that the Indians would escape than that they would resist. Given these facts, his next step was the logical one. He decided to attack.

At about twelve noon on June 25, 1876, Custer divided his command into three groups. Captain Frederick W. Benteen commanded one. He was to lead his men through the hills to the southeast and "pitch into anything he might find." This may have been a gesture toward obeying Terry's orders, but since Benteen had about 125 men, it greatly weakened Custer's command.

The second group Custer placed under the command of Major Marcus A. Reno. It was composed of about 140 men. The third, consisting of more than two hundred men, was commanded by Custer himself. Together they headed toward the location where they supposed the village to be. Shortly after two o'clock, they were within about four miles of the Little Bighorn.

When the soldiers were still in the hills above the Little Bighorn, they noticed a band of about forty warriors, whom they thought were fleeing. Still convinced that the Indians' only desire would be to escape, Custer ordered Reno to move down to their left—the soldiers were upstream from the village—and attack them, while he marched more or less parallel to the river, remaining in the hills out of sight. Shortly after that, he saw for the first time the village itself and realized at last how great was the concentration of Indians. At that moment, he regretted having sent Benteen off. Calling his bugler, John Martini, he ordered him to find Benteen and tell him to return as quickly as possible.

According to a statement later made by Gall, the Hunkpapa, "We saw the soldiers early in the morning crossing the divide [between the Rosebud and the Bighorn watersheds]. When Reno and Custer separated, we watched them until they came down into the valley. A cry was raised that the white men were coming, and orders were given for the village to move immediately." The Indians were reacting to an attack on their camp as they usually did. Their first thought was always for the safety of their women and children, so they were planning to retreat rather than to counterattack. But Reno ironically carried out his orders too well. He "swept down so rapidly on the upper end of the village," Gall said, "the Indians were forced to fight. Sitting Bull and I were at the point where Reno attacked. Sitting Bull was big medicine. The women and children were hastily moved downstream where the Cheyennes were camped."

"These men who came with Long Hair," Sitting Bull later said, confusing Reno with Custer, "were as good men as ever fought. When they rode up their horses were tired and they were tired. When they got off from their horses they could not stand firmly on their feet. They swayed to and fro—so my young men have told me—like the limbs of cypress in a great wind. Some of them staggered under the weight of their guns. But they began to fight at once; but by this time, as I have said, our camp was aroused, and there were plenty of warriors to meet them."

Sitting Bull may have exaggerated the fatigue of Reno's men, although in later discussions Custer was accused of having gone into battle with tired troops, but he did not exaggerate their courage. They had crossed the river to the flat western side where the village was located, when the volley of bullets struck them and stopped their charge. Forming a skirmish line near the river, they tried to hold the ground they had initially gained, but the Indians began slipping past Reno's left flank and threatened to take him from the rear. So he withdrew a short distance to some cottonwoods, but this position was not much of an improvement. Bullets and arrows flew among the white men. They did not cause many casualties, but the trees were protecting the Indians as well as the Americans, and enabling them to get closer and closer.

Reno now had to make a critical decision: to fight where he was or cross back over the river and take refuge in the hills on the other side. Either course seemed suicidal. Where he was, he could hardly hope to withstand the increasing hordes of Indians who were attacking him. Yet there were Indians between him and the river, and at this point the banks were about four feet high, not easy to negotiate either on foot or on horseback. In an act that probably saved his command from annihilation, he gave the order to retreat. The men fought their way to the river, often in hand-to-hand combat, and then slithered down the banks, into the water, and up the other side. For a short time while they were making the crossing, they were relatively helpless, and the Indians took full advantage of the situation. Out of his original force of approximately 140 men, Reno lost almost thirty killed or wounded.

His men were demoralized, and the retreat to the hills was ragged and without a rear guard. A few courageous men tried to restore some form of order, but the soldiers were unnerved by the initial resistance of the Indians. For days they had envisioned no greater disaster than the possibility that the Indians might escape. This thought had been impressed on them by all their officers from the commanding general down. And then on that bright June afternoon, when victory seemed near at hand, they had suddenly faced unbelievable numbers of angry warriors. Many of the men were raw recruits, and they were completely unprepared for the shock.

If the Indians had pressed their attack, they might have wiped out Reno's command, but many of the warriors began riding downstream toward the village, and some of the women began to strip the bodies of the dead soldiers and also to mutilate them. Martini, meanwhile, had carried Custer's message to Benteen, who was returning from his fruitless scout as quickly as he could. The first action he saw was Reno's, so he dashed to his aid and threw his men around the major's units until they could regroup.

Custer went along the hills until he came opposite the village. According to some of the Indian accounts, he saw the women and children fleeing down the river, thought the village had been routed, and chased them. He was near the Cheyennes' end of the camp, and they were among the first to attack him. Some of them got between him and the women and children, while others closed in on him from the rear. The fighting was intense, and both the reports of the Indians and the evidence of the bodies showed that much of it was hand-to-hand. To add to the confusion of the desperate battle, the feet of the men and horses stirred up great clouds of dust that could be seen for miles away. It blew in the faces of the fighters, blinding them and making it difficult to tell friend from enemy. After the battle, the Indians found that some of their own dead had died from arrow wounds. Reno's men heard the fighting in the distance, and Captain Thomas B. Weir volunteered to lead his company to Custer's aid, but Reno refused to let him endanger himself and his men. Nevertheless Weir disobeyed orders and went forward, reaching a spot now called Weir's Point, from which he could see the dust of the battle in the distance. Other companies joined him there, but the appearance of warriors along the slopes of the promontory from which they were watching forced them to retreat back to their original position.

Custer's men fought as best they could against the warriors and leaders like Crazy Horse and Gall, but their efforts were of no avail. With slightly more than two hundred men and no howitzers or Gatling guns, they could not oppose the thousands of warriors who opposed them. Judging from the positions of the bodies when they were later examined, it looked as though the men had split up company by company, fighting to the last in a battle in which no quarter was given.

Custer had started the campaign dreaming of glory. Now he lay dead on the slopes above the Little Bighorn. No one knows for a certainty who killed him. He died with one bullet in his chest and another through his head. Perhaps one Indian fired both shots. Perhaps two did. Perhaps—and this has happened on other occasions— one of his soldiers seeing his own end near and remembering the forced marches, the drive for glory often at the expense of the men, and recognizing the trap into which Custer had led them, felt a final moment of anger and pulled the fatal trigger. In any event, Custer was dead, and so were his entire command. Not a single American survived.

That part of the battle lasted about an hour. Reno's men were unaware of what had become of Custer, and later many of them testified they thought he had withdrawn or perhaps had gone off to join Terry, but they did not have much time for speculation. At nightfall, the Indians temporarily broke off the fighting, but the exhausted Americans, burdened with their wounded and short of horses, could not escape. They were trapped until either the Indians came back and killed them or Terry arrived.

The fires glowed in the village and cast shadows against the tepees. Overhead the stars glimmered in the clear prairie night, and the occasional neighing of a horse could be heard. In the lodges of the dead there was mourning, for the Indians had lost many warriors during the course of the fighting. But there was also rejoicing and celebrating over the greatest victory the Sioux and Cheyennes had ever won against the white men. Yet for all the jubilation in their hearts, for all Sitting Bull's pride in his prophecy and the praise that was heaped upon him, for all the brave deeds done that day by Crazy Horse and Gall and the other warriors, the Indians' fate had not been altered. What was the loss of a few hundred men to a nation that numbered millions? The wave of white men was engulfing the Indians, and ten victories like the one at the Little Bighorn would not have changed the Indians' future. As they danced around the campfires, they were unaware that they were celebrating, not a battle won, but some of their last few days of freedom.

XIV

The Fading of Hope

WHAT would you do if you were fresh from the fields of Iowa or Illinois or the streets of Philadelphia or Boston and had believed what the posters and the recruiting sergeant had told you? *Ho! For the Plains!* the posters had said in large type—the plains, that romantic land on the edge of the goldfields—and the sergeant had promised you excellent food, prancing horses to ride, a handsome uniform, and a life of glory, anything to get you to put your signature on the enlistment papers. Now you were pinned down in the hills alongside the Little Bighorn, smeared with filth and blood, Indians on every side of you, and down on the river bottom the bodies of your dead companions, the sound of their dying screams still loud in your ears.

What you would do is either run or dig—run in flight from the horror or dig deep into the earth for safety. And that was the choice faced by the men of the Seventh Cavalry on the night of June 25. They could not run; that would have been the equivalent of suicide. So they spent the hours of darkness scratching shallow rifle pits into the dirt, using what tools they had or digging with their bare hands until their fingers were torn and bloody. Where the dirt was too hard to be removed, they made crude breastworks out of packs and dead animals, heaving on stiff legs and limp tails in the blackness and cursing under their breaths as the bodies refused to budge. In the slack moments, when they were not listening to the moans of the wounded, a few of them prayed to whatever god they thought had power to save them. It looked as though divine intervention alone would get them off that hillside alive.

"At every bend of the road," Libbie Custer had remarked as they left Fort Abraham Lincoln, ". . . my husband glanced back to admire his men, and could not refrain from constantly calling my attention to their grand appearance. The soldiers, inured to many years of hardship, were the perfection of physical manhood. Their brawny limbs and lithe, well-poised bodies gave proof of the training their out-door life had given. Their resolute faces, brave and confident, inspired one with a feeling that they were going out aware of the momentous hours awaiting them, but inwardly assured of their capability to meet them." Now Custer was dead, his body stripped of its clothing, a crumpled, naked mass lying in the dust of the slope leading down to the Little Bighorn, and the men clinging to the hillside were now anything but "inwardly assured of their capability." Any dreams of glory they may once have had were long since vanished to be replaced with the hope of mere survival.

Daylight came quickly to the Little Bighorn, too quickly for the embattled Americans. A single shot rang out, and the fight was resumed. Reno had placed his wounded in a small depression where they were under the care of a civilian doctor, who had contracted with the army to supply medical service. To the north, he had five companies in a semicircle. Another troop, behind the barricade of dead mules and horses erected during the night, guarded the east; and Benteen, with his own soldiers and the men from the pack train, held a rise in the ground that pointed south. The west was covered by the flanks of Benteen's men and the northern semicircle.

The Indians were determined to wipe out this remnant of the Americans. It offered no threat to the village, being incapable of attack, and so they had no need to move their lodges. They came up from the valley to enjoy the sport, sending volleys of arrows and bullets into the small huddle of men. The Americans fired back, but the Indians were elusive targets, hiding behind clumps of sagebrush and taking advantage of every irregularity in the ground.

They correctly sensed that Benteen held the weakest point, so they concentrated much of their fire on him. Closer and closer they came and then began to mass for a charge. Realizing what they were doing, Benteen ordered his men to counterattack. Out they jumped from their fragile hiding places and dashed toward the Indians, shouting and yelling and firing their guns. It was a feeble gesture with no strength behind it, but it served its purpose. Startled by this display of aggressiveness, the Indians temporarily drew back, and the pressure on Benteen's front was relieved.

But the Indians soon realized the nature of the feint and began to attack again. Under the hot June sun, they once more crept closer and closer to the Americans, preparing for the final charge in which they would overrun the enemy and demolish them. Once again the Americans tried to hit the infrequent targets presented by the Sioux and Cheyennes but were unable to halt their advance.

Benteen talked to Reno. Their only chance, he thought, lay in another, more general, charge. His feint had worked once. Perhaps if all the men took part this time, they could gain a slight respite from the Indians' attack. All the men joined in the shouting and yelling as they dashed from behind their flimsy defenses and ran directly toward the enemy in what was only a gigantic, but nevertheless noble, bluff. Once again the Indians were startled and, picking up their dead and wounded, drew back to the valley. The Americans sustained the charge for about eighty-five yards, and then Benteen gave the order to withdraw, because they could not hold the position they had won. The Indians, initially thrown off balance by the charge, regrouped and came back again. Once more the deadly circle closed around the Americans as the Indians drew nearer and nearer.

There was no water on the slope, and the lack of it was causing great distress among the Americans. Fighting hard under the bright sun, their throats became ragged with thirst and dust. The suffering was especially acute among the wounded, and their piteous requests for water added to the horror of the day. At last a number of men, unable to bear the sad cries any longer, volunteered to make the dangerous trip to the Little Bighorn. Four sharpshooters were assigned the duty both of guarding them and distracting the Indians as they slipped along a small ravine leading down the slope. By a miracle, the Indians failed to notice them, and they came back with their canteens and camp kettles filled with water made tepid by the sun. Not much water could be carried by a few men, but at least it helped.

The day belonged to the Indians, or so they thought. Yesterday they had annihilated Custer's command, and today they would destroy Reno's. If not today, well, they could wait until tomorrow. There was no hurry; the white men could not escape.

Then came a sudden reversal in their fortunes. Terry's plan called for a two-pronged attack on the village, and the second prong under Terry and Gibbon was arriving from the north. The Indians discovered the advancing blue column, and this time, because they were not surprised as they had been by Reno's first charge, some of the warriors prepared to block the way of the advancing white men, while the women and children hastily took down the lodges, rounded up the horses, and fled.

As the afternoon wore on, Reno and Benteen noticed that the attacks made on them were becoming less and less severe and that the Indians seemed to be withdrawing, but they did not know why. Then they observed the village begin to move, but fearful of a ruse, they remained where they were. As a last token of defiance, the Indians touched fire to the grass in the valley, thus destroying the forage for the Americans' horses. The smoke rose in clouds against the evening sky, and then everything was quiet. Reno decided it was safe to move downhill to get away from the stench of the dead animals and closer to the water, so at last the men were able to drink all they needed.

Lieutenant James H. Bradley was leading Terry's advance. Off in the distance, he saw the smoke and realized he must be nearing the village. Then he came across an Indian trail that he supposed had been made by some Sioux, but after following it a short distance, he found beside it some equipment that had belonged to the Crow scouts he had loaned to Custer. A little farther on, he saw three men on the opposite side of the Little Bighorn and thought they might be the scouts themselves. By using smoke signals, he demonstrated that he was friendly, and his own scouts went forward and spoke to them. "Presently our Indians came back," he wrote in his journal, "and, as they came, shouted out at the top of their voices a doleful series of cries and wails that the interpreter . . . explained was a song of mourning for the dead. That it boded some misfortune there was no doubt; and when they came up, shedding copious tears and appearing pictures of misery, it was evident that the occasion was of no common sort." They brought the first report the Americans received of Custer's defeat.

"Did we doubt the tale?" Bradley asked. "I could not; there was an undefined vague something about it, unlooked for though it was, that commanded assent, and the most I could do was to hope that in the terror of the three fugitives from the fatal field their account of the disaster was somewhat overdrawn. But that there had been a disaster —a terrible disaster—I felt assured."

The news was of such importance that Bradley thought he should give it to Terry in person. "I therefore rode back," he said, "until I met the command, which was halted just before I came up, and narrated to the General the ghastly details. . . . He was surrounded by his staff and accompanied by General Gibbon . . . and for a moment there were blank faces and silent tongues and no doubt heavy hearts in that group. . . . But presently the voice of doubt and scorning was raised, the story was sneered at, such a catastrophe was wholly improbable, nay, impossible; if a battle had been fought, which was condescendingly admitted might have happened, then Custer was victorious, and these three Crows were dastards who had fled without awaiting the result and told this story to excuse their cowardice. General Terry took no part in these criticisms, but sat on his horse silent and thoughtful, biting his lower lip and looking to me as though he by no means shared in the wholesale scepticism of the flippant members of his staff."

Terry marched farther that day but did not reach the battlefield until June 27. Then from the survivors in Reno's command and the silent evidence of soldiers' bodies, he confirmed the reports of the Crow scouts.

*　　*　　*

The reaction of the United States to the news of Custer's defeat was one of incredulity, then of horror, and finally of rage. "The announcement of the annihilation of Custer and this large body of men," wrote one commentator, ". . . shocked the entire country, and was telegraphed around the world as a great disaster. I remember reading on the morning of July 5 . . . the headline of a newspaper, printed in the largest kind of type and running across the entire page the single word, 'Horrible.' "

Few editors had type quite large enough to reflect the public's feelings when Terry and Gibbon sent the news to the outside world. From the newest immigrant and the lowliest laborer to the highest officials, all were stunned and shared a common sense of bewilderment. Part of the emotion was based on sympathy for Custer, one of the most glamorous figures in the army and now a corpse on the Great Plains. Part of it was caused by the normal human reaction to the sudden destruction of more than two hundred men. (Indian losses did not create this effect.) Much of the shock, however, resulted from the blow to the nation's pride. Americans like to win, but this time they had lost and lost badly. Those "savages," whom so many scorned as inferior beings, had destroyed what had been regarded as one of the finest regiments of American cavalry. This was humiliating. The defeat, of course, had not been a massacre. Custer, fully armed, had deliberately attacked the village, and the Indians had destroyed him in self-defense. But "massacre" was what the public promptly labeled it, and the word still clings to the engagement. Its use helps to cover up the ineptness of the American command.

Yet at the moment there was little the army could do about what had happened. The nation was of no mind to turn back from its originally planned invasion of the Sioux's territory. The miners were flocking into the Black Hills in greater numbers, and as early as May they had laid out the city blocks in Deadwood. Treaty or no treaty, they were going to extract the gold from those mountains, and nothing could have kept them away except aggressive military action against the Americans, and that would not have been supported by public opinion. But Terry and Gibbon could not continue the Indian campaign with their shattered forces and had to march back to their starting point on the Yellowstone and await reinforcements. Crook, too, at the end of June was momentarily stalled. Shaken by his experience at the Rosebud, he wanted the Fifth Cavalry to arrive before he attempted again to enter the land held by the independent Indians.

The Indians themselves were not certain what to do next. At the approach of Terry, they had taken down their lodges and retreated without fighting, which was their usual practice under such circumstances. If they had remained, could they have won against Terry as they had won against Custer? Perhaps. They were weary and had used up much of their ammunition, but they outnumbered him, and by charging down on him or setting up ambushes, they might have been able to inflict serious injury on his command. On the other hand, he had Gatling guns and these could have made a substantial difference, because they were even more effective than howitzers.

In any case, however, the Indians had no plans for a large-scale campaign against the white men. They had formed their enormous camp and shared their common resentment against the Americans, but after the Battle of the Little Bighorn, they could not hold the camp together. Without some artificial source of supply, it was impossible to feed that many people and animals in one place for any length of time. Rich as the prairies were, they did not contain that much forage and game. So the bands began to split up again.

That did not mean the Indians, having won their great victory, became passive. Quite the contrary, as many a scalped corpse in the Black Hills testified. They struck in small groups wherever they noticed a weakness. A small miners' camp, a freight train, an undermanned detachment of soldiers—all these were targets for Indian attacks.

They also recruited more Indians from the agencies. News of the Little Bighorn spread rapidly in the red world as well as the white, and it proved to some that the Indians' warriors were the equal of the Americans' soldiers. Perhaps, after all, there was hope that the invaders could finally be defeated. However unsound this reasoning, based as it was on a single victory without knowledge of the almost limitless power of the United States, it led many warriors to slip away from the agencies and join the independent Indians.

Nor did the Sioux and Cheyennes restrict their recruiting efforts to the members of their own tribes. Some of them envisioned a great union of tribes, joined by their common hatred of the white men—something that had never happened. The agent at the Blackfeet agency in Montana—the Blackfeet and the Sioux were not normally friendly—reported that early in June the chiefs under his supervision "were invited to attend a council . . . composed of representatives of various tribes, viz. Santees, Yanktons, Chippewas, Crees, Mandans, Assinaboines, and also emissaries from the hostile camp of Sioux, under Sitting Bull. The messages were conveyed to these chiefs by the delivery of a cartridge and a piece of tobacco, signifying war or peace, and was carried to them by an Assinaboine messenger. Little Plume, the head-chief, went to the council, which lasted five or six days, and from him I learned that many of those present, especially the Santees and Yanktons, denounced the whites, calling them 'dogs and cowards: that they ought to be wiped out, and soon would be.' These chiefs [from the Blackfeet agency] took the precaution to halt their people and camp about 25 miles from the council-ground, so as to prevent communication between them and the unfriendly ones. On hearing the words above cited, and learning the hostile purpose of the council, they immediately withdrew, declaring 'the Sioux were their enemies, and that they would fight them if they ever came to this country, and that the whites were their friends, and they would help them whip the Sioux.' They then returned to their camp and went hunting with their people.

"A few days after the council broke up," the agent continued, "a young Peigan went some distance from the main camp in search of a couple of stray horses, and encountered two Santees, who fired at him from a coulie; the boy called out to them that he was a Peigan and not to shoot, but they fired a second time, wounding him, so that he died three weeks after in great pain. The murder caused intense feeling, and would have resulted in war, but for my earnest counsel and interference for peace." Just as the Sioux had earlier whipped the Cheyennes with their bowstrings when they refused to join the struggle against Carrington, they were now regarding every Indian who was not an ally as a foe. In their rage, they were ready to fight the world.

While the Sioux were recruiting more warriors, Crook remained in camp, waiting for reinforcements and news from Terry. On July 1, largely to pass the time, he made a four-day scout into the Little Bighorns. "Immense blocks of granite, some of them hundreds of feet high towered above us," Bourke wrote about the second day of their trip, "with stunted pine clinging to the scanty soil at these bases; above all loomed the majestic cone of the Cloud Peak, a thousand feet beyond timber line. . . . At every twenty or thirty feet of horizontal distance there was a cascade . . . so choked up with large fragments of granite that the current, lashed into fury, foamed like milk. The sun's rays were much obscured by the interlacing branches of the majestic spruce and fir trees shading the trail, and the rocky escarpments looming above the timber line." But such trips, no matter how magnificent the scenery, did not help subdue the Sioux and Cheyennes.

The period of waiting, however, was not entirely wasted. Although the men and officers spent much of their time hunting and fishing, they also got practice moving camp—like the Indians, they could not stay long in one place—and drilled until the new recruits began to act more like veterans.

Although the Indians could not successfully attack Crook's large camp, they were still scouring the country for smaller detachments of white men. On July 7, they came across the trail of about twenty-five soldiers, commanded by Lieutenant Frederick W. Sibley, who had been sent out by Crook to scout the country for the Indian village. The trail led toward the mountains, because Grouard, who was with Sibley, had noticed the Indians first and believed the white men's only hope to escape was to flee to the Bighorns. The Indians followed the Americans, who might have eluded them if they had not stopped for a brief rest and some coffee. But this delay gave the Indians a chance to corner them among some trees. The Indians fired into the woods, made several charges, and shot at the Americans' horses in an effort to destroy their means of transportation. The death of one of their leaders, who was struck by an American bullet, momentarily discouraged them, but they were confident of victory. The grass was slightly damp from a recent thunderstorm, and once it dried out they could set fire to it and drive the Americans out of the thicket and into the open. As they waited the Americans' gunfire became less and less and finally was stopped altogether. The American horses were still there, so the Indians were certain the white men's resistance had been overcome, and they charged again. But the wood was empty, for the Americans had retreated on foot.

The Indians pursued them, but Grouard, by circling through the mountains, led them safely back to Crook. "When they reached camp," Bourke wrote, "the whole party looked more like dead men than soldiers of the army; their clothes were torn into rags, their strength completely gone, and they faint with hunger and worn out with anxiety and distress. Two of the men, who had not been long in service, went completely crazy and refused to believe that the tents which they saw were those of the command; they persisted in thinking that they were the 'tepis' of the Sioux and Cheyennes, and would not accompany Sibley across the stream, but remained hiding in the rocks until a detachment had been sent out to capture them and bring them back."

Emboldened by this rout of a group of soldiers, the Sioux and Cheyennes decided to try to drive Crook away by harassing his camp. On July 10, the date that Crook first received dispatches telling about Custer's defeat, they crept up on the soldiers at night and set fire to the grass. For about ten nights in a row, they repeated these tactics, waiting until dark covered the plains and then attempting to stampede the soldiers' herd, attack the sentinels, and burn the grass. Although they suffered some casualties, they "destroyed an immense area of pasturage, not less than one hundred miles each way," Bourke wrote, "leaving a charred expanse of territory where had so lately been the refreshing green of dainty grass, traversed by crystal brooks; over all that blackened surface it would have been difficult to find so much as a grasshopper." The air was filled with particles of soot, which made breathing difficult. But then it began to rain heavily. The torrents of water drenched the prairies, settling the soot and made further fires impossible.

On July 13, seven companies of the Seventh Infantry arrived to reinforce Crook and brought with them a wagon train of supplies and dispatches informing Crook that the Fifth Cavalry under Colonel Wesley Merritt had been ordered to join them. Soon Crook would have no further reason for delaying his campaign.

But the Indians were not waiting for the Americans to take the offensive. In spite of the rain that had interrupted their harassment of

Crook's camp, they were busy raiding. As Merritt was approaching the Red Cloud agency on one leg of his march to meet Crook, a group of Cheyennes noticed his wagon train and two couriers. The infantry guarding the train were riding inside the wagons and were thus hidden from sight. So the Cheyennes apparently mistook it for a civilian train headed for the Black Hills and planned to attack it.

Unfortunately for the Cheyennes, the main body of troops happened by sheer chance to be nearby and out of view. Reversing the Indians' own tactics, they let their train and couriers serve as decoys to draw the Cheyennes closer to them. These soldiers, like many others, hated the Indians as much as the Indians hated the white men. One of them later wrote a description of the approaching warriors. "Here you are, beggarly, treacherous rascals," he said. "For years you have eaten of our bread, lived on our bounty. You are well fed, well cared for; you, your papooses and ponies are fat and independent; but you have heard of the grand revel in blood, scalps, and trophies of your brethren, the Sioux. It is no fight of yours. You have no grievances; but the love of rapine and warfare is the ruling passion, and you must take a hand against the Great Father, whom your treaty binds you to obey and honor. And now you have stuffed your wallets with his rations, your pouches with heavy loads of his best metallic cartridges. . . ."

Attitudes such as this prevailed among many Americans and accounted for much of the self-delusion, the hypocrisy, and the bloodshed. They pictured themselves as kindhearted, benevolent people, much sinned against by the Indians. No Colonial governor of pre-Revolutionary times ever spoke out as viciously against the colonists' aspirations for freedom as the Americans talked about the Indians' love of their own way of life or with greater misunderstanding or less objectivity.

So, filled with the hatred that only the self-righteous can feel, Merritt's soldiers charged from their hiding place, their polished equipment flashing in the summer sun. Although the Indians were taken by surprise, they fought back. One of them wheeled his horse, dropped to its far side, and from under the horse's belly fired a shot that almost struck Colonel Merritt. But the finest individual horsemanship could not carry the field, and the Indians were forced to retreat with several casualties.

Nevertheless the Indians' harassment continued throughout July, 1876. Crook's men, with the prairie burning around them, had felt the pressure; so, too, had Merritt's men, attacked as they marched to the

Red Cloud agency; but none suffered more than the miners in the
Black Hills. Crazy Horse himself was leading the raids on them, and
each scalp he took was a blow in defense of the Pah Sappa. But one
miner more or less was like a mere shovelful of earth dug from the
prairie; it made little difference.

*   *   *

While the Indians continued to raid and skirmish, Terry had been
reinforced by the Fifth Infantry under Colonel (brevet rank major
general) Nelson A. Miles, and the Americans were ready to take to
the field again. On August 3, Crook marched twenty miles to Goose
Creek, where he was to meet Colonel Merritt and the Fifth Cavalry.
(Goose Creek flows near the present-day Sheridan, Wyoming.) Crook
now had nearly two thousand men in his command, a force sufficient
to repel any body of Indians that might come against it. But its very
size presented serious problems, as William F. (Buffalo Bill) Cody,
who was serving as a scout with Merritt, pointed out.

"In form, as in face," Finerty said about Cody, "he had hardly a
peer on the American continent. He was dressed in full frontier fashion—buckskin breeches, long riding boots, blue shirt, colored necker-
chief and broad, white sombrero, with the usual snake band. His long,
silky, brown hair, with a suspicion of dark auburn glinting through it,
fell over his shoulders in graceful profusion, and his dark, exceedingly
expressive and handsome eyes seemed to blaze with martial ardor."

Crook invited him to attend a meeting of the senior officers to plan
their strategy for the coming weeks. Finerty, of course, was not invited
to attend, but like a good newspaperman he interviewed Cody as soon
as the conference was over. Cody was not optimistic. "He would not,
of course, say anything about what had passed in the General's tent,"
Finerty wrote, "but I remember that he felt doubtful of striking any
Indians with the force we then had.

" 'If they want to find Indians,' said he, 'let them send a battalion,
which I am willing to guide, and I'll engage we'll have our fill of
fighting before reaching the Little Missouri. The hostiles will never
face this outfit unless they [the officers] get it in some kind of a hole,
and there are plenty of them in this country. Crook ain't going to run
into them, though. He served in Arizona too long for that.' "

Cody had summed up the army's problem. The Sioux and Cheyennes were not going to commit suicide by massing a large force and
attacking two thousand well-armed Americans. They could not effi-
ciently move the necessary number of warriors, much less control

them during the ensuing battle. On the other hand, they could easily elude a column of that size. It had to march so slowly and its presence was so easily noticeable that they could avoid it without difficulty.

Nevertheless Crook had no option but to do what he could with his large force—after the Battle of the Rosebud and Custer's defeat, he did not dare divide it—and march down the Tongue, a river so crooked that in one day the column crossed it thirteen times. Then he moved over to the Rosebud and passed the place where they had battled the Cheyennes and Sioux. The area was now deserted, but as the officers examined the canyon down which they had almost gone in their feint, they were doubly grateful they had escaped from Crazy Horse's trap. Then after then stopping at the former location of the village, they struck a trail that took them down the Rosebud.

Because the visibility was ruined by a combination of smoke and fog, they were forced to camp for one day. To make up for lost time, Crook next ordered a night march. ". . . a night march in the Indian wilderness of the North is one of the most impressive incidents of war," Finerty wrote. "It is Weird [he capitalized the word for emphasis], *outré*, awe-inspiring. The vastness of untamed nature is around you, and its influence is insensibly felt. You are on the track of a mysterious enemy. The country over which you are marching is to you an unread chapter. You see something like a black shadow moving in advance. You are conscious that men and animals are moving within a few paces, and yet you cannot define any particular object, not even your horse's head. But you hear the steady, perpetual tramp, tramp, tramp of the iron-hoofed cavalry, broken by an occasional stumble and the half-smothered imprecation of an irate trooper; the jingle of carbines and sling-belts, and the snorting of the horses as they grope their way through the eternal dust which the rider can feel in his throat like the thick, stinking vapor of a champion London fog. Once in a while a match, struck by a soldier to light his pipe, would flash in the gloom like a huge fire-fly, and darkness would assert itself again.

"In this manner," he continued, "we proceeded for quite a time when all of a sudden a tremendous illumination sprang up from behind us and lit almost the whole line of the valley. Reflected in it, we could see the arms glistening as our battalion moved steadily along, and the bluffs, left and right, seemed like giants keeping watch and ward upon the pass. We turned in our saddles to observe the phenomenon and beheld a flood of flame [from a fire which had probably been set by the Indians], which, rushing like a charging battle-line storming some fated town, burst over the mountain crest behind us, twenty miles away, flinging its lucid banner to the very arch of the firmament, almost as if the gates of hell had been flung open. . . . I have seen some magnificent freaks of fire in my time, including the Chicago disaster . . . but that sudden outburst of flame in the Plutonian gloom of the Rosebud Valley surpassed, in lurid splendor, anything that I have ever imagined or beheld." If the Indians could not hold their country against the invasion, they were determined at least to make travel through it as difficult as they could for the Americans.

Soon the moon rose, "and its chaste luster tamed down the infernal glow on the southward hills." At two o'clock Crook let his men rest. The next day, according to Finerty, "A cold disagreeable rain, accompanied by a chilling north wind, set in, and after a tramp of twenty-two miles we halted in a cross cañon, where, fortunately, some grass remained, lit fires amid the gigantic rocks cut into fantastic columns and corners by the action of waters which had subsided countless ages ago, and made ourselves as comfortable as it was possible to be in the most inhospitable country outside of Iceland or Siberia."

As Cody had predicted, they saw no Indians; but the next day, their scouts noticed dust rising in the distance. It was Terry's column, which had marched up from the Yellowstone. The two generals, frustrated in their attempts to engage the Sioux, joined forces. Although this made it even less possible that they would encounter the Indians, it seemed the practical thing to do, and together, they marched over to the Powder, and followed it to the Yellowstone, where Crook was to pick up fresh supplies brought in by steamboat.

Since late June, when Custer was defeated, the army had been able to accomplish little. Weeks had gone by while Terry and Crook had waited for reinforcements, and when they finally went into the field, their two-pronged campaign had failed to produce any result except fatigue for officers, men, and animals. Yet the Sioux and Cheyennes were no better off either. Because of the soldiers, they could not roam through their country freely, the miners were still entering the Black Hills, and the concentration of warriors capable of meeting the Americans in force had broken up. As the hot August sun beat down on the northern plains, the war had ground to a stalemate.

Instead of the aggressive, conclusive campaign the Americans had wanted, both Terry and Crook were at the Yellowstone, and there were not enough supplies on hand to equip the two columns to take the field again. After days of further waiting while Terry scoured every

nearby post for what it could spare, Crook finally secured enough
rations for a fifteen-day march, and he and Terry agreed on their
campaign for the coming weeks. Crook, who was the more experienced Indian fighter, would march south and try to pick up the trail
they had seen earlier; and Terry, a well-loved general but not as
accustomed to the wilderness, would patrol along the Yellowstone to
prevent the Indians from fleeing north. When the weather became
colder and he was forced to withdraw to winter quarters, the Fifth
Infantry under Colonel Miles would remain at a cantonment they were
building at the juncture of the Tongue and the Yellowstone.

Always aware of the need for traveling fast and light when pursuing
Indians, Crook plunged back into the wilderness. During the first days
of the campaign, the rain drenched the soldiers. At night they had
trouble making fires from the soaked wood, and their bedding and
clothing were soggy. But they picked up an Indian trail and began
following it.

By September 4, they reached the Little Missouri but still had not
found the Indians and were running short of supplies. Earlier Finerty
had commented on the differences between Crook's command and
Terry's. "Terry's men," he wrote, "moved with 205 wagons, Sibley
and A tents, together with a pack train, while Crook's command had
only rations on their mules, and all the clothing they possessed on
their frames. Terry's troops applied to Crook's a nickname unfit for
ears polite, but which unmistakably referred to the dilapidated condition of the rear portion of their pantaloons. . . . Crook is severe, and
I'd rather be with Terry as regards food, shelter, and clean flannel, but
he goes for the Indians as one of themselves would do, and has shown
that an American army can stand, without much growling or the
slightest approach to mutiny, more than any other troops upon this
earth."

On September 5, they had marched another thirty miles and "were
within 160 miles of Fort [Abraham] Lincoln, and about 200 from the
northern edge of the Black Hills," Finerty wrote. "To accomplish
either march, we had half rations for two and a half days only. I
interviewed General Crook on the subject. This is what occurred.

" 'You are sending in a courier, General?'

" 'Yes, to Fort Lincoln. He will carry some mail and telegrams for
the command,' Crook answered.

" 'What do you propose to do now, General?'

"He paused for a moment, and, pulling his peculiar beard, said very slowly: 'We are five full marches from Fort Abraham Lincoln. We are seven at least from the Black Hills. By going to the Missouri [where Fort Abraham Lincoln was located] we lose two weeks' time. By marching on the Hills we gain so much. I march on the Black Hills to-morrow. Between going to and coming back from Fort Lincoln we should lose more than half our horses.'

" 'How many rations have you left?'

" 'Only two days' and a half half rations, but we must make them last for seven, at least. It must be done. The Indians have gone to the Hills and the agencies. The miners must be protected, and we must punish the Sioux on our way to the south, or leave this campaign entirely unfinished.'

"I looked at him in some amazement, and could not help saying, 'You will march 200 miles in the wilderness, with used-up horses and tired infantry on two and one-half days' half rations!'

" 'I know it looks hard,' was the reply, 'but we've got to do it, and it shall be done. I have sent a telegram for supplies to General Sheridan. The wagons will meet us at Crook City or Deadwood [in the Black Hills]. If not, the settlements must supply our wants. Nobody knows much about this region, but it looks fair. We'll kill some game, too, perhaps, to make up for short rations. Half rations will be issued after to-night. All will be glad of the movement after the march has been made. If necessary,' he added, 'we can eat our horses.'

"This suggestion," Finerty added, "fell upon me like a splash of ice water."

*   *   *

While Crook was deciding to continue his campaign in spite of the shortage of supplies, the United States was taking steps to lay a cloak of legality over the seizure of the Black Hills. On September 7, 1876, yet another commission opened a council at the Red Cloud agency. The government was not in a conciliatory mood. In August Congress had passed legislation providing for the negotiation of a new treaty— really an amendment to the Treaty of 1868—but on harsher terms than were offered the year before. The Indians were to cede to the United States the western portion of the lands reserved to them forever by the earlier treaty; they were to give up the Black Hills; they were to agree to agencies located on the Missouri River, where they did not want to go; and they were to consider moving to Indian Territory, now Oklahoma. In return, the government would continue to give them rations until they could support themselves. Certain other benefits would also accrue to the Indians, benefits that for the most part they did not want in the way of schools and agricultural assistance.

The Indians were in a difficult position. The Americans had destroyed the means by which they could support themselves and had substituted another—farming—which was out of keeping with their tradition. Naturally they had failed at it and become dependents. Now the government was saying it would no longer support them unless they gave up more of their lands. The choice it offered the Indians was simple: Sign or face starvation. The only other alternative was to join the independent Indians and fight the forces of Crook and Terry. It was not much of a choice, but even then the Indians delayed signing the papers and held a council of their own apart from the white men.

After seven days, the commissioners became impatient, but one of the chiefs came to the agency and told them, "You are wise men and you have had time. Our councils may not seem of much importance to you, but to us it seems a very serious matter to give up our country. You must have patience and bear with us."

Finally they met again with the commissioners for two days of argument. As they had done so many times in the past, the Indians recounted their grievances, listing the broken promises and complaining about the distribution of faulty rations. The commissioners remained adamant. The Indians must sign the new amendment. The commissioners also were not overly conscientious about explaining its terms and slurred over some of them in a vague way. Even when they set a time for the feast they had promised after the signing of the treaty, the Indians were reluctant. Some refused to put their marks next to their names, and one chief did so holding a blanket in front of his eyes so he could not see the paper.

Article Twelve of the Treaty of 1868 had specifically stated: "No treaty for the cession of any portion or part of the reservation herein described which may be held in common shall be of any validity or force as against the said Indians, unless executed and signed by at least three fourths of all the adult male Indians, occupying or interested in the same. . . ." The language could not have been clearer or more definite, but the government that had written that article paid absolutely no attention to it. None whatsoever. It wanted the Black Hills, and it was going to take the Black Hills—in fact, it had already taken them—and since it could not obtain the signatures of three-fourths of the adult males, it settled for considerably less. The commission secured the marks of the leading chiefs at the agencies and the marks of two leaders from each band. This was a paltry percent of the number required to give the treaty the force of law, but the United States government did not care. Might was the law, and the United States government had the might. The commissioners all considered themselves honorable and patriotic Americans, but on that September day at the Red Cloud agency, they ground the word of the United States into the dust of the prairie.

They then rushed to the Spotted Tail agency and to other agencies, secured a few more marks beside the names of Indians, and regarded their mission as completed. But even the commissioners felt a sense of injustice. "We hardly know," they wrote in their final report, "how to frame in words the feelings of shame and sorrow which fill our hearts as we recall the long record of the broken faith of our Government. It is made more sad, in that the rejoicings of our centennial year [1876] are mingled with the wail of sorrow of widows and orphans made by a needless Indian war, and that our Government has expended more money in this war than all the religious bodies of our country have spent in Indian missions since our existence as a nation."

*   *   *

Because the independent Indians had not signed the new treaty—if the word "treaty" properly describes the commissioners' document— and were unaffected by it, Crook continued his campaign against them. Although he had not fought with them, his marches were putting heavy pressure on them. They could not devote themselves to hunting, as they usually did, and they could not move freely through the country. Crook's men, however, were suffering also. On the morning of September 8, Finerty "observed a small group of soldiers by the side of the trail busily engaged in skinning a dead horse and appropriating steaks from its hinder parts. This was the beginning of our horse rations. The men were too hungry to be longer controlled, and the General wisely ordered that as many horses as would be necessary to feed the men be selected by the officers and slaughtered day by day. It was a tough experiment, but there was no help for it, and anything outside of actual cannibalism was preferable to slowly starving to death. Some of the men, before they began to destroy the horses for food, had taken to splitting the fat leaves of cacti, and when wood was procurable [they once traveled eighty-six miles and did not see a stick] they roasted them at the camp fires. This induced a species of dysentery, from which a large portion of the command suffered during the remainder of the march."

Faced with this shortage of food, Crook sent Anson Mills, who had commanded the advance down the Rosebud, with about 150 men and fifty pack mules to the Black Hills. They were to get supplies and return as quickly as possible. On September 8, as he was moving rapidly toward the Black Hills, Mills came across an Indian trail and decided to follow it. The village that had made it was led by a Sioux named American Horse and was composed of more than thirty lodges. They were from the Spotted Tail agency and carried certificates of good conduct from the agent there, but like so many Indians in the summer and fall of 1876, they had left the agency to resume their old life. Among their possessions was a glove marked with the name of Captain Myles Koegh, who had died with Custer at the Little Bighorn, a letter addressed to a private in Custer's regiment, and in their herd were several horses carrying the brand of the Seventh Cavalry. But that victory, although less than three months old, was now something of the past, and American Horse's band, like the other independent Sioux and Cheyennes, was simply trying to evade Crook's large column. As long as they knew where it was, they thought themselves safe.

On the evening of September 8, they were camped at a place called Slim Buttes. They had erected their tepees on a flat area of ground. Behind them were some bluffs that overlooked the campsite, and near the lodges was a brush-covered ravine. All was peaceful at the camp. Not far away, the horses grazed quietly, and the smoke curled skyward from the fires at which the women were cooking supper. American Horse believed everything was well. In the tepees were quantities of buffalo meat, a few buffalo tongues, and many baskets of cherries, plums, and other fruit, some fresh and some dried, and American Horse believed everything was well. But unknown to him, Mills's command was camped only four miles away, and Mills himself, accompanied by Grouard, was reconnoitering the village and deciding he had sufficient men to attack it.

On the morning of the following day, the Sioux suddenly heard the sound of their herd stampeding. The Americans had raided it, but they failed to cut the horses off from the camp, and many of the animals ran toward it. Then came the sound of rifle shots as the bullets began to pierce the tepees. There was no time to untie the flaps. Drawing their knives, the Indians slit the buffalo skins and canvas from which

they were made and dashed outside. Some ran for the bluffs and others
to the ravine, both of which offered them cover while they returned the
Americans' fire.

Mills had little difficulty entering the village but had a great problem
staying there. The Indians' bullets were whistling among his men, and
he realized for the first time that the camp was larger than he had
thought. Although he threw up breastworks to protect his soldiers, he
needed help. So he sent a messenger with an order to bring up his pack
train and a request to Crook for assistance. Taking a detachment of
men from his column, Crook rushed to Mills's aid.

In spite of the initial surprise, the Indians held the advantage. They
had retreated to strong positions, and they had enough warriors to
engage Mills's force. But as they counterattacked, Crook arrived. Just
as Mills had found more Indians than he had supposed he would, the
Indians discovered there were now more soldiers than they had expected, and Crook's men were able to drive them back and keep them
away from the village.

After considerable fighting, the stiffest remaining resistance was
offered by the Indians in the ravine. They were close to the white men,
so they could take good aim, and they were also unable to escape. The
soldiers, therefore, concentrated their attention on them. Women and
children were in the ravine among the warriors, and as the bullets
poured in among them, they began singing an Indian death chant, and
the children wailed piteously. Crook ordered the firing halted and,
using the scouts as interpreters, offered them a chance to surrender.
Several of the women took this chance to save their lives. "Then,"
wrote Finerty, "our troops re-opened with a very rain of hell upon the
infatuated braves, who, nevertheless, fought it out with Spartan courage against such hopeless odds, for nearly two hours. Such matchless
bravery electrified even our enraged soldiers into a spirit of chivalry
and General Crook, recognizing the fact that the unfortunate savages
had fought like fiends in defense of wives and children, ordered another suspension of hostilities and called upon the dusky heroes to
surrender."

American Horse, "a fine-looking broad-chested Sioux, with a handsome face and a neck like a bull," had been shot in the abdomen. He
and the other warriors who were still alive had taken refuge in a cave
in the ravine. Hearing the scouts repeating Crook's offer to accept
their surrender, he crept to the opening of the cave and presented his
rifle, butt forward, to the general, saying he would surrender if Crook

would spare the lives of the other warriors. Some of the soldiers who had lost friends in the fight protested, but Crook promised that none of the Indians would be harmed.

"This message having been interpreted to American Horse," Finerty wrote, "he beckoned to his surviving followers, and two strapping Indians, with their long, but quick and graceful stride, followed him out of the gully. The Chieftain's intestines protruded from his wound, but a squaw—his wife, perhaps—tied her shawl around the injured part and then the poor, fearless savage, never uttering a complaint, walked slowly to the little camp fire, occupied by his people, about 20 yards away, and sat down among the women and children. The surgeons examined the wound, pronounced it mortal, and during the night American Horse, one of the bravest and ablest of the Sioux chiefs, fell back suddenly and expired without uttering a groan."

The next day the Indians attacked again, but Crook's column was far too powerful for them. Because the women whom Crook had captured confirmed his fears that some of the Sioux were planning to fight the white men in the Black Hills, he was anxious to get to that area as quickly as possible. The march was long and hard—it was afterwards called the "horsemeat march"—but food taken from the Indians' camp helped extend the men's rations, and they also found the Indian horses better eating than their own worn-out animals. Sometimes they were as short of firewood as they were of food, traveling for miles without seeing a tree they could use as fuel, but they reached the Black Hills without encountering any more Indians.

For all intents and purposes, the Americans' summer campaign was over. It had not been a glorious one, but it had practically ended the war against the Sioux and the Cheyennes. The Indians had scored an astounding victory when they had defeated Custer; but faced with the enormous numbers of troops the government had put into the field, they could not follow it up. Although the Americans had not been able to strike the final, decisive blow they wanted—a single battle that would conclude the struggle—they had occupied the Black Hills and started a merciless, grinding process that should bring the end.

XV

The End of the Struggle

THE cool of autumn crept across the plains. As the days grew shorter, the coats of the remaining buffalos began to thicken, and the first of the migrating birds started to appear on their way south. The season of hope, when the horses were fat, travel easy, and game plentiful, was over, and in its place was coming the lean period of winter. Soon the Sioux who were away from the agencies would be huddled inside their tepees, and when they went to their doorways and opened the flaps, instead of seeing the lush prairie grass, they would find only the white wasteland stretching in every direction. That would be the time of snow blindness, of hunger, and even of despair. Yet in 1876 the winter that was approaching was not merely a change of season that again would eventually give way to spring; it was winter for the Sioux as a free nation.

Colonel Nelson A. Miles, whom Terry had left with the Fifth Infantry to patrol the Yellowstone, did not intend to spend the months idly. As he later wrote, "Preparations were made for the accommodation of the entire command during the winter, but I felt sure that simply to hibernate and allow the Indians to occupy the country meant a harassing and unendurable existence for the winter; besides giving great encouragement to the Indians by permitting them to believe themselves masters of the situation while we were simply tolerated upon the ground we occupied. My opinion was that the only way to make the country tenable for us was to render it untenable for the Indians; and with that view I made all the preparations necessary for the protection of our stores, and every possible provision for the comfort of our troops when they should be able to rest. I also made the most careful preparations for a vigorous, active, and severe winter campaign."

He wanted action, and he soon got it. While he was stocking his cantonment for the winter, one of his supply trains was attacked and forced to return to its starting point at Fort Buford. Several companies were then assigned to protect it, and although the Indians again appeared, it got through safely on its second attempt. But the men found a note, written in English, on the trail. "I want to know," it said, "what you are doing traveling on this road. You scare all the Buffalo away. I want to hunt in this place. I want you to turn back from here. If you don't I will fight you again. I want you to leave what you have got there and then turn back from there." It was signed, "I am your friend, Sitting Bull." At the end was this postscript: "I mean all the rations you have got and some powder. I wish you would write as soon as you can."

Whether the note was written at Sitting Bull's dictation by some half-breed in the band or whether it was a joke played by one of the army's scouts cannot be determined. But it expressed Sitting Bull's attitude toward the white men. He continued to regard them as interlopers, and he wanted them to leave.

The note obviously had no effect on the Americans' plans. Having received information that the Indians were on the move, Miles left the juncture of the Tongue and Yellowstone Rivers on October 17 to try to intercept them. As he drew near their camp, two friendly Indians came toward his command under a flag of truce. Although Sitting Bull was as unfriendly as ever to the Americans, some of the other Indians wanted to learn what Miles might have to say and persuaded him to talk with the American officer.

"We met," Miles continued, "and after some conversation he desired to know what the troops were remaining in that country for, and why they did not go back to their posts or into winter quarters. He was informed that we were out to bring him and his Indians in, and that we did not wish to continue the war against them, but that if they forced the war it would end, as all Indian wars had ended and must end, by their putting themselves under the authorities at Washington. He was told that he could not be allowed to roam over the country, sending out war parties to devastate the settlements. He claimed that the country belonged to the Indians and not to the white men, and declared that he had nothing to do with the white men and wanted them to leave that country entirely to the Indians. He said that the white man never lived who loved an Indian, and that no true Indian ever lived who did not hate the white man. He declared that God Almighty made him an Indian and did not make him an agency Indian either, and he did not intend to be one."

As they talked, Miles observed him closely. "He was a strong, hardy, sturdy looking man of about five feet eleven inches in height, well-built, with strongly marked features, high cheek bones, prominent nose, straight, thin lips, and a strong under jaw, indicating determination and force. He had a wide, large, well-developed head and low forehead. He was a man of few words and cautious in his expressions, evidently thinking twice before speaking. He was very deliberate in his movements and somewhat reserved in his manner. At first he was courteous, but evidently void of any genuine respect for the white race. Although the feeling was disguised, his manner indicated his animosity toward those whom he had to meet. During the conversation his manner was civil and to some extent one of calm repose. He might have been mistaken for a mild, plain-spoken, inoffensive man until I had developed the other side of his character."

A good diplomat, Sitting Bull first tried to accomplish with words what the Indians had not succeeded in accomplishing with guns and bows: the removal of the Americans from their lands. But failing in this, he became angry. He was particularly infuriated when Miles, who had obtained the information from some agency Indians, told him where he was planning to go to hunt buffalos.

At this statement, Sitting Bull "evidently suspected treachery on the part of some of his people . . . ," Miles wrote. "This fact enraged him so that he finally gave an exhibition of wild frenzy. His whole manner appeared more like that of a wild beast than a human being; his face assumed a furious expression; his jaws were closed tightly; his lips were compressed, and you could see his eyes glistening with the fire of savage hatred."

And so the two men stood facing each other, each representing his own culture and his own purpose. The Indian was determined to save his land for his people and his people's children so they could continue to live the only life they cared about. The white officer was determined to carry out his mandate, and behind him stood the miners, greedy for the Black Hills, the farmers, who were already tilling soil once occupied by the Indians, and the millions of Americans, who looked on the West as their own and were resolved to take possession of it. The

physical space between the two men was only a few feet; the ideologi-
cal difference between them was infinite. They could never have come
to an understanding.

Some of the warriors were becoming both restless and curious, and
a few of them gathered near Sitting Bull. This worried Miles, because
it about doubled the six men who were supposed to serve as guards for
each leader. He also thought that one of the warriors had handed
Sitting Bull a carbine, which the Sioux had slipped under his robe,
while Miles had only his service revolver to protect himself. Believing
it was impossible to come to terms, Miles broke off the meeting and
returned to his camp.

The next day he moved his men in the direction of the Indian
village. Some of the warriors wanted to fight Miles, but others were
still not certain. Here they were in the heart of the country with winter
coming on, and yet the white soldiers continued to plague and harass
them. Perhaps it would be better to go to an agency at least for the
cold season. As a result of this dissension, Sitting Bull and some of the
other leaders came out under a flag of truce to speak to Miles again.

But neither side was willing to yield to the other. Sitting Bull was
adamant about not going to an agency and wanted no white men in the
country except for a few trading posts. Miles, of course, insisted that
the Indians submit to the white men's will. Realizing there was little
chance of reaching an agreement, Miles had already lined his men up
in military formation. Although he was outnumbered, he could afford
to take an offensive position, because he had artillery with him. One of
the Indians had meanwhile gotten close enough to the Americans to
see that they were prepared to fight and that the artillery had been
uncovered and aimed in their direction. He reported this to Sitting
Bull, and the information, of course, increased Sitting Bull's suspicion.
After more unfruitful argument, Miles, in a state of exasperation, gave
Sitting Bull an ultimatum. He had fifteen minutes in which to accept
the Americans' terms or face a battle.

Sitting Bull raced back to the village and called on the Indians to
fight. Within a few minutes, the white soldiers began shooting. In
self-defense, the Indians set fire to the prairie, hoping that the
grass would start burning around the soldiers and prevent them from
advancing. But it did not. The soldiers charged, and the Indians
were compelled to move their camp and fall back.

The battle lasted for two days. The Indians fought desperately. At
one time, they surrounded Miles's entire command, which was forced

to form a square to prevent the Indians from overrunning it. But it was of no use. As Miles remarked later, "The engagement demonstrated the fact that Indians could not stand artillery, and that there was no position they could take from which the artillery could not dislodge them."

It seemed senseless to the Indians to continue fighting. They had retreated about forty miles, and Miles was still pursuing them. Once more they sent out envoys with a flag of truce to talk with Miles, and approximately two thousand of them agreed to go under an escort to an agency. Miles had accomplished much of his purpose, and as he could not shepherd two thousand Indians south and fight the remainder, he broke off the battle. Sitting Bull and many other Sioux still preserved their independence, but their numbers had been seriously depleted by Miles's vigorous action.

*   *   *

While Miles was fighting in the north, Crook remained active in the south and looked forward to a winter campaign, too. In a move calculated to weaken the Indians, he surrounded the Red Cloud agency toward the end of October and confiscated the Indians' horses. This was a blow to the Indians and had no moral or legal justification. But Crook was determined to bring the hostilities to a quick end, and one way was to deprive the independent Indians of possible reinforcements from the agency. Without horses, they could not leave. But even well mounted, their enthusiasm for continuing the struggle was waning. This was reflected in the comparative ease with which Crook could now enlist scouts from among the Cheyennes and Sioux. In the summer of 1876, he had been unable to secure the number of volunteers he wanted, but in the fall this had changed. Many of the agency Indians were ready to throw in their lot with the Americans, and Crook could enlist as many as he wanted.

So the grinding process continued, with Miles campaigning in the north, Crook in the south, and the solidarity of the Indians shattered. Only a few important bands remained free, and they were hunted men. Among these was Dull Knife's village of Cheyennes. In November, Crook ordered Colonel Ranald MacKenzie into the field. From information obtained from a captive Cheyenne boy, the Americans had learned the approximate location of the Indians' villages. The first one they struck was Dull Knife's. Later the Indians said they had known the soldiers were approaching and should have fled, but one of the band had inflamed the imagination of the younger men and persuaded them to stay and fight. It was a disastrous decision. "In the gray twilight of a cold November morning (the 25th)," Bourke later wrote, "MacKenzie with the cavalry and Indian scouts burst like a tornado upon the suspecting village . . . and wiped it from the face of the earth. There were two hundred and five lodges, each of which was a magazine of supplies of all kinds—buffalo and pony meat, valuable robes, ammunition, saddles, and the comforts of civilization in very appreciable quantities. The roar of the flames exasperated the fugitive Cheyennes to frenzy; they heard the dull thump, thump, of their own medicine drum, which had fallen into the hands of the Shoshones [among the scouts]. . . . Seven hundred and five ponies fell into our hands and were driven from the field; as many more were killed and wounded or slaughtered by the Cheyennes the night after the battle, partly for food and partly to let their half-naked old men and women put their feet and legs in the warm entrails."

Following that fight, the little remaining strength of the Cheyennes was only a shattered remnant of what it had once been. In June, 1876, they had charged down on Custer and Reno, helping to win one of the greatest Indian victories since General St. Clair's defeat in 1791. After November, those who had escaped from MacKenzie's attack and did not join Crazy Horse's band of Sioux began to come to the agencies and surrender.

The winds howled over the prairies, and the snows drifted deep, but the weather was no longer the Indians' protector. Usually this was a time of peace, when even the warring tribes did not raid each other, and the old men proudly related their stories by the fire. But the Americans did not respect this rule of the Indians' existence. In spite of the cold, their soldiers were marching over the prairies just as though it were summer and the time of the Sun Dance had passed.

Crazy Horse was the next to be harried. Many of the Cheyennes, who had once been his allies, were turning against him and offering to serve as the white men's scouts. They knew his ways and the places where he liked to hunt and camp, making it easier for the Americans to track him. The Sioux, too, were abandoning him. Spotted Tail, the Brulé, had gone to the agency years ago but had maintained neutrality in the continuing struggle. Now he told the white men he thought he could personally persuade Crazy Horse to surrender.

Miles also was in the field again. On January 7, having fought several skirmishes, he was marching through the snow up the Tongue River when he captured a warrior and some women and children.

From them he learned the location of Crazy Horse's camp and, on the following day, prepared to attack it. The Indians had taken up positions on the heights above the river valley, and as the white men advanced, they shouted taunts and boasted of the victory they would soon enjoy. But as the fight opened, the soldiers stripped the canvas from the two pieces of artillery they had with them. The guns boomed, the shells exploded among the Indians, and they fell back; but in spite of their initial consternation, they recovered and soon surrounded the soldiers.

Miles considered one high bluff on the left of the troops the most important point. It was held by a group of Sioux led by a medicine man named Big Crow. He had whipped both himself and the Indians into a frenzy. Thinking "that his medicine was so strong that the white men could not hurt him," Miles wrote, "he rushed out in front of the warriors, attired in the most gorgeous Indian battle costume of the brightest colors, and with a headdress made of the waving plumes of the eagle falling down his back, jumped up and down, ran in a circle and whooped and yelled. Our men turned their guns upon him, but for several minutes he was unharmed, notwithstanding their efforts to reach him with their rifles."

Then the infantry charged the bluff. "Charge" may be too strong a word. The snow was so deep and the soldiers were so encumbered with their heavy clothing that they could not move faster than a slow walk. As the men plodded forward, the snow started falling again, drifting down on the valley of the Tongue and adding "an inexpressible weirdness to the scene." During their advance, the soldiers kept on firing. One of their bullets struck Big Crow and he fell in the snow dead. Because he had boasted that his medicine had made him invincible to the Americans, his death turned the Indians into a panic. Only a short time before, they had been hurling insults at the Americans, confident of their ability to win. Now they were fleeing up the valley. Miles did not try to follow them because the snow was too deep, and if he became separated from his artillery, he would be overwhelmed. Nevertheless, as he later said, "While the engagement was not of such a serious character as to cause great loss of life on either side, yet it demonstrated the fact that we could move in any part of the country in the midst of winter, and hunt the enemy down in their camps wherever they might take refuge. In this way, constantly pursuing them, we made them realize that there was no peace or safety for them while they remained in a hostile attitude."

The Americans now enjoyed all the advantage of the initiative. They could attack or withdraw whenever they wished, and the Indians could only remain on the defensive. As they slept in their tepees, they never knew if the coming dawn would bring the sound of rifle shots and the whistling of bullets through their lodges. The Cheyennes were discouraged by the endless and uneven struggle; and in February, when one of Miles's scouts went to the village with some of the Americans' captives and an offer of peace, many of them decided to surrender.

As Crazy Horse looked around his camp, he could see it getting smaller and smaller. More families had left, and new recruits no longer came from the agencies to join him, bringing with them the supplies he needed, particularly ammunition. As the Indians that winter discussed their future, Sitting Bull remained firmly against surrender. He had repeatedly said he would not become an agency Indian, and all the hardships and disasters had not caused him to change his mind. Crazy Horse, however, was beginning to weaken. He could remember when he had led the decoys that had lured Fetterman to his death, the long and successful fight over the Bozeman Trail, the day he had turned back Crook on the Rosebud, and the great battle on the Little Bighorn. But in the long winter evenings, he was not boasting about these triumphs, for they had proved fruitless. The white men were stronger than ever before, more aggressive, more difficult to defeat.

Then came the final blow. Red Cloud, who had led the fight against Carrington and forced the Americans to abandon their forts, responded to the white men's promise to give him additional authority at the agency if he succeeded in persuading Crazy Horse to surrender. He, too, began sending messengers to the weary Oglala, urging him to give up. What could a man do against a powerful enemy when even his friends were against him? In April, 1877, Crazy Horse reached his decision. He would hold out no longer, and on May 6, he surrendered at the Red Cloud agency.

Bourke visited him that evening with Frank Grouard. "I saw before me," he wrote, "a man who looked quite young, not over thirty years old [he looked younger than he actually was], five feet eight inches high, lithe and sinewy, with a scar in the face. The expression of his countenance was one of quiet dignity but morose, dogged, tenacious, and melancholy. He behaved with solidity, like a man who realized he had to give in to Fate. . . ."

Through no fault of his own, he had been defeated. He had fought bravely, persistently, and well. But decades ago the course had been set, and the best he could do was to run it to the end with dignity. That he had done, and now he sat in his tepee in the spring evening, lonely and defeated.

* * *

Sitting Bull refused to follow the example of Crazy Horse. Miles could press him on the north, Crook attack from the south, and the agency Indians try to persuade him to surrender, but all this did not shake his determination. Yet he could not remain in his old haunts, crisscrossed as they were by marching columns of soldiers, ready at any moment to attack him. No tribe could live under the constant threat of destruction. So he took the only choice left to him and moved with his band across the Canadian border, where the Americans could not pursue him.

This may have temporarily solved Sitting Bull's problem, but it was not a satisfactory solution for either Canada or the United States. For the village remained close to the border, leaving the American settlements and agencies in the north still open to attack by raiding parties. The Canadian authorities, on the other hand, were already having troubles with their own plains Indians and did not want to add to the numbers for which they were responsible. So while they were willing to provide an asylum for the band as long as they behaved themselves, they would have preferred to have had the Indians return to the United States.

In June, 1877, the Catholic bishop of Dakota visited the camp. He told the leaders he did not represent the American government officially but that he had been assured any promises he made would be carried out. A representative of the North West Mounted Police was at the conference, and Sitting Bull asked him if he could expect protection. The officer replied that he could as long as he did not misbehave. Whereupon Sitting Bull said, "What would I return for? To have my horses and arms taken away? What have the Americans to give me? Once I was rich; . . . but the Americans stole it all in the Black Hills. I have come to remain with the White Mother's [Queen Victoria's] children." As long as the Canadians would permit him to live both free and at peace, he had at that time little to gain by returning to the United States and submitting to the restrictions of reservation life.

The United States, however, was not at all satisfied to leave Sitting Bull alone. Chief Joseph was leading the Nez Percés in their famous an dramatic confrontation with the white men, and the resurgence of warfare was breeding restlessness among the agency Indians. If they broke out, the independent camp just across the border could provide a focal point for the resistance.

The restlessness spread to the Red Cloud agency, and in August, Crazy Horse, who had temporarily adjusted well to agency life, began to regret his earlier decision. Reflecting the opinion of many Americans, Bourke wrote, "Crazy Horse began to cherish hopes of being able to slip out of the agency and get back into some section farther to the north, where he would have little to fear, and where he could resume the old wild life with its pleasant incidents of hunting the buffalo, the elk, and the moose, and its raids upon the horses of Montana." Therefore, the Americans, growing more anxious than ever to break up Sitting Bull's village, started to make arrangements with the Canadian government to meet with him.

While these negotiations were going on, trouble was brewing between Crazy Horse and the white men at the Red Cloud agency, and rumors began to circulate that he was preparing to flee. Fear on both sides did not breed good judgment. Crook, on a flying visit to Red Cloud, ordered Crazy Horse's arrest, but on September 4, when the soldiers arrived at his camp, they found he had fled the night before to the Spotted Tail agency. There they took him into custody and brought him back to Fort Robinson and put him in the guardhouse. He drew a knife, an Indian seized his wrist, the soldiers grabbed for him, and in the ensuing struggle he received a mortal wound in the abdomen. Whether it came from a bayonet or his own knife has never been known. In either case, the result was the same. The great leader of the Oglalas was dead.

Mourn for him, as his people did. But Crazy Horse, a farmer? Crazy Horse, a begging recipient of rations? Crazy Horse, a reservation politician, maneuvering between the Indians and the white agents? Of course not. If what the medicine men preached was true, he was now where the buffalo grazed once more, great herds of buffalo, as great as they had been before the white men first came. And if what the medicine men said was not true? Then at least his eyes and ears were closed to the degradation of his people.

But the death of Crazy Horse did not ease the government's determination to catch Sitting Bull and put him where he could be more closely watched. On October 17, the American commission, headed by General Terry and accompanied by officials of the Canadian government, met with Sitting Bull and some of the other leaders. Almost anyone could have foreseen the result. The Americans would not agree to permit Sitting Bull to return on terms that were acceptable to him. Nor was he going to come back on any terms that were acceptable to them. Proud and angry, he rebutted every argument the Canadians and Americans offered.

Although the council went on for several days, going over the same ground again and again, Sitting Bull summarized his point of view in a single speech. At one point, he rose, conspicuously shook hands with the Canadians, ignored the Americans, and started speaking.

"My fathers," he said, "you know well how the Americans have treated us, and what they have done for us. They take me for their son, but they have come behind me with their guns. When first our nation learned to shoot with the gun to kill meat for our children and women it was by the English we were taught; but since that time I [used in the American sense of "we"] have been in misery; I tell you the truth: Since I was raised I have done nothing bad. The Americans tried to get our country from us; our country, the Black Hills country, was filled with gold; they knew that the gold was there. I told them not to go into it. I did not wish to leave my golden country; I had not given them the land any more than you would have given it. The Great Almighty and the Queen know that there is no harm in me and that I did nothing wrong.

"At the present time in my own country," he continued, "my people suffer from the Americans. I want to live in this country and be strong and live well and happy. I knew that this was our Great Mother's house when I came here with my people. Now I see plainly that there are no more deer, elk or buffalo on the other side of the line: All is blood. I don't believe you will do me harm, as long as I behave.

"Today you heard the sweet talk of the Americans. They would give me flour and cattle and when they got me across the line they would fight me. I don't want to disturb the ground or the sky. I came to raise my children here. God Almighty always raised me buffalo meat to live on. We will pay for what we want here. We asked the Americans to give us traders, but instead of this we got fire balls. All of the Americans robbed, cheated, and laughed at us. Now we tell you all that the Americans have done to us and I want you to tell our Great Mother all. I could never live over there again. They never tell the truth; they told me that they did not want to fight, but they commenced it."

Beneath the poor translation, Sitting Bull's meaning was clear. He would trust the Canadians, but not the Americans, whom he hated. Under no circumstances that he could foresee would he exchange the freedom of Canada for the restrictions offered by the United States, and he threw himself on the mercy of the northern country.

The reaction of the Canadians was temperate. They would not permit American soldiers to enter Canada and capture Sitting Bull, a reasonable stand to take against the intrusion of foreign troops on their soil. Neither would they accede to the Americans' request that they force Sitting Bull to move farther north away from the border. That was an internal matter, and they were not going to be dictated to. Also there was a humane consideration. The Sioux, for all their hardiness, might have had difficulty surviving in colder weather. On the other hand, they would not establish a permanent reservation for the Sioux, nor would they issue them regular rations.

The commissioners, of course, were not satisfied, but the surrender that fall of Joseph and the Nez Percés made the control of Sitting Bull less urgent. Although some of the Nez Percés managed to reach the Sioux camp, the fear of a general outbreak abated, and therefore the Sioux seemed to present less of a threat to the Americans.

That winter it was cold in Canada, even colder than on the American plains, but at least the Indians were free. They neither had to obey an agent nor fear they would be attacked by soldiers. The North West Mounted Police made certain they did no raiding on Canadian territory but otherwise treated them sympathetically.

When spring came and the prairie turned green again, the Indians hunted the buffalos. Again they came dashing down on the herds, the feet of their horses pounding against the dirt, the animals snorting in terror, and the great thundering noise of the stampeding herds broke the quiet of the wilderness. Then came the butchering, the slicing of the still warm carcasses and the preservation of the meat and hides.

Yet it was not truly the old life. To exist according to their traditional way, the Indians required land, hundreds of square miles of it to support the game they required for subsistence. And Canada already had tribes of its own, tribes who had lived there before the Sioux arrived and who were already making full use of the resources of the Canadian plains. Competition for the remaining buffalos mounted. In former times, the Sioux had fought for any extra space they needed, but this was no longer possible. To have done so would have led the Canadians to expel them.

Their only source of additional supplies, therefore, was the land just south of the border. Groups of warriors would enter the United States, quickly shoot some buffalos or raid the horse herds of the Crows, then vanish north again. The army's strategy was to patrol the area north of the Yellowstone, engage the Indians whenever they could, or at least drive them again into Canada, where food was scarce. Soon, Washington hoped, the Indians would be worn out and forced to submit.

In the early summer of 1879, Sitting Bull's camp was reported to be south of the border again, and in the middle of July Miles marched north from Fort Peck on the Missouri on a new campaign. With him, he had the newspaper correspondent, Finerty, whom he had met during the earlier campaign when Finerty had been with Crook.

"The country through which we moved from the Missouri," Finerty wrote, "was rich and pastoral in its appearance. It is not unlike some of the better portions of Minnesota, and was then one of the best buffalo ranges in North America. This, no doubt, accounts for Sitting Bull's interest in keeping so fine a country for himself and his people. It is true that the wily savage was, to all intents and purposes, a British subject, but his influence crossed the line, and no settlers would venture on Milk River until the implaccable savage was thoroughly whipped and humbled." That was what Miles proposed to do if he could just find him.

Sitting Bull had indeed moved south of the border with a raiding party, and on July 17, some of the warriors were riding near Frenchman's Creek in the area where Grouard had earlier led the raid on the Metís. They suddenly found themselves under attack from Miles's advance guard, two companies of Indian scouts under Lieutenant W. P. Clark. They fought back but could not hold their own and were forced to retreat twelve miles toward their main camp. Clark pursued them, but he wisely sent a message to Miles requesting reinforcements. Otherwise the larger body of Indians might have been able to defeat him.

Miles came up as quickly as possible with seven companies of the Fifth Infantry, now mounted on horses captured from the Indians in an earlier campaign, and seven companies of the Second Cavalry. These reinforcements alone would probably have defeated the Sioux. But the major in charge of ordnance, "by making great efforts, brought up two Hotchkiss guns," Finerty reported, "and shelled the stubborn hostiles with such good effect that they broke and ran like hares. They hate the sound of cannon and dread its long range power." Of course, they did. Artillery could always win the day.

That night "the rain came down in blinding, bewildering splashes," Finerty wrote. "The wind blew a hurricane. The thunder absolutely shook the ground. The night was pitch-dark, except when the fierce and fitful flashes of forked lightning revealed the fast-moving ranks for a second, and then left them wrapped in impenetrable blackness, except for a peculiar phosphorescent glow on the horses' ears." In this drenching rain, the Indians rode sadly north. The water poured down around them, the creeks and rivers rose, and the sound of thunder echoed across the prairie. The gods were exerting themselves that night, but not on the side of the Sioux and their allies. They had been defeated again and driven back to Canada, where there was peace but no food.

Shortly after this fight, the Americans were visited by a major, named Walsh, from the North West Mounted Police. He was assigned to the Indians, serving almost as their agent. He had been ordered to keep the Americans informed of any hostile movements on the part of the Sioux, but he did not regard hunting buffalo as hostile. The Indians, he said, were hungry. When Miles pointed out that several of the Sioux were wanted for murder, Walsh replied he should submit the problem to the dominion government for investigation. When Miles claimed the Indians had a number of stolen horses, Walsh said he would help recover them if they were properly identified. Miles complained about the Metí traders and said he would confiscate their property if he found them selling ammunition to the Indians on American soil. Walsh replied that they only sold ammunition for hunting and that furthermore he had no instructions regarding their trade. A perfect diplomat, at least on this occasion, he even refused to become aroused when one of the Americans made a sneering remark about Braddock's defeat. The visit ended on a friendly note—Walsh even invited Finerty to visit Sitting Bull's camp—but the Americans would obviously receive no help from him as long as the Indians did not wage war on Canadian territory.

Since international law prevented Miles from attacking the main camp of the Sioux, he descended on the Metís who were in the United States. He sent out troops that surrounded their camps and gathered them together in one place. There were about a thousand of them, along with some eight hundred carts and their horses, tents, and herds. He held them for a while, largely to punish them, and then sent them out of the country. In this way, he hoped to harass one of the Indians' important sources of supplies.

On July 23, the soldiers fought a skirmish with a small band of Indians, but it was becoming apparent that the Sioux could not cross the border in force. Miles's soldiers and Hotchkiss guns had them trapped in the north. By thus compelling them to go hungry, Miles hoped to drive them into submission.

Without any prospect, therefore, of seeing a large engagement, Finerty, always the good newspaperman, decided to accept Major Walsh's invitation to visit Sitting Bull's camp. With the major and four members of the North West Mounted Police, he rode through some of the finest pastureland he had ever seen, including, in his opinion, even the best of the Montana ranges. The mosquitoes, however, tormented them terribly. By day, they would often gallop their horses in the hope that the breeze would blow them away, and at night they wrapped themselves tightly in their blankets, preferring to swelter in the heat than to endure the bites.

A ride of about twenty miles on the second day brought them close to the camp. "I confess to having felt a queer sensation," Finerty wrote, "when on mounting a high point, looking nearly northward, I saw, five miles away, a large village of white tepees covering the valley. It was the camp of Sitting Bull, but I then saw only a small part of it. Hardly had we descended the hill, when the rude wooden buildings, which were once a half-breed trading post, and were then occupied by the police and a Canadian trader, stood before us, and a squad of mounted Sioux made a wild rush to meet us."

The Indians were delighted to see Major Walsh alive, because they had heard a rumor that he and two Sioux he had with him had been murdered in Miles's camp, but they recognized Finerty's blue shirt and broad-brimmed white hat as part of a soldier's usual dress and looked at him with hostility. At the time, they were engaged in a scalp dance, having killed a Cheyenne, which certainly belied their complete peacefulness, but this did not seem to bother Major Walsh. The dance took up a good part of the day, and more and more warriors joined in, executing, according to Finerty, "the most grotesque steps and figures, while the old men beat the tom-tom and the shrill voices of the thronging squaws added to the satanic uproar."

Finally they finished the dance and held a council. "Major Walsh," Finerty wrote, "had chairs placed for himself and me under the shade of his garden fence. The chiefs seated themselves on the ground, after the Turkish fashion. Behind them, rank after rank, were the mounted warriors, and still further back, the squaws and children. The chiefs were all assembled, and I inquired which was Sitting Bull. 'He is not among them,' said Major Walsh. 'He will not speak in council where Americans are present, because he stubbornly declares he will have nothing to do with them. You will see him, however, before very long.'

"Soon afterward, an Indian mounted on a cream-colored pony, and holding in his hand an eagle's wing, which did duty for a fan, spurred in back of the chiefs and stared solidly, for a minute or so, at me. His hair, parted in the ordinary Sioux fashion, was without a plume. His broad face, with a prominent hooked nose and wide jaws, was desti- tute of paint. His fierce, half bloodshot eyes gleamed from under brows which displayed large perceptive organs, and, as he sat there on his horse regarding me with a look which seemed blended of curiosity and insolence, I did not need to be told that he was Sitting Bull.

" 'That is old Bull himself,' said the Major. 'He will hear every- thing, but will say nothing until he feels called upon to agitate some- thing with the tribe.'

"After a little, the noted savage dismounted, and led his horse partly into the shade. I noticed he was an inch or two over the medium height, broadly built, rather bow-legged, I thought, and he limped slightly, as though from an old wound. [That was the wound he had received so many years ago and which had lamed him for life.] He sat upon the ground, and was soon encircled by a crowd of young war- riors with whom he was an especial favorite, as representing the unquenchable hostility of the aboriginal savage to the pale faces."

There were many tribes at the council, Sans Arcs, Miniconjous, Oglalas, Hunkpapas, and others, as well as Indians who were not Sioux—and there were many great leaders, like No Neck, Sitting Bull's rival. They listened closely while Walsh explained that they should not go south of the border. "Your hunting parties must not cross the boundary in search of buffalo and other game," he said, according to Finerty. "Wait until they come here. . . . Your young men can chase them after they come into the White Mother's country. I know your meat is nearly gone, and if the buffalo do not cross the line, then I don't know what can be done for your relief. One thing is certain—you cannot be permitted to violate the laws. I am willing to do all I can to aid you, within the law."

While he was speaking, a warrior rode up and spoke to the Hunk- papas. The interpreter asked what news he had brought, and the Indi- ans told him that one warrior had been killed and another wounded in an encounter with Miles's scouts. "Your young men will not hear what I say," Walsh said. "Therefore they must suffer the consequences. If they had kept here, as I asked them, nothing fatal would have occurred to them. So long as you remain deaf to my counsel, so long will there be death at your doors and mourning in your tepees."

After learning that Finerty was not a soldier but a reporter who could carry their words to the American people, one of the leaders of the Oglalas stood up and spoke. "When my people go hunting over there," he said, pointing to the south, "they are met with fire. My women are killed and my children starve. My grandmother [the Queen of England] says I must not go to war, and I obey her. I see my people starving, and I go to kill the buffalo. The Great Spirit made no lines. The buffalo tastes the same on both sides of the stone heaps [marking the boundary]. I can find no change. Why then do the Americans meet us with fire when we only wish to feed ourselves and our women and children? The Great Spirit has given me a stomach—He has given me the buffalo. I see the buffalo near the stone heaps and I must not shoot him, even while my children cry for his meat. The Great Spirit never meant to tempt me with the buffalo so near while my people are hungry."

The speech expressed the Indians' views well. Before the coming of the white men, they had been able to roam the prairies north and south. Now the Canadians and Americans had arbitrarily placed piles of stones across the plains, and the Indians were expected to observe those markers even if their women and children starved. Yet no white man would have done so.

After the council, Walsh and Finerty went back to his house, and in the evening Sitting Bull's wife and Jumping Bull came to see them, but Sitting Bull remained outside breaking young horses. "He was an excellent rider," Finerty wrote, "and a thorough paced Indian in every characteristic. He had, however, one grand virtue, which all must acknowledge—Sitting Bull never begged. He may have been acting a part, but it was, at least, a dignified and consistent one."

The following day, Finerty examined the village. "Arms and ammunition were plentiful," he wrote, "but food of any kind was scarce. The Indians did not seem to trouble themselves about concealing their strength; on the contrary, they seemed to glory in it, and the young warriors wore an air of haughty hostility whenever I came near them. Their leaders, however, treated me respectfully. Sitting Bull only stared at me occasionally, but was not rude, as was often his habit when brought in contact with people he supposed to be Americans, whom he hated with inconceivable rancor. He said to Larrabee the interpreter, 'That man [meaning me] is from the other side. I want nothing to do with Americans. They have my country now. Let them keep it. I never seek anybody. Least of all do I seek Americans.'"

From his observation of the camp, Finerty concluded, "Many of the high-minded and most of the vicious men among the Indian nations of the Northwest found their leader in Sitting Bull, who, although often unpopular with his fellow-chiefs, was always potent for evil with the wild and restless spirits who believed that war against the whites was, or ought to be, the chief object of their existence. This was about the true status of the agitator in those days. He had strong personal magnetism. His judgment was said to be superior to his courage, and his cunning superior to both. He had not, like Crazy Horse, the reputation of being recklessly brave, but neither was he reputed a dastard. Sitting Bull was simply prudent, and would not throw away his life, so long as he had any chance of doing injury to the Americans. . . . In manner he was dignified, but not stiff, and when in good humor, which occurred pretty often, he laughed with the ease of a school boy." He could laugh, but not at Americans. His hatred for them was as deep as it had ever been.

Yet a hatred and a strong will cannot overcome hunger. "The Indians," Finerty wrote, "appeared to be pretty short on meat supply during my stay in their camp, but the poor creatures had no more idea of the imminence of the famine which subsequently compelled their surrender than so many children. The faithful squaws went out on the wooded bluffs and gathered all kinds of berries to make up for the lack of animal food. Yet it was the intense humanity of Major Walsh that absolutely kept the wretched people from eating their horses. I knew then that the reign of Sitting Bull would not be long in the land."

On his return to the United States, Finerty learned that Miles had been ordered to end his active campaigning and limit his soldiers to patrolling the Missouri. Naturally the officers were annoyed by this restriction, but more fighting would have accomplished little. As Finerty had foreseen, the noose was tightening. A few less buffalo on the Canadian plains, and the end would come.

In February, 1880, a band of Indians slipped across the border, forded the Missouri, and headed toward the Tongue and Rosebud Rivers, their old haunts. Although the earth was shrouded with snow, the loose white cover rounding the features of the land, everything was familiar to the Indians. They had traveled and camped there too often to be confused by the weird winter shapes that the country had assumed. Each tributary of the rivers, each grove of cottonwoods and willows was familiar to them, for here is where they had lived and hunted. But despite their knowledge of the territory, they were aliens in their own land. The army learned of their expedition, a detachment of soldiers cornered them in a ravine and held them there until more troops could come up and force their surrender.

In March, another band rode over the border on a raid against Fort Custer at the confluence of the Bighorn and Little Bighorn Rivers. After capturing about fifty horses, they headed through the snow back to Canada, but the army was in pursuit. On the evening of April 1, the soldiers caught up with them and surprised them. The Indians took up such a strong position that the Americans could not dislodge them, but the soldiers succeeded in recovering the stolen horses and took five prisoners.

Using these captives and the ones seized earlier in the year as hostages, Miles began to bargain with some of the Canadian camp to surrender. Eight warriors came south to negotiate with him. To demonstrate the power of the Americans he showed them his telegraph, first darkening the room by hanging blankets over the windows so they could see the sparks. Then he let them use the telephone he had installed at the post. "They appeared," Miles later wrote, "to be as much struck with awe as if they had been in the presence of the Almighty, for . . . when an Indian cannot understand anything he gives it a spirit, or believes it to possess a spirit. If it shows some power that he cannot equal or excel, it inspires his reverence. After rejoining their companions and talking the matter over, they gave the telephone a very pretty name; they called it the 'whispering spirit.' On returning to their camp, some two hundred miles north, it is needless to say that they were strong advocates of peace, urging the surrender of the camp."

Miles undoubtedly overestimated the effect of his display of American ingenuity on the Indians. Certainly they were impressed by the white men's mechanical devices, but hunger was the greater advocate of peace. All they saw ahead of them were short rations in this relentless, effective, and inglorious war of the stomach. Starvation is a deadly, implacable enemy. It can creep past the most alert sentinel, and no warrior, no matter how brave, can count coup on it. Several bands decided they could fight it no longer, came south, and surrendered.

However much he hated the Americans, Sitting Bull was losing to them. He had been preaching resistance, and earlier he and his camps had been a focal point for the Indians who did not want to go to the agencies. But his influence was rapidly waning. Some of the young men might be fired by his words, but the older warriors were growing weary of a strategy that led them only to hunger or death.

At times, the Indians' condition was desperate. In his official report of 1880, Walsh wrote, "The conduct of these starving and destitute people, their patient endurance, their sympathy, the extent to which they assisted each other, and their strict observance of all order would reflect credit upon the most civilized community. I am pleased to inform you, as no doubt it will give you pleasure to know, that the greatest good feeling and consideration was extended to these poor sufferers at Wood Mountain Post. [Wood Mountain, where the Indians were located, is a succession of clay hills near the border.] The little that was daily left from their table was carefully preserved and meted out as far as it would go to the women and children. During those five or six weeks of distress I do not think that one ounce of food was wasted at Wood Mountain Post; every man appeared to be interested in saving what little he could, and day after day they divided their rations with those starving people."

This was not much of a life. With no regular rations, the Indians were dependent on the uncertain buffalo herds that no longer moved over the prairies in the great numbers they used to and on the charity of the Metís, who sometimes helped them. Once in a while, when the hunting was good, the tepees were filled with meat, but more often they were not.

By the early summer of 1881, even Sitting Bull knew the situation could not continue. He visited the Canadian post at Qu'Appelle, on the river of the same name, and begged the Canadian authorities to give his people a reservation. But the answer was, No. The American Indians had a reservation waiting for them south of the border if they would only comply with the demands of the United States government. Sitting Bull then asked for food. Once again the government repeated what it had said before, that it would not supply rations on a regular basis. Finally the officials at Qu'Appelle gave them enough provisions to return to Wood Mountain.

Sitting Bull would have gladly charged down on an enemy, the hooves of his horse raising the prairie dust, the bullets whistling around him, and the yelling of the warriors in his ears, but—there was no enemy to charge, only the quiet—yet deadly—courtesy of the white men's bureaucracy. A war shield could fend off an enemy arrow; it was no protection against an official's "no." Nor could any amulet, regardless of the power of the medicine man who made it, deflect that simple word. No poet would ever have written the end of the Sioux as fate did. There should have been a great battle like the one at the Little Bighorn with the warriors lined up to face the white men, and the hills ringing with the sound of rifle shots and the thunder of artillery. No matter if the Sioux lost—they had to lose—but let them lose gloriously, outnumbered and pounded by the big guns yet fighting to the end, their horses exhausted, their ammunition spent, but the air filled with the smell of powder. Not this shabby, dreary finale to a noble struggle.

But the way of poets and the way of life are not the same. On his return to Wood Mountain, Sitting Bull asked the North West Mounted Police for food. The officer in charge refused. Sitting Bull threatened to resort to violence, but it was an empty threat. There were no longer thousands of massed warriors as there had been at the Little Bighorn, just a handful of immediate followers, numbering in the end less than two hundred, who remained faithful to the ideal of resistance. The police reminded Sitting Bull that they had done everything in their power to help him but that if he started fighting, he would be regarded as the nation's enemy.

Louis Le Garé, a trader who had been feeding the Sioux at his own expense hoping for later reimbursement from the Canadian and American governments, offered to help transport them. Sitting Bull had always said he would never become an agency Indian, but years ago, almost at the time he was born, whatever gods ruled over his life dictated that in the end he would be one. He could not escape the many forces that had been set in motion so far back in the past.

Le Garé supplied the great, clumsy, two-wheeled wagons used by the Metís to carry their belongings. It was a sad contrast to the swift-moving warriors of the past, mounted on their ponies. The drivers cracked their whips, the dray animals pulled at their harnesses, the wheels rolled, and the carts moved slowly forward. Around them were the wide expanses of the prairie where free men once roamed. But the people with the wagons had only one place to go. That was south across the line marked with the piles of stones.

"I am thrown away," Sitting Bull told the Canadians.

XVI

Peace and Bullets

WHEN Sitting Bull surrendered in 1881, he and his immediate followers, who made up a band of about 150, were kept in custody at Fort Randall, South Dakota, until May, 1883. They were then moved to the Standing Rock agency, which occupied a plateau on the west bank of the Missouri almost at the present North Dakota line. The Indians arrived by steamboat, and the lieutenant in charge of them lost little time in transferring them to the authority of the Indian agent, James McLaughlin.

Unlike many of the agents, McLaughlin was a man of strong character, but he quickly found Sitting Bull was one, too. His months in the custody of the army had done nothing to break his spirit. The day after his arrival at Standing Rock, he came to McLaughlin's office, according to the agent, and "solicited a council, whereupon, with the greatest *sang froid*, he commenced his harangue by announcing a code of regulations by which he and his people desired to be governed, stating that he did not intend to plant anything that season, but would look around and see how it was done, so that he would be prepared to commence next year; that he did not want ration tickets, but would be 'big chief' and draw all supplies in bulk for himself and his people. He also asked to be placed first on the rolls of the agency. . . . He also presented a paper, which he had prepared in duplicate, asking that his appointment of eleven chiefs and thirteen headmen be confirmed. His request for the appointment of these twenty-four chiefs and headmen out of a total of thirty-four adults which constituted his party did not

seem to him unreasonable, as his argument in support of his application, which he urgently set forth in their presence, was that they were
all hereditary chiefs, good and true men—true to him and superior to
any of the old chiefs of the agency; that the Great Father had written
to him before he left Fort Randall to the effect that he, Sitting Bull,
was now to return to his own country and to live among his people;
that he would be the head man, the big chief of the agency; that a
good house would be built for him to live in; that he and his people
would have cattle and wagons, horses and buggies; that he might
gather his people from all the other agencies and have everything he
desired."

Sitting Bull was determined to get all he could from the agent in the
way of privileges and rations, but McLaughlin was not prepared to be
bluffed in this fashion. "I heard his inflated nonsense to the end," he
wrote, "and then gave him some sound advice, telling him that to be
honest with him I must be frank, and must therefore say to him that
the Great Father never wrote him any such letter as he claimed, in fact
never wrote him any letter or made any such promises as he stated, or
authorized any such promises to be made; that the Great Father recognized the most industrious Indian who was endeavoring to benefit
his condition and set a good example of his people as the biggest chief,
and that he and his people would receive their proportionate share of
all goods and supplies that came to this agency for distribution among
the Indians; that he would be assisted and encouraged in every way
possible with the means at my disposal, and be treated in all respects
in the same manner as other Indians at the agency, but that he must
not expect anything more than others equally deserving.

"After hearing my reply," McLaughlin went on, "he was considerably crestfallen, and replied that he was greatly surprised at the very
beginning. I thereupon carefully and clearly explained to him his
status, together with the rules and regulations governing the Indian
service, which I informed him I should endeavor mildly but strictly to
enforce, and that it was better for me to put him on the right path in
the beginning than to allow him to labor under such erroneous ideas as
he had just expressed."

This was not the reaction Sitting Bull had expected, but he had to
put up with it. McLaughlin then had about twelve acres plowed for
Sitting Bull's band and told him to report for work with his people. "I
sent two white employees to instruct them, staking off a separate piece

of ground for each family," McLaughlin wrote. "Sitting Bull worked
with the others, using a hoe, but rather awkwardly, and in two days
they had their fields nicely planted."

When McLaughlin asked Sitting Bull if he found farming difficult,
the Sioux answered, "No," but this was not the sort of life he enjoyed.
A warrior with a hoe? Sitting Bull's hands were accustomed to gripping a gun or a bow, not the smooth, straight handle of an agricultural
instrument. Scratching the dry dirt of the plains was not like counting
coup on an enemy. Walking to and from the field was not like riding
down on the enemy or a Crow camp. It was ignominious.

The seizure of the Black Hills and the Powder River country had
not satisfied the white men. Millions of them were still looking for land
into which they could sink their plows and make a living for themselves and their families, and John Deere and Cyrus McCormick had
transformed the prairies into potential farms. Even after the Treaty of
1876, the Sioux still retained a single large reservation, consisting of
more than twenty-two million acres. That was far too many acres,
many people thought, for the Indians to own. They could never farm
that much land, so it should be opened up to settlement by the white
men.

In 1882, while Sitting Bull was at Fort Randall, Congress authorized the appointment of another commission to divide this one reservation into five separate reservations and at the same time negotiate
the purchase of more than ten million acres, or almost half the original
area. The price to be offered was far less than most impartial observers thought the land was worth. Furthermore, the commission was
far from scrupulous in explaining the terms of the new agreement to
the Indians, and many of those who signed it did not know what they
were doing.

Fortunately for the Indians, they had a friend in Congress, Henry L.
Dawes, the Senator from Massachusetts. He did not approve of the
techniques used by the commission and held up ratification of the new
agreement, largely on the ground that the commission had not obtained the number of signatures required by the Treaty of 1868. He
also secured passage of legislation setting up a second commission to
investigate the conduct of the first and to renegotiate the agreement.

When Dawes, who headed the new group, arrived at Standing Rock,
Sitting Bull thought he saw an opportunity to gain recognition and
improve his position among the agency Indians. Although he had not
been present at the previous council, which the commission was in-

vestigating, Sitting Bull asked permission to speak at the council. Rising to his feet, he recited the wrongs he had suffered, made demands on behalf of his band of Hunkpapas, insisted on being recognized as a chief on the agency, and committed the blunder of accusing the commissioners of being drunk. Dawes was sympathetic to the Indians, but Sitting Bull did not appeal to that sympathy. Instead he antagonized the commissioners, who compelled him to apologize for his conduct.

This performance did not raise Sitting Bull in the esteem of the officials. McLaughlin, who was one of the better agents and married to a Santee, said in his report that year, "Sitting Bull is an Indian of very mediocre ability, rather dull, and much the inferior of Gall and others of his lieutenants in intelligence. I cannot understand how he held such sway over or controlled men so eminently his superiors in every respect, unless it was by his sheer obstinacy and stubborn tenacity. He is pompous, vain, and boastful, and considers himself a very important personage. . . ."

Nor was his standing high among the other Indians. Before his surrender, he had been deserted by all but a relatively few of them, that little band that had finally followed him back over the border into the United States. The others had wearied of his stubborn opposition to the inevitable and the suffering it had brought them. They had not heeded his counsel in the north, and they were not ready suddenly to heed it now. Watching him futilely struggle with McLaughlin and quarrel with the commissioners, they knew he could accomplish nothing for them. So he remained a lonely, bitter figure, with little influence at Standing Rock and resentful of his decline.

Only one group lionized him, and that, curiously enough, was the American public against whom he had fought so long. Now that the Indians were defeated, the Americans, including those who had fought them with the greatest bitterness and the least sympathy, sentimentalized them and made heroes of them, not in any way that benefited or helped them but in a purely impractical and romantic fashion. Somehow Sitting Bull had become the best known of the Sioux warriors and therefore became the symbol of the Indians' resistance. Visitors to Standing Rock wanted to meet Sitting Bull. When the Northern Pacific Railroad was at last completed—work on it had started again in 1880—he took part in the ceremonies, and he was a member of Buffalo Bill's Wild West Show, being greeted by enthusiastic audiences who purchased the autographed photographs he sold them.

Yet it was not a happy existence. He had said earlier that he would never be an agency Indian, but now he was one, subservient to the agent's rules and orders, yet all the time resentful. Still a warrior at heart, he naturally regretted the old days when Indians could live like Indians instead of following a synthetic mockery of the white men's existence. What future was there in farming for a man who had spent his life as a warrior? The talents of Sitting Bull were not adaptable to an agency.

*   *   *

The Dawes commission having failed to produce a new agreement, at the end of 1887 the Indians still retained a reservation including most of the present state of North Dakota west of the Missouri River. This was far more land than they could then farm, and in the view of many Americans, particularly those with a stake in the economic development of the West, it represented an intolerable state of affairs. So they now came up with a new scheme. The Indians were to give up more than half their reservation, and the remainder was to be divided into five separate reservations. What were the Indians to receive in return? The head of each family would receive on application an allotment of 160 acres—others a little less—to which he would have title personally. The land that was returned to the public domain was to be sold to white men at fifty cents an acre, the proceeds to be placed in a fund for the Indians. They were also to receive a million dollars, paid over ten years, some miscellaneous farming tools, seeds, and two milk cows and a pair of oxen for each family. This time, however, the congressional act specifically stated that the agreement must conform to the Treaty of 1868 in that the commissioners negotiating it would have to secure the signatures of three-fourths of the adult males.

The proposal won the support of those who sympathized with the Indians, for they saw in it an opportunity to establish the Indians as independent farmers, a goal for which they had long strived. Those with no interest in the Indians' welfare welcomed it, because the fifty-cent-an-acre land was sure to sell quickly and attract settlers to Dakota.

McLaughlin, however, did not like it. "The agreement proposed," he wrote wryly, "was not the sort of proposition I would make to a friend of mine, but the people who were pressing it did not regard the Indian in the light of a friend." He had been made an *ex officio* member of the commission while they were at Standing Rock. Finding this inconsistent with his responsibilities as the Indians' agent, he obtained permission from the Secretary of the Interior not to serve.

"Being relieved as a member of the commission," he wrote, "enabled me to meet freely with the Indians as their agent, and, although I did not oppose it, they, being close observers, concluded that the provisions of the act did not meet my views, and the longer the commission remained at the agency, the more pronounced the Indians expressed themselves in opposition. . . ."

After thirty-two days at Standing Rock, the commission obtained only twenty-two signatures. ". . . it put me in a delicate position," McLaughlin later wrote, "for it was very clear that Secretary [of the Interior] Villas and other influential members of the administration were very desirous that the act be ratified by the Indians. I, also, was desirous of an agreement that would permit the lands not necessary for the support of the Indians to be utilized; but I was the agent for the Standing Rock Indians, and knew that they were not offered any sort of fair compensation, and was convinced that a further trimming of their possessions would set them back by producing in them a sullen disposition."

The commission visited two more agencies after Standing Rock and, not obtaining much better results, returned to Washington. In October, an Indian delegation went to the capital. Sitting Bull had not been among the Indians' spokesmen at the council at Standing Rock, but McLaughlin took him on the trip, too. The journey was inconclusive. After several days of discussion, a minority recommended accepting the Americans' original terms, but the majority held out for an increase in price from the proposed fifty cents an acre to $1.25. As the government considered this too high, the delegation returned to the agencies. The effect on the Indians of this new effort to take their lands was not good, and many of them, including Sitting Bull, were in an angry and sullen mood.

*   *   *

Even those Americans friendly to the Indians knew they could not resist the pressure forever; and in 1889, the year Congress passed the legislation admitting South and North Dakota as states, they recognized that the time of decision had come. The government had decided to offer somewhat more generous terms to the Indians. The heads of families would be eligible for 320 acres each, instead of the 160 previously offered, and the price of the land to be sold was raised from fifty cents an acre to $1.25 for land sold during the first three years, after which the price would drop to seventy-five cents an acre for the next two years, and then down to the original fifty cents. The thinking behind this complicated provision was that the best land would be sold first. The funds thus obtained would be held in trust for the Indians' use. There were some other concessions, too, but the principal point noted by most persons friendly to the Indians was this: They would probably never get a better offer; and if they did not sign the new agreement, they might well be forced to sell their land on poorer terms. That was the mood of the country, and the Indians would be wise to give in.

This was the message brought by the new commission. General Crook, who was a member and who knew the Indians well, made this clear to them. It was either sign or expect worse. At the Pine Ridge agency, which the commission visited first, the Indians were practically united in their opposition to the new agreement. They did not understand the complicated provisions for pricing their land, and they were suspicious of any treaty offered by the white men, no matter how generous its terms might appear to be. But the commission, largely because of Crook's leadership, gradually broke them down. They were allowed to dance, they were given feasts, and when they were finally in a better mood, the commission spoke to the leaders individually, persuading them they had better sign. One by one, the leaders gave in, and this commission obtained the necessary number of signatures.

Standing Rock was the last agency to be visited. The commission arrived by steamboat on July 25 and held a brief council with the Indians the following day. The Indians then asked for an adjournment so they could discuss the question among themselves. Like so many others, McLaughlin was certain that they could expect no better terms from the government, but he was afraid they would not sign. Talking to the commissioners in private, he persuaded them to agree to work for some concessions from Congress on behalf of the Indians. These included payment of $200,000 for horses seized by the army in 1876. In return, he agreed to use his influence with the Indians to get them to sign.

For three days, the commission met with the Indians, and four of their leaders, John Grass, Mad Bear, Big Head, and Sitting Bull's old rival, Gall, talked against signing the new agreement. Sitting Bull, of course, was also opposed, but the commission would not let him speak. The Indians knew that McLaughlin's position had changed from the previous year, but even this did not cause them to change their minds.

Finally McLaughlin arranged to talk with Grass privately. Tension was so high at the agency, and the Indians were so suspicious, that they met at night in a vacant building where no one could see or hear them. "I told him," McLaughlin later wrote, "that the time had come to recede from the position taken the previous year; that the agreement must be accepted or Congress might pass the law regardless of the attitude of the Indians in the premises. Grass was an honest man and always stood for the best interests of his people, but in order to meet my views now, he would have to recede from the position he had maintained in council and in private for a long time. I told him that if the act was not concurred in, a worse thing might happen; that legislation might be enacted that would open the reservation without the consent of the Indians. . . ."

Grass finally saw McLaughlin's logic and agreed to urge ratification of the agreement, but he emphatically refused to talk to Gall or the other leaders, so McLaughlin spoke to them and explained what he had said to Grass. They, too, finally understood the truth of what McLaughlin was saying.

"The council the next day," McLaughlin later wrote, "was the biggest held at Standing Rock in many years. It was held within an enclosure made by placing branches of trees, which would temper the sun's rays for the people and orators, around three sides of a large parallelogram. The fourth side was bounded by the wall of the warhouse, and the platform upon which the commissioners and officials sat was directly in front of the doors leading into the building. . . . Grass did most of the talking, and he changed his base with the facility of a statesman." Then Gall talked in favor of the new agreement, followed by Mad Bear and Big Head, after which the council adjourned until the next day. Most of the Indians were now convinced they should sign.

Sitting Bull was furious. From the first, he had preached resistance to this new demand of the white men, and the arguments advanced by Crook and taken up by Grass and the other leaders had not made him change his mind. McLaughlin had not even bothered to talk to him, knowing that he could not win him over and also being certain that, although he could cause trouble, he was no longer an important influence.

The next day, every Indian who could get to the agency was present at the council. McLaughlin, fearful of a disturbance, had Two Bears place his band around the semicircle of Indians, and he instructed his Indian police to be on the alert for trouble. When the paper was ready to be signed, Sitting Bull rode up. He was still able to muster about twenty followers, the last Indians faithful to his views, and they tried to stampede the council. But McLaughlin's precautions and the unity of the other Indians prevented him from succeeding.

To reduce the chance of trouble, McLaughlin had arranged to have the Indians walk through the warehouse after signing the paper, thus leaving the council ground. Grass was the first to sign and then Mad Bear. Gall was to sign third, but he lost his nerve and hesitated for fear of reprisals by Sitting Bull's followers. While he hesitated, Bear Face of the Hunkpapas stepped ahead of him. As they prepared to leave through the warehouse, Sitting Bull tried once more to create a disturbance and break up the council. But the Indian police rushed to the front of the building and drove him away.

That was the end. The Indians' resistance was broken. The white men had what they wanted. The others came up and signed, and the great reservation provided for in the Treaty of 1868 was a memory of the past.

* * *

On January 1, 1889, an eclipse of the sun took place in Utah, and the passage of that shadow and the momentary darkening of the earth directly influenced the fate of the Sioux in Dakota Territory. While the eclipse was going on, a Paiute medicine man named Wovoka fell into a trance. On regaining his senses, he spoke of the vision he had seen, a strange vision in which the white men's Christ returned to the earth, the white men disappeared because they had killed him, the Indians took over, and the buffalo herds once more roamed the prairies in great numbers.

It was a curious mixture of Christianity, which Wovoka had learned from several sects, and an appeal to Indian aspirations. Wovoka, who was obviously anxious for fame, had already won a good reputation as a medicine man, and his introduction of this new faith, based on his vision, increased it. Indians began to travel distances to see him and learn more about what he preached. According to him, this new world would not arrive until sometime in 1891, but those who danced what he called the Ghost Dance would see it ahead of time in their visions.

The new faith caught on. The Sioux, as well as many other tribes, sent delegations to Wovoka, and when they returned to their agencies, they taught their fellows how to perform the dance.

One Indian described its meaning to an army inspector. "This dance," he said, "is not a war-dance but a religious one. The Indians, men, women and children, dance in a ring, call on Jesus to come, to hasten his coming, and say that they are ready. They expect him to remove the white man, bring back the buffalo, and raise the dead Indians . . . they believe that Christ will come, but he is traveling slowly with all the dead Indians and buffalo. They expect him to be here in April or May of next year [1891]. When he gets here the white people will disappear from this reservation and from the United States. This removal is to be effected by Jesus alone, and the Indians are not to assist but look on."

Many of the Indians paid no attention to this new faith. If a Messiah was coming, let him come, and so much the better. Their lives would be improved. But they would not participate in the Ghost Dance or take the new faith seriously. Others, however, were excited by the hope of a new world in which the Indians would regain their former importance. ". . . it is true," the inspector added, "that many of the Indians are neglecting their usual business, eating their cattle, presenting ponies to the pseudo apostles, etc., but in this respect they are not unlike certain Christians of enlightened New England who, abandoning home, lands and friends, went to Boston not many years ago with their ascension robes expecting to be taken up in the air by Christ. Their disappointment and disgust, when they found out they had been deceived by overwise prophets, were probably about as great as the Indians will experience when they awake and learn they have been deluded."

Other white men, however, took the new faith more seriously and were fearful that the Ghost Dance would lead to a general outbreak. Worried reports began to reach Washington, communications started to flow back and forth between the office of the Commissioner of Indian Affairs and the agencies, and tension mounted. Naturally those who were the strongest proponents of the new faith were those who were the least satisfied with their lives at the agencies and were therefore regarded as the biggest troublemakers. This increased the concern of the white men.

Sitting Bull, of course, espoused the Ghost Dance. On the agency, he had been pushed aside by McLaughlin, superseded by men like Grass and Gall, and disregarded at the council of 1889. At first the Ghost Dance did not worry McLaughlin. On June 18, 1890, he reported to the Commissioner of Indian Affairs that he had ". . . every confidence in the good intentions of the Sioux, as a people. They will not be the aggressors in any overt act against white settlers, and if *justice* is only done them no uneasiness need be entertained." He had, however, some reservations about Sitting Bull and thought that perhaps he and a few of the other "leaders of disaffection" might have to be removed from the agency.

But a few months later, McLaughlin was more gravely concerned. " 'Sitting Bull' is high priest and leading apostle of this latest Indian absurdity," he wrote the Commissioner of Indian Affairs. "In a word, he is the chief mischief maker at this agency, and if he were not here this craze so general among the Indians would never have gotten a foothold at this agency. . . . He had announced that those who signed the Agreement ratifying the Act of March 2nd, 1889, opening the Sioux reservation [the agreement signed the previous year], will be compelled to accept a small corner to be set apart and subdivided into small tracts for them to settle upon, where they will be obliged to remain and support themselves, but those who have refused to ratify the Act, or, who have ratified but will now oppose surveys and refuse to accept allotments, will have all the unoccupied portions of the reservation to hold in common and continue to enjoy their old Indian ways. . . ." Crook had ignored Sitting Bull and McLaughlin's police had broken up his attempt to disrupt the council, but he was not yet through with the white men or with that agreement that disposed of so much of the Indians' land. His motives were not simple. In part, he was still the same stubborn man who had always preached resistance to the Americans even at the cost of near starvation. In part, he was also genuinely concerned about the new agreement and the loss to the Indians. He also undoubtedly saw in the Ghost Dance a chance to regain his standing among the Indians. Then, too, he was influenced by a woman named Catherine Weldon, who was an admirer of his. Interested in the cause of the Indians, she had come to Standing Rock in 1899 to see him, and she kept on encouraging him in the position he had taken.

McLaughlin would not give Sitting Bull a pass to visit the Ghost Dance leaders at other agencies, so Sitting Bull invited an Indian named Kicking Bear from the Cheyenne River agency to come and see him. Kicking Bear, according to McLaughlin, was the "Chief Medicine Man of the Ghost Dance among the Sioux." On October 9, McLaughlin sent a detachment of thirteen of his Indian police and the captain and second lieutenant to Sitting Bull's camp on the Grand River, forty miles from the agency's headquarters. They were to arrest Kicking Bear and escort him from the reservation, ". . . but they returned,"

McLaughlin wrote the Commissioner of Indian Affairs, "without executing the order, both officers being in a 'dazed' condition and fearing the powers of Kicking Bear's medicine." Only a few months before, McLaughlin had been absolutely confident of the reliability of his police. Now they would not obey orders.

On October 14, McLaughlin sent the lieutenant and one policeman back to see whether Kicking Bear had left. He had not, but promised to do so immediately. Sitting Bull, however, had no intention of discontinuing the Ghost Dance, although he agreed to talk with McLaughlin first. Word came to the agent, however, that he was still leading the dances, and on October 17, McLaughlin officially recommended that Sitting Bull be arrested and confined in some military prison away from the reservation. He did not feel any urgency, however, and suggested that the authorities should wait until winter.

Disregarding McLaughlin's orders, Sitting Bull continued to lead Ghost Dances, taking pleasure in once again finding himself the center of an important Indian activity. One day in November, he had assembled about forty men, twenty-five women, and thirty-five girls, all of whom were dancing in front of some two hundred spectators, when suddenly McLaughlin and the post interpreter appeared.

"I did not attempt to stop the dance then going on," McLaughlin reported, "as in their crazed condition under the excitement, it would have been useless to accomplish it. . . ." So he waited until the next morning, when he spoke to Sitting Bull and a number of his followers. He began by outlining what the government had done for them and "assured them what this absurd craze would lead to and the chastisement that would certainly follow if these demoralizing dances and disregard of department orders were not soon discontinued."

Sitting Bull replied that although he knew McLaughlin disliked him personally—certainly a true statement—he thought the agent had the Indians' best interests at heart. Therefore he would make McLaughlin an offer. He and McLaughlin would make "a journey to trace from this agency to each of the other tribes of Indians through which the story of the Indian Messiah had been brought and when we reached the last tribe or where it originated if they could not produce the man who started the story and we did not find the new Messiah, as described, upon the earth, together with the dead Indians returning to reinhabit this country, he would return convinced that they (the Indians) had been too credulous and imposed upon. . . ." McLaughlin admitted that the idea was novel but added that it would be "similar to the attempt to catch up the wind that blew last year." As a counter-proposal, he told Sitting Bull to come to the agency. He would give him a whole day and night "in which time I thought I could convince him of the absurdity of this foolish craze and the fact of his making me the proposition he did was a convincing proof that he did not fully believe in what he was professing and endeavoring so hard to make others believe." Although Sitting Bull did not promise to come to the agency, McLaughlin left convinced that the number of participants in the Ghost Dance was declining and that Sitting Bull was losing influence again.

To the Commissioner of Indian Affairs he suggested that the Indians at the Grand River camp, where Sitting Bull was holding forth, be given a chance to renounce the Ghost Dance and come to the agency. Those who refused could remain where they were, but he requested authorization to withhold their rations. "Something looking toward breaking up this craze should be done and now, that cold weather is approaching, is the proper time. Such a step as here suggested would leave Sitting Bull with but few followers, as all or nearly all would soon report for enrollment and thus he would be forced in himself." Sitting Bull had defied McLaughlin as he had defied other Americans in the past, but once again he had failed to reckon with their superior strength. He had his small band of followers at the remote camp on the Grand River, but that was all. McLaughlin could draw on the resources of the entire federal government. If an open confrontation occurred, there was little question who would win.

McLaughlin knew what he wanted to do, but his plans were being swept away by forces over which he had no control. 1889 had brought a change of administration to Washington, and as the Indian agencies were regarded as part of the patronage system, several new agents had been assigned to the Sioux. These new men lacked both experience and perspective, and so while McLaughlin remained relatively calm, some of the others, now thoroughly frightened, wanted help from the army. One of these was Daniel F. Royer, a former member of the territorial legislature who was the newly appointed agent at Pine Ridge. On November 15, Royer telegraphed the Acting Commissioner of Indian Affairs that his agency was out of control and that a thousand troops were needed to restore order. This request brought the army's active intervention.

McLaughlin believed the military would function only at those agencies where the civilian authorities had lost control, but Miles, who was now a general, thought otherwise. At a banquet, he happened to meet William Cody, and, knowing that Cody was acquainted with Sitting Bull, commissioned him to arrest the Indian. McLaughlin was frantic at this turn of events. He still intended to take Sitting Bull into custody but wanted to wait until winter, when the bad weather would make it more difficult for the Indians to resist. When Cody arrived at Standing Rock, McLaughlin was able to divert him long enough—first by entertaining him and then by misleading him as to Sitting Bull's whereabouts—to have his orders rescinded.

But the respite was only temporary, and time was running out. The army ordered Lieutenant Colonel William F. Drum, the commander at Fort Yates, to arrest Sitting Bull. Fortunately, Drum and McLaughlin worked well together—Fort Yates was close to the agency—and Drum was willing to follow McLaughlin's advice. So at least he did not act independently. But Sitting Bull himself, unaware of the agent's determination to stop the dance, was planning to visit friends at another agency. When McLaughlin received word of his proposed trip, he believed he could delay no longer and issued orders to Lieutenant Henry Bull Head, of the Indian police, to make the arrest.

Sitting Bull had two log cabins a few rods apart at the Grand River settlement. At daybreak on December 15, 1890, thirty-nine policemen rode up. Ten entered one cabin, and eight the other. They found him in the larger of the two and told him he was under arrest. Taken by surprise, Sitting Bull replied simply, "All right; I will go with you; I will put on my clothes."

But then he began to play for time. McLaughlin had instructed the police to take a light wagon with them, put Sitting Bull into it immediately, and leave the camp as quickly as possible. But the police had failed to bring the wagon, so Sitting Bull asked them to saddle his favorite horse. This caused more delay. He also asked one of his wives to go to his other house and get some clothing for him. This cost more time, and meanwhile his followers began to assemble.

They were not willing to have their leader taken away from them, and although the policemen argued with them, they refused to withdraw. Suddenly two of Sitting Bull's most devoted followers charged through the crowd. One of them fired his gun, and the bullet struck Lieutenant Bull Head in the right side. He, in turn, fired and hit Sitting Bull. Two more shots immediately rang out. Another mortal bullet struck Sitting Bull, and the second shot hit a policeman. The three men fell in a heap, and Sitting Bull was dead.

General fighting then broke out. The police were able to drive the Indians back toward some woods. Then they occupied one of Sitting Bull's houses and were able to hold it for about three hours until the cavalry arrived and relieved them.

The long struggle was over. Sitting Bull had always said he would never be an agency Indian, and now he no longer was one. No white man would ever again tell him what he could or could not do, no longer would he have to subsist on the Americans' rations, often short and always given with condescension. If the faith of his fathers held, he had left Standing Rock for the place where the buffalo surged across the plains in countless numbers and an Indian could live as an Indian should.

And if that faith did not hold true, and he was condemned to an endless nothingness? Then at least he did not see or hear about the horrors at Wounded Knee, when the Seventh Cavalry shot down helpless men and women, so many of them that they were buried in a mass grave. And he did not see his people waging their almost hopeless struggle against an inept—and often corrupt—bureaucracy, unable to reconcile their traditions and culture with those imposed on them.

He died in tragedy, but in doing so, he avoided even greater tragedy. At the last, he died asserting his independent right to do what he wanted, and he died still preaching resistance to the white men. That had been his creed since he first met them. It was his creed when the two bullets entered his body.

No matter how bravely they fought, the Indians could not withstand the devastating effects of artillery. This is a Gatling gun of 1879. Because the Gatling guns could be fired more rapidly, they superseded the earlier howitzers.

In the Sioux's society, competition for leadership was always keen. This is Gall, an outstanding warrior who was one of Sitting Bull's principal rivals among the Hunkpapa Sioux.

Unlike the Sioux, the Americans were able to transport supplies on the Missouri River, an important logistical advantage. This is the steamer *Far West*, which supported General Terry during the campaign of 1876.

This typical Sioux village was near the Pine Ridge agency. The heavy concentrations of people and livestock made it necessary for the Indians to move frequently in search of game and fodder if they did not receive rations.

After the "horsemeat march" of 1876, General Crook set up his field headquarters at Whitewood, South Dakota. Both the men and the equipment were worn out, and many of the horses had been destroyed for food.

This picture of Custer's Black Hills expedition shows an army column in marching formation. Being in the center, the wagon train was well protected. Because of the absence of fast shutter speeds, the photographer had to ask the men to pose for this picture.

This is the same wagon train passing through Castle Creek
Valley in the Black Hills. Because of the terrain, it has been
forced to string out in single file, making it much more difficult
to defend in case of attack. This often happened when traveling
with wagon trains.

Pack animals could move faster and over more rugged terrain than wagon trains. Consequently they were commonly used by both the military and civilians for carrying their supplies.

One of the great Sioux leaders, Red Cloud forced the Americans to abandon the forts they built to protect the Bozeman Trail to Montana. But he was never able to capitalize on the fruits of his victory.

A lawyer by profession, General Alfred H. Terry was commissioned during the Civil War. Remaining in the army, he commanded the troops that fought the Sioux on the northern plains, finally driving them either to surrender or take refuge in Canada.

In spite of the Americans' pledge that the Black Hills would be reserved for the Sioux for all time, as early as 1876 Deadwood, South Dakota, was a flourishing community. For nothing could prevent the prospectors' search for gold.

Flamboyant and anxious for publicity, General George Armstrong Custer became well known to the American public as an Indian fighter. His lack of caution led to his disastrous defeat at the Little Bighorn, an event that shook the nation. The photograph is by Brady.

The army's Indian scouts were invaluable in guiding the troops through the unknown wilderness and in locating the Sioux. This Crow was assigned to Custer's command but escaped the debacle at the Little Bighorn.

An unassuming man, General George Crook was relentless in his pursuit of the Indians. To gain mobility, he often marched with a minimum of equipment, which caused hardships to his men. But they admired him, because he never reserved any special privileges for himself.

The graves of the unknown soldiers who were with Custer at the Little Bighorn reveal the extent of the Americans' defeat. It was one of the greatest victories the Indians ever won against the white men.

Originally built as a trading post, Fort Laramie helped protect travelers on the Emigrant Trail to the West. It was also the site of important conferences with the Indians. This picture was taken in 1876.

Whenever possible, army columns were accompanied by ambulances for the transportation of the sick and wounded. But when ambulances were not available, the wounded were carried in a horse travois like this one.

Following the summer campaign of 1876, General Nelson A. Miles was assigned to patrol the northern Missouri River. His aggressive tactics contributed to the surrender of many Sioux and the retreat of the remainder to Canada. The photograph is by Brady.

Acknowledgments

Many persons play a role in the writing of any book, and this one was no exception.

The staff of the National Archives and Records Service—that wonderland for all those interested in America's past—gave me much assistance. I am especially grateful to Robert Kvasnicka of the Natural Resources Branch, who searched out many records for me.

The National Archives and Records Service also supplied the illustrations.

The Yale Library provided much information, and the staff of the Public Documents Room were particularly helpful in locating material for me.

Mid-America graciously gave me permission to quote the words that Sitting Bull spoke when Father De Smet visited his camp.

As usual, William Targ was a sympathetic and helpful editor, one for whom it is a pleasure to work. I also appreciate the personal interest that Jane Kronick has taken in this and others of my books.

Mrs. C. R. Horton, Jr., as she has done so many times, carefully read the manuscript and offered me her suggestions.

Harriet A. Transue supervised the final preparation of the manuscript for the printer while I was flat on my back with a detached retina.

My friends, Harriet McKissock, Ruth and Helen Collings, and Peter Brandon, helped me with the proofs, although they are not responsible for any errors that may have occurred; and another friend, Burke Meehan, also povided me with needed assistance.

Notes

In some of the direct quotations, I have taken the liberty of correcting obvious typographical errors without reproducing the original mistakes and following them with *sic*s. Also, to make it easier reading I have broken up some of the quotations into shorter paragraphs.

CHAPTER I

THE GREAT BARRIER

Much Indian history will never be known. It has long since disappeared with the passage of time and cannot now be recovered. For the Indians had no written material to store in archives, where historians could later delve to recapture the past and, hopefully, to reconstruct the truth. What they knew about their history was passed on by word of mouth, and everyone knows that the memories of old men and women are indeed fragile. Whole events are often forgotten and others distorted.

The Sioux, however, had a practical method of refreshing their memories. Many of the leading families kept "winter counts." These consisted of buffalo skins on which they painted pictures, in a spiral moving out from the center. Each picture represented what they considered to be the major event that had befallen the group during that particular year. Using these points of reference, arranged in chronological order as a framework, the Sioux could reconstruct their past lives and give the information to their children. Obviously there was no provision for detail, but the principal happenings could be recalled in order. Subsidiary events would be remembered as having occurred in the year of so-and-so. Because some of the events were known to the white men also, the "winter counts" could often be dated according to the white men's calendar.

Stanley Vestal, the noted Western writer, did extensive work among the Sioux when the breach between the past and the present was not as great as it is now. Every student of the Sioux owes him a heavy debt, and in this chapter I have relied heavily on his work for the account of Sitting Bull's youth. When I refer to Vestal by name alone, I am referring to his biography.

In describing the Sioux's customs, one of my principal sources has been Hassrick's book.

In this book, I have used the spelling "tepee," which is currently preferred. The word comes from *ti pi, ti* meaning "dwell" in Sioux, and *pi* meaning "used for." This became "teepee" and eventually "tepee." A "lodge" and a "tepee" are the same. "Lodge" also means the family that occupies the tepee. Thus "a village of five lodges" means a village of five families as well as five tepees. They were remarkable shelters, for it was possible to make them warm in winter and cool in summer.

A good description of the political problems in the opening years of Andrew Jackson's administration can be found in Marquis James's two-volume life of the president. Although some historians now disagree with James's contention that Jackson worked with Sam Houston for the future annexation of Texas, his book is well written and makes interesting reading. Another good book on the period is Schlesinger's.

Much has been made of Jackson's advocacy of the Indians' removal to the West. Although the number of Indians who died as a result has sometimes been exaggerated, the act was an extremely cruel one. Yet paradoxically it may have fostered the preservation of the Indian culture. If they had been allowed to remain in the East, they would undoubtedly have either been annihilated or completely assimilated within a short time. Their removal west, however, set a precedent for treating them as a people apart.

The geographer's description of the United States comes from Mitchell, p. 177. Washington Irving's description of the Great Plains appears in *Astoria* on pp. 167–68 in the edition I have cited in the bibliography. Irving's several books on the West are of particular interest, because he was a writer who visited Oregon for the express purpose of reporting what he found.

The reader who wants to pursue further the effect of firearms and horses on the Plains Indians may enjoy Secoy's book *Changing Military Tactics on the Great Plains*. Although short in length, it is a detailed and scholarly study of the subject.

Those who are surprised to find that Sioux children were not disciplined may be interested in knowing that this is true of other primitive peoples. A friend of mine who spent considerable time living with the Eskimos told me that perhaps nature was so rigorous that it served as the disciplinary force. A child who disobeyed the mild injunctions of its parents was usually punished by nature. Among the Sioux, many of the disciplines were direct, not indirect, responses to the demands of nature, and nature served as the enforcer.

The traveler who stops at Grand Detour, Illinois, can visit the site of John Deere's blacksmith shop, where he created his first plow. The area has been designated a National Historic Landmark and contains displays showing parts of Deere's original blacksmith shop. There is also a forge equipped with the tools used in the nineteenth century.

The development of mechanized farming had an enormous impact on the United States. The year Sitting Bull was born, nine-tenths of the population worked in agriculture, producing food and other farm products for themselves and the remaining one-tenth. The energies of the nation were primarily absorbed in this one effort. With mechanization, however, much of this manpower was released for other work. One effect, for example, was the Union victory in the Civil War. Secretary of War Stanton said: "The reaper is to the North what Slavery is to the South. By taking the place of regiments of young men in western harvest fields, it released them to do battle for the Union at the front and at the same time kept up the supply of bread for the nation and the nation's armies. Thus, without McCormick's invention I feel the North could not win and the Union would have been dismembered." A review of the history of the reaper is contained in *McCormick Reaper Centennial Source Material* issued by the International Harvester Company. Also available in some libraries is a two-volume life of McCormick by William T. Hutchinson.

The exhilaration and visions that resulted from the self-mutilation involved in the Sun Dance is a curious psychiatric phenomenon not limited to the Sioux. Among the greatest practitioners of it in the United States were Los Hermanos Penitentes, who at Eastertime practiced self-flagellation and ended their ceremonies by crucifying one of their members. Although they used ropes instead of nails to attach the body to the cross, the experience was a painful one. I once witnessed a modified penitente ceremony and was among those who helped to lash the man to the cross, a criminal offense to which I plead guilty now that the statute of limitations has long since run out. (For sensitive readers, I used the words "modified ceremony" advisedly. We did everything we could to cause as little discomfort as possible to the "Christ.") For those who would like better to understand the impulses that drive men to such acts, I recommend Dr. Karl Menninger's book, *Man Against Himself*. As usual, Dr. Menninger writes clearly and well and describes the self-destructive urges that lie not only in the Sioux and Los Hermanos Penitentes, but in many of us as well. Many of today's business executives, for example, actually boast about their ulcers and regard them as the signs of their office. This is all the same thing.

The comments on the Sun Dance come from Dodge's *Thirty-Three Years Among Our Wild Indians*, p. 149.

The custom of counting coup is also closely related to the instinct for self-destruction. Absolutely nothing was gained by Slow's action. On the contrary, he jeopardized the success of the other Sioux by prematurely revealing their presence and forcing them to leave their ambush sooner than they intended, and he certainly jeopardized his own life for no practical purpose. Striking the fleeing Indian with his coup stick had no effect whatsoever on the outcome of the fight, but it brought Slow and his family great honor—greater honor than if he had killed the warrior from a distance. Yet the effect of this attitude on the Sioux as fighters should not be underestimated. Although they might be rash, they were dangerous enemies. On the other hand, their love for bravado often cost them needless lives and sometimes undermined their value in battle.

CHAPTER II

WOUNDED IN BATTLE

The story of Sitting Bull killing the captive Crow woman was told to Stanley Vestal by a Sioux Indian, Red Hail. It is an unusual incident and reveals both Sitting Bull's sense of kindness and his determination to do what he thought was right. Red Hail did not say what occurred afterwards, but certainly the women must have been angry to have been deprived of their captive by a boy in his teens. Yet Sitting Bull was willing to face their wrath. Perhaps even more important, he was capable of withstanding it. This seems to demonstrate that he had already earned standing among his elders.

In connection with this incident, it should be noted that the Sioux did not ordinarily torture their prisoners. They might torture themselves in the Sun Dance and other ceremonies, but they did not think they could propitiate their gods by hurting others.

A brief discussion of prostitution occurs in Hassrick's book. Among the Sioux it did not exist. Their society had neither room nor a need for it. Later, when the Indians met with the traders, some of the tribes became extremely loose in offering women to the white men, but it was the white men's civilization, not the Indians', that made this commerce possible and profitable.

An amusing sidelight on the Kearny council was the appearance of an official Sioux flag, which was displayed along with the American. It showed two bands crossing diagonally. Beneath the cross were clasped hands, and above it were nine stars. Apparently somebody in the army or one of the traders thought the ceremony would be more impressive if the Sioux had a flag of their own and therefore stitched one up for them. Needless to say, it was never used again. The incident, however, illustrates the white men's tendency to interpret the Indians' wishes in the light of their own culture.

I have described the howitzer at considerable length, so the reader will understand what this weapon was and how it worked. It played an extremely important part in the wars against the Indians, because when the Americans had one with them, they enjoyed great superiority of firepower over their enemies. An interesting sidelight is that Frémont took one with him on his expedition. When the army learned what he was doing, Washington ordered him not to, because his was to be a peaceful mission. He had already left, however, and the story goes that Mrs. Frémont purposely failed to forward the message to him. Like many wives, she was concerned about his safety.

Descriptions of the council held at Fort Laramie can be found in Hyde's *Spotted Tail's Folk*, pp. 33–48, in Grinnell's *The Fighting Cheyennes*, pp. 100–1, in Nadeau, pp. 61–82, and in Hafen's *Fort Laramie*. The treaty has been called by various names: the Fort Laramie Treaty, the Horse Creek Treaty, and the Fitzpatrick Treaty, after the Indian agent who was one of its promoters and who was present. The Jesuit's description of the parties during the council appear in De Smet, Vol. 1, p. 682, and the description of distributing the gifts, Vol. 1, pp. 682–83.

Brave Bear's name must have been difficult to translate into English, because it appears in various forms such as Scattering, Whirling, or Conquering Bear. Obviously the name was intended to describe him as a mighty warrior.

Many readers will recognize in Grattan the type of officer who, in later wars, got themselves fragged. Impetuous and bold, they risk the lives of their men needlessly to secure glory for themselves. The question then arises, why did so many volunteer to serve under him? Some did not. One noncommissioned officer, who sensed the recklessness of the expedition, positively refused to volunteer. As for the others, they were probably motivated by one factor: boredom. In spite of the scenes offered by movies and television shows, life at most army posts in the West was intolerably boring, because there was almost nothing to do but drink. And most of the soldiers did a lot of that, although a few like Harney were teetotalers. Lucien would have had no trouble obtaining the bottle of whisky he took on the expedition, for there was always plenty of it around. It was the army's equivalent of the modern USO, a source of entertainment. How the army can rid itself of personnel like Grattan is a difficult problem to resolve. It is not easy to teach a man both to fight— and when not to fight.

Those who are familiar with the Apache Wars will probably recognize a similarity between Lieutenant Grattan and Lieutenant Bascom, another brash young officer who started years of needless warfare with the Chiricahua Apaches.

The details of the Grattan affair are somewhat obscured by the absence of any firsthand account from the American side and also by the desire of many participants, either direct or indirect, to cover up their own actions. For example, the army dismissed the evidence offered by Bordeau on the ground that his wife was a Sioux and therefore he was prejudiced. Even Fleming on various occasions changed his accounts somewhat slightly, slanting them in his own favor.

There were numerous reports made about the affair to the army and to Congress, and the House *33rd. Congress, 2nd. Session, Executive Document Number 63* contains many of them. Among those who have done well at correlating the events and the points of view are Nadeau, pp. 83–110, Grinnell in *The Fighting Cheyennes*, pp. 104–8, and Hyde in *Spotted Tail's Folk*, pp. 48–54.

Several variations of Lucien's name occur. These are discussed by Hyde in *Spotted Tail's Folk*, p. 51.

It is difficult to evaluate Harney's role. He was a gruff, tough soldier with a certain sense of fair play, limited somewhat by his simplistic view of the military objectives. He certainly started on his expedition imbued with the army's opinion that Grattan had been massacred. His subsequent attitude shows that he may have been basically a better man than his first actions on the campaign make him appear.

Sitting Bull's encounter with the Crow chief was well remembered by the Sioux, not only for Sitting Bull's bravery, but for the wound he sustained. The reader who is accustomed to the Siouan war tactics shown in the movies and on television may be surprised to find the Indians standing in line when they fought the Crows. Actually their tactics went through a period of evolution, as they obtained horses and guns and then again as the guns improved in quality. Standing in line and holding their shields in front of them was an early stage in this development.

Colonel Dodge in *Our Wild Indians*, pp. 450–51, gives a brief description of the change in tactics: "Thirty years ago [about 1850], the rifle was little used by mounted Indians, as it could not be reloaded on horseback, but many of them were armed with guns of the most nondescript character, old Tower muskets, and smooth-bores of every antique pattern. Powder and lead were easily obtained from the traders. The former was carried in a horn, the latter was cut into pieces, which were roughly hammered into spherical form. These bullets were purposely made so much smaller than the bore of the gun as to run down when dropped into the muzzle. When going into a fight, the Indian filled his mouth with bullets. After firing he reloaded in full career, by turning up the powder horn, pouring into his gun an unknown quantity of powder, and then spitting a bullet into the muzzle. There was very little danger to be apprehended from such weapons, so loaded, and the troops did not hesitate, even with the sabre alone, to rush on any odds of Indians.

"Then came the revolver, which multiplied every soldier by six, and produced such an inspiring moral effect on the troops, and entirely a depressing effect on the Indians, that the fights became simply chases, the soldiers attacking with perfect surety of success ten or twenty times their numbers.

"After some years, the Indians began to obtain and use revolvers, and the fighting became more equal.

"It remained, however, for the breech-loading rifle and metallic cartridges to transform the Plains Indians from an insignificant, scarcely dangerous adversary into as magnificent a soldier as the world can show. Already a perfect horseman, and accustomed all his life to the use of arms on horseback, all he needed was an accurate weapon, which could be easily and rapidly loaded while at full speed."

That later stage, of course, is the subject of most movie and television shows. A more detailed description of this change is contained in Secoy's book.

The story of Sitting Bull's being wounded in the foot was well known among the Sioux because of his lifelong limp. The story is told by Vestal, pp. 28–30, and by Grouard, p. 33.

CHAPTER III

THE HANGING OF THE WARRIORS

The history of Kansas from its creation as a state until the end of the Civil War is a fascinating part of American history. Passions rose to great heights, as that strange figure, John Brown, rode on his death-dealing errands, and the pro-slavery forces retaliated. The story of the fighting and also the intense political rivalries is well told in Castel's book, which deals largely with the period from 1861 to the conclusion of the Civil War.

The term "Jayhawker," although applied first to the Abolitionist raiders of Kansas and now to all Kansans, is of obscure origin. There seems to be evidence that it first appeared in California during the Gold Rush of 1849 and then moved east, despite numerous stories to the contrary.

Marriage among the Sioux was not sanctified as it is among the whites, being a much more informal occasion. Divorce, too, was easier to obtain. If he had some cause, such as infidelity, of which to complain, the husband simply beat a drum and announced to the band that any one of them could have his wife. That meant she was divorced. In her turn, if she grew to dislike her husband, she could simply leave the tepee and return to her parents. This casualness, however, did not mean that the Sioux did not value a good marriage. On the contrary, they did, and a couple who were well suited to each other received the respect of the band.

The story of the Sioux's attack on the Assiniboin family is not a pretty one, but neither is warfare. There is no question that the Indians could be brutal in their attacks, just as the white men could. Among some of the older Sioux, Sitting Bull's adoption of the young boy was remembered as a sign of his humanity, as indeed it was. But also some such act was demanded of him if he hoped to continue to ascend in the Siouan society. More often, the brother to be adopted was chosen from among the man's own band rather than from among the enemy. The important point was that the adoptee should be an unfortunate one.

The reader who is interested in learning more about the ceremonies of the Sioux and more especially about their fascinating social structure will find a good and clear account in Hassrick's book.

The battle with the Crows in which Jumping Bull lost his life was recorded by Sitting Bull in the series of pictures he drew to depict his own life and was related to Vestal by his Indian informants. Today it is difficult to understand why some of the younger warriors did not come to Jumping Bull's aid, particularly after the Crow had discharged his gun and therefore no longer held that advantage. But the Sioux still followed a tradition of individual combat. That should not seem peculiar to anyone with a European background. The reader has only to open the pages of the *Iliad* to find many parallels with the individual fighting of the Sioux, including the hurling of taunts before the actual fighting began.

The passage of the Homestead Act did more than open up lands for settlement; it also had a profound effect on the spirit of many Americans. When I was a boy, I hardly knew any young cowhand who did not have in the back of his mind that someday he would have enough money to buy a few head of cattle of his own and be able to take out a homestead on some good source of water. Many of them already had a specific place picked out. (Conversely, many ranchers were desperately afraid that they would lose a supply of water to some homesteader and did everything they could to keep them out.) As far as I know, most of those cowhands never realized that dream, but it nevertheless affected their attitudes. For it gave them the feeling that eventually they would be on their own; and that, in turn, filled them with a sense of independence. Gates's book, although issued in the unattractive format of an official government document, is a fascinating account of the development of public land law. It is also a discouraging one. No matter what Congress did to provide for equitable treatment, some crooks always found their way around it.

There are numerous accounts of the Sioux uprising in 1862. One is contained in Robinson's book. Although his story is not contemporary, he knew many of the soldiers who were involved in putting it down. The statement of the former Commissioner of Indian Affairs on making cash payments to the Indians appears on page 211. Meyer has written an excellent history of the Santee Nation and has followed them into the twentieth century. The subtitle of his book, *United States Indian Policy on Trial*, indicates its tenor. An interesting adjunct of his book is an appendix that contains the text of many of the treaties made with the Santees. He also includes the text of the letter from the bishop to Lincoln. It is an excellent summation of the Indian problem in Minnesota and elsewhere.

A contemporary account is Harriet McConkey's. She did not participate in the events but did talk to many eyewitnesses. *Mary and I*, by Stephen R. Riggs, is a firsthand account of what took place. Riggs was a missionary to the Indians and chaplain to Sibley's forces. He was extremely interested in the Sioux and developed a method of writing their language. His comments on Lincoln's appointments appear on pp. 171–72, his remarks on the delay in paying the annuity on pp. 174–75, and his description of the trial on pp. 208–9. The charitable remarks about the uprising were written by his daughter, Martha, and appear on p. 204. She is also author of the quotation that appears at the beginning of this book.

The description of the hanging comes from Buck, pp. 268–69. His book is also graphic and takes up individually the various battles that were fought. His account is a contemporary one. The mistaken identity was uncovered by Riggs, but although he was a minister and interested in the Sioux, he did not seem to be upset.

The recommendation of the Commissioner of Indian Affairs against carrying out the executions is contained in the *Message of the President of the United States to the Two Houses of Congress at the Commencement of the Third Session of the Thirty-Seventh Congress*, Vol. II, p. 62.

CHAPTER IV

UNPROVOKED ATTACKS

The comments of the Commissioner of Indian Affairs on the attitude of the Western Sioux, as well as the report of the Indian agent on his meeting with the Indians at St. Pierre, are contained on pp. 71–72 of the *Message of the President of the United States to the Two Houses of Congress at the Commencement of the Third Session of the Thirty-Seventh Congress*, Vol. II.

The reader may be surprised that Sibley, with such a large army, could draw so close to the band of Sioux without being discovered. Generally speaking, the Sioux, as well as many other tribes, were extremely poor at keeping out scouts except in unusual circumstances. Otherwise they would not have been so susceptible to surprise attack and to the raids of their enemies. Considering the constant danger in which they lived, this may appear strange, but it probably results from two causes. One was the busyness of their lives; they just did not have the men to spare. For example, it would have taken a rather large group of warriors properly to guard a fast-moving buffalo hunt. The other reason was lack of organization. Although the Sioux had a complicated hierarchy, more complicated than some of the tribes, the emphasis was still on individuality. Hence it would have been difficult to assign scouts and sentinels for every day and night of the year. Who would want to be sitting peacefully on a knoll when the rest of the band was chasing the buffalo?

A good account of Sibley's campaign is contained in Robinson. The soldier who described the first battle was Abraham VanOsdel, who wrote his memories down in an article that appeared in the *Monthly South Dakotan* in October, 1899. He is quoted at length in Robinson, pp. 319–20.

Sitting Bull's attack on the baggage train is one of the events that he portrayed in his series of autobiographical pictographs. These, of course, show single incidents, and they can be correlated with other events only by considering the individual situations and then determining when the incident would logically have occurred. Because of the year in which it happened and the circumstances surrounding it, his capture of the mule almost surely happened during the Sioux's effort to outflank Sibley. The pictures fell into the hands of a white man in 1870 and are in the Bureau of American Ethnology. Some of them are reproduced in Vestal's book.

The arrival of Sully's men without the Indians' hunting party's learning that they were in the vicinity is another instance of the Indians' not having scouts out and thus exposing themselves to surprise attack. The death of Sitting Bull's first white victim was recorded in his pictographs.

The soldier's summation of the military situation in the United States at the end of 1863 appears in Ware's book, p. 1.

The effect of Chivington's aggressive drive against the Cheyennes is, of course, not directly measurable. But there is little question that several attacks made by the men under his command, with his encouragement, contributed greatly to the ill-feeling that led to the wars of 1864. The facts are somewhat difficult to ascertain accurately because of the conflicting versions given by the participants. Even the original theft of the contractor's livestock could not be proved one way or the other. For a good synthesis of the events that took place, the reader may wish to consult Grinnell's *The Fighting Cheyennes*, starting on p. 137.

Ware was stationed at Camp Cottonwood in 1864. His book was written long after the event, but he said it was based on notes he made at the time, and there is no reason to doubt his claim. In some instances his version differs from those that found their way into the official records, but he certainly captured the spirit of what took place. His description of the council occurs on pp. 106–7, of the Americans' demands on p. 113, and Spotted Tail's reply on pp. 114–15.

Sitting Bull's two encounters with the white men, including the one in which he was wounded, were recorded by him in his pictographs. They probably occurred after the battle at the Killdeer Mountains during Sully's march to the Yellowstone River.

Mrs. Kelly's graphic story is contained in her book. The paragraphs from her letter to Captain Fisk appear on p. 275, her description of the battle and the flight on pp. 99–103 and of the plight of the Indians on pp. 106–7.

The Sand Creek Massacre was a disgrace and deeply influenced the Indians' attitude toward the Americans, as well it might. The truth that finally emerged was murky, and the recollections of those who participated did not always agree. The report of the joint committee appointed by Congress contains the testimony of many persons involved in the massacre as well as in the events that led up to it. Chivington and Anthony must bear the principal blame for the atrocities, but a reading of the evidence indicates that their actions reflected the sentiments of many of their superiors. In *The Fighting Cheyennes*, Grinnell, pp. 177–80, includes an account of Chivington's attack told by an occupant of the Indians' camp, George Bent. Grinnell also devotes several chapters to the fighting that took place in 1864. They will make interesting reading for anyone who wants to pursue the subject further. He does not, however, deal with Sully's campaign farther north. For a defense of Chivington, read Dunn, pp. 342–82.

CHAPTER V

ACTION IN THE POWDER RIVER VALLEY

The failure of the younger warriors to exercise restraint and remain hidden in the sand hills at the battle outside Fort Rankin reveals one of the great weaknesses of their culture. The emphasis on individual glory often caused them to engage in foolish acts that did not serve the tribe as a whole and, as in this case, sometimes cost them victory.

The Indians' inability to take a fortified position such as the stockade was typical. They labored under two disadvantages. Usually they were not as well armed as the white men and therefore had difficulty getting inside the ring of fire that the Americans could lay down. (It must be remembered, too, that many Indians were not very good shots; they simply did not have enough ammunition for extensive target practice the way the white men did.) They also did not have the discipline to hold a siege. The idea of maintaining a constant guard night and day and cutting off all reinforcements and supplies was not in their nature. If they could have effectively learned this technique of warfare, the settlers would have suffered much more grievously than they did.

In saying that the Sioux lacked discipline, I am talking about discipline in the strictly military sense. It took much self-discipline to engage in the Sun Dance or perform some of the other feats that were part of their way of life, but their existence forced them ordinarily to operate in small units. Therefore their society had not devised effective ways of controlling large groups. This was no handicap when they were fighting other Indians, but it created problems for them when they were battling the Americans, who were better organized. On the other hand, the Indians were adept at the sort of attacks they made along the Platte, when small groups could act independently. In turn, this was the type of warfare that the Americans could not carry on.

Grinnell, in *The Fighting Cheyennes*, pp. 182–203, gives a good description of the fighting that took place after Chivington's attack. Some of his information came from George Bent, who was with the Indians. Some of these half-breed sons of traders led tragic lives. The traders took Indian wives, partly out of love, partly out of loneliness, and partly out of business motives, because a family connection with a particular tribe was always helpful to them. But the children grew up in two worlds, one Indian and one white, and sometimes had difficulty choosing between them. Bent had been to a white man's school, but he preferred to live with the Indians and share their fate. Ware was one of the soldiers who arrived at Fort Rankin during the second attack on Julesburg. The quotation is from his book, pp. 366–67.

Grinnell, in *The Fighting Cheyennes*, pp. 204–15, gives a brief and clear account of the Sawyer expedition and the Powder River campaign. Johnson's book, *The Bloody Bozeman*, gives an interesting history of the trail and the early development of Montana. She, of course, includes material about Connor and Sawyer. Hafen's book, *Powder River Campaigns and Sawyer's Expedition*, contains the official reports of the men involved, the orders that were issued, Captain Palmer's account of Connor's expedition (originally published in 1887), Holman's reminiscent account of Sawyer's expedition (originally published in 1924), and other source material. The book is Volume XII in the invaluable *Far West and Rockies Series*, a scholarly undertaking to collect in one place pertinent material about the opening of the West.

Dodge's, Connor's, and Pope's orders will be found on pp. 29, 36, and 43, respectively. The description of the mountains comes from Palmer, p. 117, of the Pawnees, pp. 120–21, and of the cutting out of the soldier's tongue, p. 131. Cole's complaint was contained in his official report, p. 82. As is often common in such cases, the various accounts of the same event are as interesting for their differences as for their similarities. For example, Holman does not mention the Arapahoes' attempt to regain their horses from Connor, a fact that he may possibly not have known. On the other hand, he throws some light on the inability of Sawyer and the military escort to get along together and on some of the mistakes they made, particularly during their fight with the Arapahoes. Grinnell, in *The Fighting Cheyennes*, p. 209, says that Red Cloud was present when the Indians were negotiating with Sawyer and told the white men they would have to go farther south. Grinnell probably learned this from one of his Indian sources, but unfortunately the statement is not documented. None of the white men made reference to either his presence or his speech. If the event actually occurred—and it may well have—it was a dramatic portent of the battles to come. Dodge's official report, made after an inspection trip, comments on the presence of George Bent and the threats he made.

CHAPTER VI

FORTS IN THE WILDERNESS

There are several versions of what took place at Fort Laramie. Olson, pp. 33–37, does a good job of comparing them. Some of them are extremely dramatic, with Red Cloud refusing to be introduced to Carrington or walking out of the conference because of the Colonel's appearance. Carrington himself does not say this. Yet if some such dramatic action had actually occurred, he probably would have, because it would have been good substantiation of his later claims that he had been sent out to guard the Bozeman Trail with insufficient forces and supplies.

His own account, which appears in the *50th. Congress, 1st. Session, Senate Executive Document 33*, says that he told several Indians what he had been ordered to do and that they had told him there would be trouble. But he does not mention any particular dramatic outburst or occasion.

Document 33 (I will not quote its full, laborious title in the remainder of these notes) contains the testimony that Carrington later offered in his own defense and consists largely of reports that were filed at the time. His orders to his men before he reached Laramie, June 13, 1866, appear on p. 4, the warning of the friendly chief on p. 5, his two messages to headquarters on June 6, 1866, on p. 6, and his message of July 31, 1866, on p. 13.

The description of the beleaguered army detachment is taken from Frances Carrington, pp. 73–81. It was written out for her later by one of the participants. I give it in detail not only because it shows what Carrington was up against, but also because it was typical of hundreds of such fights that took place on the plains. It is a particularly graphic account and shows how both the white men and the Indians did much of their fighting. At the time she was at Fort Philip Kearny, Mrs. Carrington was married to another officer who was killed during the bloody summer of 1866. Her account—in spite of grounds for prejudice in favor of her future husband—appears to be a fair one. It is also interesting to see an active fort through the eyes of a woman.

Carrington's report of July 30, 1866, describing the "false security" felt by the army and the emigrants appears on p. 13 of *Document 33*. The description of the arrival at the fort and of the fort itself is from Frances Carrington, pp. 86–87. Reports of the many attacks against the fort and the road are also contained in *Document 33.* Starting on page 39, this same document contains Carrington's official report, dated January 3, 1867, describing Fetterman's defeat. The quotations from Carrington are taken from this. Although this was a major disaster for the Americans, Carrington made no effort to cover up what had occurred, and his account seems factual and straightforward. The description of the mood prevailing in the fort after the defeat is taken from Frances Carrington, pp. 150–51. (Her first husband was killed with Fetterman.) Of course, no white man left an eyewitness account of the battle, because they were all killed. But Grinnell in *The Fighting Cheyennes,* pp. 237–44, gives an account of the battle as he heard it from the Indians. Mari Sandoz also tells the Indians' version as she heard it in *Crazy Horse,* pp. 197–204.

For the events following the defeat of Fetterman, I have continued to rely on Colonel Carrington's official report. Frances Carrington gives an excellent description of conditions in the fort after the battle. In particular, she gives a sense of the desolation after Fetterman's defeat as well as the high courage of men like John Phillips. The description of the snowstorms appears in her book on pp. 158–61. Page 176 contains the report made by the Commissioner of Indian Affairs to Congress.

Some sources are quite critical of Carrington. For example, Ostrander specifically states that Carrington's troubles did not come from his having too few men and supplies. (See the *Bozeman Trail Forts,* pp. 13–14.) And William Murphy claims that Fetterman did not receive the order to remain close to the fort. Some of those present also accuse Carrington of deserting his men in the early attack that led him to be cautious.

CHAPTER VII

THE STRUGGLE FOR THE ROAD

According to Stanley Vestal's Indian informants, Sitting Bull did not take part in Red Cloud's struggle to regain control of the Bozeman Trail, although the outcome of that fight definitely affected his own future. But the Hunkpapas were too far removed from the scene. If the Sioux had been able to mass as a single unit against the Americans, the outcome might not have been different, but the war would have been far longer and costly.

One must feel sorry for the men stationed at Fort Philip Kearny and Fort C. F. Smith, facing the invisible enemy. It was not as though even normal conditions in the army were good. On the contrary, the pay was low, the food often poor, and the discipline exacting and cruel. Flogging was still common, and men were even branded as a punishment. In at least one case, a man was cashiered out while at a post in the middle of the Indians' territory without even providing him a means of getting home. Add to this the cold, the possibility of death, and the scurvy that racked the troops, and one has to admire the soldiers' courage and perseverance.

The statement by the Indian agent about the difficulty of solving the Indian problem with war was written by John B. Sanborn, who had been a major general in the Volunteers but had later accepted an appointment as agent among the Cheyennes. It was written on May 18, 1867, and appears on pp. 111–13 of the *40th. Congress, 1st. Session, Senate Executive Document No. 13*. What he pinpoints is the inability of officers trained in classical European warfare to come to grips with the guerrilla warfare of the Indians. Without permanent villages, supply bases, and other strategic points to be captured, the Indians presented an elusive foe. Furthermore, their mobility often enabled them to avoid attack when outnumbered and to attack only when they enjoyed superiority.

The Hayfield Fight was not well documented at the time, perhaps because the only commissioned officer present was killed. Certainly the frontiersman who played such a role in leading the men to victory was not interested in producing a detailed report for army headquarters—he would have gained little by it and he probably was not accustomed to writing anyway—and the commanding officer at the fort seems to have shown an extraordinary lack of interest either in the fight itself or in the safety of the men involved. Roy E. Appleman has presented a clear picture of what happened in his chapter in *Great Western Indian Fights*, written by members of the Potomac Corral of the Westerners. He has done a similarly excellent job with the Wagon Box Fight, which was better documented, as well as with Fetterman's disaster. The Hayfield Fight and the Wagon Box Fight were primarily important because of their psychological impact on the Americans, many of whom had come to believe that the army could do nothing successfully. Relatively unimportant though they were, these two fights proved that the soldiers were not always beaten when the odds were against them.

Olson's book, pp. 58–82, has a good account of the peace commission of 1867 and its activities. The speech of the chief at the council at Fort McPherson is from Stanley, Vol. 1, pp. 202–3, and Sherman's answer to the Indians appears on pp. 210–11.

Hancock's campaign is discussed in detail by Grinnell in *The Fighting Cheyennes*, pp. 245–62. This was another extraordinary military blunder, resulting from Hancock's ignorance of the Indians and their ways. The reader who is interested in learning how a single general could put the

Indians on the warpath again will be interested in reading Grinnell's account. It is a pathetic case of how human errors kept contributing to war on the plains. In the same book, pp. 263–76, Grinnell also discusses the council held by the commission with the southern Indians in more detail than I have space to.

The commissioner's speech at Fort Laramie is taken from Stanley, Vol. 1, pp. 264–66. The Crow chief's reply appears on pp. 268–70, and the description of the chief talking can be found on pp. 272–73. This council, like so many others held with the Indians, was an exercise in futility, for there was really no meeting ground. Both sides were talking about something entirely different and about entirely different values. No wonder the councils were not productive of better results. Stanley's assessment of Red Cloud's absence appears on pp. 290–91.

For some reason, a second *e* crept into the spelling of "Kearny" during the existence of the fort, and the name was often written Kearney in contemporary reports. The proper spelling of the name of the officer after whom it was named was only one *e*, and that is the form used by most writers today.

Chapter VIII

The Outcome of the Treaties

For all the goodwill of many of its members, the peace commission had an impossible task to perform. Caught between the conflicting desires of the settlers, the army, the Indians, and the public, it could not find a solution that was acceptable to all sides. Its negotiations with Red Cloud and the Sioux are well described in Olson's book, and Grinnell tells about the negotiations with the Cheyennes in *The Fighting Cheyennes*.

De Smet's mission to the Hunkpapas was an extraordinary undertaking for a man of his age—or of any age, for that matter. Yet neither his bravery nor his faith could reconcile the fundamental differences between the Americans and the Indians, and for all practical purposes, he might just as well have stayed in St. Louis. Even the best efforts of the finest men are sometimes not equal to a problem.

The quotation describing his mission in the Northwest appears in Vol. 1, p. 72 of his *Life, Letters, and Travels*. His meeting with the Hunkpapas appears in Vol. 3, pp. 899–919, from which the quotations have been taken. Although he was obviously a sincere and honest person, the suspicion lingers that he was sometimes carried away in describing the receptions he received among the Indians. Certainly they welcomed him in a way they did not accord many other whites, but this probably was the result of his sincerity and not so much because of the ideas he had to offer.

In some respects, his account differs from that of Galpin's, but not in any major aspect. Galpin includes Sitting Bull's speech, however, and De Smet does not mention it. Although I have placed direct quotations around the speeches and have repeated them as they appear in both De Smet's words and Galpin's, the reader should remember that these are condensations. Neither Indians nor white men spoke so briefly on formal occasions.

The report of Red Cloud signing the treaty is contained in the letter from Dye to Brevet Brigadier General G. D. Ruggles, November 20, 1868, National Archives and Records Service, Record Group 75, letters received, Upper Platte Agency, W1184–1868. A good account is given in Olson, pp. 79–82.

The writer who covered the Sheridan's campaign was DeB. Randolph Keim. His book is especially interesting because he is able to escape the dry language of so many official reports and to add many details that were officially unimportant. He describes the expedition's first night out on pp. 88–90 and the Beaver River on pp. 96–97.

Custer was an interesting, although not very complex, person. He was a type that frequently appears in the military forces, an asset in some circumstances and a serious liability in others. When swift, immediate action was called for, Custer could perform, but in more delicate situations, he was unable to think ahead or even to consider the long-run consequences of what he did. As a result, he could be a hero at one moment and a blunderer at the next. This was reflected in his handling of the men under his command. Some of them apparently loved him, but to control others he had to resort to brutal discipline, such as shooting deserters or flogging others. For flogging was permitted in the army, and the descriptions of it make unpleasant reading. Two circumstances combined to make Custer as well known as he is. One was his dramatic death, and the other was the promotional use of an imaginative painting of his "last stand." A beer company acquired it from a foreclosed saloon and, sensing its advertising value, distributed copies of it widely. But the real importance in Custer lies in his being an example of a type, although in his case both the virtues and the defects were highly exaggerated.

There are numerous books about him. One that the reader might enjoy is Monaghan's. The quotation about his return to the army appears on pp. 216–17 of his own *My Life on the Plains*. That book, of course, places him in a favorable light, but there is one point in it I do not understand. Before joining Sheridan he was out on the plains hunting buffalo and managed to shoot his own horse. This is a constant danger but also about the worst thing that a cavalryman can do. Yet Custer tells it about himself. Perhaps he liked the drama of being left alone on the plains with no means of transportation, or perhaps he was more fundamentally honest about himself than he is often considered.

The description of Custer setting out for the Washita River appears in Keim, pp. 102–3. Custer's *My Life on the Plains* contains the description of his catching up with Elliot on pp. 310–11, the night before the battle on p. 324, the beginning of the fight at the Washita on pp. 334–45, and the advance toward the deserted village on pp. 372–73.

Custer's account is a dramatic one, but most authorities are agreed that he greatly overestimated the number of Indians opposing him, a common failing among military commanders. (In the Bison edition of *My Life on the Plains*, pp. 353–55, Quaife provides a detailed discussion of the number of Indians that possibly faced Custer.) The episode clearly illustrated both his virtues and his failings. Considering that he was attacking a camp completely by surprise and that the trees provided cover for him, he lost a rather large number of men. Many persons have also questioned his lack of effort to locate and rescue Elliot. On the other hand, his decision to march down the valley instead of up it was a masterful maneuver that probably saved many American lives.

Grinnell in *The Fighting Cheyennes* tells about the fight, using the information he received from his Indian informants. They told him about the Indian who discovered the Americans approaching in the distance, and they also told him about the fate of Elliot's command.

The description of the troops returning appears in Keim, p. 121, and the remark of the scout on p. 111.

The massacre at the Washita River had two-fold significance in the story of the Sioux. It revealed once again the futility of sending inexperienced army commanders out to kill Indians, because they often killed the wrong ones. It also revealed much about Custer's character. It makes the manner in which he finally died more understandable.

Chapter IX

An Adopted Brother

The story of Red Cloud is a tragic one. His determination to close the Bozeman Trail and the success with which he carried out his plan were unusual in Indian history. The Indian tradition ordinarily called for sporadic warfare waged for limited objectives, a fortunate tradition for the Americans, because otherwise the conquest of the West would have been far more difficult and costly. If the tribes had united under their ablest chiefs and if they had fully sensed the importance of such things as roads and railroads to the white men, they probably could have checked the Americans' advance for many years. Red Cloud showed what they could do when they were under a capable leader who had a broader objective than usual.

His ultimate defeat came because he did not understand the Americans' process of negotiations—not just the meaning of the specific treaty, but the whole process. He could not cope with the gradual whittling away of provisions, nor did he ever understand that the government could not truly control its own people in spite of all its promises. He was the inevitable victim of events that, given the spirit of the times, no one could have reversed.

His story deserves a full book, and it has received at least two of them. I would particularly recommend James C. Olson's *Red Cloud and the Sioux Problem* and George E. Hyde's *Red Cloud's Folk*.

It is interesting to note that at one of the councils the army quartermaster set up a large tent for the negotiators. Red Cloud, however, refused to use it. On a matter of such grave importance, he insisted on negotiating where his people could hear what was said by both sides. White men's governments might learn from the example set by the chief.

Grouard's story of his experiences with the Sioux is told in his book, pp. 30–90. In his book, he relates how his father went to the South Seas and married a native girl, but Mari Sandoz in *Crazy Horse*, p. 426, gives various versions of his birth as repeated to her by people who had known Grouard, some of them versions Grouard himself had told them. These made him partly black, and they were probably more nearly true than the romantic tale he put down in print.

Although Grouard was not present at the council that decided his fate, he was able to repeat Sitting Bull's speech, because Jumping Bull was so proud of it that he kept resaying it. The text appears on p. 35 of Grouard's book.

There are many differences between Grouard's account of the battle with the Crows, which appears on pp. 46–48 of his book, and the version that Vestal learned from his Indian informants, which is on pp. 113–17 of his book. In Grouard's account, for example, the Sioux and the Crows were almost evenly matched in numbers. In Vestal's version, the Sioux outnumbered the Crows by about three to one. Because Grouard heard about the battle from Jumping Bull, who was there at the time, I have followed his account. Both sources, however, agree that such a battle took place and that once again Sitting Bull distinguished himself for his bravery.

The incident involving the Flatheads appears in Vestal, pp. 118–24, but Grouard does not mention it. Perhaps he had forgotten it, or perhaps the event occurred before or after the time that Grouard spent with the Indians.

Grouard's anticipation of the torture appears on p. 55, and the description of the torture on pp. 55–56. Although he referred to it as "torture" and considered it a test of his physical courage—which, indeed, it was—it was also a religious ceremony of great importance. Its meaning is discussed in Joseph Epes Brown's book, pp. 85 and 96. Hassrick, pp. 227–29, gives a good description of the sweat bath. In his account, Grouard says the Indians removed 480 pieces of flesh. This was undoubtedly an exaggeration, for the number was usually far less. Also he says that he took the sweat bath after, not before, the ceremony. Usually the sequence was the other way around, because the sweat bath purified, and therefore prepared, the warriors for the ceremony.

In describing the events that took place during Grouard's life with Sitting Bull, I have not attempted to present them in chronological sequence, because the chronology did not mean anything. In the Indians' life, as I have pointed out in the text, only the present had significance. By including these incidents, I have tried to give the reader an idea of existence with Sitting Bull as seen by a white man. Grouard's remark concerning the importance of food appears on p. 56 and his description of his nearly starving on p. 80.

CHAPTER X

SURVEYORS IN THE NORTH

The story of the building of the Western railroads is a lurid and dramatic one. Their construction was marked by all sorts of speculation and downright peculation, as well as mismanagement, which cost bondholders and stockholders millions of dollars. Often, too, they were conceived with more enthusiasm than realism. The West, of course, did not have the necessary capital, so control of them gradually shifted to the East and to Europe, and conflicts grew up between the users and the absentee owners. But their construction was also marked by deeds of daring and heroism. The reader who wishes to refresh his memory about their history may find Riegel's book of interest, although there are a number of other good ones.

Problems of chronology develop in this chapter. Vestal's informants gave him a detailed picture of Sitting Bull's fight with the soldiers guarding the surveying party and placed it in the year 1872. That would mean that Sitting Bull would have fought against Major E. M. Baker. Grouard, however, who was with Sitting Bull at the time, says the fight occurred against Custer, and the evidence supports him. In the first place, the two fights that took place in 1872 were both relatively minor, and both Grouard and Vestal described a major battle. As Grouard shortly afterwards became a scout for the Americans, it can be assumed that he would have been able to recognize the Seventh Cavalry. Furthermore he says he heard the band playing "Garry Owen," which was Custer's favorite tune and which he liked to have the band play before going into battle. Custer also identifies the Sioux against whom he fought in the second battle as Hunkpapas and says that Sitting Bull was with them. His information came from his scouts, who talked with the Indians across the river during the early stages of the fight. Confusing the case further, Vestal says on p. 132 that "the northern plains were quiet during 1873. . . ." This was one of those unfortunate misstatements that the best of historians sometimes make, because 1873 was the year in which the guards on the surveying parties were increased and in which Custer engaged the Sioux. The evidence lies on the side of Sitting Bull having fought Custer in 1873.

If this is the case, however, Grouard's chronology may also be wrong. He says that the incident involving the Metís came after the fight with Custer, not before. But the report of the Superintendent of Indian Affairs for Montana Territory for 1872 specifically mentions Sitting Bull's one trip to Fort Peck and the Indians' trade with the Metís. It is probable, therefore, that Grouard's memory reversed the two events.

Those who are interested in learning more about the activities of the Metís will enjoy reading Joseph Kinsey Howard's book, which deals with them at some length. The book also contains a discussion of the Americans' attempts to take over western Canada. The arrogance with which we have sometimes treated our northern neighbor is unbelievable, and it is a wonder that they are as friendly toward us as they are.

The report of the commission sent to Fort Peck in 1872 appears on pp. 456–58 of the *Report of the Commissioner of Indian Affairs* for that year, and the report of the Superintendent for Indian Affairs for Montana Territory appears on pp. 274–76.

Custer's campaigns on the southern plains are important, for they illustrate his character at both its best and its worst and thus help throw light on what transpired later. Therefore I have treated some of them at length. His attack on Black Kettle's village was certainly not a very valiant attack, but rather the action of someone completely unfamiliar with the situation. His later campaign, however, showed a different side of him, for he certainly used his head and acted with restraint in recovering the two

American girls. I cannot help wishing, however, that he had expressed a bit more regret over the deaths of the two hostages. Aside from trying to ascertain the truth—and for that we can be grateful to him—all he says is, "The affair was a source of deep regret to all." The quotations that I have used appear on pp. 567–68 and pp. 570–71 of *My Life on the Plains*. Milo Milton Quaife, the editor of the volume, emphasizes the importance of understanding Custer's winter campaign, because he behaved wisely. It was an exciting moment when Custer was trying to take his hostages. "Even at this date," he wrote, "I recall no more exciting experience with Indians than the occasion of which I now write." The reader may wish to consult Custer's own book to learn more about the details.

In dealing with the Indian battles, it is always a temptation for writers to say that so-and-so was "in command." This, of course, was not the case. In the individualistic society of the Sioux, no one was in actual command. The leading warriors played prominent roles in helping the bands decide what they were going to do, but no one was in command in the European military sense. This was both a strength, because it gave the Indians flexibility, and a weakness, because it prevented them from taking coordinated action.

The episode of Sitting Bull's smoking his pipe under the Americans' fire was given to Stanley Vestal by his Indian informants. They place it, however, the year before, but for the reasons I have already given, it probably occurred during the fight with Custer.

If any reader thinks that Sitting Bull's demonstration of bravado was foolish—which indeed it was—let him remember that white men do the same. More than one American officer has risked his own life and the lives of the men under him to gain recognition for bravery—and a medal and promotion—when the military results were clearly not worth the cost.

The description of the Indians' weapons given by the commission sent to Fort Peck appears on p. 458 of the *Report of the Commissioner of Indian Affairs* for 1872, and the commissioner's summation of the Sioux problem appears on pp. 3–4 of his report for 1873.

Custer's official report of his two battles is reprinted in Elizabeth Custer's *Boots and Saddles*, pp. 280–90.

CHAPTER XI

A SEARCH FOR GOLD

The Report of the Commissioner of Indian Affairs for 1873 makes melancholy reading. One after another, the agents reported the problems among their Indians, and they were numerous. In this chapter the quotation from the report from Devils Lake appears on pp. 227–28, from the Sisseton agency on pp. 225–26, from the Upper Missouri agency on p. 333, from the Yankton agency on p. 238, the telegram from the Red Cloud agency on p. 241, and the report from the Ponca agency on p. 242.

The statistics about the United States that I have cited are from Watson. As well as any descriptions, they tell what was happening in the United States.

Those who are interested in knowing more about Crazy Horse might enjoy reading Mari Sandoz's book about him. She presents a good picture of the Sioux's way of life.

Grouard's story of leaving the Hunkpapas is told on pp. 53–54 of his book. It was a sad end to his effort to help the Sioux.

In describing the expedition into the Black Hills, I have drawn heavily on the U.S. Senate, *43rd. Congress, 2nd. Session, Document No. 32*, "A Letter from the Secretary of War Transmitting a Report of the Expedition to the Black Hills under the Command of Bvt. Maj. Gen. George A. Custer." This contains many of the dispatches sent by Custer while he was on the expedition. It is the source of all but one of the quotations of his that I have used. The pages from the Black Hills Order and Dispatch Book in the Beinecke Library at Yale contain some additional dispatches that do not appear in the Senate Document. Maguire's *New Map and Guide to Dakota and the Black Hills* reprints the text of the journal of George A. Forsyth, an officer with the expedition.

The quotation from Custer's letter appears in Elizabeth Custer's *Boots and Saddles*, pp. 298–99, and her own description of the returning men is on pp. 192–93.

Those who want more information about the expedition will find Jackson's account a good one. Considerable controversy developed later over Custer's intent in notifying the world of the discovery of gold, and his detractors said he quickly selected a messenger to take the news to Fort Laramie. Jackson refutes this contention in detail. As I have said in the text, my personal opinion was that Custer desired the publicity that would arise from the news. Nothing but the discovery of gold would make the expedition a real success in the eyes of the nation. It is doubtful, in my mind, that Custer gave a second thought to the effect the discovery would have on the Indians.

Chapter XII

Victory at the Powder River

The army has been accused of violating the Treaty of 1868 by entering the Black Hills, while punishing civilians who attempted to do the same. Actually the question was not that simple. After describing the area reserved for the Indians, Article 2 of the treaty states, ". . . and the United States now solemnly agrees that no persons except those herein designated and authorized to do so, and *except such officers, agents, and employees of the Government as may be authorized to enter upon Indian reservations in discharge of duties enjoined by law*, shall ever be permitted to pass over, settle upon, or reside in the territory described in this article. . . ." The treaty clearly prohibited civilian settlements or other encroachments, but with the words I have italicized the government reserved for itself the right to send its own agents onto the reservation. Custer's Black Hills expedition and the subsequent expedition under Jenney may not have been in keeping with the spirit of the treaty, but a strong case can be made that they did not technically violate it.

The story of the Russell party was later told by Annie D. Tallent in her book, *The Black Hills: Or the Last Hunting Ground of the Dakotahs*, a condensation of which appears in her *First White Woman in the Black Hills*. A good summary of this period in Black Hills history can be found in Peattie, pp. 71–102.

Jenney's report appears in U. S. Senate, *44th. Congress, 1st. Session, Executive Document Number 51*. The quotations I have used appear on pp. 11, 12, 19, 34, 63 and 56.

The report of the agent at Standing Rock can be found on pp. 244–45 of the *Annual Report of the Commissioner of Indian Affairs for 1875*. The report for the Spotted Tail agency is on p. 254 and for the Red Cloud agency on p. 250. The comments on the reaction of the Indians to the situation in the Black Hills appears on p. 246. The reader of these reports, however, will be struck by the general unawareness of the agents of the seriousness of the Black Hills issue. Or perhaps, being political appointees, the agents did not dare question the policy of the administration that had given them their jobs.

The commissioners' instructions for negotiating with the Sioux appear on p. 185 of the *Annual Report of the Commissioner of Indian Affairs for 1875*. The reluctance of the Indians at Standing Rock to attend the conference appears on p. 246. Grouard's description of his mission to the camp of Crazy Horse and Sitting Bull is contained on pp. 85–87 of his book. Pages 184–205 of the report of the Commissioner of Indian Affairs contains the report of the commission that went to the Red Cloud agency, and the quotations are from those pages. In translation the chiefs often use the words "I" and "my." It should be remembered that that is not the way they thought. They were not in any sense like kings who owned their lands. They were merely spokesmen for their people.

The conference, of course, was doomed from the start. Some of the commissioners thought its failure was accentuated by well-meaning white men who had emphasized to the Indians the potential value of the Black Hills, but this view overlooked the principal point: The Indians did not want to sell the Black Hills, and they were tired of making treaties with the Americans.

The army officer who noted that war would come in the spring was Bourke. The quotation appears on p. 244 of his book.

Excerpts from Watkins's report and a description of the subsequent actions of the government are contained in U.S. Senate, *44th Congress, 1st Session, Executive Document No. 81*. Watkins's great mistake was in underestimating the number of Indians.

There is doubt about the identity of the camp that Reynolds attacked. Grouard was certain it was Crazy Horse's. "I knew this village by the horses," he later wrote. "Knew every horse that was there." To anyone familiar with livestock, this is strong identification. He also talked to a woman who was wounded there. Although she told him the location of Sitting Bull's camp, he does not report talking to her about Crazy Horse. Bourke does say, however, that someone did discuss the subject with the wounded woman and that she said the camp was Crazy Horse's. These are two strong, on-the-spot pieces of evidence, whereas Bourke's is second-hand.

Other writers have argued that the camp was composed of Oglalas with He Dog and Cheyennes with Two Moon. Mari Sandoz in *Crazy Horse*, pp. 304–7 and 426, makes out a good case for this. She is particularly convincing because of her statement that He Dog had been with Crazy Horse, which would account for Grouard's recognizing the horses.

Whether He Dog was on the way to the agency, as he later claimed, is debatable. Bourke noted the camp contained enough ammunition "for a regiment" and that the explosions in the burning tepees were large enough to be a hazard. This would certainly indicate that Two Moon had been to the agency and was now coming out to trade, for it does not seem likely in that severe cold that he would have been coming out to hunt. Whether He Dog merely joined him for a short time and then intended to go on to the agency or whether he planned to return to Crazy Horse with him is an open question. In any case, according to Miss Sandoz, after the attack he did the latter.

There is no need, I think, for those who sympathize with the Indians to apologize for their obtaining supplies at the agencies and then fighting again. Where else were they going to get the goods, particularly guns and ammunition, they needed? If they could get them from the Americans, what was wrong with that? After all, this was a war, and they were fighting for their lives.

A point that is not debatable is the importance of the Indians' victory. Their turning back the force under Crook was an outstanding achievement.

Both Bourke and Grouard give dramatic accounts of the campaign. The quotation describing the march from Fort Fetterman to Fort Reno appears in Bourke, p. 256, the description of Fort Reno on p. 259, the trip into more mountainous country, pp. 259–60, the camp in which Crook stayed in the beaver lodge, pp. 260–61, the bivouac at Lodge Pole Creek, p. 279, and Crook's reasons for turning back on p. 281.

Chapter XIII

The Greatest Victory

The story of the farmers' frontier is well told in Fite's *The Farmer's Frontier, 1865–1900*. Pages 22–23 talk about the growth of farming in the section of country once occupied by the Indians, and pp. 75–93 describe the development of the large farms in the valley of the Red River. This aspect of our national history, which so often is related in dull statistics or the more lively but parochial reminiscences of individuals, comes to life in this book with a full sense of historical perspective.

The cattle industry played a less significant part in the opening of this area to the white men. The severe winters and the impracticality of grazing herds of cattle among buffalo-hunting Indians meant that the ranchers could not spearhead the drive into these lands, although later, of course, they became extremely important in this region. That is not to say, however, that there was no cattle in Wyoming and Montana before the final conquest of the Indians.

It is important to remember that Sheridan did not expect his three columns to meet in the Yellowstone country and conduct a joint campaign. He had assumed that if he escalated the war by sending out larger forces, the other side could, or would, not do the same. Any observer of the events in Southeast Asia almost a hundred years later will notice the clear parallel and will wonder why Americans keep repeating the same mistakes. The description of snow-blindness is from Bradley, p. 13, the start of the Dakota Column from Elizabeth Custer, pp. 263–64, and Crook's start from Bourke, p. 291.

The movement of the Indians before the Battle of the Rosebud is described by Mari Sandoz in *Crazy Horse*, pp. 308–16, and in other sources as well. It is surprising indeed that the agents did not learn what was happening, but the agency Indians were loyal to their fellows. When Crook went to the Red Cloud agency to enlist scouts, an incident that I have not described in the text, he had difficulty persuading them they might fight on the Americans' side. He thought this was the work of the agents. Actually it was loyalty. (It should also be noted that while he was there, he complained vigorously about the treatment the Indians were receiving.)

The description of the Bighorns is taken from Bourke, p. 292. Vestal reports that Sitting Bull was the chief dancer at the Sun Dance that June.

The Battle of the Rosebud has been the subject of much discussion and controversy. Most authorities agree that Crazy Horse was there and was the guiding spirit. Vestal says that Sitting Bull was also there, although he provides little information about Sitting Bull's actions. He sets the date of the Sun Dance as June 14, 1876, only three days before the battle took place. It hardly seems likely that Sitting Bull would have recovered in time to participate in the active fighting, for the Sun Dance was no small experience. He undoubtedly was still back in the camp. This does not mean, however, that he did not make an important contribution. As the medicine man who had had the vision of victory, he significantly added to the Indians' morale, and the camp in which he lived was the center of the planning that went on. The sight of him gave courage to the others and kept up their determination to fight the Americans.

In Crook's earlier attack on He Dog's village, Reynolds had been clearly to blame for the forced withdrawal. If he had done what he had been ordered to—and there was no reason not to—Crook would have carried the day. But at the Rosebud, Crook was personally in command. Finerty, p. 93, blames the Crow scouts for his defeat by not finding the Indian's camp and therefore making impossible the sort of attack Crook had planned. But they probably could not have located the camp, because the Sioux and Cheyennes also had their scouts out. In fact, their first encounter was with the Crows. Later Royall said Crook had fought poorly at the Rosebud, and Crook replied by accusing Royall of not having returned to the main body of troops when he was repeatedly ordered to do so. (See Crook's *Autobiography*, p. 196.) In this instance the evidence does not substantiate Crook. Yet Crook had no reason to be ashamed. There were not as many Indians as some have claimed—perhaps a thousand to fifteen hundred—but that was many more than the total number of warriors thought to be fighting the white men. Furthermore Crook had not even reached the camp. He was caught by surprise, not through any fault of his own, but because of extraordinarily bad intelligence. Given this situation, he fought a good battle and was fortunate to get his troops out with only about fifty-seven killed and wounded, not counting the casualties among the scouts. His later wait at the wagon train can only be explained, I think, as I have explained it in the text. He was in a state of shock. This hesitancy to resume fighting, it should be noted, was not typical of either his previous or later career. Those who criticize him for it should remember that Sheridan's strategy did not call for Crook to meet Terry at an appointed date. They were really individual campaigns, and therefore Crook did not feel obliged to support Terry any more than Terry had felt obliged to support Crook. Those who partially blame Crook for Custer's disaster should remember that perhaps if Terry had come up faster, Crook would not have been in trouble.

Crazy Horse later told Crook what his battle plan was, which adds to the interest of the account. Bourke reported it in describing the battle.

Crook was fortunate—and so is anyone who studies him—in having good writers with him. For this account, I have drawn heavily on Bourke and Finerty. The description of the camp on the Rosebud comes from Bourke, p. 310, the battleground, Finerty, p. 83, the charge, Bourke, p. 312, the canyon, first Bourke, p. 315, then Finerty, pp. 90–91, and finally Crook's decision, Finerty, p. 93–94.

Few battles have generated as much controversy as Custer's defeat on the Little Bighorn, and the subject can make a book in itself. In fact, many have been written. In *The Custer Myth*, Graham includes a bibliography of more than six hundred books and articles on the subject compiled by Fred Dustin, and more have been written since. There are several reasons for this interest. Custer himself was a glamorous, well-known figure and was rated by many as one of the great Indian fighters of his time, a judgment with which I am not entirely in accord. Spectacular, yes, and well publicized, largely through his own efforts, but there were Indian fighters in the army who certainly understood the enemy better than Custer did. His death produced numbers of investigations, because people, including his detractors, of which there were many, wanted to know what actually happened. As no white men lived to tell the story, no evidence is available from that side.

Numerous Indian accounts exist, and they are sometimes contradictory. This is largely a result of their manner of fighting. They obviously had no written commands that could later be produced or any chain of command that might make it possible to trace "orders." Although they fought in a more coordinated fashion than usual, they still waged the battle as individual bands of individual warriors.

The controversy was further heightened by the popular attitude toward Reno. Because many people could not understand how Custer could have been defeated, they turned their attention to the senior surviving officer. Reno's court-martial produced considerable evidence from those who were present before and just after Custer's annihilation, but nothing, of course, that pertained directly to the general's personal disaster. The strange verdict of the court did little to quiet the controversy. "The conduct of the officers throughout was excellent," the court of inquiry said, "and while subordinates, in some instances, did more for the safety of the command by brilliant displays of courage than did Major Reno, there was nothing in his conduct which requires animadversion from this Court." That verdict was hardly designed to settle the question, and Reno remained under a cloud.

In the text, I have not discussed Custer's relations with President Grant, which may have had some bearing on his action. He had just testified against Grant's Secretary of War, who was accused of wrongdoing. This had brought Grant's wrath down on his head, and Grant had ordered him removed from his command. Only the intercession of Sheridan and Terry brought about his restoration. Some have argued that this made him even more eager than usual to gain fame and approval. I have not treated the subject, because I think it might only have been a question of intensifying his normal attitude. Nothing in Custer's action at the Little Bighorn was inconsistent with what he had repeatedly done before.

The question of who killed Custer has been debated for years. White Bull claimed to have done it after a hand-to-hand fight in which he finally seized Custer's service revolver and shot him with it. It seems to me that he could also have been killed by one of his own men. Much of his career indicates that he was the kind of officer to whom that sometimes happens. But the full discussion of this possibility is the subject of a different book.

Those who are interested in studying the battle in detail will find many books listed in the bibliography. This, however, is far from all-inclusive.

In the part of the text dealing with the beginning of this expedition, the reaction of the officer in the Montana Column to a possible fight is from

Bradley, pp. 102–3, the reaction of the men to Reno's report is from General Godfrey's article that appeared in *Century Magazine*, January, 1892. It is reprinted in full in Graham's *The Custer Myth*, and the quotation appears on pp. 120–30. Custer's reaction can be found in his letter to Libby in Merrington, p. 305. Terry's order is reprinted in many of the accounts. The officer with Gibbon who expressed doubt about there being any chance of their seeing action is from Bradley, p. 143.

Sitting Bull's account of the battle appeared in the New York *Herald*, November 16, 1877, and is reproduced in Graham's *The Custer Myth*, pp. 65–73. Gall's appeared in the St. Paul *Pioneer Press*, July 18, 1886, and is reproduced in Graham, pp. 89–92. Graham also includes many other Indian accounts but wisely warns his readers that in weighing them, "one should be wary," if only because of the inaccuracies that occurred in translation. They do, however, make fascinating reading.

CHAPTER XIV

THE FADING OF HOPE

After the Battle of the Little Bighorn, Major Reno came in for more than his share of criticism. General Miles, for example, in his *Personal Recollections* dubbed him "the running Reno" and claimed that Custer's defeat resulted from Reno's failure to continue the attack. "It is not expected that five troops could have whipped that body of Indians," he wrote, "neither is it believed that that body of Indians could have whipped twelve troops of the Seventh Cavalry under Custer's command, or if his orders had been properly executed. The fact that after Custer's five troops had been annihilated, the Indians who came back and engaged the seven troops were repulsed, and that they failed to dislodge these troops is proof that the force was amply strong, if it had only acted in full concert. No commanding officer can win victories with seven-twelfths of his command remaining out of the engagement when within sound of his rifle shots."

But that judgment begs a number of important points. Who split the command in the first place? Not Reno, but Custer, and he not only divided the command, he sent Benteen off to an area where there were no Indians at all. Could Reno have sustained his attack? In view of what happened to Custer, it is doubtful, particularly as he had fewer men than his commander. Reno was not a brilliant officer, but he probably did about as well as possible under the circumstances, and although he lost many men, he saved the majority.

Setting aside questions of Custer's personality, the basic problem was
that he blindly attacked an enemy that was too many for him. This was a
repetition of the Battle of the Washita, where he did the same thing. That
time, however, the Indians were not concentrated in a single camp, and
therefore he did not have to fight them all at once. It should be remembered
that his faulty estimate of the size of the Indian camp was shared by
everyone else in the army at the time. But he can be criticized for not
using his scouts more effectively or paying more attention to them when
they tried to warn him of his danger.

After the battle, Reno's men unsuccessfully petitioned to have him
made commander of the regiment.

Elizabeth Custer's description of the regiment will be found on p. 264
of her book, and Bradley, pp. 154–55, contains the command's reaction
to the news.

The commentator describing the effect of the news on the United States
is Miles, p. 212, and his remarks are in no way exaggerated. The United
States was stunned by Custer's defeat and its pride badly shaken. The
efforts of the Sioux to stir up the Indians on the Blackfeet agency, and
other tribes as well, is recounted in the *Annual Report of the Commissioner of Indian Affairs, 1876,* p. 86. If the Indians could have buried
their ancient hostilities and united against the white men, they could not
have ultimately won, but they would have made the Americans' final
victory far more difficult.

The description of the Bighorns during Crook's exploratory trip comes
from Bourke, p. 326, the return of Sibley's scout, p. 332, and the burning
of the prairie, p. 334.

Sibley's scout is described by Bourke, who did not accompany it, and
Finerty and Grouard, who did. Although they do not differ on any major
points, they are interesting to compare because they reveal differences in
attitudes and background. Grouard's makes it clear that the soldiers could
not have survived without the help of the scouts. Finerty and Bourke give
somewhat more credit to the army.

The quotation reflecting the attitude of the Americans toward the Indians is taken from King, p. 30. Charles King had an unusual career.
Severely wounded in the arm by an Apache bullet in 1874, he continued
on active duty until 1879. In 1880, he produced his first book. He had
become professor of military science at the University of Wisconsin and
wrote a series of newspaper articles describing life in the army fighting the
Indians. These proved so popular, they were later reprinted in book form.
After that he completed almost seventy additional volumes, many of them
novels dealing with Western life. Although hardly great art, his books are
important, because he knew what he was writing about. He also reflected
the popular attitudes toward the army and the Indians. The quotation that

I have used, although reflecting an extreme point of view, was undoubtedly held by the majority of Americans.

Finerty, Bourke, Grouard, and King all provide good descriptions of Crook's campaign and of Terry's too, when Crook was with him. The descriptions of William Cody are from Finerty, pp. 153–54, Crook's night march and the fire, pp. 158–60, Terry's and Crook's commands, pp. 179–80, and Crook's deciding to continue to the Black Hills instead of making the shorter march to Fort Abraham Lincoln, pp. 182–83. Finerty does not point out that that march would not only have been easier, it would have been much safer, because it would have led Crook away from the Indians. The comparison between Crook and Terry was not exaggerated. Terry was an able, well-liked officer, but Crook was the more aggressive fighter.

The report of the commissioners who presented the new treaty will be found in the *Annual Report of the Commissioner of Indian Affairs, 1876*, pp. 330–57. The pathetic comment of the chief who tried to explain the Indians' desire to continue their own council longer appears on p. 335 and the comment of the commissioners themselves on p. 343. The conference is also treated at length in U.S. Senate, *44th. Congress, 2nd. Session, Executive Document Number 9.* Olson has a good summary of what took place and presents reasons for the Indians' capitulation, pp. 224–30. There are various legalistic excuses for the United States having openly violated Article 12 of the Treaty of 1868, but that is what they are, "legalistic." One of them, of course, is that some of the Indians had also violated the treaty, and therefore the Americans had a right to do so, too. Under the circumstances, that was not the best reason. I realize that from a practical point of view the government had gotten itself into a box. It could not control its own voters, who were marching into the Black Hills in spite of the Treaty of 1868, so it had to have some sort of new arrangement. But that does not eliminate the cold, blunt fact that it deliberately violated its own word nine years after it had given it.

Crook's march to the Black Hills is described by Bourke, Finerty, Grouard, and King. The quotation about the soldiers eating the first horse comes from Finerty, p. 185, and the fight with American Horse, pp. 190–91.

CHAPTER XV

THE END OF THE STRUGGLE

Miles's plans for his winter campaign are described on p. 218 of his book. He was a relentless fighter during this campaign, and his use of infantry against the mounted Indians was remarkably skillful. Both he, pp. 225–28, and Vestal, pp. 193–202, describe the conference with Sitting Bull. Miles tells it from his point of view, Vestal from the point of view of the Indians quite a few years later, but there is not much essential difference between the two accounts except for Vestal's stress on Sitting Bull's desire for peace. The quotations from Miles appear in the section of his book that I have indicated.

The story of MacKenzie's attack on Dull Knife's village is told in Bourke's *On the Border with Crook* and at greater length in his *Mac-Kenzie's Last Fight with the Cheyennes—a Winter Campaign in Wyoming*. As with other references to Bourke in these notes, I have drawn on *On the Border with Crook* for the description of the battle. The quotation appears on p. 392. On pp. 389 and 394–96 Bourke describes the comparative ease with which Crook was then able to obtain Indian scouts. Most commanders used Indians as trackers, but Crook, while serving in Arizona, had learned to use them to do much of the actual fighting. It was his employment of Apaches to fight Apaches that largely accounted for the final defeat of that tribe. Washington, however, was uneasy about the arrangement, being uncertain that Indians would make reliable allies. Crook was finally relieved of his command in a dispute over his Apache scouts.

Grinnell, p. 369, tells why the Cheyennes remained where they were instead of retreating. His account of the battle is on pp. 359–82 and of the subsequent surrender of more Cheyennes on pp. 383–97. Bourke and he disagree on one important point. Bourke says that the Indians who escaped turned to Crazy Horse for help, but Crazy Horse refused to give them any. Grinnell states the contrary. I suspect Grinnell in this case was right. Mari Sandoz, p. 338, says that Dull Knife had not participated in the Custer fight and did not want to have anything to do with the independent Indians. Bourke reports, however, that they discovered in the camp clothing marked with the names of members of the Seventh Cavalry.

Miles's description of his campaign against Crazy Horse's camp appears on pp. 236-39 of his book, and the quotations are taken from them.

The picture of Crazy Horse at the Red Cloud agency comes from Bourke, pp. 412-13. There were other surrenders that spring, such as Two Moon's and Lame Deer's, both Cheyennes. But they followed the pattern of the others, and that of Crazy Horse had greater consequences, for it spelled an end to this phase of the war.

Sitting Bull's answer to the bishop appears in Black, p. 185.

The actions of the peace commission are described in Black, pp. 185-88, Vestal, pp. 223-33, and in the *Annual Report of the Commissioner of Indian Affairs, 1877.*

Crazy Horse's restlessness is described by Bourke, p. 418, and by Sandoz, pp. 389-412. Olson, pp. 240-46, discusses the circumstances leading up to his death and the causes. There is little hope that Crazy Horse could have permanently adjusted to agency life. It was just too different from what he had always known and loved.

Miles, pp. 306-19, describes the border campaigns of 1879 and 1880. The Indians' reaction to the telegraph and telephone appear on pp. 317-18. Finerty, pp. 241-68, also tells about the campaign in 1879. The position of the Canadian government was a difficult one of trying to maintain impartiality. It did extremely well at it, although it frustrated the Americans. The backing of Great Britain made it possible to carry it out. As one commentator remarked, the Mexican government could not have kept American troops out of its territory under similar circumstances— and did not during the wars against the Apaches.

Finerty tells about his visit to the Canadian camp of Indians in his book, pp. 268-97. Miles was quite astonished when Finerty told him he had decided to accept Walsh's invitation, for the trip held considerable danger. Of course, he could never have made it at all without Walsh's protection. As it was, he stayed only a short time, because some of the Indians were upset by his presence. Black gives a picture of the Indian problem from the Canadian point of view. Finerty's description of the country north of Missouri appears on p. 253 of his book, the effect of artillery, p. 256, the camp, p. 272, Sitting Bull at the conference, p. 274, Walsh's remarks, pp. 277-78, Sitting Bull's status among the Indians, pp. 283-84, and the shortage of food, p. 289. Black reproduces the excerpt from Walsh's report, p. 188, and also Sitting Bull's comment to the Canadian authorities, p. 189. Further details about his surrender can be found in both Allison and Wade. Allison says that by the time Sitting Bull himself surrendered, he had so few followers that the American Government did not care whether he gave himself up or not.

CHAPTER XVI

PEACE AND BULLETS

In the last chapter I felt somewhat like a Victorian novelist, gathering all the loose ends at the close of a long story. In this case, I had to deal with the many separate bands of Indians whose actions, although taken independently, had a direct effect on each other. For the surrender of one band made more inevitable the surrender of the next. By the end of the chapter, the Indians had almost all reported to the agencies except for about two hundred who remained in Canada and whose decendants are still living there. The fate of Dull Knife's band was exceptionally tragic. They were sent to Indian Territory—"exiled" would perhaps be a better word than "sent"—and later made a disastrous effort to return. They were finally held captive at Fort Robinson, where the army tried to starve them into submission. They broke out of jail, and the army pursued them and massacred more than half their number. The reader will find a good brief account in *Great Indian Fights*, pp. 295–302.

With the opening of this chapter, armed resistance has come to an end. Never again will the Sioux and Cheyennes in force take up their guns and bows, and the whole battle has shifted to the council ground and the deliberations of officials in Washington, some of them well-meaning and some of them not. In spite of a few humanitarians, the Indians lost much of their land, and the reader has only to pick up a map that shows the present reservations to see how much.

Nor did they receive adequate compensation, and I am speaking not only of the money paid them. For the Americans have been unable to provide them with an adequate substitute for their own culture. In saying this, I am not suggesting that the Indians' problems would be solved if by some miracle we could arrange to have them return to their old ways. Such a course would be both impractical and impossible, and at this point in time it would accomplish little. Even the Indians themselves would not be happy. And so the Indian question remains with us, and I regret that personally I see no immediate solution in sight, although many have been proposed. I can only say that the subject is extremely complex, but much of the thinking about it is simplistic.

In this chapter, I have not dealt with Indian policy from 1883, the time that Sitting Bull came to Standing Rock, to 1890, the year of his death, because he played little part in forming it. His continued opposition to the white men provided a center of resistance to their demands, but his influence had waned. Vestal, pp. 237–70, presents quite a different picture, but I do not think the evidence supports it.

The two quotations from McLaughlin appear on p. 49 of the *Annual Report of the Commissioner of Indian Affairs, 1883*. The U.S. Senate, *48th. Congress, 1st. Session, Executive Document No. 283* contains the report of the commission headed by Dawes. For those who would like to know more about the government's Indian policy during this period, I would suggest Olson's book, pp. 286–305, Hyde's *A Sioux Chronicle*, pp. 107–245; and for the Santees, Meyer's book, which discusses their treatment in detail. None of it makes happy reading.

The reader may be surprised at the lionization of Sitting Bull by those he had lately fought, but he should not be. The Americans' attitude toward the Indians has always been inconsistent. Even today there is at least one state where successful politicians like to have their pictures taken with Indian acquaintances before Election Day. It will get them votes, although many of their constituents and they themselves would like to strip the Indians of their remaining lands. It is all part of our mixed-up feelings about our frontier period.

The provisions of the agreement proposed in 1888 are set forth in the *Annual Report of the Commissioner of Indian Affairs* for that year, pp. lxiii–lxv. These pages also show the number of signatures obtained at each agency. McLaughlin's comments are on pp. 275–76 of his book, and he also describes the trip to Washington on pp. 277–80. It should be noted that he was not against the sale of the land but against the terms offered.

The report of the last commission is contained in U.S. Senate, 51st. Congress, 1st. Session, Executive Document No. 51. Crook's *Autobiography*, pp. 284–89, describes his part in the proceedings. McLaughlin, pp. 280–88, also tells what happened. The quotations are from pp. 284–85. Sad as it may have been, the white men who worked to get the Indians to sign were undoubtedly doing the right thing. The nation was determined to take the Indians' land away from them and would have done so anyway.

McLaughlin, p. 289, had this to say: "The history of treaty-making with the Sioux is the history of the treaty-making with all the Indians. The treaties were made for the accommodation of the whites, and broken when they interfered with the money-getters. There never was time in the history of this country when the government could not have obtained any reasonable concession from the Indians, if it had treated the red men honestly; and I know of few—and those only isolated cases—Indian outbreaks which were not preceded by acts of oppression practiced by the civilized people on the barbarians; and like barbarians those same people revenged themselves. There is no possible justification for the barbarities practiced by the Indians when they were aroused to dig up the hatchet, but the Indian wars generally have been in the nature of fierce reprisals for injuries sustained. That the Indian has not always discriminated between the innocent and the guilty in taking his revenge, is certain—else had there been no Minnesota massacre. If his sense of justice had led him to fine discrimination in these matters, the red man would long ago have made an attack on the national Capitol."

At the National Archives and Records Service in Washington—a truly remarkable place and a joy to scholars in American history—they have a special file in which they have collected much of the material in their possession leading up to the tragedy at Wounded Knee. In writing this chapter, I have drawn on the report of Major Wirt Davis, Inspector of Small Arms Practice, who made a special trip to ascertain the significance of the Ghost Dance among various tribes. He filed his report in December, 1891, when the Ghost Dance had reached a crisis. Obviously, from his study, many of the Indians did not take the new faith seriously. The other reports from this file on which I have relied heavily are McLaughlin's, dated June 18, October 17, November 2, November 29, and December 16, 1890. The latter relates what happened when the police attempted to arrest Sitting Bull. The *Annual Report of the Commissioner of Indian Affairs, 1891*, pp. 325–38, also contains much of the material submitted by him to Washington.

As a former law enforcement officer, I cannot help commenting on the ineptness of Bull Head's performance. Every policeman knows, or should know, the importance of removing the prisoner quickly from the scene of the arrest, especially if he is surrounded by his family and friends. His failure to do as he was ordered and take the wagon resulted in the death of five Indian police, the wounding of two more, and the death of Sitting Bull and seven of his supporters. On his behalf, however, it can be said that the art of police work was not advanced in his time, and many other policemen might well have made the same mistake.

It is also sad to note that the Americans had learned nothing from their previous experience with an Indian who started a new faith based on Christianity. That was the Apache Noch-ay-del-klinne, in 1881. The mishandling of him and his followers also unnecessarily cost many lives.

For those readers who would like a more detailed study of the events leading up to Sitting Bull's death and the massacre at Wounded Knee, I would recommend Utley's excellent book, *The Last Days of the Sioux Nation*.

Bibliography

The following are some of the most important sources consulted in the preparation of this book.

ALLISON, E. H., *The Surrender of Sitting Bull.* Dayton, Ohio, The Walker Litho. and Printing Co., 1891.

ASHER, CASH, *See* Red Fox.

ATHEARN, ROBERT G., *High Country Empire: The High Plains and Rockies.* Lincoln, Nebraska, University of Nebraska Press, 1960.

AUDUBON, JOHN JAMES, *Audubon and His Journals,* Maria Audubon, ed., 2 vols. New York, Dover Publications, Inc., 1960.

BANNING, GEORGE HUGH, *see* Banning, William.

BANNING, WILLIAM, with Banning, George Hugh, *Six Horses.* New York, The Century Company, 1930.

BLACK, NORMAN FERGS, *History of Saskatchewan and the Old North West.* Regina, Saskatchewan, North West Historical Company, 1913.

BLACK ELK, *The Sacred Pipe,* recorded and edited by Joseph Epes Brown. Baltimore, Maryland, Penguin Books, 1971.

BOURKE, JOHN G., *MacKenzie's Last Fight with the Cheyennes—A Winter Campaign in Wyoming and Montana.* Governor's Island, New York Harbor, The Military Service Institution, 1890.

———, *On the Border with Crook.* Glorieta, New Mexico, Rio Grande Press, 1969.

BRADLEY, JAMES H., *The March of the Montana Column: A Prelude to the Custer Disaster,* Edgar I. Stewart, ed. Norman, Oklahoma, University of Oklahoma Press, 1961.

BRIMMER, FREDERICK, ed., *Scalps and Tomahawks: Narratives of Indian Captivity.* New York, Coward-McCann, Inc., 1961.

BRININSTOOL, E. A., *Troopers with Custer*. Harrisburg, Pennsylvania, The Stackpole Company, 1952.

BRONSON, EDGAR BEECHER, *Reminiscences of a Ranchman*. Lincoln, Nebraska, University of Nebraska Press, 1967.

BROWN, DEE, *Bury My Heart at Wounded Knee*. New York, Holt, Rinehart & Winston, 1970.

BROWN, JOSEPH EPES. *See* Black Elk.

BROWN, MARK H., *The Plainsmen of the Yellowstone: A History of the Yellowstone Basin*. New York, G. P. Putnam's Sons, 1961.

———, and FELTON, W. R., *Before Barbed Wire: I. A. Huffman, Photographer on Horseback*. New York, Henry Holt and Company, 1956.

———, *The Frontier Years*. New York, Bramhall House, 1955.

BUCK, DANIEL, *Indian Outbreaks*. Minneapolis, Minnesota, Ross & Haines, Inc., 1965.

BULL, JOSEPH WHITE, *The Warrior Who Killed Custer: The Personal Narrative of Chief Joseph White Bull*. Lincoln, Nebraska, University of Nabraska Press, 1968.

BURDICK, USHER L., *The Last Battle of the Sioux Nation*. Fargo, North Dakota, Usher L. Burdick, 1929.

CARRINGTON, FRANCES C., *Army Life on the Plains*. Philadelphia, J. B. Lippincott Company, 1911.

CASEY, ROBERT J., *The Black Hills and Their Incredible Characters*. Indianapolis, The Bobbs-Merrill Company, 1949.

CASTEL, ALBERT, *A Frontier State at War: Kansas, 1861–1865*. Ithaca, New York, Cornell University Press, 1958.

CHAPEL, CHARLES EDWARD, *Guns of the Old West*. New York, Coward-McCann, Inc., 1961.

CHITTENDEN, HIRAM MARTIN, and RICHARDSON, ALFRED TALBOT, *Life, Letters and Travels of Father Pierre-Jean De Smet, S. J. 1801–1873*, 4 vols. New York, Francis P. Harper, 1905.

CLARK, THOMAS D., *Frontier America: The Story of the Western Movement*. New York, Charles Scribner's Sons, 1969.

CODY, WILLIAM P., *An Autobiography of Buffalo Bill*. New York, Rinehart & Company, 1920.

COOK, JAMES H., *Fifty Years on the Old Frontier*. Norman, Oklahoma, University of Oklahoma Press, 1957.

COURSEY, O. W., *See* Tallent, Annie D.

CROOK, GEORGE, *Autobiography*, edited and annotated by Martin F. Schmitt. Norman, Oklahoma, University of Oklahoma Press, 1946.

CUSTER, ELIZABETH B., *"Boots and Saddles" or, Life in Dakota with General Custer*. Williamstown, Massachusetts, Corner House Publishers, 1969.

CUSTER, GEORGE ARMSTRONG, "Battling with the Sioux on the Yellowstone." *The Galaxy*, Vol. XXII, No. 1 (July, 1876).

——, *My Life on the Plains*, edited and with an introduction by Milo Milton Quaife. Lincoln, Nebraska, University of Nebraska Press, 1966.

——, Pages from Black Hills Order and Despatch Book. MS Coe Collection. New Haven, Connecticut, Beinecke Library, Yale University.

DEBARTHE, JOE, *Life and Adventures of Frank Grouard*, edited and with an introduction by Edgar I. Stewart. Norman, Oklahoma, University of Oklahoma Press, 1958.

DENIG, EDWIN THOMPSON, *Five Indian Tribes of the Upper Missouri: Sioux, Arickaras, Assiniboines, Crees, Crows*, edited and with an introduction by John C. Ewers. Norman, Oklahoma, University of Oklahoma Press, 1961.

DE SMET, PIERRE-JEAN. See Chittenden, Hiram Martin.

DEVOTO, BERNARD, *Across the Wide Missouri*. Boston, Houghton Mifflin Co., 1947.

——, *The Course of Empire*. Boston, Houghton Mifflin Co., 1952.

——, *The Year of Decision: 1846*. Boston, Little, Brown and Co., 1943.

DODGE, RICHARD IRVING, *The Black Hills*. Minneapolis, Minnesota, Roos & Haines, 1965.

——, *The Plains of the Great West*. New York, Archer House, Inc., 1959.

——, *Thirty-Three Years Among Our Wild Indians*. New York, Archer House, Inc., 1959.

DRAGO, HARRY SINCLAIR, *Great American Cattle Trails*. New York, Bramhall House, 1965.

DUNN, J. P., JR., *Massacres of the Mountains*. New York, Archer House, Inc., no date. (Originally published in 1886.)

EASTMAN, CHARLES A., *Indian Boyhood*. Boston, Little, Brown and Co., 1930.

EASTMAN, MARY, *Dahcotah: Life and Legends of the Sioux*. Minneapolis, Minnesota, Ross & Haines, Inc., 1962.

EDWARDS, ELSA SPEAR, "Fifteen Day Fight on Tongue River." *Annals of Wyoming*, Vol. 10, No. 2 (April, 1938), pp 51–59.

EWERS, JOHN C., *The Blackfeet: Raiders on the Northwestern Plains*. Norman, Oklahoma, University of Oklahoma Press, 1958. *See also* Denig, Edwin Thompson.

FELTON, W. R. *See* Brown, Mark H.

FINERTY, JOHN F., *War-Path and Bivouac or The Conquest of The Sioux*. Norman, Oklahoma, University of Oklahoma Press, 1961.

FITE, GILBERT C., *The Farmers' Frontier, 1865–1900*. New York, Holt, Rinehart & Winston, 1966.

FORSYTH, GEORGE A., *The Story of the Soldier*. New York, D. Appleton and Co., 1900.

FOSTER-HARRIS, *The Look of the Old West*. New York, Viking Press, 1955.

FRAZER, ROBERT W., *Forts of the Old West*. Norman, Oklahoma, University of Oklahoma Press, 1966.

GARDINER, DOROTHY, *West of the River: A History*. New York, Thomas Y. Crowell Co., 1963.

GARRAGHAN, GILBERT J., "Father De Smet's Sioux Peace Mission of 1868 and the Journal of Charles Galpin." *Mid-America*, Vol. XIII, No. 2 (October, 1930), pp. 141–63.

GATES, PAUL W., *History of Public Land Law*, with a chapter by Robert W. Swenson. Washington, D.C., U.S. Government Printing Office, 1968.

GODDARD, JEANNE M., and KRITZLER, CHARLES, compilers. *A Catalogue of the Frederick W. and Carrie Beinecke Collection of Western Americana*. Vol. I, Manuscripts. New Haven, Connecticut, Yale University Press, 1965.

GODFREY, EDWARD SETTLE, *Field Diary*, edited and with introduction and notes by Edgar I. Stewart and Jane R. Stewart. Portland, Oregon, Champoeg Press, 1957.

GOLDFRANK, ESTHER S., *Changing Configurations in the Social Organization of a Blackfoot Tribe During the Reserve Period*. Seattle, Washington, University of Washington Press, 1945.

GRAHAM, WILLIAM ALEXANDER, *The Custer Myth: A Source Book of Custeriana*. Harrisburg, Pennsylvania, The Stackpole Co., 1953.

———, *Reno Court of Inquiry*, with an introduction by William Alexander Graham. Pacific Palisades, California, Privately printed, 1951.

———, *The Story of the Little Big Horn*. New York, Bonanza Books, 1959.

GRESHAM, JOHN C., "The Story of Wounded Knee." *Harper's Weekly*, Vol. XXXV, No. 1781 (February 7, 1891), pp. 106–7.

GRINNELL, GEORGE BIRD, *Blackfoot Lodge Tales: The Story of a Prairie People*. Lincoln, Nebraska, University of Nebraska Press, 1962.

———, *The Fighting Cheyennes*. Norman, Oklahoma, University of Oklahoma Press, 1956.

———, *When Buffalo Ran*. Norman, Oklahoma, University of Oklahoma Press, 1966.

GROUARD: *See* De Barthe.

HAFEN, LEROY R., *Colorado Gold Rush: Contemporary Letters and Reports, 1858–1859*. Glendale, California, The Arthur H. Clark Company, 1941.

———, and HAFEN, ANN W., *Powder River Campaigns and Sawyer's Expedition of 1865*. Glendale, California, The Arthur H. Clark Company, 1961.

———, *Relations with the Plains Indians, 1857–1861*. Glendale, California, The Arthur H. Clark Company, 1959.

———, and YOUNG, FRANCIS MARION, *Fort Laramie and the Pageant of the West, 1834–1890*. Glendale, California, The Arthur H. Clark Company, 1938.

HAGAN, WILLIAM T., *American Indians*. Chicago, University of Chicago Press, 1961.

HAMILTON, W. T., *My Sixty Years on the Plains*. Norman, Oklahoma, University of Oklahoma Press, 1960.

HANS, FRED M., *The Great Sioux Nation*. Minneapolis, Minnesota, Ross & Haines, Inc., 1964.

HART, HEBERT M., *Pioneer Forts of the West*. Seattle, Washington, Superior Publishing Company, 1967.

HASSRICK, ROYAL B., *The Sioux: Life and Customs of a Warrior Society*. Norman, Oklahoma, University of Oklahoma Press, 1965.

HAWGOOD, JOHN A., *America's Western Frontiers*. New York, Alfred A. Knopf, 1967.

HOLLOWAY, W. L. (original copyright owner; no author), *Wild Life on the Plains and Horrors of Indian Warfare*. New York, Arno Press & The New York Times, 1969.

HOWARD, JAMES H. *See* Bull, Joseph White.

HOWARD, JOSEPH KINSEY, *Strange Empire*. New York, William Morrow & Co., 1952.

HYDE, GEORGE E., *Red Cloud's Folk*. Norman, Oklahoma, University of Oklahoma Press, 1937.

———, *A Sioux Chronicle*. Norman, Oklahoma, University of Oklahoma Press, 1956.

———, *Spotted Tail's Folk: A History of the Brulé Sioux*. Norman, Oklahoma, University of Oklahoma Press, 1961.

INTERNATIONAL HARVESTER COMPANY, *McCormick Reaper Cenntenial Source Material*. Chicago, Illinois, International Harvester Company, 1931.

IRVING, WASHINGTON, *Astoria or Anecdotes of an Enterprise Beyond the Rocky Mountains*. New York, John W. Lovell Co., no date.

JACKSON, DONALD, *Custer's Gold: The United States Cavalry Expedition of 1874*. New Haven, Connecticut, Yale University Press, 1966.

JACKSON, HELEN HUNT, *A Century of Dishonor*. New York, Harper & Row, 1965.

JAMES, MARQUIS, *The Life of Andrew Jackson*. Indianapolis, Indiana, The Bobbs-Merrill Co., 1938.

JOHNSON, DOROTHY M., *The Bloody Bozeman*. New York, McGraw-Hill Book Company, 1971.

JOHNSON, M. L., *Trail Blazing*. Dallas, Texas, Mathis Publishing Co., 1935.

JOSEPHY, ALFRED M., JR., *The Indian Heritage of America*. New York, Alfred A. Knopf, 1968.

———, *The Patriot Chiefs*. New York, Viking Press, Inc., 1961.

KEIM, DEB. RANDOLPH, *Sheridan's Troopers on the Borders: A Winter Campaign on the Plains*. New York, George Routledge and Sons, 1885.

KELLY, FANNY, *Narrative of My Captivity Among the Sioux Indians*. Chicago, R. R. Donnelly & Sons Co., 1891.

KING, CHARLES, *Campaigning with Crook*. Norman, Oklahoma, University of Oklahoma Press, 1964.

KINSLEY, D. A., *Favor the Bold: Custer: The Indian Fighter*. New York, Holt, Rinehart & Winston, 1968.

KRITZLER, CHARLES. *See* Goddard, Jeanne M.

LAMAR, HOWARD ROBERTS, *Dakota Territory, 1861–1899: A Study of Frontier Politics*. New Haven, Connecticut, Yale University Press, 1956.

LANCASTER, RICHARD, *Piegan*. Garden City, New York, Doubleday & Company, Inc., 1966.

LAVENDER, DAVID, *Bent's Fort*. Garden City, New York, Doubleday & Company, 1954.

LONGSTREET, STEPHEN, *War Cries on Horseback: The Story of the Indian Wars on the Great Plains*. Garden City, New York, Doubleday & Company, 1970.

LOWIE, ROBERT H., *Indians of the Plains*. New York, McGraw-Hill Book Company, 1954.

MACCLINTOCK, WALTER, *The Old North Trail: Life, Legends and Religion of the Blackfeet Indians*. Lincoln, Nebraska, University of Nebraska Press, 1968.

McCONKEY, HARRIET E. BISHOP, *Dakota War Whoop*. Minneapolis, Minnesota, Ross & Haines, 1970.

McCRACKEN, HAROLD, *George Catlin and the Old Frontier*. New York, Bonanza Books, no date.

McGILLYCUDDY, JULIA B., *McGillycuddy: Agent*. Stanford, California, Stanford University Press, 1941.

McGREGOR, JAMES H., *The Wounded Knee Massacre From Viewpoint of the Sioux*. Minneapolis, Minnesota, The Lund Press, Inc., 1940.

McLAUGHLIN, JAMES, *My Friend the Indian*. Boston, Houghton Mifflin Company, 1910.

MAGUIRE, N. H., *New Map and Guide to Dakota and the Black Hills*. Chicago, Rand McNally & Co., no date.

MANLEY, WILLIAM LEWIS, *Death Valley in '49*, with a foreword by John Stephen McGroarty. New York, Wallace Hebberd, 1929.

MARQUIS, THOMAS B., interpreter, *Wooden Leg: Warrior Who Fought Custer*. Lincoln, Nebraska, University of Nebraska Press, 1962.

MERINGTON, MARGUERITE, *The Custer Story: The Life and Intimate Letters of General George A. Custer and His Wife Elizabeth*. New York, The Devin-Adair Company, 1950.

MERRILL, JAMES M., *Spurs to Glory: The Story of the United States Cavalry*. Chicago, Rand McNally & Co., 1966.

MEYER, ROY W., *History of the Santee Sioux: United States Indian Policy on Trial*. Lincoln, Nebraska, University of Nebraska Press, 1967.

MILES, NELSON A., *Personal Recollections*, with an introduction by Robert M. Utley. New York, Da Capo Press, 1969.

MILLER, DAVID HUMPHREYS, *Ghost Dance*. New York, Duell, Sloan and Pearce, 1959.

MISHKIN, BERNHARD, *Rank and Warfare Among the Plains Indians*. Seattle, Washington, University of Washington Press, 1940.

MITCHELL and HINMAN, *An Accompaniment to Mitchell's Reference and Distance Map of the United States*. Philadelphia, Pennsylvania, Mitchell and Hinman, 1835.

MONAGHAN, JAY, *Custer: The Life of General George Armstrong Custer*. Boston, Little, Brown and Company, 1959.

MOONEY, JAMES, *The Siouan Tribes of the East*. New York, Johnson Reprint Corporation, 1970.

MORGAN, DALE L., *Rand McNally's Pioneer Atlas of the American West*. Chicago, Rand McNally & Co., 1956.

MURPHY, WILLIAM, "The Forgotten Battalion." *Annals of Wyoming*, Vol. 7, No. 2 (October, 1930), pp. 383–401; Vol. 7, No. 3 (January, 1931), pp. 441–42.

NADEAU, REMI, *Fort Laramie and the Sioux Indians*. Englewood Cliffs, New Jersey, Prentice-Hall, Inc., 1967.

NEIHARDT, JOHN G., *Black Elk Speaks*. Lincoln, Nebraska, University of Nebraska Press, 1961.

NELSON, BRUCE, *Land of the Dacotahs*. Lincoln, Nebraska, University of Nebraska Press, 1964.

NURGE, ETHEL, ed., *The Modern Sioux: Social Systems and Reservation Culture*. Lincoln, Nebraska, University of Nebraska Press, 1970.

OLSON, JAMES C., *Red Cloud and the Sioux Problem*. Lincoln, Nebraska, University of Nebraska Press, 1965.

OSTRANDER, ALSON, B., *An Army Boy of the Sixties: A Story of the Plains*. Yonkers-on-Hudson, New York, World Book Co., 1924.

———, *The Bozeman Trail Forts Under General St. George Cooke in 1886*. Seattle, Washington, Major Alson B. Ostrander, 1932.

PEATTIE, RODERICK, ed., *The Black Hills*. New York, Vanguard Press, 1952.

Potomac Corral of the Westerners, Members of, *Great Western Indian Fights*. Lincoln, Nebraska, University of Nebraska Press, 1960.

QUAIFE, MILO MILTON. *See* Custer, George A.

REMINGTON, FREDERIC, *Frederic Remington's Old West*. New York, Dial Press, 1960.

———, "The Sioux Outbreak in South Dakota." *Harper's Weekly*, Vol. XXXV, No. 1779 (January 24, 1891), pp. 57, 61, 62.

RICHARDSON, ALFRED TALBOT. See Chittenden, Hirma Martin.

RIEGEL, ROBERT EDGAR, *The Story of the Western Railroads*. Lincoln, Nebraska, University of Nebraska Press, 1964.

RIGGS, STEPHEN R., *Mary and I: Forty Years with the Sioux*. Minneapolis, Minnesota, Ross & Haines, 1969.

ROBBINS, ROY M., *Our Landed Heritage: The Public Domain, 1776–1936.* Lincoln, Nebraska, University of Nebraska Press, 1962.

ROBINSON, DOANE, *A History of the Dakota or Sioux Indians.* Minneapolis, Minnesota, Ross & Haines, Inc., 1967.

RUSSELL, CARL P., *Guns on the Early Frontier.* New York, Bonanza, 1957.

RUSSELL, CHARLES M., *Trails Plowed Under.* Garden City, New York, Doubleday, Doran & Company, 1928.

RYAN, J. C., ed., *Custer Fell First: The Adventures of John C. Lockwood.* San Antonio, Texas, The Naylor Company, 1966.

SANDOZ, MARI, *Crazy Horse: The Strange Man of the Oglalas.* Lincoln, Nebraska, University of Nebraska Press, 1942.

———, *Love Song to the Plains.* Lincoln, Nebraska, University of Nebraska Press, 1966.

SCHLESINGER, ARTHUR W., JR., *The Age of Jackson.* Boston, Little, Brown and Company, 1945.

SECOY, FRANK RAYMOND, *Changing Military Patterns on the Great Plains.* Seattle, Washington, University of Washington Press, 1971.

SEYMOUR, CHARLES G., "The Sioux Rebellion." *Harper's Weekly,* Vol. XXXV, No. 1781 (February 7, 1891), p. 106.

SIBERTS, BRUCE, *Nothing but Prairie and Sky: Life on the Dakota Range in the Early Days.* Norman, Oklahoma, University of Oklahoma Press, 1954.

STANDING BEAR, LUTHER, *Land of the Spotted Eagle.* Boston, Houghton Mifflin Company, 1933.

———, *My People the Sioux.* Boston, Houghton Mifflin Company, 1928.

STANLEY, HENRY M., *My Early Adventures and Travels,* Vols. 1 and 2. New York, Charles Scribner's Sons, 1895.

STEWART, EDGAR I., *Custer's Luck.* Norman, Oklahoma, University of Nebraska Press, 1955. *See also* Bradley, James H.

SWENSON, ROBERT W. *See* Gates, Paul W.

TALLENT, ANNIE D., *The First White Woman in the Black Hills,* collected and edited by O. W. Coursey. Mitchell, South Dakota, Educator Supply Co., 1923.

TARG, WILLIAM, ed., *The American West.* New York, World Publishing Co., 1946.

TEBBEL, JOHN, *The Compact History of the Indian Wars.* New York, Hawthorn Books, Inc., 1966.

U.S. Commissioner of Indian Affairs, *Annual Reports for the Years 1846–1891.* Washington, D.C., Government Printing Office.

U.S. House of Representatives, *33rd. Congress, 2nd. Sessions, Report No. 63.*

U.S. National Archives, *Register of Letters Received, Office of Indian Affairs.*

———, *Special Case 188.* Land Division, Office of Indian Affairs.

U.S. Secretary of War, *Annual Report for the Year 1891.* Washington, D.C., Government Printing Office, 1891.

U.S. Senate, *Message of the President of the United States to the Two Houses of Congress at the Commencement of the Third Session of the Thirty-Seventh Congress.* Washington, D.C., Government Printing Office, 1862.

———, *40th. Congress, 1st. Session, Executive Document No. 13.*

———, *43rd. Congress, 2nd. Session. Executive Document No. 32.*

———, *44th. Congress, 1st. Session, Executive Document No. 51.*

———, *44th. Congress, 1st Session, Executive Document No. 81.*

———, *48th. Congress, 1st. Session, Executive Document No. 70.*

———, *48th. Congress, 1st. Session, Report No. 283.*

———, *50th Congress, 1st. Session, Executive Document No. 33.*

———, *51st. Congress, 1st Session, Executive Document No. 51.*

UBBELOHDE, CARL, *A Colorado History.* Boulder, Colorado, Pruett Press, 1965.

UTLEY, ROBERT M., *Custer Battlefield National Monument, Montana.* Washington, D.C., National Park Service, 1969.

———, *The Last Days of the Sioux Nation.* New Haven, Connecticut, Yale University Press, 1965.

VESTAL, STANLEY, *New Sources of Indian History, 1850–1891.* Norman, Oklahoma, University of Oklahoma Press, 1934.

———, *Sitting Bull: Champion of the Sioux.* Norman, Oklahoma, University of Oklahoma Press, 1957.

———, *Warpath and Council Fire: The Plains Indians' Struggle for Survival in War and in Diplomacy 1851–1891.* New York, Random House, 1948.

VICTOR, FRANCES F., *Eleven Years in the Rocky Mountains and Life on the Frontier.* Hartford, Connecticut, R. W. Bliss and Co., 1881.

WADE, F. C., "The Surrender of Sitting Bull." *The Canadian Magazine* (Toronto), Vol. XXIV, No. 4 (February, 1905).

WARE, EUGENE F., *The Indian War of 1864.* New York, St. Martin's Press, 1960.

WATSON, GAYLORD, *The United States of America: A Collection of Facts, Dates, and Statistics.* New York, Gaylord Watson, 1875.

WEBB, WALTER PRESCOTT, *The Great Plains.* New York, Grosset & Dunlap, 1931.

WELLMAN, PAUL I., *The Indian Wars of the West.* Garden City, New York, Doubleday & Co., Inc., 1947.

WHITMAN, S. E., *The Troopers: An Informal History of the Plains Cavalry, 1865–1890.* New York, Hastings House Publishers, 1962.

WHITTAKER, FREDERICK, "General George A. Custer." *The Galaxy,* Vol. XXII, No. 3 (September 1876).

WYMAN, WALKER D. *See* Siberts, Bruce.

YOUNG, FRANCIS MARION. *See* Hafen, LeRoy R.

Index

Index

435